The Guru Guide

The Best Ideas
of the
Top Management Thinkers

Joseph H. Boyett
and
Jimmie T. Boyett

John Wiley & Sons, Inc.
New York • Chichester • Weinheim • Brisbane • Singapore • Toronto

Published by John Wiley & Sons, Inc.
Published simultaneously in Canada.

This publication is designed to provide accurate and authoritative information in regard to the subject matter covered. It is sold with the understanding that the publisher is not engaged in rendering legal, accounting, or other professional services. If legal advice or other expert assistance is required, the services of a competent professional person should be sought.

Library of Congress Cataloging-in-Publication Data:

Boyett, Joseph H.
    The guru guide : the best ideas of the top management thinkers /
Joseph H. Boyett & Jimmie T. Boyett
        p.   cm.
    Includes bibliographical references (p. 341) and index.
    ISBN 0-471-18242-7 (cloth : alk. paper)
    1. Management. 2. Leadership. 3. Business. I. Boyett,
Jimmie T. II. Title.
HD31.B7193   1998
658—dc21   97-41058
                                                         CIP

Printed in the United States of America.

10 9 8 7 6 5 4 3 2

To our grandchildren

Megan Elizabeth Reeves
Benedict William Luongo
Kayla Nicole Reeves

who have taught us that a grandparent's love is truly exponential.

Contents

Introduction vii

Chapter 1 Leadership 1

Chapter 2 Managing Change 47

Chapter 3 The Learning Organization 81

Chapter 4 Creating High-Performance
Organizations Through Teamwork 129

Chapter 5 The Pursuit of Market Leadership 175

Chapter 6 Managing and Motivating People 233

Chapter 7 Business, Work, and Society 293

Notes 325

Bibliography 341

The Gurus 357

Index 381

Introduction

Y ou need quick access to state-of-the-art management information, right? Of course you do. There is just one problem. In today's hectic corporate world, you simply have too much to do and too little time to sift through hundreds of books and thousands of articles to find the advice you need. Which books should you read? What articles could provide you with some insight? Whose writings should you seek on the Internet? Who is the authority on a particular issue? What advice does he or she offer? How do the ideas of one authority complement or conflict with those of another? Most importantly, whose ideas about how to manage and run businesses really produce results? Under what circumstances do their ideas work or not work? You need a guide to help you answer these questions. Congratulations. You have just found it.

The Guru Guide has been designed to provide you with a clear, concise, and informative introduction to the wisdom of the world's top business advisors. You are holding in your hands a highly opinionated but informative guide to the skills, ideas, and concepts of the world's top business thinkers of the 1990s. But we have designed this guide to be more than just a digest of current thought about business. The ideas of each business thinker are linked and cross-linked with those of other experts who agree or disagree. We have identified the ideas that coincide and those that conflict. We show you how some of the world's most important management theories and concepts have evolved. We report on the gurus' methods and the results they say they have obtained. Finally, we provide an evaluation of their strengths and weaknesses.

We set out on the journey to produce this book with a few simple questions in mind. What could we learn from the world's best-known management gurus that might help us—and you—succeed? What tidbits of knowledge could we discover that, if faithfully followed, would make work less stressful and careers more bulletproof? How can a company become a better steward of stockholder wealth, a more energetic customer servant, or simply a better corporate citizen? What business strategies make companies invincible or nearly invincible? Which management gurus make sense? Which rehash old bromides? In this book we have provided a road map to guide you through the bewildering maze of management advice. There are plenty of wrong turns and blind alleys, and we have specifically pointed them out. In regard to a wide range of important topics we have searched out and recommended the best routes, and we have warned you about the dead ends.

Do we cover everything about management? No, of course not. Just walk into your local bookstore and peruse the seemingly endless shelves of business books. Search Amazon.com on the Internet and you will find nearly 700 "best-sellers" on the topics of management and leadership alone. The complete list of books on management is so long it will probably crash your browser the way it did ours. Given the huge volume of business books out there, not to mention the hundreds of thousands of articles, we had to be selective. Even then, we reviewed over 200 books and some 3,000 articles to prepare the guide you are about to read. You read that right: over 200 books and more than 3,000 articles, and we still left some things out.

OUR GURUS

You may wonder how we finally decided whose ideas to include and which topics to cover. We started out by making a list of what we thought were some of the most important and enduring management issues. Some topics, such as leadership and managing change, were obvious choices. Other topics made it to the initial list but were later dropped for one reason or another. For example, reengineering was on our initial list, but we dropped it because we felt it was too faddish. After much discussion and debate, we finally settled on the topics covered in this volume: leadership, managing change, learning, teams, strategy, motivation, and future organizational designs.

Once we had our topics, we began looking for our gurus. We narrowed down our search in most cases to business gurus of the 1980s and '90s. We gave the most emphasis to those who had written significant books or articles in the last five years. We checked the best-seller lists to see what businesspeople were reading, and we asked our friends, clients, and associates to recommend people they thought had unique insights. In total, we selected 79 gurus for this guide. Some of them are arguably the best thinkers in their field. Others may not necessarily be the greatest thinkers, but their bank accounts attest to their popularity. In alphabetical order, here are the gurus we selected:

Karl Albrecht	Sumantra Ghoshal	David P. Norton
Christopher Argyris	Thomas F. Gilbert	James O'Toole
K. W. (Ken) Bamforth	Robert K. Greenleaf	Glenn M. Parker
Christopher A. Bartlett	Gary P. Hamel	William A. Pasmore
Warren Bennis	Michael Hammer	Thomas J. (Tom) Peters
Warren Blank	Charles Handy	Paul E. Platten
Lee G. Bolman	David A. Hofrichter	Michael E. Porter
Juana Bordas	William N. Isaacs	C. K. Prahalad
Adam M.	F. Robert Jacobs	Edgar H. Schein
Brandenburger	Laurie Beth Jones	Peter R. Scholtes
Jill Carpenter	M. Patricia Kane	Donald A. Schön
John Case	Robert S. Kaplan	Jay R. Schuster
James Champy	Jon R. Katzenbach	John P. Schuster
Jay A. Conger	Manfred F. R. Kets	Peter M. Senge
Daryl Conner	de Vries	Henry P. Sims, Jr.
Stephen R. Covey	Daniel Kim	Douglas K. Smith
Aubrey C. Daniels	John P. Kotter	John P. (Jack) Stack
Terrence E. Deal	Edward E. Lawler III	Paul Strebel
Max DePree	Charles C. Manz	Noel M. Tichy
Peter F. Drucker	Henry Mintzberg	Michael Treacy
Fred Emery	Allan M. Mohrman, Jr.	Eric Trist
Richard Farson	Susan Albers Mohrman	Marvin R. Weisbord
Thomas P. Flannery	James F. Moore	Etienne Wenger
Jay W. Forrester	Linda Moran	Margaret J. Wheatley
Timothy J. Galpin	Ed Musselwhite	Fred Wiersema
Howard Gardner	Barry J. Nalebuff	John H. Zenger
John W. Gardner	Burt Nanus	Patricia K. Zingheim

Our gurus are drawn from leading research and teaching centers, such as the Aspen Institute, Center for Effective Organizations at the University of California, Center for Organizational Learning at MIT, Center for Creative Leadership, Institute for Research on Learning, and University of Southern California's Leadership Institute. They include business professors from Harvard, MIT, Stanford, Yale, Case Western Reserve, the London School of

Business, the European Institute for Business Administration (INSEAD), and the University of Southern California. And our gurus represent some of the largest and best-known management consulting firms, including CSC Index, McKinsey & Company, the Hay Group, the Tom Peters Group, and Zenger Miller.

Our gurus are the best and/or most popular business writers and thinkers around today. You won't agree with everything they have to say—we don't either—but we are confident that they will stimulate your thinking about management, point you in new directions, and challenge many of your best-loved assumptions about what makes businesses work and how they should be led.

ORGANIZATION OF THIS BOOK

We have organized our gurus' ideas into seven chapters. Each chapter covers an important management issue and summarizes the best current thinking by our panel of gurus on that issue.

Chapter 1, "Leadership," examines the current thinking of some of the world's best-known management gurus on the changing role of leaders in the modern organization. In this chapter we summarize three major shifts in leadership roles and responsibilities that our gurus say are now under way—strategist to visionary, commander to storyteller, and systems architect to change agent and servant. We conclude this chapter with an overview of the best advice our gurus have for how you can learn to lead.

In **Chapter 2, "Managing Change,"** we turn to a central problem all leaders must face today, one of leading their companies through major change. We summarize six reasons our gurus give for employee resistance to change and seven tips they provide for overcoming that resistance. We conclude this chapter with an overview of a process that at least some of our gurus think is the ultimate in change wisdom and the long sought-after answer to the problem of gaining organization-wide commitment to major change.

Chapter 3, "The Learning Organization," deals with one of the most popular business topics of the early 1990s—organizational learning. We open this chapter with a summary of current thinking about why and how individuals and organizations learn. We then present three competing approaches for understanding and improving organizational learning.

Chapter 4, "Creating High-Performance Organizations," is about teams. What types of teams can and should an organization create? When are teams useful and for what? What does a team-based organization look like? How are teams implemented? What are the keys to success in making the transition from a traditional organization to a high-performance, team-based organization? How do the roles and responsibilities of managers and supervisors change as organizations implement team systems? What skills do managers, supervisors, team leaders, and team members need? We summarize the answers provided by America's top team gurus and give eight tips they offer for team success.

In Chapter 5, "The Pursuit of Market Leadership," we summarize five different views on business strategy, beginning with the preeminent view of the 1980s and ending with the most popular views of the mid-1990s. We show how one reigning strategy guru is replaced by another, year after year, as America's CEOs keep searching for the magic elixir that will make their companies bulletproof. We conclude this chapter with a summary of the key ideas put forth by the most recent gurus to land on *Business Week*'s "hot new strategists" shortlist.

Of course, strategies are worthless unless they can be implemented, and implementation requires the dedication, support, and commitment of people. Chapter 6, "Managing and Motivating People," tackles that most difficult of issues. In this chapter, we go all the way back to 1978 to discuss the ideas of Thomas F. Gilbert, a guru who many think wrote the definitive book about managing people in organizations. After discussing some of Gilbert's most controversial ideas, we present his model for understanding human behavior in organizations, a model many consider to be the best ever created. In the remainder of this chapter we discuss the flow of information in organizations—who our gurus think should know what, when, and how—and the best methods for delivering financial and nonfinancial consequences for performance. In a concluding section, we summarize the consensus of top compensation gurus on what constitutes the most desirable compensation systems for most American businesses today.

In our concluding chapter, "Business, Work, and Society," we examine the views of the business guru of all business gurus, Peter Drucker, on the obsolescence of capitalism and rise of the postcapitalist, knowledge society. We then compare the thinking of two of the world's most popular gurus on the implications of Drucker's knowledge society, particularly in the ways companies must be organized and careers must be managed.

Finally, at the end of this book you will find biographies for all of our gurus, including in many instances, postal addresses, telephone numbers, and e-mail addresses where they can be reached.

SOME GUIDANCE ON WHAT FOLLOWS: HOW THE CHAPTERS ARE ORGANIZED

Throughout *The Guru Guide* we have tried to summarize as clearly, succinctly, and objectively as possible the key ideas of each guru. Our personal opinions are expressed in sections entitled "Our View" and preceded by the following icon:

OUR VIEW

At the beginning of each chapter, we use the following icon to identify the gurus covered in that chapter. For example, the chapter on managing change begins as follows:

OUR CHANGE MANAGEMENT GURUS

James Champy
Daryl Conner
Richard Farson

At the end of each chapter, we provide a summary of the key ideas presented in that chapter and indicated by the following:

KEY POINTS

You can read this book straight through, from beginning to end, covering the topics in the order we present them, or you can go directly to a topic that interests you. You can read the chapters in any order you wish, since each chapter has been designed to stand on its own. We therefore encourage you to start with whatever topic is of most interest to you at the moment. If you are interested in specific gurus, check the index or the guru lists at the beginning of each chapter to find out where they appear in the book and proceed accordingly. You are in control of how you read this book. In fact, this advice is a good summary of the message contained herein. You are in control, or at least you had better be.

So here it is—an unbiased but highly opinionated look at the best and worst the most notable management gurus have to offer. We wish you good reading and, of course, good management. If you have comments about *The Guru Guide* or suggestions concerning how we might make it better, contact us through our web site.

Joseph H. Boyett
Jimmie T. Boyett

Web site: http://www.Jboyett.com
E-mail: Boyett@Jboyett.com

Karl Albrecht, author of *Service America! Doing Business in the New Economy*

Christopher A. Bartlett, coauthor of *Managing across Borders*

Warren Bennis, founding chair of the University of Southern California's Leadership Institute

Warren Blank, president of the Leadership Group

Lee G. Bolman, coauthor of *Leading with Soul*

Juana Bordas, founding president and CEO of the National Hispana Leadership Institute

James Champy, author of *Reengineering Management*

Jay A. Conger, chair of the University of Southern California's Leadership Institute

Stephen R. Covey, author of *The Seven Habits of Highly Effective People*

Terrence E. Deal, coauthor of *Leading with Soul*

Max DePree, chair of the board of directors, Herman Miller Co. and author of *Leadership Jazz*

Peter F. Drucker, professor of social science and management at the Clairmont Graduate School and author of *Concept of the Corporation*

Richard Farson, author of *Management of the Absurd*

Howard Gardner, author of *Leading Minds*

John W. Gardner, founder of Common Cause, presidential advisor, and author of *On Leadership*

Sumantra Ghoshal, coauthor of *Managing across Borders*

Robert K. Greenleaf, author of the 1970 essay "The Servant Leader"

Laurie Beth Jones, author of *Jesus CEO*

Jon R. Katzenbach, coauthor of *Real Change Leaders*

Manfred F. R. Kets de Vries, author of *Life and Death in the Executive Fast Lane*

John P. Kotter, author of *The Leadership Factor*

Burt Nanus, coauthor of *Visionary Leadership and Leaders*

James O'Toole, author of *Vanguard Management*

Margaret J. Wheatley, author of *Leadership and the New Science*

Leadership

We begin this book with perhaps the most popular topic in all of business literature—leadership. Every business guru, it seems, has written at least one book and/or a collection of articles on the topic. Even when the topic isn't specifically leadership, but something else, such as managing diversity, managing change, total quality, reengineering, or strategy, a sizable portion of the narrative comes down to how and why people lead the particular effort under discussion or fail to do so. Leadership is *the* catchall subject of business discourse, but perhaps we shouldn't be too surprised.

People have been arguing about and writing about leaders and leadership for at least 2,000 years. Even the Bible contains an opinion. For example, Matt. 15:14 warns that "if the blind lead the blind, both shall fall into the ditch," which, by the way, is good cautionary advice for those who want to learn how to lead by following the advice of some of our leadership gurus.

It is easy to understand why so many gurus and aspiring gurus tackle the issue of leadership. Providing leadership wisdom has become a very lucrative occupation, with some of the best-known gurus earning more than

$500,000 per month for dishing out advice. American corporations dole out an estimated $15 *billion* per year on training and consulting for their up-and-coming leaders. As you might expect, that amount of money attracts a lot of interest in the leadership game and is responsible for the profusion of literature on the topic—including a lot of junk that can be found in books and articles purporting to reveal the 7, 8, 9, or 100 secrets somebody you may or may not have heard of knows about leadership.

Faced with the enormous volume of writing, research, videos, multimedia, and executive short courses on leadership, and even after tossing out the obvious junk, we had to be selective in preparing this chapter. Consequently, we offer this disclaimer. Unlike two of our leadership gurus who claimed that after reading their book you will be "equipped with *all* of the information and answers you need to become an effective, inspiring leader" (emphasis added), we will say only that after you read this chapter you will be equipped with *some* of the most important information and answers about becoming a leader. We will start where most other writers on leadership have started for thousands of years—with the characteristics of leaders.

THE ESSENTIAL CHARACTERISTICS OF LEADERS

Almost all of our leadership gurus provide a list of attributes or characteristics that leaders do or should possess. These are the yardsticks against which the rest of us should be able to measure the mettle of our character and consequently our leadership potential. Throughout this chapter, we provide lists of leadership characteristics from the writings of some the best-known gurus. We invite you to score your own leadership potential by checking off the *characteristics, attributes, megaskills,* and *ingredients of leadership* that you possess; but we warn you that the standards laid out by our gurus are stringent. We will begin with one of the best-known names in the leadership business—Warren Bennis. His list of basic leadership ingredients appears in Exhibit 1.1.

Bennis is a professor of business administration at the University of Southern California and the best-selling author of *On Becoming a Leader* and numerous other works on leadership. If anyone knows what it takes to be a leader, Bennis does.

EXHIBIT 1.1. **Warren Bennis's Basic Ingredients of Leadership**

✔	BASIC INGREDIENT	WHAT IT MEANS
	Guiding vision	You have a clear idea of what you want to do—professionally and personally—and the strength to persist in the face of setbacks, even failures.
	Passion	You have an underlying passion for the promises of life, combined with a very particular passion for a vocation, a profession, a course of action. You love what you do.
	Integrity	Your integrity is derived from self-knowledge, candor, and maturity. You know your strengths and weaknesses, are true to your principles, and have learned from experience how to learn from and work with others.
	Trust	You have earned people's trust.
	Curiosity	You wonder about everything and want to learn as much as you can.
	Daring	You are willing to take risks, experiment, and try new things.

Source: Warren Bennis, *On Becoming a Leader* (New York: Addison Wesley, 1989/1994), pp. 39–42.

We hope you have these basic ingredients. Now let's see if you have mastered the seven megaskills of leadership as outlined by Burt Nanus in *The Leader's Edge* (see Exhibit 1.2). Nanus is a professor emeritus of management at the University of Southern California's School of Business Administration, former director of research at USC's Leadership Institute, and coauthor with Warren Bennis of the 1985 business best-seller *Leaders: The Strategies for Taking Charge.*

Next, in Exhibit 1.3, we have a list of characteristics from James O'Toole, former vice president of the famous Aspen Institute, where many leaders have been trained. O'Toole was also a director of the Leadership Institute at USC.

Next we list Stephen Covey's seven habits of successful people and eight characteristics of principle-centered leaders. (See Exhibits 1.4. and 1.5.) Covey is the author of the best-selling book *The Seven Habits of Highly Successful People,* in which he introduces the philosophy of people-centered leadership, and more recently *Principle-Centered Leadership.* He

EXHIBIT 1.2.   Burt Nanus's Seven Megaskills of Leadership

✔ MEGASKILL	WHAT IT MEANS
Farsightedness	You keep your eyes firmly fixed on the far horizon, even as you take steps toward it.
Mastery of change	You regulate the speed, direction, and rhythm of change in the organization so that its growth and evolution matches the external pace of events.
Organization design	You are an institution builder whose legacy is an organization capable of success in realizing the desired vision.
Anticipatory learning	You are a lifelong learner who is committed to promoting organizational learning.
Initiative	You demonstrate an ability to make things happen.
Mastery of interdependence	You inspire others to share ideas and trust each other, to communicate well and frequently, and to seek collaborative solutions to problems.
High standards of integrity	You are fair, honest, tolerant, dependable, caring, open, loyal, and committed to the best traditions of the past.

Source: Burt Nanus, **The Leader's Edge: The Seven Keys to Leadership in a Turbulent World** (New York: Contemporary Books, 1989), pp. 81–97.

EXHIBIT 1.3.   James O'Toole's Characteristics of Values-Based Leaders

✔ CHARACTERISTIC	WHAT IT MEANS
Integrity	You never lose sight of your goals or compromise your principles. You are simultaneously principled and pragmatic.
Trust	You reflect the values and aspirations of your followers. You accept leadership as a responsibility, not a privilege. You serve.
Listening	You listen to the people you serve, but you are not a prisoner of public opinion. You encourage dissenting opinions among your advisors. You test ideas, explore all sides of issues, and air the full range of opinion.
Respect for followers	You are a leader of leaders. You are pragmatic to your core but believe passionately in what you say and do.

Source: James O'Toole, **Leading Change: The Argument for Values-Based Leadership** (New York: Ballantine, 1996), pp. 23–34.

EXHIBIT 1.4. Stephen Covey's Seven Habits of Highly Successful People

✔ Habit	What It Means
Be proactive.	You take responsibility for your own behavior. You don't blame circumstances, conditions, or your conditioning for your behavior. You choose your response to any situation and any person.
Begin with the end in mind.	You can visualize the future that you want to achieve. You have a clear vision of where you want to go and what you want to accomplish. You live your life according to some deeply held beliefs, principles, or fundamental truths.
Put first things first.	You live a disciplined life. You focus heavily on highly important but not necessarily urgent activities such as "building relationships, writing a personal mission statement, long-range planning, exercising, . . . preparation—all those things we know we need to do, but somehow seldom get around to doing, because they aren't urgent" (Covey 1990, p. 154). You say no to things that seem critical but are unimportant.
Think win/win.	You have an "abundance" mentality. You believe there is plenty for everybody. You don't believe that one person's success requires another person's failure. You look for synergistic solutions to problems. You seek to find solutions in which all parties benefit.
Seek first to understand, then to be understood.	You listen with the strong intent to fully, deeply understand the other person both emotionally and intellectually. You diagnose before you prescribe.
Synergize.	You are creative. You are a trailblazer and a pathfinder. You believe the whole is greater than the sum of its parts. You value differences between people and try to build upon those differences. When presented with two conflicting alternatives, you seek a third, more creative response.
Sharpen the saw.	You seek continuous improvement, innovation, and refinement. You are always seeking to learn.

Source: Stephen R. Covey, *The Seven Habits of Highly Effective People: Powerful Lessons in Personal Change* (New York: Fireside, 1990), pp. 63–309 and Stephen R. Covey, *Principle-Centered Leadership* (New York: Summit, 1991), pp. 40–47.

EXHIBIT 1.5.　**Stephen Covey's Eight Discernible Characteristics of Principle-Centered Leaders**

✔	CHARACTERISTIC	WHAT IT MEANS
	Continual learning	You seek training, take classes, listen, ask questions.
	Service orientation	You "see life as a mission, not as a career."
	Radiate positive energy	You are cheerful, pleasant, happy, optimistic, positive, upbeat, enthusiastic, hopeful, and you believe in people.
	Believe in other people	You don't overreact to negative behaviors, don't carry grudges, and don't label, stereotype, or prejudge people.
	Lead a balanced life	You are balanced, temperate, moderate, wise, sensible, simple, direct, nonmanipulative, physically active, socially active, and well read. You are not a zealot, fanatic, martyr, or addict. You don't brood. You take praise and blame proportionately and are genuinely happy for others' successes.
	See life as an adventure	You are a courageous, unflappable, totally flexible explorer who savors life.
	Synergize	You are a productive, "smart working" change catalyst.
	Engage in physical, mental, emotional, and spiritual exercise for self-renewal	You engage in aerobic exercise. You like reading, writing, and creative problem solving. You are emotional but patient. You listen with empathy and show unconditional love. You pray, meditate, fast, and read scripture.

Source: Stephen R. Covey, *Principle-Centered Leadership* (Summit, 1991), pp. 33–39.

is also chair of the Covey Leadership Center. Let's see if you have the right habits of success and characteristics to make you a principle-centered leader.

Max DePree offers his opinions about the attributes of leadership in his book *Leadership Jazz*. As the retired CEO of Herman Miller, Inc., he brings the perspective of real experience to our group of gurus, describing leadership attributes as shown in Exhibit 1.6.

Finally, we include a list of leadership attributes provided by someone with both a business and government perspective. John W. Gardner served as secretary of health, education, and welfare, an advisor to six presidents,

EXHIBIT 1.6. **Max DePree's Attributes of Leadership**

✔	Attribute	What It Means
	Integrity	You demonstrate integrity in your behavior.
	Vulnerability	You trust in the abilities of other people. You allow people who follow you to do their best.
	Discernment	You exhibit keen insight, wisdom, and judgment.
	Awareness of the human spirit	You understand the cares, yearning, and struggles of the human spirit.
	Courage in relationships	You face up to tough decisions. You act with ruthless honesty.
	Sense of humor	You have a broad perspective on the human condition that accounts for many points of view. You have a compassionate sense of humor.
	Intellectual energy and curiosity	You accept responsibility for learning frantically.
	Respect for the future, regard for the present, understanding of the past	You are able to move constantly back and forth between the present and the future. You build upon the work of your elders.
	Predictability	You do not follow whims.
	Breadth	Your vision of what the organization can accomplish has room for contributions from all quarters. Your vision is "large enough to contain multitudes."
	Comfort with ambiguity	You make sense out of chaos.
	Presence	You stop to ask and answer questions. You are patient. You listen to problems. You seek to understand nuances. You follow up on leads.

Source: Max DePree, **Leadership Jazz: The Art of Conducting Business through Leadership, Followership, Teamwork, Touch, Voice** (New York: Dell, 1993), pp. 222–225.

and a business professor at Stanford University. He is the author of *On Leadership,* in which he maintains that the following attributes of leadership in Exhibit 1.7 apply to leaders in both the public and the private sector.

In addition to providing lists of habits, attributes, and characteristics, our gurus use a lot of descriptive words and phrases about leaders. Exhibit 1.8

EXHIBIT 1.7. **John Gardner's Attributes of Leadership**

✔	ATTRIBUTE	WHAT IT MEANS
	Physical vitality and stamina	You have a high energy level and are physically durable.
	Intelligence and judgment-in-action	You can combine hard data, questionable data, and intuitive guesses to arrive at a conclusion that events prove to be correct.
	Willingness (eagerness) to accept responsibilities	You have an impulse to exercise initiative in social situations. You step forward when no one else will.
	Task competence	You have knowledge of the task at hand.
	Understanding of followers/constituents and their needs	You understand the various constituencies with whom you work.
	Skill in dealing with people	You can appraise accurately the readiness or resistance of followers to move in a given direction. You make the most of their motives and understand their sensitivities.
	Need to achieve	You have a driving pressure to achieve.
	Capacity to motivate	You communicate persuasively. You move people to action.
	Courage, resolution, steadiness	You are willing to take risks. You never give up. You stay the course.
	Capacity to win and hold trust	You have an extraordinary ability to win the trust of people.
	Capacity to manage, decide, set priorities	You perform the traditional tasks of management—formulating goals, setting priorities, framing a course of action, selecting aides, and delegating—very well.
	Confidence	You continually nominate yourself for leadership tasks. You have confidence that others will react positively to your offer of leadership.
	Ascendance, dominance, assertiveness	You have a strong impulse to take charge.
	Adaptability, flexibility of approach	You can shift swiftly and without hesitation from a failing tactic to another approach, and if that does not work, to still another.

Source: John Gardner, **On Leadership** (New York: Free Press, 1990), pp. 48–53.

EXHIBIT 1.8. Evaluating Your Leadership Potential. Are You Really . . .

❏ A good listener	❏ Credible	❏ Hard-working	❏ Reliable
❏ A risk taker	❏ Curious	❏ Hopeful	❏ Respectful
❏ A visionary	❏ Daring	❏ Humble	❏ Responsible
❏ Active	❏ Decisive	❏ Humorous	❏ Restless
❏ Adaptable	❏ Dependable	❏ Intelligent	❏ Self-confident
❏ Ambitious	❏ Direct	❏ Loyal	❏ Sensible
❏ An achiever	❏ Disciplined	❏ Mature	❏ Sensitive
❏ Assertive	❏ Dominant	❏ Moderate	❏ Simple
❏ Aware	❏ Driven	❏ Open	❏ Social
❏ Balanced	❏ Empathetic	❏ Optimistic	❏ Solicitous
❏ Cheerful	❏ Energetic	❏ Passionate	❏ Spiritual
❏ Committed	❏ Enthusiastic	❏ Patient	❏ Stable
❏ Competitive	❏ Fair	❏ Physically fit	❏ Tenacious
❏ Conceptual	❏ Farsighted	❏ Pleasant	❏ Trustworthy
❏ Conscientious	❏ Firm	❏ Positive	❏ Unflappable
❏ Constant	❏ Flexible	❏ Pragmatic	❏ Upbeat
❏ Courageous	❏ Goal-oriented	❏ Proactive	❏ Vulnerable
❏ Creative	❏ Happy	❏ Productive	❏ Wise

shows you a few. Check off those that apply to you and continue to assess your leadership potential. Be honest.

Don't Worry If You Don't Fit the Leadership Profile— You Just Might Be Leader Material Anyway

If after reading this laundry list of attributes and characteristics and checking off those that apply to you, the phrases "able to leap small buildings in a single bound" and "that pretty much leaves me out" come to mind, you are not alone. Most people find this roll call of superlatives somewhat daunting. But take heart. Some of our gurus consider this to be much ado about nothing.

For all of their lists of must-have traits and characteristics, there is much disagreement among our gurus about their real value and necessity. The really necessary attributes, say our gurus, might be some of the traits we listed above, none of them, all of them some of the time, none of them most of the time, and so on. Some gurus even contradict themselves—John Gardner, for example. He offers his list of leadership attributes and then writes that "research has demonstrated over and over that we must not think rigidly or mechanically about the attributes of leaders. The attributes required of a leader depend on the kind of leadership being exercised, the context, the nature of followers, and so on."[1]

Some gurus think that there may indeed be a select few attributes or characteristics that really matter, with the rest being somewhat optional or situation-dependent. For example, Manfred F. R. Kets de Vries, once described as a European "corporate pathology expert," writes that most researchers would agree that traits such as *conscientiousness, energy, intelligence, dominance, self-confidence, sociability, openness to experience, task-relevant knowledge,* and *emotional stability* are important. Beyond that limited area of common agreement, however, he says that "the myriad theories diverge, and it is easy to lose oneself in the academic hair-splitting."[2]

Peter Drucker, the grand old man of management guruship, goes even further. He rejects the possibility of finding even a few fundamental traits. According to him, the whole discussion of characteristics and traits is a waste of time.

"Leadership personality," "leadership style," and "leadership traits" do not exist. Among the most effective leaders I have encountered and worked with in a half century, some locked themselves into their office and others were ultra-gregarious. Some (though not many) were "nice guys" and others were stern disciplinarians. Some were quick and impulsive; others studied and studied again and then took forever to come to a decision. Some were warm and instantly "simpatico"; others remained aloof. Some spoke of their family; others never mentioned anything apart from the task in hand. Some leaders were excruciatingly vain—and it did not affect their performance. . . . Some were self-effacing to a fault—and again it did not affect their performance as leaders. . . . Some were as austere in their private lives as a hermit in the desert; others were ostentatious and pleasure-loving and whooped it up at every opportunity. Some were good listeners, but among the most effective I have worked with were also a few loners who listened only to their own inner voice. The one and only personality trait the effective ones I have encountered did have in common was something they did not have: they had little or no "charisma" and little use either for the term or for what it signifies.[3]

◆◎ OUR VIEW

So who is right and who is wrong? In our view, Drucker is closer to reality. While there may be a few characteristics that many leaders hold in common, such as the desire to lead, the willingness to take risks, a need to achieve, and so on, these characteristics aren't necessarily shared by all leaders. There may be some characteristics that we would like our leaders to have, such as honesty, ethics, and a concern for the welfare of followers, but we can easily identify leaders who exhibit none of these traits—Hitler, for example. Maybe we can understand leaders better if we focus less on the traits of leaders and more on the relationships between leaders and followers. That's what Warren Blank and his colleagues at the Leadership Group in Chapel Hill, North Carolina, recommend.

HEADS IT'S LEADERSHIP; TAILS IT'S SOMETHING ELSE

Here's a little quiz. What do the following leaders have in common?

Susan B. Anthony	Thomas Edison	Adolf Hitler
Mary Kay Ash	Michael Eisner	Lee Iacocca
Attila the Hun	Henry Ford	Thomas Jefferson
Jan Carlzon	Robert Galvin	Steve Jobs
Andrew Carnegie	Mohandas Gandhi	John Kennedy
Jesus Christ	Stanley Gault	Martin Luther King
Robert Crandall	Louis Gertsner	Bobby Knight
King David	Bill Gore	Helmut Kohl
Max DePree	Andy Grove	Edwin H. Land

Abraham Lincoln	Jean-Luc Picard	Ted Turner
George C. Marshall	Ronald Reagan	Bill Walsh
J. P. Morgan	John D. Rockefeller	Sam Walton
J. Robert Oppenheimer	Anita Roddick	Jack Welch
George C. Patton	Theodore Roosevelt	Lee Kwan Yew
Ross Perot	Sitting Bull	Andrew Young

Stumped? Well, here are some hints.

- Forget about personal characteristics, behavioral traits, or leadership styles.
- Forget about what these people did or said or when they lived.
- Ask yourself what one thing made all of these people leaders.

Why were the people we listed above leaders?

The one thing all of these leaders had in common was **willing followers.**

We know that sounds simple, but it's true. Having willing followers is the only thing that clearly differentiates leaders from nonleaders. Leaders have willing followers. Nonleaders don't. And no one is a leader until he or she acquires willing followers. "Followers," writes Warren Blank, "are the underlying element that defines all leaders in all situations. . . . Lincoln, Lenin, King, Perot, Ash, and Wachner . . . were leaders when they gained followers. . . . Followers are allies who represent the necessary opposite side of the leadership coin."[4]

At first glance, the idea that leaders have followers and nonleaders don't hardly seems extraordinary. In fact, it may seem obvious. What is not so obvious about this fact are the implications that result from changing our perspective.

When we stop viewing the leader-follower relationship as something that is commonplace and uninteresting and begin making the relationship itself central to our understanding of leadership, we gain new insights. When we focus on the leader-follower *relationship* rather than on the leader's personal traits, behaviors, or habits, we begin to see leaders and leadership in a new light. Warren Blank translates this new perspective into what he calls "nine natural laws of leadership." We summarize three of these here because they provide an interesting new perspective on leadership. All nine of Blank's natural laws are listed in Exhibit 1.9.

EXHIBIT 1.9. **Warren Blank's Nine Natural Laws of Leadership**

---

1. A leader has willing followers-allies.
2. Leadership is a field of interaction.
3. Leadership occurs as an event.
4. Leaders use influence beyond formal authority.
5. Leaders operate outside the boundaries of the organizationally defined procedures.
6. Leadership involves risk and uncertainty.
7. Not everyone will follow a leader's initiative.
8. Consciousness—information processing capacity—creates leadership.
9. Leadership is a self-referral process. Leaders and followers process information from their own subjective, internal frame of reference.

Source: Warren Blank, *The Nine Natural Laws of Leadership* (New York: AMACOM, 1995), p. 10.

Natural Law #1:
A Leader Has Willing Followers-Allies

Blank's first natural law is that leaders must have followers. Obvious, you say. Yes, but think about the implication of that simple statement. If a leader must have followers to be a leader, then a lot of the leader's activity has to do with getting the backing of people, that is, getting followers. Blank says, "Most people who aspire to lead ask the wrong initial questions. 'How do I lead?' or 'What do I have to do to be a leader?' reveal a mistaken belief that leadership is made up of parts. The correct questions are 'How do I get others to follow me?' 'What are the needs of others?' and 'How do I gain allies?' "[5] Laurie Beth Jones, the author of *Jesus CEO,* makes the point this way:

> Leaders who are intent upon accomplishing anything worthwhile have to enroll others in their cause. I find too many managers who have staffs who are employed on paper but are not emotionally enrolled in the mission. . . . To enroll others means that you make sure your entire staff is "hitched" to you, and to each other, before you take off in a big puff of smoke, leaving everyone behind. Jesus constantly checked his staff's commitment, asking them "Are you with me?" and then waited for the answer.[6]

Natural Law #2: Leadership Is a Field of Interaction

Blank's second natural law is derived from the first. If leaders need followers, then leadership isn't just about character. It is largely about a relationship between leader and followers. Blank refers to this relationship as "an undivided wholeness that resembles a dance . . . the interacting ebb and flow between leader and follower." He adds that "leadership is better understood as a field of interaction. It is not so much personal as it is interpersonal. . . . Jack Welch's . . . tough-mindedness was not what made him a leader. Rather it was the people who followed him. . . . [The] leadership at Microsoft is not Bill Gates's innovativeness but the unity or connection between Gates and his people."[7] Therefore, a central task of all leaders is to build a solid working relationship with others. Blank cites Jesse Jackson's comment that "leaders do not choose sides but rather bring sides together."[8] Consequently, "field-conscious . . . leaders continually build bridges and establish common ground so that others become more receptive to the leadership initiatives."[9]

Natural Law #3: Leadership Occurs As an Event

As we all know, relationships don't necessarily last. Therefore, if leadership is a relationship, leaders may not remain leaders forever; a leader today may not be a leader tomorrow. That's not what we expect of leaders. When most of us think about leadership, we tend to view it as a continuous process—one in which leaders lead, followers follow, and the whole process goes on and on as long as the leader is alive or chooses to lead. Blank argues that this is not what happens at all.

> Leadership occurs as an event. Leader-follower fields [of interaction] begin, have a middle, and they end. They occur as discrete interactions each time a leader and follower join. . . . Leadership can appear continuous if a leader manifests multiple leadership events. . . . The bulk of leadership events, however, have a shorter shelf-life. They occur as brief leader-follower interactions in specific circumstances.[10]

Consequently, leaders can have roller-coaster careers. Lee Iacocca can become president and leader of Ford, be fired, and come back as a leader at Chrysler. Steve Jobs can excel at Apple and fail at NeXT. Blank explains:

> Leadership is best understood as a discontinuous reality. . . . The field [of interaction] exists only as long as leaders have followers. Breaks exist between leadership events just as a motion picture is made up of separate frames and spaces exist between the letters in words such as
>
> l | e | a | d | e | r | s | h | i | p[11]

So there you have it. If you want to understand leadership, don't focus so much on characteristics and personality traits. Leadership is an event, not a trait. It is about what you do with who you are, more than just about who you are. In short, leadership is first about understanding your strengths and weaknesses and then about taking on leadership roles and responsibilities in which you connect with followers in a special way. So what are the roles and responsibilities of leaders? What do leaders do? How do leaders differ from managers? As you might expect, our gurus have a lot to say about these issues.

LEADER ROLES AND RESPONSIBILITIES— WHAT LEADERS DO

Perhaps the best way to explain what leaders do, or at least what our gurus think leaders do or should do, is to use a device most of them use. Our gurus compare the roles, responsibilities, habits, and actions of the traditional manager on one side, with those of the servant, virtual, visionary, charismatic, group-centered, quantum, postheroic, new-science leader on the other. Exhibit 1.10 shows the comparison drawn from the works of many of our leadership gurus. As you read the list, notice the difference in what the leader emphasizes versus what the manager emphasizes.

Another way to distinguish between leaders and managers is to examine the language our gurus use in talking about leaders. When speaking of

EXHIBIT 1.10. **Managers versus Leaders**

MANAGERS	LEADERS
Do things right	Do the right thing
Are interested in efficiency	Are interested in effectiveness
Administer	Innovate
Maintain	Develop
Focus on systems and structure	Focus on people
Rely on control	Rely on trust
Organize and staff	Align people with a direction
Emphasize tactics, structure, and systems	Emphasize philosophy, core values, and shared goals
Have a short-term view	Have a long-term view
Ask how and when	Ask what and why
Accept the status quo	Challenge the status quo
Focus on the present	Focus on the future
Have their eyes on the bottom line	Have their eyes on the horizon
Develop detailed steps and timetables	Develop visions and strategies
Seek predictability and order	Seek change
Avoid risks	Take risks
Motivate people to comply with standards	Inspire people to change
Use position-to-position (superior-to-subordinate) influence	Use person-to-person influence
Require others to comply	Inspire others to follow
Operate within organizational rules, regulations, policies, and procedures	Operate outside of organizational rules, regulations, policies, and procedures
Are given a position	Take initiative to lead

Sources: Writings of Warren Bennis, Burt Nanus, Robert Townsend, John P. Kotter, Manfred F. R. Kets de Vries, Warren Blank, Jon R. Katzenbach, and others.

them, our gurus say things that most tradition-minded managers find strange, to say the least.

Leadership requires love.
The best leaders are servants.
You lead by giving to others.

As strange as it may seem to say that leadership requires love or that leaders must be servants and gift givers, such statements reflect the thinking of many of our gurus about what is required of today's leader. Needless to say, what our gurus ask of leaders today is quite different from what we have expected of our leaders in the past. Our gurus ask for a different rhythm for a leader's activities, a different leadership mind-set, a different focus for the executive's daily tasks, and most especially a different relationship between leaders and employees, customers, and stakeholders. Our gurus raise new expectations. They de-emphasize leadership activities once thought important and emphasize different roles and responsibilities for the leader. They outline at least three fundamental shifts in the leader's duties and responsibilities: (1) from strategist to visionary, (2) from commander to storyteller, and (3) from systems architect to change agent and servant. Each of these shifts represents an important change of emphasis in leader behavior that many, if not most, of our gurus support. We summarize them in the following pages.

Leadership Role Shift #1: From Strategist to Visionary

Since at least the 1920s, top managers have focused much of their time and attention on developing and implementing business strategy. In a 1994 article in the *Harvard Business Review,* Christopher Bartlett of Harvard and Sumantra Ghoshal of the London Business School noted that "from Alfred Sloan to Lee Iacocca, the powerful, even heroic image of the CEO as omniscient strategist is ingrained in business history and folklore."[12] In the past, traditional senior managers "explored business synergies," "balanced strategic portfolios," and sought to "articulate strategic intent." Strategy-making has long been seen as a key leadership function, but that's not what our gurus think leaders should be spending their time on today.

Almost without exception, our gurus want today's leaders to focus more on developing a vision for their organization than on designing a business strategy. The problem, say our gurus, is not that business strategies aren't needed but that strategies alone are no longer enough. "Traditionally," explain Bartlett and Ghoshal, "top-level managers have tried to engage employees intellectually through the persuasive logic of strategic analyses. But clinically framed and contractually based relationships do not inspire the extraordinary effort and sustained commitment required to deliver consistently superior performance."[13] People aren't engaged by strategies. They don't form any strong emotional attachment to them. Strategies answer *what* but don't answer *why*, and knowing why is more important. Leaders must go beyond the what, say Bartlett, Ghoshal, and most of our other gurus, to create "an organization with which members can identify, in which they share a sense of pride, and to which they are willing to commit. In short, senior managers must convert the contractual employees of an economic entity into committed members of a purposeful organization."[14]

Karl Albrecht, author of the best-seller *Service America* and *The Northbound Train: Finding the Purpose, Setting the Direction, Shaping the Destiny of Your Organization,* puts the need for vision this way:

> In many ways the crisis in business today is a crisis of meaning. People aren't sure of themselves because they no longer understand the why behind the what. They no longer have the sense that things are well defined and that hard work will lead to success. More and more people have feelings of doubt and uncertainty about the future of their organizations, and consequently about their own careers and futures. More and more organizations and their people are in a crisis of meaning. . . . Those who would aspire to leadership roles in this new environment must not underestimate the depth of this human need for meaning. It is a most fundamental human craving, an appetite that will not go away.[15]

Our gurus make it clear that a vision is something more than the rallying cry to increase market share, bloody the competition, or double last year's profits. It is more emotional than analytical. In short, it is something that touches the heart, not just the mind. A vision, says Karl Albrecht, is a "shared image of what we want the enterprise to be or become. . . . It . . . provides an aiming point for a future orientation. It answers the question, 'How do we want those we care about to perceive us?' The vision statement . . . implies an element of noble purpose and high values, of something considered especially worthwhile."[16]

Burt Nanus describes a vision as a "realistic, credible, attractive future for your organization . . . an idea so energizing that it in effect jump-starts the future by calling forth the skills, talents, and resources to make it happen [and] a signpost pointing the way for all who need to understand what the organization is and where it intends to go."[17] Jay Conger, author of *The Charismatic Leader,* describes a vision as a mental image that portrays a desirable future state, an ideal, or a far-reaching dream.[18] Warren Blank likens it to a "unique wide-angle and long-range lens of awareness [that enables people] to see into the future and to comprehend big picture possibilities."[19]

According to our gurus, a good vision:

Gives meaning to the changes expected of people
Evokes a clear and positive mental image of a future state
Creates pride, energy, and a sense of accomplishment
Is memorable
Is motivating
Is idealistic
Offers a view of the future that is clearly and demonstrably better
Fits the organization's history, culture, and values
Sets standards of excellence that reflect high ideals
Clarifies purpose and direction
Inspires enthusiasm
Encourages commitment
Reflects the uniqueness of the organization
Is ambitious
Grabs attention
Focuses attention
Guides day-to-day activities
Screens out the unessential
Energizes people to transcend the bottom line
Provides meaning and significance to daily activities
Bridges the present and the future
Moves people to action

In *Leadership and the New Science,* Margaret Wheatley likens a vision to an intentional force field that permeates the organization like a wave of energy. All employees who bump up against this field, she says, are influenced by it. Their behavior is shaped by these "field meetings" and made congruent with the organization's goals.[20]

Visions are sometimes expressed simply:

3M	To solve unsolved problems innovatively
Fannie Mae	To strengthen the social fabric by continually democratizing home ownership
Girl Scouts of America	To help a girl reach her highest potential
Hewlett-Packard	To make technical contributions for the advancement and welfare of humanity
Mary Kay Cosmetics	To give unlimited opportunity to women
Merck	To preserve and improve human life
Nike	To experience the emotion of competition, winning, and crushing competitors
Sony	To experience the joy of advancing and applying technology for the benefit of the public
Wal-Mart	To give ordinary folk the chance to buy the same things as rich people
Walt Disney	To make people happy.[21]

However, a few words are rarely enough. We usually need to hear a more lengthy explanation from an articulate leader to grasp the full power of a compelling vision.

Great Vision Statements from Great Leaders

Henry Ford said this about his vision for democratizing the automobile:

> I will build a motor car for the great multitude. . . . It will be so low in price that no man making a good salary will be unable to own one and enjoy with his family the blessing of hours of pleasure in God's great open spaces. . . . When I'm through, everybody will be able to afford one, and everyone will have one. The horse will have disappeared from our highways, the automobile will be taken for granted [and we will] give a large number of men employment at good wages.[22]

Walt Disney described his dream for Disneyland this way:

> The idea of Disneyland is a simple one. It will be a place for people to find happiness and knowledge. It will be a place for parents and children to spend

pleasant times in one another's company; a place for teachers and pupils to discover greater ways of understanding and education. Here the older generation can recapture the nostalgia of days gone by, and the younger generation can savor the challenge of the future. Here will be the wonders of Nature and Man for all to see and understand. Disneyland will be based upon and dedicated to the ideals, the dreams and hard facts that have created America. And it will be uniquely equipped to dramatize these dreams and facts and send them forth as a source of courage and inspiration to all the world.

Disneyland will be something of a fair, an exhibition, a playground, a community center, a museum of living facts, and a showplace of beauty and magic. It will be filled with the accomplishments, the joys and hopes of the world we live in. And it will remind us and show us how to make those wonders part of our lives. [23]

Here is Sir Winston Churchill's famous vision for Britain's finest hour:

Hitler knows he will have to break us on this island or lose the war. If we can stand up to him, all Europe may be free, and the life of the world may move forward into broad, sunlit uplands. But if we fail, the whole world, including the United States, including all we have known and cared for, will sink into the abyss of a new Dark Age, made more sinister and perhaps more protracted by the lights of perverted science. Let us therefore brace ourselves to our duties and so bear ourselves that if the British Empire and its Commonwealth last for a thousand years, men will still say, "This was their finest hour." [24]

And finally, Martin Luther King expressed his dream for America in these words:

I say to you today, my friends, that in spite of the difficulties and frustrations of the moment I still have a dream. It is a dream deeply rooted in the American dream.

I have a dream that one day the nation will rise up and live out the true meaning of its creed: "We hold these truths to be self-evident; that all men are created equal."

I have a dream that one day on the red hills of Georgia the sons of former slaves and the sons of former slave owners will be able to sit down together at the table of brotherhood.

I have a dream that one day even the State of Mississippi, a desert state sweltering in the heat of injustice and oppression, will be transformed into an oasis of freedom and justice.

I have a dream that my four children will one day live in a nation where they will not be judged by the color of their skin but by the content of their character.

I have a dream today. . . .[25]

All of these visions are compelling and forceful. They have what James Collins and Jerry Porras, coauthors of *Built to Last: Successful Habits of Visionary Companies,* call the *gulp factor.* "When it dawns on people what it will take to achieve the [vision], there [is] an almost audible gulp."[26]

Honing Your Own Vision

If the prospect of having to reach such heights of visionary insight and imagination for your organization leaves you breathless, you are not alone. Unfortunately, our gurus aren't much help when it comes to explaining how a Churchill gets to his finest hour, how a Disney conceives of Disneyland, or a King evolves a dream. All they say is that the visioning process is long, difficult, and uncertain. For example, Jay Conger describes it as a "fragmented, evolutionary . . . largely intuitive [and] incremental . . . creative process."[27] Jon R. Katzenbach, a consultant with McKinsey & Company and coauthor of *Real Change Leaders,* calls the process murky and uncertain; and Burt Nanus describes it as messy, introspective, and difficult to explain—even for the person who conceives the vision.[28]

Even when our gurus try to get more specific, what they offer doesn't help much. For example, Burt Nanus provides a four-step process consisting of a series of questions that you and your visioning team can answer to construct a vision for your organizations. (See Exhibit 1.11.) He tells us to begin by *taking stock*—by asking questions such as, What business are we really in? What are the current values of the organization? Do people agree or disagree on a direction for the organization? Then we are supposed to *test reality* by asking, Who are the major stakeholders? and Are their needs being met? Next, Nanus tells us to *establish the vision context* by asking, What future developments might affect the vision? and What are some future scenarios? Finally we have to develop alternatives and *choose the vision.*

EXHIBIT 1.11. **Burt Nanus's Systematic Approach to Developing a New Vision**

Process Steps	Major Issues	Questions to Ask
Taking stock—understanding the current status of the organization	What business are we really in?	1. What is the current stated mission or purpose of your organization? 2. What value does the organization provide to society? 3. What is the character of the industry or institutional framework within which your organization operates? 4. What is your organization's unique position in that industry or institutional structure? 5. What does it take for your organization to succeed?
	How do we operate?	1. What are the values and the organizational culture that govern behavior and decision making? 2. What are the operating strengths and weaknesses of the organization? 3. What is the current strategy, and can it be defended?
	The vision audit	1. Does the organization have a clearly stated vision? If so, what is it? 2. If the organization continues on its current path, where will it be heading over the next decade? How good would such a direction be? 3. Do the key people in the organization know where the organization is headed and agree on the direction? 4. Do the structures, processes, personnel, incentives, and information systems support the current direction of the organization?
Testing reality—drawing the boundaries for the vision	Who are the major stakeholders and what are their needs?	1. Who are the most critical stakeholders—both inside and outside your organization—and of these, which are the most important? 2. What are the major interests and expectations of the five or six most important stakeholders regarding the future of your organization?

EXHIBIT 1.11. (Continued)

PROCESS STEPS	MAJOR ISSUES	QUESTIONS TO ASK
		3. What threats or opportunities emanate from these critical stakeholders?
		4. Considering yourself a stakeholder, what do you personally and passionately want to make happen in your organization?
	How should the new vision be bounded?	1. What are the boundaries (time, geographic, social) to your new vision? 2. What must the vision accomplish? How will you know when it is successful? 3. Which critical issues must be addressed in the vision?
Establishing the vision context—positioning the organization in its future external environment	What future developments are likely to influence your vision statement?	1. What major changes can be expected in the needs and wants served by your organization in the future? 2. What changes can be expected in the major stakeholders of your organization in the future? 3. What major changes can be expected in the relevant economic environments in the future? 4. What major changes can be expected in the relevant social environments in the future? 5. What major changes can be expected in the relevant political environments in the future? 6. What major changes can be expected in the relevant technological environments in the future? 7. What major changes can be expected in other external environments that could affect your organization in the future?
	Which future developments are likely to have the greatest impact on your organization's future direction if they were to occur as expected?	Priority One = Greatest impact Priority Two = Next greatest impact Priority Three = Third greatest impact Priority Four = Least impact

PROCESS STEPS	MAJOR ISSUES	QUESTIONS TO ASK
	What three or four scenarios are possible given the occurrence of the developments with the highest impact (Priority One developments)?	Write four or five narrative descriptions of the future. Either start with the present and describe what will happen chronologically up to the future time or pick a future period and describe what it is like, especially as to how the world got to the way you envision it.
Choosing the vision— defining and packaging the new vision	What are several alternative visions?	Of all of the possible directions you could take over the next five to seven years, which ones offer the greatest promise of dramatically improving your position and achieving the greatest success for you and for your key stakeholders?
	Which of the possible visions best fits the criteria for a good vision? (Nanus suggests a method for scoring and weighting alternatives on pages 121–126 of his book *Visionary Leadership*.)	1. Is the vision future oriented? 2. Will it lead to a better future for the organization? 3. Does it fit with the organization's history, culture, and values? 4. Does it set standards of excellence and reflect high ideals? 5. Does it clarify purpose and direction? 6. Will it inspire enthusiasm and encourage commitment? 7. Does it reflect the uniqueness of the organization, its distinctive competence, and what it stands for? 8. Is it ambitious enough?

OUR VIEW

There is nothing wrong with Nanus's steps and questions. They are at least as good as, and in many respects, better than most visioning processes our gurus peddle. Still, we can't help but think that something is missing. Would Disney have gotten to his Fantasy Kingdom this way? Would this have been the way King arrived at his dream? Probably not. In fact, when Nanus works laboriously through his own process to derive a vision for a fictitious pet-food company, he comes up with this glorious vision: "harnessing the research capacity of our parent company to become the innovation leader in our industry, with the goal of no more than 40 percent of our revenues in seven years coming from existing product lines."[29] Somehow this just doesn't seem to have the zing of Ford's vision of a car for the masses or Churchill's finest hour.

Even when our gurus offer simpler suggestions for arriving at visions, we usually find ourselves at a loss. Take, for example, the "five-whys" process James Collins and Jerry Porras propose in a 1996 article in the *Harvard Business Review*. "Start with the descriptive statement 'We make X products' or 'We deliver X services,' " they suggest, "and then ask, 'Why is that important?' five times. After a few whys, you'll find that you're getting down to the fundamental purpose of the organization."[30] Well, maybe.

We invite you try Nanus's process, the five-whys process, and even the tongue-in-cheek Handy-Dandy Vision Crafter (see Exhibit 1.12) suggested by Thomas Stewart in a 1996 article in *Fortune*. These tricks or treats, multistep processes, and batteries of questions offered by our gurus may help you zero in on a vision, or they may not. Just don't expect them to produce

---

EXHIBIT 1.12. **Handy-Dandy Vision Crafter**

Our vision is to be a _____
premier; leading; preeminent; world-class; growing (choose one)

company that provides _____
innovative; cost-effective; focused; diversified; high-quality (choose one)

_____
products; services; products and services (choose one)

to _____
serve the global marketplace; create shareholder value; fulfill our covenants with our stakeholders; delight our customers (choose one)

in the rapidly changing _____
information-solutions; business-solutions; consumer-solutions; financial-solutions (choose one)

industries.

Source: Thomas A. Stewart, "A Refreshing Change: Vision Statements That Make Sense," **Fortune,** September 30, 1996, p. 195.

a vision the same way you, as a master chef, might create an exquisite, well-cooked meal.

On the whole, we don't put much faith in being able to develop a high-quality vision by using any of these step-by-step visioning methods. The results are usually pretty unemotional and unexciting, which is just the opposite of what a true vision is supposed to be. There's also no guarantee of greater success just by involving a lot of people in some kind of visioning conference. Jon Katzenbach argues that "calling people together to talk vision for an afternoon is bound to feel contrived and unproductive, if not downright silly."[31] Like Warren Bennis, we can't help but think that "just as no great painting has ever been created by a committee, no great vision has ever emerged from the herd."[32] When it comes to visioning, you are pretty much on your own.

In most cases, the gurus have you begin the visioning process by focusing on the organization you want to lead. In our opinion, that's a mistake. How can you develop a compelling vision for an organization until you have a compelling vision for your own life—a better understanding of your own values, needs, expectations, hopes, and dreams? When Walt Disney described Disneyland, he wasn't speaking about an amusement park; he was describing his happy place. It was highly personal and expressed his values, needs, expectations, and dreams.

Martin Luther King gave voice to his personal dream—a dream that ultimately ignited a movement with a higher purpose, but one that began with a personal vision. Like Disney and King, you must start with yourself. Ultimately, getting to a vision is about being brutally honest about who you are and who you want to be.

How do you do that? Here are a few ideas from Juana Bordas, a senior program associate with the Center for Creative Leadership in Colorado Springs and founding president and CEO of the National Hispana Leadership Institute.[33]

1. Find a quiet, safe, reflective environment where you can get away from day-to-day activities and do some serious reflection. Bordas suggests a church, garden, mountain top, under an oak tree in your backyard, the seashore, a park, or in your most comfortable chair surrounded by plants and soothing music. Leave the cellular telephone behind.
2. Reflect on your early childhood and how it shaped your development. Look for patterns, motivations, and values that you have as a result of

the way you were raised. Bordas suggests that you think about all of the following:

- *Family composition:* What were your birth position, family rules, expectations, and economic status? What feelings do you have about your family? What traditions did you have? Think about personal characteristics you feel are genetic or inherited.

- *Gender significance:* Being male or female certainly influences the way we think and what we believe is possible. To grasp the significance of gender, write down 10 ways your life would be different if you were a member of the opposite sex.

- *Geographic influences:* Where were you born? Even different regions within a country have diverse cultures and lifestyles. Ask people who were born in a different region or country about the customs, pastimes, and aspects they consider unique about growing up in that area.

- *Cultural background:* For some people, cultural identity is a key to understanding who they are, while others have little awareness of their heritage. What would you describe as your culture? How significant has this been in shaping your life? How has your culture woven the fabric of your purpose as a leader?

- *Generational influences:* Events that occur during the particular period of time in which people are born shape their lives and give identity to their generation. One need only to talk to a baby boomer to understand the importance of generational influences, such as television or computers. Certain influences are so pervasive that the majority of people's lives are touched by them, such as the changing role of women in the workplace and in the family, the advent of the global marketplace, or the demographic changes that are taking place in America. How have these and other experiences of your generation affected your beliefs, standards, expectations?

3. Draw a time line of your life and list your major activities and jobs in chronological order. For each point along the time line, list the skills and talents that you exhibited as you moved through life. Group these skills by category—people-related, technical, intellectual, communication, and so on. What were your greatest strengths? Which skills and talents did you enjoy using? In what areas did you excel? What

came easy to you? What have you learned? What is the deeper meaning behind your experiences? What inspired you and why?

4. Think of moments in your life when you made significant decisions
that may not have seemed most logical or expedient at the time but
just "felt right." What do these periods of intuition, hunches, perceptions, and feelings tell you about what you truly value?

5. Ask yourself, What would I do even if I didn't get paid for it? What do
I dream about doing? What is my passion? What would I do if I won
the lottery, had only six months to live, or could live in good health for
100 years? And yes, your answer can be to play golf, travel, or shop
'til you drop.

Don't be surprised if developing a compelling vision for your own life
turns out to be difficult. Warren Bennis warns that "if knowing yourself and
being yourself were as easy to do as to talk about, there wouldn't be nearly
so many people walking around in borrowed postures, spouting second-
hand ideas, trying desperately to fit in rather than to stand out."[34] Good or
bad, it seems that most of us just muddle through life, never setting a specific course. Reluctant to pick a course, we trust our lives to happenstance
rather than our own judgment. We follow those who have developed a compelling personal vision, particularly if they are able to express that vision in
a way that connects with our own aspirations. Ultimately, that's how King,
Disney, Ford, Churchill, and all of the other great visionary leaders succeeded. They knew who they were and they connected with others. They
had a compelling personal vision others could share. They expressed what
others couldn't, which, according to our gurus, is what you have to do if
you want to lead.

Leadership Role Shift #2: From Commander to Storyteller

The second leadership role shift is derived from the first. Visionary leaders
must behave differently from master strategists. Strategy can be and often
is implemented by the leader barking orders. Buy this. Sell that. Add this
product. Cut that one. Invest here. Starve that unit for funds. Staff up.
Downsize. It's all about commanding. Our gurus are quick to point out,
however, that realizing a vision requires different behavior on the part of

the leader. Martin Luther King didn't issue an order, then suddenly realize his dream. Disney didn't beat the "happy place" into being. While strategists may demand and command, visionaries must excite and entice. The second shift in the leadership role requires that leaders stop being commanders and become master storytellers.

The term *storyteller* probably conjures up images of ancient prophets or gentle grandparents spinning farfetched and entertaining yarns. Our local grocery offers storytelling for preschoolers each Wednesday afternoon. Youngsters from the neighborhood gather around a kindly older woman who enchants them with tall tales about little people. That's the image most of us have of storytellers and storytelling. It doesn't seem like a task for leaders. Yet storytelling is exactly the task many of our gurus recommend to modern leaders.

The greatest advocate of the leader as storyteller is the psychologist Howard Gardner. In his 1995 book *Leading Minds,* Gardner maintains that "a key—perhaps *the* key—to leadership . . . is the effective communication of a story."[35] In his examination of well-known and less-well-known leaders throughout history, Gardner finds that many of them distinguished themselves early in life by their ability to tell stories. "Many others make the mastery of storytelling—whether through persuasive oratory or through well-crafted written documents—a primary goal."[36] Stories, says Gardner, are a "fundamental part of the leader's vocation."[37]

Of course, just any old story told any old way will not do. Leadership storytelling is a craft. Told correctly, stories can connect with, motivate, inspire, and rally followers to the support of the leader's vision. Told in the wrong way, they simply bore. As you might expect, our gurus, particularly Gardner, have some ideas about what constitutes the right stories and the right way to tell them. Here are some of their storytelling basics.

The Best Stories Address the Topic of Identity

Gardner notes that from birth, we all search for answers to a few basic questions, such as Who am I? Where did I come from? What group do I belong to and why? Where is my life going? What things in life are really true, beautiful, and good? These are questions about identity, and the most powerful stories that leaders tell are those that provide answers to questions concerning personal, social, and moral choices. If you go back and reread the visions expressed by Disney, Churchill, and King, you will see that they are all about answers to a few basic questions about identity.

The Most Powerful Identity Stories Reflect Traits the Leader Embodies

Leaders must "walk the talk." They can't just express a personal, social, and/or moral identity and then not live it. Their words and actions must mesh. In his book, Gardner contrasts Richard Nixon, who championed law and order but whose administration was responsible for illegal acts, to Martin Luther King, Jr., whose personal actions were consistent with his call for followers to withstand pain and criticism.[38] Nixon's story—and his reputation—was diminished, while King's was enhanced by his behavior and the behavior of their closest associates.

All Leader Stories Must Compete with Existing Stories for Attention

"The audience is not simply a blank slate . . . waiting for the first, or for the best, story to be etched on its virginal tablet," writes Gardner. "Rather, audience members come equipped with many stories that have already been told and retold in their homes, their societies, and their [professions]."[39] A new story must push its way through the competing masses of stories out there already. If it is to gain prominence, the new story must grab our attention and then surpass, transplant, or suppress competing explanations of who we are, what we do, and what we believe. Every leader/storyteller faces the same challenge. How different must or can the story be to existing stories in the same organization? A new story will likely encounter strong resistance and be rejected if the identity it expresses is too new, or if its answer to the question Who are we? departs too drastically from past and accepted answers to that question. As Gardner notes, "by and large, members of a society are not—except in times of crisis—searching for an unfamiliar story or a new form of understanding. Indeed the situation is almost the opposite."[40] On the other hand, if the story sounds too familiar, its impact will be minimal. It will just be absorbed into the mass of stories that have gone before. As we noted earlier, the leader-follower relationship is dynamic. Leaders and followers play roles in a drama that unfolds over time. No story stands alone. Every story becomes part of the continuing saga. The best leaders understand that and craft their stories accordingly.

Stories Are More Readily Accepted If They Are Geared to the Unschooled, Five-Year-Old Mind

In our first half decade of life, most of us are like sponges, absorbing anything and everything we can in a desperate effort to answer critical identity questions. By the age of five, we are already well along in the process of self-definition and identification. We have had little, if any, formal education—are unschooled, in Gardner's terms—and yet we have developed powerful notions about our existence. We see ourselves as being part of some groups but not of others. We hold certain beliefs, attitudes, and values, yet we reject others. Some behaviors seem perfectly natural to us. Others seem extraordinarily strange.

Stories are the containers, or vessels, for the answers we are developing to our identity questions. Even at a young age, we create and consume stories, particularly simple stories that provide a sharp contrast between good and evil. Gardner calls these Star Wars stories in which "two forces or individuals (A and B) are opposed to each other (as in the series of *Star Wars* movies). There may well be a protracted struggle between A and B. In the end, A—generally identified with the good—is likely to prevail, though there are instances where B triumphs, most often temporarily. In nearly all cases, the child identifies strongly with the individual(s) and the cause(s) of Force A."[41]

As we mature, most of us develop the capacity to absorb much more complicated stories, especially those on subjects in which we have had formal training. Yet we continue to find Star Wars stories appealing. Successful leaders recognize and may choose to exploit our sensitivity to such narratives when they are dealing with large heterogeneous groups. Gardner explains that "it is often the leader who can . . . speak directly to the 'unschooled mind'—that succeeds in convincing an audience of the merits of his or her program, policy, or plan."[42] Ronald Reagan was a master at telling stories that appealed to the five-year-old mind, which may in part explain his success.

In Storytelling, Form Is As Important As Content

Finally, our gurus urge would-be leader storytellers to polish their delivery. Jay Conger suggests that the best leader storytellers "create engaging dialogues with their audiences, structure their talks like symphonies, and use their personal energy to radiate excitement about their plans."[43] Champion storytellers elicit reactions such as:

> I enjoy listening to him—it can be very exciting at times.
>
> He fills the room with ideas, challenges . . . hell of a job stimulating, exciting you and the group. He's very engaging. He puts the force of his personality behind his ideas, and he gets you moving toward an idea as quickly as he can. You know he's found something important. He engages by building to a crescendo.
>
> He has so much enthusiasm that it spills over [in his talks]. He was always enthused, always high, but now it's right off the scale.[44]

Leadership, say our gurus, is partially a game of language. Would-be players must master the tools of rhetoric, including the use of metaphors and rhythmic speech patterns. Repetition, rhyme, rhythm, balance, and alliteration grab the listeners' attention, spark an emotional reaction, and cut through the daily babble. People remember the message. More important, stories connect the listener with the leader storyteller. Powerful and effective storytelling is the second major shift in leadership roles.

Leadership Role Shift #3: From Systems Architect to Change Agent and Servant

Our final leadership role shift draws equally from the other two. There would be no need to communicate a vision if it were already well-known, widely accepted, and aggressively pursued. People don't need leaders to get them to do what they are already doing. The new leadership is about change, and that is very different from what has gone on in the past.

Since the early twentieth century, top managers in most businesses have created systems to define, measure, and control middle-manager and employee behavior. These systems were designed to create the organization man and woman who would do things the company way. The idea was to produce stability, consistency, and predictability. Christopher Bartlett and Sumantra Ghoshal describe this traditional organization:

> From atop the hierarchy, the leader [looked] down on order, symmetry, and uniformity—a neat step-by-step decomposition of the company's tasks and

responsibilities. From the bottom, frontline managers [looked] up at a phalanx of controllers whose demands soak up most of their energy and time. The result, as General Electric's chairman and CEO Jack Welch puts it, [was] an organization with its face toward the CEO and its ass toward the customer.[45]

In such a structure, information and capital requests flow to the top, where executives make decisions, allocate resources, set priorities, assign responsibilities, and control the management of resources. Top managers are the only true entrepreneurs. Ideas from the bottom are subjected to an extensive documentation and review process from which they rarely emerge. The whole system is "vertically driven . . . financially oriented, and authority-based."[46]

The problem with such a system, according to our gurus, is that it fragments a company's resources, creates vertical communication channels that isolate business units and prevent them from sharing their strengths with each other, and on the whole, makes the company less than the sum of its parts. People focus solely on the chain of command and the tasks in their job description. Bartlett and Ghoshal write

The systems that ensured control and conformity also inhibited creativity and initiative. Stripped of individuality, people often engaged in the very behaviors that the system had been designed to control. At best, the resulting organizational culture grew passive; with amused resignation, employees implemented corporate-led initiatives that they knew would fail. At worst, the tightly controlled environment triggered antagonism and even subversion; people deep in the organization found ways to undermine the system that constrained them.[47]

Today, say our gurus, that type of system will lead to disaster. For example, James Champy, the cofounder of the reengineering movement with Michael Hammer and author of the book *Reengineering Management: The Mandate for New Leadership,* suggests that

In the Rough Weather we're sailing in today, . . . you must have a culture that encourages qualities like relentless pursuit (to match our customers' elusiveness), bottomless resources of imagination (to create needs our customers may not know they have), and both smooth teamwork and individual autonomy (to match their demanding standards). You cannot have a culture of obedience to chains of command and the job slot. It just won't work. The markets will punish you for it.[48]

Based on their observation of top management behavior in such companies as 3M, Canon, Intel, ABB, GE, and Komatsu, Ghoshal, Bartlett, Champy, and many other leadership gurus offer an alternative organizational structure and leadership role. They maintain that leaders in these companies create cultures that encourage entrepreneurship at the front line, build competence across internal boundaries, and encourage people to continually question business strategy. These leaders achieve these goals by acting as change agents and by serving others. (For a more detailed discussion of the kind of structures these leaders prefer, see Chapter 7, "Business, Work, and Society.")

Acting As Change Agents

First, these new leaders act as agents of change that force people to think about and prepare for an uncertain future. These leaders don't just accept challenges to conventional wisdom—they demand them. For example, Bartlett and Ghoshal describe how Goran Lindahl, a member of ABB's top-level executive committee, uses bimonthly meetings with ABB's worldwide business heads to "shake things up and create an environment for learning."

> Instead of show-and-tell budget reviews, Lindahl uses the meetings for contingency planning exercises. He might, for instance, ask them to consider the opportunities or threats that could arise if certain environmental laws are enacted, the implications for ABB's investment in developing countries if North-South conflicts erupt, or the impact on the company's global supply network if trade negotiations reach some assumed resolution. Through such hypothetical scenarios, he hopes to prepare his executives, stimulate their thinking, and generate fresh initiatives.[49]

The new leader focuses less on directing and controlling worker behavior and more on developing employee initiative and supporting employee ideas. 3M's chairman and CEO, Livio D. DeSimone, describes the new role of the leader as "one of creation and destruction—supporting individual initiative while breaking down bureaucracy and cynicism,"[50] essentially removing barriers to progress. The leader is out front, not pulling followers by some imagined chain, but rather clearing the path. The leader works for the followers, not the other way around. At the extreme, the leader becomes more of a servant to those he or she leads than a commander, or a controller or systems designer.

Serving Others

This idea of the *servant-leader* is actually drawn from the teachings of the late Robert K. Greenleaf, former director of management research at AT&T. In the mid-1960s, Greenleaf discovered the writings of Hermann Hesse, the German-Swiss Nobel Prize–winning author. One of Hesse's books, *Journey to the East,* made an enormous impression on Greenleaf and inspired him to create a new approach to leadership. Greenleaf described his discovery in a 1984 commencement talk at Alverno College in Milwaukee.

> *Journey to the East* is an account of a mythical journey by a band of men on a search to the East. . . . The central figure of the story is Leo, who accompanies the party as the servant who does the menial chores, but who also sustains them with his spirit and his song. He is a person of extraordinary presence. All goes well with the journey until one day Leo disappears. Then the group falls apart in disarray, and the journey is abandoned. They cannot make it without the servant Leo. The narrator, one of the party, after some years of searching, finds Leo and is taken into the order that had sponsored the search. There he discovers that Leo, whom he had first known as a servant, was in fact, the titular head of the order, its guiding spirit, a great and noble leader.
>
> There has been much speculation on Hesse's life and work, some of it centering on this story which critics find most puzzling. But to me this story clearly says: The greatest leader (who may be a "little" person) is seen as servant first because that is what he is deep down inside. Leadership is bestowed on the person who is, by nature, a true servant. Leadership is something given or assumed, that could be taken away. Leo's servant nature was the real person, not bestowed, not assumed, and not to be taken away. Leo was servant first.[51]

Greenleaf later elaborated on the concept of the servant as leader in a number of his writings, the most famous of which is *Servant Leadership.*

He is regarded as the creator of the modern empowerment movement in business and has had significant influence on a number of management gurus. Here are some of the key ways Greenleaf's servant-leader differs from his or her traditional counterpart.

- The traditional leader asks subordinates questions about results, processes, methods, and behavior—questions like, Did you do this? Did you do that? What is the status of. . . ? The servant-leader asks questions that help uncover what he or she can do to help. How might I be of help? What is it that you need from me? What resources do I have that would be of use to you?[52]
- The traditional leader measures organizational productivity in output per man-hour or some other quantitative indicator. The servant-leader thinks that the most productive organization is the one in which "there is the largest amount of voluntary action; people do the right things, things that optimize total effectiveness, at the right times—because they understand what ought to be done, they believe these are the right things to do, and they take the necessary actions without being in-structed."[53]
- The traditional CEO sees people, at best, as a valuable resource, sees himself as chief, and sees his role as generating profits for stockhold-ers. The servant-leader internalizes the belief that "people are first," sees himself or herself as "first among equals," and sees his or her role as one of "facilitating and fostering the leadership capabilities of others."[54]
- The traditional leader is seen as a stern taskmaster, often with ques-tionable and self-serving ethics. The servant-leader emphasizes ethi-cal behavior and living a holistic life. Employees describe the servant-leader as a person who is trusting, accepting, open to new ideas, resilient, wise, insightful, imaginative, positive, and who possesses a sense of humor and the ability to laugh.[55]
- The traditional leader promotes internal competition. The servant-leader believes that "competition must be muted, if not eliminated. Serving and competing are antithetical."[56]
- The traditional leader assembles a task force to analyze a problem and make a recommendation, then disappears while the task force does its job. The servant-leader puts together a task force to make a recom-mendation, "but also listens, teaches, and helps the members of the

task force ask the right questions so that together they can discover answers that represent everyone."[57]

- The traditional leader has no time for people. The servant-leader makes time for people.

- The traditional leader mediates disputes. The servant-leader not only mediates disputes but also "notices a person whose views are not being heard because of a communication style that unnecessarily irritates others. A servant-leader takes the time to offer sensitive and supportive coaching in a way that preserves the message but eliminates distancing mannerisms—helping not only the individual but also strengthening the team."[58]

- The traditional leader attempts to get followers to follow policies and do things the company way. The servant-leader interacts with followers "to make sure that good ideas are brought into the open, are considered seriously, and where possible tested, so that eventually shared visions develop."[59]

- Traditional leaders view the organization as a pyramid and themselves as the chief architect and master builder. Servant-leaders view the organization as a garden and themselves as gardeners.

- Traditional leaders demand obedience and seek to recreate people in their own image. "The servant-leader always empathizes and always accepts the person, but sometimes refuses to accept the person's effort or performance as good enough. . . . [T]he servant-leader has too much respect for herself or himself and cares too much for others to let them perform at less than their best level." The servant leader says that "I enable and empower you through my love and patience and my firmness. I love you enough not to let you do less than your best. But I don't shame you into it: I invite you into it."[60]

- The traditional leader believes that the ultimate test of leadership is bottom line, financial results. The servant-leader believes that the ultimate test of leadership is answering the questions "Do those served grow as persons; do they, while being served, become healthier, wiser, freer, more autonomous, more likely themselves to become servants? And what is the effect on the least privileged in society; will [they] benefit, or at least, will [they] not be further deprived?"[61]

The servant-leader is sharply different from the leader most of us have known. Chances are you have never had a servant-leader as a boss and, consequently, you have no role model. If, as the gurus argue, you need to adopt a more people-oriented style to be a successful leader, how do you develop those skills? What training should you have? What degree should you acquire? Where you do start to mold yourself into this powerful twenty-first-century leader? Can you learn to lead? We will close this chapter on that last important question.

CAN YOU LEARN TO LEAD?
FACTORS AFFECTING LEADERSHIP ABILITY

It seems perfectly obvious that you can learn to lead. After all, nearly three-fourths of American companies send people to leadership classes every year. Psychologists and anthropologists videotape would-be leaders in action, survey their coworkers, peers, bosses, and associates, and give the aspiring leaders feedback to help them become more "self-aware." Macho types climb rocks and have wilderness experiences under the guidance of New Age personal-growth specialists who help them "go beyond their limits" in order to "develop a passion for leadership." Practically every business school offers executive education to teach leadership theory. In addition, all of our gurus teach their own brand of leadership, and many even run their own leadership schools. Of course you can learn to lead. Companies wouldn't be pouring so much money into training classes if you couldn't. Would they? Our gurus wouldn't be offering so many courses in leadership if it wasn't something just about everybody could learn. Would they?

If you ask our gurus—the very people who are teaching most of the leadership courses—whether they think leadership can be taught, you will probably get an interesting response. "Yes," they will say, and then equivocate, "Well, maybe sometimes." For every Warren Bennis who maintains that "you can't teach leadership. . . . Leadership is character and judgment [and] two things you can't teach are judgment and character,"[62] you will encounter a Peter Drucker who states flatly that "leadership must be learned and can be learned."[63]

So, what is going on here? Can we learn to be leaders or not? The answer is yes and no. We can learn techniques, skills, ways of communicating, and so on easily and in short order. We can master the theories, strategies, and tactics of leadership that are taught in short courses and multiweek seminars.

What we can't easily acquire are the feelings, intuition, emotion, subtleties, desires, caring, empathy, exhilaration—the passion of and for leadership—that will make us leaders. Think of it this way. The tricks of the leadership trade that you can learn in a short course are the polish that can help bring out your leadership shine. They can make you a better leader, but they can't make you a leader if you aren't one already. So how do you become a true leader, complete with all of the feelings, intuition, desires, and so forth that distinguish us from the polished nonleader? Here is what our gurus think.

Genetics and Early Childhood

Most of our gurus think your leadership potential is helped along if you are born with reasonably good mental and physical capacities and have early childhood experiences that put the leadership fire in your belly. Beyond intelligence and physical energy, there is a great debate about the impact of genetics on leadership potential. Some gurus think leadership is built into your DNA. Others disagree. However, there is less controversy over the importance of early childhood experiences.

Most of our gurus agree that what happened to you in the first few years of your life makes a real difference. The early experiences that seem to matter most are the successes and failures, encouragement and criticism, experimentation, discipline, and so on that either helped you develop a sense of confidence and need for achievement or prevented you from doing so. While most of these experiences are positive, they don't have to be. Manfred Kets de Vries concluded from his clinical work with leaders that a considerable percentage of them developed a drive to lead because they experienced early traumas.

> Because of the hardships they have encountered, many of them seem to be on a mission: they are going to prove the world wrong; they are going to show everyone that they can amount to something. Many of them, suffering from what could be called the Count of Monte Cristo complex (after Alexander Dumas's novel), go even further: they have a very strong need to get even for the wrongs done to them at earlier periods in their lives.[64]

Education

Our gurus think you need the right kind of education to learn to lead. Notice that we are talking about education, not training. There is an important difference, as psychologist Richard Farson notes in *Management of the Absurd: Paradoxes in Leadership.*

> *Training* . . . leads to the development of skills and techniques. . . . Education, on the other hand, leads not to technique but to information and knowledge, which in the right hands can lead to understanding, even to wisdom. And wisdom leads to humility, compassion, and respect—qualities that are fundamental to effective leadership.
>
> Training makes people more alike, because everyone learns the same skills. Education, because it involves an examination of one's personal experience in the light of an encounter with ideas, tends to make people different from each other. So the first benefit of education is that the manager becomes unique, independent, the genuine article.[65]

Some of our gurus want potential leaders to have an education that goes well beyond the subjects, such as marketing, finance, and information systems, that form the backbone courses of most business schools. Lee Bolman and Terrence Deal, coauthors of *Leading with Soul: An Uncommon Journey of Spirit,* prefer to have potential leaders steep themselves in poetry, literature, music, art, theater, history, philosophy, and even dance.[66] John Gardner expands this idea further by suggesting that would-be leaders should be exposed to "the whole range of liberal arts from science to literature, from mathematics to history [so they can absorb] through literature, religion, psychology, sociology, drama, and the like, the hopes, fears, aspirations and dilemmas of their people, . . . understand what our ancestors valued and fought for; [and] know through history and biography the extraordinary outlines of the human story. . . ."[67]

Experience

Third, the gurus maintain that you need leadership experience early in your career. In his book *A Force for Change* John Kotter writes that the leaders he has met "almost always have had opportunities during their twenties and thirties to actually try to lead, to take a risk, and to learn from both triumphs and failures."[68] Such experiences seem essential in developing a wide range of leadership skills and perspectives, because they teach people about both the difficulty of leadership and its potential for producing change. These experiences help "them see that management techniques alone do not work when it comes to adapting organizations to shifting environments. [They even provide] people with insight into their own relative strengths and weaknesses pertaining to leadership."[69]

Kets de Vries found that the global business leaders he interviewed had similar early career experiences.

> Over and over again, when I interview global business leaders and ask them where they learned how to lead, they tell stories about how, in their late twenties or early thirties, they were sent to Argentina, Taiwan, Australia, or Canada to set up a plant, restructure a sales office, arrange a joint venture—you name it. They sweated taking on the assignment, they had sleepless nights over it, and they made mistakes. But most important, they were thrilled and they learned! The lessons learned while they were on their own, having to make the project work, were never forgotten. The experience taught them an incredible amount about motivation, decision making, and taking responsibility.[70]

Failure

One experience you absolutely must have to become a leader, say our gurus, is failure. Failures seem to be the spark that ignites early leadership lessons and burns them into your consciousness. Warren Bennis cites the executives he knows well who felt that they learned the most when they hit bottom and really screwed up. Problems, he says, shape leaders like weather shapes mountains; "difficult bosses, lack of vision and virtue in the executive suite, circumstances beyond their control, and their own mistakes [are] the leader's basic curriculum."[71] Bennis quotes Margaret Thatcher: "It's at that moment when the iron entered my soul that gave me the steel I needed to have the resilience to become a really first-rate leader."[72]

Targeted Training

Finally, a little targeted training may help polish your leadership style, but remember that there are real limits to what training can do for you. The Bill Gateses, Walt Disneys, and Ted Turners of this world were not created by a short course, weekend seminar, consultant's workshop, or arranged wilderness experience. That's not to say that they didn't hone some of their communication or interpersonal skills through such experiences. They just didn't become business, entertainment, or world leaders solely because of them.

Beware of the glossy training brochures and ads in your favorite business magazine that promise to make Churchills out of you or your employees in three easy lessons, with six videotapes, or after a one-hour inspirational speech. Your good sense should remind you of the old adage that warns "if it sounds too good to be true. . . ."

Should you avoid all training then? Of course not. Training can be of value if it is targeted to specific skills. For example, you may want to take courses in writing and speaking to enhance your ability to tell stories, but don't expect one training class or even a hundred to make you a leader if you aren't one already. Training can shine and polish your leadership abilities, but it doesn't build the leadership foundation. That comes long before the training.

LEADERSHIP IS ABOUT THE WHOLE OF YOU

In summary, leadership comes down to the fact that with all of the posturing and promises, no guru, regardless of his or her mettle or meddling, can make you an instant leader. Leaders aren't born—at least not full blown. Neither are they made like instant coffee. Instead, they are slow brewed. The leadership learning process is a lengthy one and proceeds in somewhat the following way:

- Genes and early childhood experiences provide the predisposition for leadership.
- A liberal-arts education lays the broad foundation of knowledge.

- Experience provides the wisdom that comes from putting knowledge to use.
- Training puts the shine on behavior in specific areas such as communication.

If you happen to be missing some genes or some early childhood experiences, if you didn't major in one of the liberal arts, if your worldly experiences haven't been that worldly, or if the training you've taken hasn't been that good, take heart. It doesn't mean that you won't be able to lead. When it comes to leadership, it's the whole of you that matters, not the bits and pieces.

KEY POINTS

- While there may be a few characteristics that many leaders hold in common, such as the desire to lead, the willingness to take risks, a need to achieve, and so on, these characteristics aren't necessarily shared by all leaders.
- The one characteristic that separates leaders from nonleaders is that leaders have willing followers.
- Leadership is largely about a relationship between leaders and followers; therefore, a central task for all leaders is to build and maintain a solid relationship with others.
- Leadership occurs as a series of discontinuous events. Therefore, a person who succeeds as a leader today may not excel in leadership tomorrow or with a different group of followers.
- The new leader must be more of a
     visionary than a strategist,
     storyteller than commander,
     change agent and servant than systems architect or engineer.
- Learning to lead is a lengthy process that stretches back to childhood. Training, seminars, short courses, and consulting can only polish the leadership qualities a person already possesses.

James Champy, coauthor of *Reengineering the Corporation*

Daryl Conner, founder and president of Organizational Development Resources

Richard Farson, author of *Management of the Absurd*

Timothy J. Galpin, author of *The Human Side of Change*

Michael Hammer, coauthor of *Reengineering the Corporation*

F. Robert Jacobs, author of *Real Time Strategic Change*

Jon R. Katzenbach, coauthor of *Real Change Leaders*

Manfred F. R. Kets de Vries, author of *Life and Death in the Executive Fast Lane*

John P. Kotter, author of *A Force for Change*

James O'Toole, author of *Leading Change*

William A. Pasmore, author of *Creating Strategic Change*

Paul Strebel, author of *Breakpoint: How Managers Exploit Radical Change*

Noel M. Tichy, author of *Control Your Destiny or Someone Else Will*

Marvin R. Weisbord, coauthor of *Future Search*

2

Managing Change

With the exception of the topic of leadership, there is perhaps no other subject in management gurudom that offers as much fascination to our pundits as the process, problems, promises, and possibilities of major organizational change. William A. Pasmore, author of *Creating Strategic Change* and professor of organizational behavior at Case Western Reserve University, expresses in these melodramatic terms the enchantment he and other gurus feel about change:

> The unfolding interplay among all [the factors surrounding change] . . . makes the process of change mysterious if not miraculous, as dynamic an achievement as any mankind could hope to accomplish. The process is beautiful to behold, enchanting in its shifts between subtlety and storminess, no more predictable in its course than the cutting of a river through granite. With its origins in our spirit and our primal acquaintance with it, change in human systems remains as thrilling to experience as the wind of a thunderstorm sweeping across an open lake. Slightly apprehensive, forever expectant, we approach change in organizations with our heads and

our hearts fully engaged, straining toward the goal like a horse pulling a heavy carriage. We will succeed; we will make the organization better; we will arrive at the moment of fulfillment in which we can look back upon our work and rest at least momentarily, with pride.[1]

To the modern guru, change is a wondrous experiment that is made even more wondrous by its necessity. "An organization's capacity to change is a key factor in its short and longer term success," writes F. Robert Jacobs, change consultant and author of the book *Real Time Strategic Change*.[2] He adds that the "most successful organizations of the future will be those that are capable of rapidly and effectively bringing about fundamental, lasting, system-wide changes."[3]

Throughout the 1980s and 1990s, our gurus preached that major, strategic, organizational change was mysterious, magical, and most importantly, vital to the success—perhaps even to the survival—of American business. American CEOs listened to the prophets of change and acted on their sage advice, launching their companies into total quality management, time-based competition, downsizing, restructuring, reengineering, and a host of other programs that brought about gut-wrenching organizational change. They initiated change, change, and more change.

America's top CEOs expressed their determination to reinvent their companies through their deeds. They spent billions on consultants—including some of our most famous gurus. They forced their managers and employees to attend thousands of hours of training. They purchased and installed billions of dollars of the latest technology. Change became the obligatory response to a full range of corporate maladies. Every major U.S. company launched some kind of change initiative, and most companies initiated more than one. Over 40% indulged themselves in 11 or more major change programs within the short span of the early 1990s.[4] Corporate change became so common in the United States and such an ordeal for American workers that by 1994 the editors of *Training* magazine felt it necessary to offer a not-so tongue-in-cheek *apology* from American management (see Exhibit 2.1).

This dismal state of affairs resulted not only from the sheer volume of change programs, but also from the quality of their results. For all the CEO huffing and expensive guru puffing, nothing much changed; and changes that were accomplished rarely lasted or reaped the results promised by their advocates—our high-priced gurus included. By most estimates, 50 to 70%

EXHIBIT 2.1.   **Weathering Change—Enough Already!**

Dear Employees:

For the last decade, we have been trying to change our organization. Because we are frightened for our economic future, we kept looking for—and finding—another program du jour. We've dragged you through quality circles, excellence, total-quality management, self-directed work teams, re-engineering, and God knows what else. Desperate to find some way to improve our profitability, we switched from change to change almost as fast as we could read about them in business magazines. All of this bounding from one panacea to the next gave birth to rampant bandwagonism. We forgot to consider each change carefully, implement it thoughtfully, and wait patiently for results. Instead, we just kept on changing while you progressed from skepticism to cynicism to downright intransigence because you realized that all of these changes were just creating the illusion of movement toward some ill-defined goal. Now we've got a lot of burned-out workers and managers tired of the change-of-the-month club and unlikely to listen to our next idea, no matter how good it might be. For our complicity in this dismal state of affairs, we are sincerely sorry.

The Management

Source: Bob Filipczak, "Weathering Change: Enough Already," *Training*, September 1994, p. 23.

---

of all corporate change initiatives launched in the 1980s and 1990s failed to achieve their objectives. More specifically, one survey in the mid-1990s found that two-thirds of all corporate restructuring efforts failed to achieve the outcomes they were designed to achieve,[5] while leading practitioners of reengineering reported that their success rates among Fortune 1,000 companies were well below 50% and perhaps as low as 20%.[6] Michael Hammer, the most prominent reengineering guru of them all, estimated that fully $20 billion of the estimated $32 billion spent by American business on reengineering in 1994 was wasted.[7]

VIVA LA RESISTANCE

Of course, the real problem with change programs was that the people who were supposed to change stubbornly resisted doing what the change advocates wanted them to do. As noted by James O'Toole, author of *Leading Change*, it seemed as if everyone was resisting change—particularly the people who had to do the most changing.[8] And the most puzzling aspect of this resistance was that people resisted not only bad or harmful change, but also change that was clearly in their own self-interest.[9] This seemingly irrational resistance is maddeningly frustrating to our gurus, but it is all too common. Consider the story told by Barry Spiker and Eric Lesser, two consultants from Mercer Management Consulting, concerning the baffling experience of one businessman who decided to do something to make work a little easier for his employees.

> The owner of a small tire shop—Bob Treadwear—once decided to invest in a set of three power drills for removing lug nuts. For years, his three mechanics had been changing tires manually, and the benefits of switching to the new drills were obvious: faster service, more control over torque, less physical strain on the worker. But a funny thing happened after Treadwear bought the drills. Within a month of their arrival, all three were out of service. One had been dropped from a lift. Another had been run over by a truck. A third had been left in a customer's trunk. The three mechanics went back to removing tires by hand.
>
> When Treadwear finally sat his mechanics down and asked them how they had managed to wreck three expensive drills in a month, they admitted that perhaps it wasn't just accidental.[10]

Treadwear's mechanics offered what was, to them, a very logical explanation for rejecting their employer's kindness—a rationale we will examine more thoroughly a little later. For now, just note that Treadwear's experience is common in both large and small organizations and is representative of the puzzling behaviors often exhibited by employees when they are faced with change. As Michael Hammer maintains, this mysterious resistance is "the most perplexing, annoying, distressing, and confusing part of [change]."[11]

This resistance is so common and so destructive to change efforts that the quest to understand it forms the bedrock of most of our gurus' approaches to managing change. Practically every change guru has a number of explanations for resistance to change, including James O'Toole's 33 hypotheses. (See Exhibit 2.2.)

As O'Toole demonstrates, there are lots of reasons for people to resist change. However, our gurus agree on six widely accepted reasons.

EXHIBIT 2.2. James O'Toole's Thirty-Three Hypotheses for Why People Resist Change

1. Homeostasis—change is not a natural condition.
2. *Stare decisis*—presumption given to the status quo; burden of proof is on change.
3. Inertia—takes considerable power to change course.
4. Satisfaction—most people like the way things are.
5. Lack of ripeness—the preconditions for change haven't been met; the time isn't right.
6. Fear—people fear the unknown.
7. Self-interest—the change may be good for others but not us.
8. Lack of self-confidence—we don't think we are up to the new challenges.
9. Future shock—overwhelmed by change, we hunker down and resist it.
10. Futility—we view all change as superficial, cosmetic, and illusory, so why bother?
11. Lack of knowledge—we don't know how to change or what to change to.
12. Human nature—humans are competitive, aggressive, greedy, and selfish and lack the altruism necessary to change.
13. Cynicism—we suspect the motives of the change agent.
14. Perversity—change sounds good but we fear that the unintended consequences will be bad.
15. Individual genius versus group mediocrity—those of us with mediocre minds can't see the wisdom of the change.
16. Ego—the powerful refuse to admit that they have been wrong.
17. Short-term thinking—people can't defer gratification.
18. Myopia—we can't see that the change is in the broader self-interest.
19. Sleepwalking—most of us lead unexamined lives.
20. Snow blindness—groupthink, or social conformity.
21. Collective fantasy—we don't learn from experience and view everything in the light of preconceived notions.
22. Chauvinistic conditioning—we are right; *they* who want us to change are wrong.
23. Fallacy of the exception—the change might work elsewhere but we are different.
24. Ideology—we have different worldviews—inherently conflicting values.
25. Institutionalism—individuals may change but groups do not.
26. *"Natura no facit saltum"*—"nature does not proceed by leaps."
27. The rectitude of the powerful—who are we to question the leaders who set us on the current course?
28. "Change has no constituency"—the minority has a greater stake in preserving the status quo than the majority has in changing.
29. Determinism—there is nothing anyone can do to bring about purposeful change.
30. Scientism—the lessons of history are scientific and therefore there is nothing to learn from them.
31. Habit.
32. The despotism of custom—the ideas of change agents are seen as a reproach to society.
33. Human mindlessness.

Source: James O'Toole, **Leading Change: The Argument for Values-Based Leadership** *(New York: Ballantine Books, 1996), pp. 161–164.*

Reason for Resistance #1: Perceived Negative Outcome

The individual or group that must change will be negatively affected by the change, or at least thinks they will be.

In *Life and Death in the Executive Fast Lane,* Manfred F. R. Kets de Vries explains that "change . . . unleashes a multitude of fears: of the unknown, of loss of freedom, of loss of status or position, of loss of authority and responsibility; and of loss of good working conditions and money."[12] In our earlier example, Mr. Treadwear's mechanics resisted using the new power drills for just such a reason. They explained that as good as the drills were, they made too much noise. The men enjoyed talking with one another as they changed tires, but with the power drills, talking was impossible. They appreciated the new drills, but they missed the conversation. So the drills had to go.

Reason for Resistance #2: Fear of More Work

Employees perceive that the change will result in their having more work to do and less opportunity for rewards.

Paul Strebel, director of the Change Program for international managers at the International Institute for Management Development in Lausanne, Switzerland, argues that employees resist change primarily because major changes alter the terms of personal compacts employees have with their organizations. Strebel has identified three common dimensions of these personal compacts: *formal, psychological,* and *social.*

The *formal* dimension "captures the basic task and performance requirements of the job as defined by company documents such as job descriptions, employment contracts, and performance agreements."[13] The formal dimension involves answers to such employee questions as:

- What am I supposed to do for the organization?
- What help will I get to do the job?
- How and when will my performance be evaluated, and what form will the feedback take?
- What will I be paid, and how will pay relate to my performance evaluation?

The *psychological* dimension of a personal compact addresses aspects of the employment relationship that are mainly implicit. This dimension involves answers to such employee questions as:

- How hard will I really have to work?
- What recognition, financial reward, or other personal satisfaction will I get for my efforts?
- Are the rewards worth it?

Finally, "employees gauge an organization's culture through the *social* dimension of their personal compacts."[14] Employees pay attention not only to what the company's leadership says about corporate values and the company's mission but also to what they do in support of their pronouncements. The social dimension of the personal compact answers such employee questions as:

- Are my values similar to those of others in the organization?
- What are the real rules that determine who gets what in the company?[15]

Major organizational change can and often does impact some or all of these dimensions of the personal compact. To the extent that employees perceive the changes to the personal compact negatively, says Strebel, they will resist the change.

Reason for Resistance #3: Habits Must Be Broken

Changes require that employees alter long-standing habits.

In *Leading Change* John P. Kotter tells the story of Frank, the manager of 100 employees in a large corporation. Frank has been told dozens of times that the company is trying to be more innovative and that his command-and-control management style is not only out of date but also "snuffs out initiative and creativity as quickly as carbon dioxide kills a fire."[16] Change zealots demonize Frank. To them, he is one of those perplexing, annoying, distressing, and totally frustrating obstructionists who stand in the way of all the good the change agents are trying to do.

Kotter is more sympathetic, arguing that Frank is not really a bad person.

To a large degree, like all of us, he's a product of his history. . . . If Frank's problem were related to only a single discrete element, change would come much more easily. But that's not the case. He has dozens of inter-related habits that add up to a style of management. If he alters just one aspect of his behavior, all the other interrelated elements tend to put great pressure on him to switch that one piece of behavior back to the way it was. What he needs is to change all of the habits as a group, but that can feel as hard as trying to quit smoking, drinking, and eating fatty foods all at the same time.[17]

Is it any wonder that Frank resists?

Reason for Resistance #4: Lack of Communication

The organization does not effectively communicate the what, why, and how of change and does not clearly spell out expectations for future performance.

Kotter reminds us that before most people can understand and accept a proposed change they seek answers to a lot of questions:

- What will this mean to me?
- What will it mean to my friends?
- What will it mean to the organization?
- What other alternatives are there?
- Are there better options?
- If I'm going to operate differently, can I do it?
- How will I learn the new skills I will need?
- Will I have to make sacrifices? What will they be? How do I feel about having to make them?
- Do I really believe this change is necessary?
- Do I really believe what I'm hearing about the direction for the future?
- Is this the right direction for us to take?
- Are others playing some game, perhaps to improve their positions at my expense?

In response to these questions, says Kotter, most companies undercommunicate by 100%, 1,000%, or 10,000%. The CEO makes a few speeches about the proposed change, the top management team sends out a few memos, and a few upbeat stories run in the employee newsletter. That's about all. Employees are left to wonder and speculate about the when, where, how, and, most importantly, the why of the change.[18]

Reason for Resistance #5: Failure to Align with the Organization As a Whole

The organization's structure, business systems, technology, core competencies, employee knowledge and skills, and culture (values, norms, beliefs, and assumptions) are not aligned and integrated with the change effort.

William Pasmore describes two change efforts in which he was involved early in his career. In the first, a product failure led to the introduction of a new product, new technology, and a new organizational design, all at the same time. Pasmore notes that "it was like starting from scratch, except that the existing labor force was used."[19]

In the second change effort, there was no new technology, no new product, and the organization remained pretty much the same. "The change effort consisted of administering an attitude survey, following which discussions were held with every group of employees to determine how the operation could be improved."[20] The same union represented employees in both change efforts, the same management team provided leadership, and the demographics of the labor forces were similar. The results of the two change efforts were, however, quite different. In the first, productivity jumped 30% and quality improved. Management and the union agreed that employee job satisfaction, commitment, and labor-management cooperation all improved. In the second change effort, attitudes improved but productivity, quality, and costs remained the same. What was the difference? Pasmore explains:

> In the first unit, there was agreement that new ways of working should be explored. Employees were given training to allow them to perform a broad range of technical tasks, and teams were formed with responsibility for controlling interdependent production processes, not just independent pieces of equipment. The supervision of the unit, its pay system and even its technical layout were designed to foster teamwork and self-direction. In the second unit, jobs, pay systems, supervision and the technology remained the same. People talked about improving the performance of the unit, but they didn't do anything to make it happen. Control of the overall process remained with the first-line supervisors. People wanted to do a better job but ultimately found that there was little they could do within the design of the organization to change things.[21]

In short, the traditional methods, processes, procedures, reward systems, structures, technologies, and so on that were not specifically targeted by the change effort remained untouched and made change impossible.

Reason for Resistance #6: Employee Rebellion

Those who resist change do so because they feel it is being forced upon them.

Daryl Conner, founder and president of Organizational Development Resources (ODR) and author of *Managing at the Speed of Change,* writes that "we do not resist the intrusion of something new into our lives as much as we resist the resulting loss of control. In fact, the phrase *resistance to change* can be considered somewhat misleading. People don't resist change as much as its implications—the ambiguity that results when the familiar ceases to be relevant."[22] In short, people don't resist change as much as they resist *being changed.* William Pasmore suggests that "our current approach to change typically combines teaching with coercion. . . . That's why programs don't work. They are change from without; somebody else's idea of how change should happen, how change should feel. Often the someone isn't even a member of the organization; it's an author or consultant who knows nothing of the lives and experiences of the people involved. Yet, people are asked to follow the advice of the guru, in a blind and cultish way. Just do the program, and don't ask questions."[23] Such a situation is a matter of *being changed,* of *losing control over one's life.* Is it any wonder people resist?

THE NECESSARY INGREDIENTS FOR SUCCESSFUL CHANGE

Our gurus invariably claim to have developed their expertise in change management from personal experiences, not just from their intellect and academic prowess. They all claim to have a lot of experience in managing change, or rather in trying to manage change but failing to do so. Drawing upon their many failures and an occasional success, our gurus have a great deal of advice on how to overcome employee resistance and manage change. Here are some of their recommendations.

Change Tip #1: Establish a Need to Change

You have to *raise the heat* if you want to get the attention of those you want to change. This tip and the two that follow are direct descendants of a well-known formula for change:

$$C = A \times B \times D > X$$

Where:
C = the probability of change being successful
A = dissatisfaction with the status quo
B = a clear statement of the desired end state after the change
D = concrete first steps toward the goal
X = the cost of change[24]

In brief, the formula states that if you want people to change you have to (A) convince them that they need to change, (B) provide a vision of how much better their lives will be if they do change, and (D) demonstrate that you know what you are doing by generating some positive results early in the change process. Arguably the most important of these ingredients is (A), waking the organization up to the need to change.

Noel M. Tichy, a professor of business at the University of Michigan and coauthor of a highly popular history of GE's transformation, *Control Your Destiny or Someone Else Will,* maintains that waking the organization to the need for change is the "most emotionally wrenching and terrifying aspect"[25] of any major organizational change. Part of what makes this step in the change process so wrenching and terrifying is the extreme intensity people have to feel before they are prepared to change.

Daryl Conner says that he always had difficulty conveying the level of intensity that people had to reach before they would change until he watched a news interview with the survivor of an explosion and fire on a North Sea oil-drilling platform. One hundred sixty-eight people lost their lives, but Andy Mochan, a superintendent on the rig, was one of the 63 survivors. Conner recalls Mochan's description of his ordeal:

> [Mochan] said that he ran from his quarters to the platform edge and jumped fifteen stories from the platform to the water. Because of the water's temperature, he knew that he could live a maximum of only twenty

minutes if he were not rescued. Also, oil had surfaced and ignited. Yet Andy jumped 150 feet in the middle of the night into an ocean of burning oil and debris.

When asked why he took that potentially fatal leap, he did not hesitate. He said, "It was either jump or fry." He chose possible death over certain death.[26]

Conner notes that Mochan didn't jump from the burning platform because he felt confident he would survive, because jumping seemed like a good idea, or because the idea of a nighttime swim in burning oil was intellectually intriguing or was a personal growth experience. Mochan jumped because he didn't have a choice. That's one of the major ingredients of change, according to Conner and most of our other change gurus.

If you want people to change, don't give them a choice. You have to raise the heat—set the once-comfortable platform on fire—if you want people to jump into the cold, dark, and scary sea of change. And it is not enough to push just a few people in your organization to jump. A majority of your employees, 75% of your managers, and virtually all of your top executives must be totally convinced that change is essential if you are to accomplish major change.[27]

But how do you convince half your workforce and nearly all of your managers that major change is essential? John Kotter thinks you must take bold and even risky actions, such as the ones listed in Exhibit 2.3.

WOW! No wonder successful change is such a challenge and so rarely occurs. If our gurus are right, you can't even get started on the road to major change until you invent or admit to a crisis horrible enough to scare the wits out of most of your people. Such an admission of impending doom can be embarrassing. After all, what you are really saying is, "I really goofed the leadership on this thing" or "We're not as good as we thought we were." And your stockholders aren't going to be happy when they hear about your company's trouble. Analysts are going to pick you apart. Yet such bold, embarrassing, risky, ego-squashing actions are just the ones our gurus think you must take to jump-start most major changes. It's a tough first assignment and one that most CEOs aren't prepared to tackle. As a result, many change efforts are doomed from the beginning. The people who must do the most changing simply don't see any reason to do so.

EXHIBIT 2.3. **Bold Ways to Convince Employees of a Needed Change**

According to Kotter, being bold means doing such things as:

- Cleaning up the balance sheet and creating a huge loss for the quarter
- Selling corporate headquarters and moving into a building that looks more like a battle command center
- Telling all your businesses that they have 24 months to become first or second in their markets, with the penalty for failure being divestiture or closure
- Making 50% of the top pay for the top 10 officers based on tough product-quality targets for the whole organization
- Exposing managers to a major weakness vis-à-vis competitors
- Allowing errors to blow up instead of being corrected at the last minute
- Eliminating obvious examples of excess (e.g. company-owned country-club facilities, a large air force, gourmet executive dining rooms)
- Insisting that more people at lower levels be held accountable for broad measures of business performance
- Sending more data about customer satisfaction and financial performance to more employees, especially information that demonstrates weaknesses vis-à-vis the competition
- Insisting that people talk regularly to unsatisfied customers, unhappy suppliers, and disgruntled shareholders
- Putting more honest discussions of the firm's problems in company newspapers and senior management speeches.

Source: John P. Kotter, *Leading Change* (Boston: Harvard Business School Press, 1996), p. 44.

Change Tip #2: Create a Clear, Compelling Vision That Shows People How Their Lives Will Be Better

We discussed corporate visions at length in the leadership chapter, so we won't dwell on them here. To reiterate, our gurus emphasize the importance of a compelling vision; it is critical to directing efforts, aligning activity, and inspiring people to take action. John Kotter predicts that "without an appropriate vision, a transformation effort can easily dissolve into a list of confusing, incompatible, and time-consuming projects that go in the wrong direction or nowhere at all."[28] Of course, there is one thing worse than having no vision at all, say our gurus, and that is having a vision that becomes nothing more than "a sloganeering, 'bumper sticker' campaign of platitudes such as 'customer-oriented, cycle-time,' and 'reengineered organization.' These platitudes become a source of ridicule, and what was meant to be a vision actually leads to deep cynicism and alienation."[29] In short, if you are only responding to the latest management fad or short-term competitive pressures, then our gurus urge you to reconsider your whole change effort. If you don't have a strong understanding of where you want to take your organization, say our gurus, then maybe you shouldn't try to take it anywhere at all.

Change Tip #3: Go for True Performance Results and Create Early Wins

Successful change programs begin with results—clear, tangible, bottom-line results—and the earlier they occur, the better. Jon Katzenbach of McKinsey & Company and coauthor of *Real Change Leaders,* writes that one of the biggest problems with change programs is unclear or off-target goals. "Far too many mobilization efforts count their progress by activities such as the number of teams mobilized, the number of ideas generated, etc."[30] Wrong, wrong, double-wrong, say our gurus. "Program goals cannot be activities. They must be performance results for customers, employees, or shareholders."[31] William Pasmore is emphatic about the need to show real results: "Organizational change is about *changing organizational performance.* The clearer the tie between what we are doing and results, the more energy, commitment, and excitement we will generate during the change process. If the tie to results is fuzzy, what we are up to will eventually meet with resistance, apathy, or support from the lunatic fringe—none of which we need. Instead, we should *start and end every change effort with performance improvement as the goal.* And then change everything that needs to be changed to make it happen."[32]

Of course, you can't afford to wait too long to show some real results. If you are implementing change in a small company or small unit of a large enterprise, our gurus want you to show some real results within 6 months. If you are changing a big organization, they allow you up to 18 months to show results, but not much longer. People need to see some fairly rapid progress to reaffirm their faith in the effort. John Kotter reminds us that "most people won't go on the long march unless they see compelling evidence within six to eighteen months that the journey is producing expected results. Without short-term wins, too many employees give up or actively join the resistance."[33]

Short-term wins do a lot to help the change process along. For example,

- They provide evidence that the sacrifices are worth it.
- They reward change agents, who can relax for a moment and celebrate.
- They provide a test of the viability of the long-term vision and provide guidance on how the vision should be fine-tuned.
- They undermine those opposed to change.
- They help retain the support of bosses for the change effort.
- They build momentum for the change effort by turning neutrals into change supporters.[34]

Ideally, such short-term results are highly visible—large numbers of people can easily see them. They are unambiguous—there is no doubt that the improvement occurred. And they are clearly related to the change effort—it is obvious that the improvement didn't occur by chance. Kotter gives several examples of what he considers good short-term wins:

> When a reengineering effort promises that the first cost reductions will come in twelve months and they occur as predicted, that's a win. When a reorganization in a transformation reduces the first phase of the new product development cycle from ten to three months, that's a win. When the early assimilation of an acquisition is handled so well that *Business Week* writes a complimentary story, that's a win.[35]

Change Tip #4: Communicate, Communicate, Communicate, and Communicate Some More

You can never do enough to get your message across to your people. Poor and/or inadequate communication is one of the chief reasons our gurus cite for failed change efforts, and it is not only our gurus who recognize the role communication plays in change. For example, in 1993 the Wyatt Company asked CEOs in 531 U.S. organizations that had recently undergone major restructuring to identify one thing they would change about their restructuring effort. Overwhelmingly, the CEOs said they would like to alter the way they communicated with their employees about the change effort.[36]

What then is the secret to successful communication? John Kotter suggests seven principles for successful communication, as described in Exhibit 2.4.

EXHIBIT 2.4. **John Kotter's Seven Principles for Successfully Communicating a Vision**

Principle	What It Means
Keep it simple.	Focused, jargon-free information can be disseminated to large groups of people at a fraction of the cost of clumsy, complicated communication.
	Bad: "Our goal is to reduce our mean time to repair parameters so that they are perceptually lower than all major competitors inside the United States and out. In a similar vein, we have targeted new-product development cycle times, order process times, and other customer-relevant processes for change."[1]
	Better: "We are going to become faster than anyone in our industry at satisfying customer needs."[2]
Use metaphors, analogies, and examples.	**Bad:** "We need to retain the advantages of economies of great scale and yet become much less bureaucratic and slow in decision making in order to help ourselves retain and win customers in a very competitive and tough business environment."[3]
	Better: "We need to become less like an elephant and more like a customer-friendly *Tyrannosaurus rex*."[4]
Use many different forums.	"Vision is usually communicated most effectively when many different vehicles are used: large group meetings, memos, newspapers, posters, informal one-on-one talks. When the same message comes at people from six different directions, it stands a better chance of being heard and remembered, on both intellectual and emotional levels."[5]
Repeat, repeat, repeat.	"All successful cases of major change seem to include tens of thousands of communications that help employees to grapple with difficult intellectual and emotional issues. A sentence here, a paragraph there, two minutes in the middle of a meeting, five minutes at the end of a conversation, three quick references in a speech—collectively, these brief mentions can add up to a massive amount of useful communication, which is generally what is needed to win over both hearts and minds."[6]

Principle	What It Means
Walk the talk, or lead by example.	**Bad:** "Division head Sally O'Rourke tells her 1,200 employees that speed, speed, speed should become the hallmark of their organization. Then she takes nine months to approve a capital request from one of her product managers, allowing the competition to grab the lion's share of the market in a new and expanding segment."[7]
	Better: "The central element in a new transformation effort at a major airline relates to customer service. Whenever the CEO receives a letter of complaint from a customer, he personally sends a response back within forty-eight hours. After a while, stories about his letters circulate throughout the company."[8]
Explicitly address seeming inconsistencies.	**Bad:** During a major cost-cutting initiative, the employees feel the pain but top management continues to lease jets for executive use and retains regal offices.[9]
	Better: Sell the jets, fancy offices, and other excesses, or at least explain why selling such luxuries at this time wouldn't make sense.[10]
Listen and be listened to.	**Bad:** "A half-dozen computerwise young sales reps would have seen immediately, had they been briefed, that the basic concept guiding new hardware and software purchases for the sales force was flawed. But they were never briefed until after the new equipment arrived. By then . . . course corrections were very costly."[11]
	Better: Hold lots of two-way discussions. "Most human beings, especially well-educated ones, buy into something only after they have had a chance to wrestle with it. Wrestling means asking questions, challenging, and arguing."[12]

1. John P. Kotter, **Leading Change** (Boston: Harvard Business School Press, 1996), p. 90.
2. Ibid. p. 91.
3. Ibid. p. 92.
4. Ibid.
5. Ibid. p. 93.
6. Ibid. pp. 94–95.
7. Ibid. p. 96.
8. Ibid. p. 95.
9. Ibid. pp. 97–98.
10. Ibid.
11. Ibid. p. 99.
12. Ibid. pp. 99–100.

William Pasmore adds that much of your communication effort may, of necessity, involve educating your employees about the business and competitive environment. If you want your employees to understand the need to change, the vision, and even the process of change itself, take a look at Exhibit 2.5. Ultimately, of course, what employees most need to know is *the truth*.

Change Tip #5: Build a Strong, Committed, Guiding Coalition That Includes Top Management

The CEO may lord it over all he or she surveys, but no CEO is accomplished enough, powerful enough, or smart enough to navigate the treach-

---

EXHIBIT 2.5. **What Employees Need to Know About Their Company**

- Employees need to know *what managers know,* including how to read the income statement and the balance sheet, what makes the numbers on each get larger or smaller, what the numbers really mean, and where the company stands today compared to where it's been historically and versus the competition.

- Employees need to know *the threats to the organization* and the plans to deal with them, including an understanding of why the plans make sense and what other alternatives were considered before deciding on this course of action.

- Employees need to understand *decision-making processes* and criteria and how much risk is acceptable.

- Employees need to understand the *consequences of making poor decisions* and what to do when the unexpected happens.

- Employees need to understand *customers' expectations* and how to better meet them.

- Employees need to be introduced to *global economics,* and why it costs so much more to do business in the United States than in Mexico or Korea.

- Employees need to know about *health-care costs* and about workers' compensation, about the costs of carrying inventory and liability insurance.

- Employees need to understand the *technical system* used to produce goods or services— how it functions and why it was designed as it was designed.

- Employees need to understand what *technical alternatives* are possible and what would be involved in applying them.

- Employees need to develop the *social skills* that allow them to take part in participative activities, including speaking up in front of others, confronting differences, understanding how to reach consensus, facilitating the participation of others, and listening.

Source: William Pasmore, **Creating Strategic Change: Designing the Flexible High-Performing Organization** (New York: John Wiley & Sons, 1994), pp. 50–54.

erous shoals of major organizational change without help. Successful change requires a sponsoring team—a guiding coalition—of executives, line managers, technical whiz kids, and informal leaders who can help the CEO articulate the vision, communicate with large numbers of people, eliminate obstacles, generate short-term wins, lead project teams, and embed the new approaches in the corporate culture. Several of our gurus identify the requirements for a good sponsoring coalition. Exhibit 2.6 summarizes them.

EXHIBIT 2.6. **Characteristics of an Effective Change Team**

- Enough of the key players in the organization must *actively support the change* to legitimize it and to overcome opposition from those who would block progress.

- The members of the guiding coalition should *share a keen sense of discomfort with the status quo.*

- The sponsors should *be in substantial agreement on a vision* for the future.

- The coalition should contain people who represent *diverse points of view* in the organization in terms of functional expertise, work experience, and so on so that informed and intelligent decisions will be made by the sponsoring team.

- Members of the sponsoring coalition must *have a good reputation* in the firm. They should be widely respected, and their opinions must be taken seriously by employees.

- The coalition should *control key resources* (time, money, people) that will be necessary for successful implementation of the proposed change and must be willing to commit these resources to the change effort.

- Members of the coalition should *control the rewards and punishments* within the organization and be willing to use them to support the behavioral changes necessary to achieve the vision.

- The coalition sponsors must *appreciate the personal sacrifices* people will have to make to accomplish the change and empathize with those who will be negatively affected by the change.

- Members of the coalition must be willing to *demonstrate public support* for the change and to convey in their words and deeds a strong commitment to realizing the vision.

- Members of the coalition must be able and *willing to meet privately* with key individuals or groups to convey strong personal support for the change.

- Coalition members must commit to being *in for the long-haul.* They must recognize that the change will take time and require sacrifice and agree to reject short-term actions that are inconsistent with the long-term goals of the change.

Source: Taken primarily from John P. Kotter, **Leading Change** (Boston: Harvard Business School Press, 1996), p. 57, and Daryl Conner, **Managing at the Speed of Change** (New York: Villard Books, 1992), pp. 114–115.

◆◎ OUR VIEW

Of course, the idea of a powerful and committed guiding coalition in total agreement about the need to change and the direction the change should take is a compelling one. Who couldn't accomplish major change with such a force on their side? But we wonder how such an ideal could be achieved? When in your organization, or any organization for that matter, do you recall the top management team ever fully agreeing to do something different? Normally, what they agree about is keeping things pretty much the same. What they disagree about is doing something completely different. Still, getting the total backing of the top team is a good idea—if you can do it.

Change Tip #6: Keep it Complex, Stupid

We know that this recommendation is counterintuitive, but the wisdom offered by increasing numbers of gurus today is that large-scale, complex change may be easier to accomplish than small-scale, incremental change. Proponents of this theory include Richard Farson, author of *Management of the Absurd,* and James Champy, author of *Reengineering Management,* who maintains emphatically that "the larger the scale of change, the greater the opportunity for success."[37]

Champy argues that when you face large-scale change, you're forced to confront the larger issues of culture and management style that exist in every organization. These issues of culture and style frequently make incremental change almost impossible to accomplish. William Pasmore recommends taking a blank-sheet-of-paper approach that frees the organization from all of the written and implied agreements about the way things have to be done. He explains:

> We can ask people to change, but when we fail to redesign the structures and systems around them, a lot of old behavior gets reinforced and new behaviors go unrewarded. Pay systems, leadership styles, job boundaries, technology, policies; if these aren't also changed, they merely serve to pull people back to where they were before the change process started. . . . We can train people in facilitation skills until we are blue in the face. Or give more stirring speeches. Or redesign the process one more time. But in most

cases what we really need to do is to change everything at the same time, as if we were designing the organization from scratch.[38]

In short, Champy, Pasmore, Farson, and many of our other gurus argue in favor of large-scale change. They have come to recognize that organizations are made up of interdependent parts. As a consequence, if you want to change one thing about an organization, you frequently must change almost everything in it. John Kotter uses the following analogy to make this point.

Imagine walking into an office and not liking the way it is arranged. So you move one chair to the left. You put a few books on the credenza. You get a hammer and rehang a painting. All of this may take an hour at most, since the task is relatively straightforward. Indeed, creating change in any system of independent parts is usually not difficult.

Now imagine going into another office where a series of ropes, big rubber bands, and steel cables connect the objects to one another. First, you'd have trouble even walking into the room without getting tangled up. After making your way slowly over to the chair, you try to move it, but find that this light-weight piece of furniture won't budge. Straining harder, you do move the chair a few inches, but then you notice that a dozen books have been pulled off the bookshelf and that the sofa has also moved slightly in a direction you don't like. You slowly work your way over to the sofa and try to push it back into the right spot, which turns out to be incredibly difficult. After thirty minutes, you succeed, but now a lamp has been pulled off the edge of the desk and is precariously hanging in midair, supported by a cable going in one direction and a rope going in the other.[39]

So what is interconnected? What do you have to change? How large-scale does the large-scale change have to be? Timothy J. Galpin of Pritchett & Associates, a Dallas-based consulting firm, identifies 10 cultural components you must address to implement change, as described in Exhibit 2.7.

If the idea of tackling all of these 10 cultural components at once makes you a little nervous, you are not alone. William Pasmore admits that changing everything at once takes a tremendous leap of faith. Undoubtedly, such

EXHIBIT 2.7. **Ten Cultural Components to Consider When Implementing Change**

1. Rules and Policies

   Eliminate rules and policies that will hinder performance of new methods and procedures.

   Create new rules and policies that reinforce desired ways of operating.

   Develop and document new standard operating procedures.

2. Goals and Measurement

   Develop goals and measurements that reinforce desired changes.

   Make goals specific to operations. For example, establish procedural goals and measures for employees conducting the process that is to be changed, rather than financial goals that are a by-product of changing the process and that employees cannot easily relate to their actions.

3. Customs and Norms

   Eliminate old customs and norms that reinforce the old ways of doing things and replace them with new customs and norms that reinforce the new ways. For example, replace written memos to convey information through the organization with face-to-face weekly meetings of managers and their teams.

4. Training

   Eliminate training that reinforces the old way of operating and replace it with training that reinforces the new.

   Deliver training "just-in-time" so people can apply it immediately.

   Develop experiential training that provides real-time, hands-on experience with new processes and procedures.

5. Ceremonies and Events

   Establish ceremonies and events that reinforce new ways of doing things, such as awards ceremonies and recognition events for teams and employees who achieve goals or successfully implement changes.

6. Management Behaviors

   Develop goals and measurements that reinforce the desired behaviors.

   Provide training that focuses on the new behaviors.

   Publicly recognize and reward managers who change by linking promotion and pay rewards to the desired behaviors.

   Penalize managers who do not change behaviors. For example, do not give promotions or pay increases or bonuses to managers who do not demonstrate the desired behaviors.

7. Rewards and Recognition

   Eliminate rewards and recognition that reinforce old methods and procedures, replace them with new rewards and recognition that reinforce the desired ways of operating.

   Make rewards specific to the change goals that have been set.

8. Communications

   Eliminate communication that reinforces the old way of operating; replace it with communication that reinforces the new.

Deliver communication in new ways to show commitment to change. Use multiple channels to deliver consistent messages before, during, and after changes are made.
Make communications two-way by soliciting regular feedback from management and
employees about the changes being made.

9. Physical Environment
Establish a physical environment that reinforces the change. Relocate management and
employees who will need to work together to make changes successful. Use "virtual
offices" to encourage people to work outside the office with customers and telecommunications to connect people who need to interact from a distance.

10. Organizational Structure
Establish an organizational structure that will reinforce operational changes. For example,
set up client service teams, eliminate management layers, centralize or decentralize work
as needed, combine overlapping divisions.

Source: Timothy Galpin, "Connecting Culture to Organizational Change," **HRMagazine,** March 1996, pp. 84–90.

a clean break with the past would send, in James Champy's words, "a
mobilization jolt of energy through the company."[40] We imagine it would
also send a chill through the spine of most CEOs.

Change Tip #7: People Do Not Resist Their Own Ideas

This may be the most important and most obvious change tip of all. Our
gurus agree that people who participate in deciding what and how things
will change not only are more likely to support the change but also are actually changed themselves by the mere act of participation. Pasmore predicts that people who help make decisions about the future of their organization "learn to think about the organization in new ways, to speak out
when they have an opinion, to deal with conflict within the team, to survive
battles with management, to communicate with their peers, to be creative,
to read, to make presentations, to write, to participate. In a word, they become citizens. Active, powerful, well-informed, conscientious citizens bent
on improving the system in which they live and work."[41]

Of course, there is nothing new about this admonition to involve employees in decision making. Our gurus have preached the gospel of participation
and involvement for decades. Participation has become the de rigueur

method for accomplishing change and a key feature of everyone's change process. Decisions about layoffs and other such nasty things may still be made in private and announced from on high to the multitudes; but that's not how we undertake major, transformative, strategic, make-us-a-great-company-once-again change in the 1990s. Today, when we are thinking about launching major change, we assemble process teams, task forces, working groups, and other assorted parallel organizations to work out the details of what will be done, when, where, how, and by whom. F. Robert Jacobs describes the typical 1990s change effort this way:

> A small, select group of people regularly meet for a period of several weeks or even months, carefully crafting plans for a new and better future for their organization. There may be a strategy development or planning and policy unit, a top leadership group, a steering committee or task force. Informed by surveys, studies, and analyses, plus additional data collected from others both inside and outside of their organization, this team of highly committed and respected people forges new ground. Others, especially senior managers and maybe the board of directors, get periodic progress reports from this group and offer comments regarding the focus and direction of their work. . . .
>
> After documenting the strategy or plan, including recommendations for change[s] that need to be made and securing senior management approval, the implementation phase begins. The plan and recommended changes are rolled out to the entire organization. The case for change is clearly communicated, necessary actions spelled out, questions asked and answered and buy-in, agreement, or compliance sought. Numerous informational meetings may be held to allay people's concerns about the impending changes and to inform them of the new ways in which they will need to do business in the future.[42]

Is this a clear textbook case of participatory change management? Yes. But does it work? No. William Pasmore describes what happened to a design team he worked with early in his career:

> [The] design team did a marvelous job of analyzing its organization, learning about alternatives, and putting together some excellent recommendations for change. Some of the recommendations were revolutionary and would have resulted in changes in the entire management system of their plant.

The plant manager, who had chartered the design team, had stated clearly in the beginning that he expected the design team to challenge his thinking. When he heard the recommendations, however, he said that he hadn't expected to be challenged that much! . . .

Eventually [the plant manager] accepted most of the recommendations of the design team, but the battle was harder than it should have been. And then when he did approve the changes and presented them to everyone in his organization in a plant-wide communication session, he was surprised to find that others didn't accept them readily. His middle managers were the most resistant because their jobs were most threatened by the proposed redesign. . . . The plant manager believed that his position gave him the authority to implement change, at least in a caring, compassionate way. He didn't demand that people change; he just said that this change was necessary for the good of the organization and that he hoped everyone would do their best to make it happen. When they didn't, he became angry with them. Why didn't they accept his decision? What happened to their loyalty? How could they go against his authority in such an important matter? He still didn't understand. And I didn't understand, because I thought I could hold a session with the middle managers to answer their questions and provide whatever support was necessary to help them through the transition. But they didn't want to go![43]

The experience of Pasmore's design team is typical of what happens in most change efforts. Most middle managers, employees, and executives are not involved in the design process in any significant way. When the design team finally announces its recommendations, the rest of the organization doesn't want to go where the design team wants to take them. And why should they? The people on the design team were actively involved in the process—they became what Pasmore terms *active citizens* of the corporation. They were transformed by the process of participation. They learned to think about the organization in all of those new ways we described earlier. But everyone else was left out—the plant manager, the middle managers, the rest of the workforce. They weren't involved in the process, so their thinking had not been transformed.

Granted, you say, people who aren't consulted about the change and don't get a chance to serve on the design team aren't going to have the kind of understanding and commitment to the proposed changes as the design team members. But you can't put everyone on the design team. You can't have 100, 500, 1,000, or 2,000 people working together simultaneously to decide on what should change and how the change should be accomplished, can you?

Our gurus disagree. In fact, they maintain that's exactly what you must do. Shut the plant down. Close the offices. Rent a large auditorium. Take everyone from board members to janitors away for three days. Involve *everyone* in revolutionary change. This startling advice may be the ultimate in change wisdom and a fitting way to end this chapter.

REAL-TIME STRATEGIC CHANGE

F. Robert Jacobs calls them real-time strategic change events. Marvin R. Weisbord, author of *Discovering Common Ground,* William Pasmore, and a number of other gurus call them "future search conferences." Regardless of what they are called, they are a way to involve literally hundreds, even thousands, of people simultaneously in major organizational change decisions. Weisbord describes the process as a group-planning meeting that "brings a 'whole system' into the room to work on a task-focused agenda."[44] Marriott, Kaiser-Permanente, Allied Signal, 3M, Ford, and many other companies have used such conferences to bring together hundreds of people at a time. Perhaps the largest such conference was sponsored by Ford in 1994, which brought together all 2,200 employees from Ford's Dearborn assembly plant.

Each search conference, or real-time strategic change event, is unique, reflecting the needs of the particular organization sponsoring the event and the preferences of the consultants that plan and facilitate the conference. F. Robert Jacobs describes such a real-time strategic change event in great detail in his book *Real Time Strategic Change.* We have included an example of a typical three-day conference in Exhibit 2.8.

A typical conference or event extends over two to three days. All or nearly all employees in the organization attend. In short, the business basically shuts down during the event.

The conference is usually held to deal with a major issue such as what the organization must do differently to be successful in the future. The purpose of the conference is to get everyone to understand the need to change,

EXHIBIT 2.8. **Real-Time Strategic Change: A Three-Day Conference Guide**

Day One

- *Introduction:* The leader of the organization welcomes the participants and reviews the purpose of the meeting.

- *Telling our stories:* Participants are assigned to table groups with people they don't know from other parts of the organization. Robert Jacobs calls these *Max/Mix* groups—the maximum mixture of individuals from diverse backgrounds. Group members share their opinions about the challenges and opportunities the organization faces and about results they want to see from the conference. After discussion, the Max/Mix group agrees upon common themes, differences, and desired outcomes as expressed by the group. They record them on large easel paper sheets and post them on the conference wall for other participants to see.

- *View from the leadership perspective:* The leader of the organization gives a short presentation on the challenges and opportunities the leadership sees the organization facing, the leadership teams' vision for the future, and key steps the leadership team feels the organization must take to realize that vision. Working from their Max/Mix groups, participants have the opportunity to ask questions to clarify but not to object to or criticize the leadership message.

- *Organization diagnosis:* The Max/Mix groups pick an organization-wide topic such as decision making, teamwork, or communication, and brainstorm about their experiences with the topic over the past year that have made them glad, sad, and mad. The results are once again recorded and posted. During lunch, participants vote on their gladdest glads, saddest sads, and maddest mads by placing check marks next to the posted results from each table.

- *Content expert input:* The participants hear from and have an opportunity to question an outside expert concerning marketplace, governmental, labor, and other trends likely to affect the organization over the next few years.

- *Customer perspective:* Participants hear from and have the opportunity to question one or more key customers about the customers' needs and expectations.

Day Two

- *Change possibilities panel:* The participants hear from and have the opportunity to question a panel of representatives from another organization who have gone through a major change.

- *Valentines:* Participants assemble in break-out groups according to department or function. These groups brainstorm and prepare a *valentine* for each of the other departments/function groups. The valentines are lists of things the department/function would like the other department/function to do differently in the future. The valentines are then posted in the main conference room for everyone to see. Jacobs calls these lists *valentines* because, as he reasons, "when we truly care about someone, we send them the best we can, which in this case is the truth."[1]

EXHIBIT 2.8. (Continued)

- *Response to valentines:* Department/functions read their valentines and prepare a nondefensive response outlining what they are prepared to do differently.

- *Organization norms:* Reconvening in their Max/Mix groups, participants brainstorm the unwritten rules of the organization. Then they pick one unwritten rule they think needs to change and communicate it to the whole group.

- *Organization strategy revisited:* The organization leaders review the vision or perspective they provided on the first day in the light of what they have heard from participants so far. They identify what portions of the strategy are open for revision by the group.

- *Participant feedback on strategy:* The Max/Mix groups discuss the strategy the leadership has presented, then draft and post their recommendations for changes.

- *Leadership turnaround on strategy:* The leadership team reviews the recommendations of the Max/Mix groups and revises the strategy.

Day 3

- *Finalized strategy:* The leadership group presents the final strategy, noting changes to which it agreed and explaining why it decided not to accept some of the recommendations from the Max/Mix groups.

- *Preferred futuring:* Participants are given 3-inch sticky notes and asked to record actions they suggest to implement the various portions of the strategy. The notes are collected and grouped according to portions of the strategy.

- *Systemwide planning:* Participants sign up to work on different portions of the strategy in break-out groups. The groups meet, brainstorm, and compile a list of actions to implement their assigned portion of the strategy. They record the two or three most important actions on large sheets of paper that are posted in the main conference room. All participants then vote on the actions they feel are most important.

- *Back home teamwork and action planning:* Participants meet with their department/ function groups and agree upon key actions they need to take as a group to improve teamwork and help implement the strategy the organization has agreed upon for the future. The department/function groups then report these commitments back to the larger group.

1. Robert Jacobs, **Real Time Strategic Change** (San Francisco: Berrett-Koehler, 1994), p. 4.

agree upon a future vision, and agree upon and make a commitment to take the first steps to realize the vision. Essentially, the conference is designed around the $C = A \times B \times D > X$ change model we mentioned earlier.

Does this kind of change process work? Does it lead to quicker and more successful strategic, large-scale change? Does it eliminate, or at least minimize, resistance? Many of our gurus swear by the process. Weisbord waxes rhapsodic about the experience:

> People arrive [at the conference] curious, expectant, eager, mystified, open—and anxious. This is, after all, a strange group, an unfamiliar methodology, and a formidable task. Each person has an agenda, though [he or she] may not know what it is or how to work with it. That is part of the discovery.
>
> We build lists, compare . . . views, listen, and seek to make order from chaos. No person has the whole. Each is tuned into different events. But you remember what I have forgotten, and together we build a very rich portrait. Each discovery brings heightened anxiety and release of energy. Early on people report being both confused by the multiple images, impressions, diversity, and eager to go deeper, explore more, find new action channels. . . .
>
> Gradually the realization sinks in that *this*—all of it—constitutes a mutual portrait of our world. It is complex, interconnected, hopeless, hopeful, unmanageable, inescapable. At the end . . . most groups fall speechless. My word for it is "awe.". . .
>
> [T]hey start a dialogue with peers on what they are doing now and what they wish to do in the future. . . . the anxiety becomes pure energy. We are moving toward renewal. We have touched down on common ground.[45]

OUR VIEW

In less poetic and breathless terms, we can say that such events and conferences do have some advantages:

1. More information is disseminated. Search conferences and real-time strategic change events generate a lot more information from more sources than you typically find in a small-group design team. When everyone, or almost everyone, in the organization provides input at the same time about an important decision, such as the direction the organization should take and how it should get there, your chances of making the right decision improve.
2. Greater buy-in and commitment. With a small group doing the design work, you have to do a lot of selling *after* decisions have been made. By necessity, you start your implementation before you have everyone on board. With search conferences and similar vehicles, you have

a much better chance of getting rapid buy-in, commitment, and ownership, since everyone has been involved in the entire design process.

3. Better coordination among different projects. Under the typical approach, change almost always has to occur in a piecemeal and sequential fashion. Different parts of the organization launch different change projects at different times, and coordination of these projects becomes a major problem for the leadership team. Inevitably, change projects in one area of the organization end up conflicting with change projects in another area. With search conferences, not only are many of the projects launched simultaneously across the whole organization, but since they have been designed at the same time and are based upon the same set of assumptions about the future of the entire organization, coordination becomes much easier.

4. Greater acceptance of change as an integral part of daily work. In the typical company, change efforts are viewed as a disruption to people doing *real work*. People who serve on design teams are taken away from their regular jobs for this special project work. While they are gone, others have to take up the slack. After attending search conferences or participating in real-time strategic change events, people are more likely to come away seeing change as an integral part of what they do each day. In short, they get the connection.

5. Change happens faster. In spite of management pressure to get something done right away, the change process typically progresses at a snail's pace. Change teams usually meet, meet, and meet for months on end, often in secret, and then spring their decisions on the rest of the organization. Planning for change and implementing change occur as distinct phases. Since the design team has to sell its recommendations to the rest of the organization, the planning stage drags out as the design team tries to make sure it has a solid case for its recommendations. Then, there is a lengthy communication and selling process before implementation can even begin. In contrast, people come away from search conferences with practical things they can do immediately to support the strategy and with the incentive to accomplish these things. Planning and implementation are inseparable, and change occurs at a fast pace in real time.

6. Faster and better results. Search conferences are much more likely to lead to early and significant results across the entire organization

since there is a lot of activity going on everywhere. In typical change efforts, design teams have to choose between making either substantial changes in a small part of the organization or limited and less significant changes across the entire organization. They just don't have the resources to do both.

In short, there is a lot to be said for real-time strategic change events—or whatever you want to call them. Are they the solution to problems in managing change? Probably not. But they are one of the latest and hottest guru ideas and a better idea than most.

KEY POINTS

- Most change meets with some level of resistance from those who must change.

- People resist not only change that is bad for them, but also change that will benefit them in the long run.

- There are many reasons why people resist change, but the most common are:

  They think the change will have a negative impact on them.

  The change alters the formal, psychological, and social relationship that the employee has with the organization.

  The change requires employees to give up long-standing habits.

  The organization does not adequately communicate why the change is necessary, what the benefits of the change will be, and/or how the change is progressing once it begins.

  The traditional organizational structure, business systems, technology, rewards, and so on are not aligned with the change effort, so they operate to oppose the change.

  They feel they are being forced to change by people and events outside of their control.

Change is more likely to succeed if these things occur:

The leaders of the organization establish and communicate a compelling reason to change.

The leaders agree upon and communicate a compelling vision for the future of the organization.

The change seeks and quickly achieves clear, tangible, bottom-line results that all can see.

The leadership team floods the organization with information about the change effort.

The change effort is led by a strong and committed top-management guiding coalition that is in full agreement about the need to change and what the change is intended to accomplish.

Everything is changed at once rather than in piecemeal fashion. Change is large-scale and addresses all of the cultural components that could impact the success of the change effort.

Everyone in the organization is involved in a meaningful way, through a search conference or otherwise, in deciding why a change is needed, what should change, and how the change should be accomplished.

Christopher Argyris, author of *On Organizational Learning*

Jay W. Forrester, professor emeritus of management at MIT's Sloan School of Management and author of *Principles of Systems*

William N. Isaacs, director of the Dialogue Project at MIT's Center for Organizational Learning

Daniel H. Kim, cofounder of MIT's Center for Organizational Learning

Edgar H. Schein, professor emeritus at MIT's Sloan School of Management

Donald A. Schön, author of *Organizational Learning: A Theory of Action Perspective*

Peter Senge, author of *The Fifth Discipline* and director of MIT's Center for Organizational Learning

Etienne Wenger, research scientist at the Institute for Research on Learning

3

The Learning Organization

n the late 1980s, Peter Senge, a relatively unknown professor of management at MIT, came to the realization that gurudom was about to pass him by. Senge later recalled in a 1991 interview how he reached this shocking conclusion:

> It sort of hit me one morning . . . while I was meditating, that the learning organization was going to be a hot area in business. I had already watched a fad cycle come and go related to work I had been doing for years with [my consulting firm] Innovation Associates. We had been teaching courses in . . . leadership since 1979, and we all sat on the sidelines and watched as other people wrote about vision, empowerment, and alignment— ideas that we had been teaching for years. That morning as I meditated it dawned on me that it was not OK to sit on the sidelines this time. It was time for a book on the subject of learning organizations, and I wanted to get it out before the whole world was talking about [organizational learning].[1]

So Senge wrote *The Fifth Discipline: The Art and Science of the Learning Organization.* Published in 1990, it was a loose collection of ideas about change, learning, and communication from such disparate sources as systems theorist Jay Forrester, quantum physicist David Bohm, organizational behaviorist Christopher Argyris, and musician-composer Robert Fritz. The ideas in the book were neither especially new nor presented in a very practical manner. Readers came away saying, "But what do we do Monday morning to put these ideas into practice?" The choice of the term *discipline,* as reflected in the title, was essentially a rhetorical device that provided a semblance of structure for the work. Senge later admitted that he did not fully understand the basic premise of the book at the time he was writing it. Even worse, Senge couched his musings in mystical terminology that was confusing and difficult for the lay reader to understand. *The Fifth Discipline* hardly seemed like the kind of book that would find a wide and willing business audience. Nevertheless, it made the best-seller list and turned Senge into "Mr. Learning Organization." This time Senge had the starring role in his own fad.

In retrospect, it is not too surprising that Senge's book was a success and that the learning organization became another in a long line of management passions. Organizational learning is the kind of topic that is perfect for gurudom. True, the book is murky, confusing, and filled with abstruse jargon, such as "Ladders of Inference," "Circles of Causality," "Left-Hand Columns," "Balancing Loops," "Archetypes," and "Micro-worlds." But the jargon lends a kind of pseudosophistication to a topic that many people find enticing—a kind of if-I-can't-understand-it-then-it-must-be-good logic. Plus, Senge presented the concept as a magical and reverential search that would achieve the utopian dream of all corporate executives—truly sustainable competitive advantage. "As the world becomes more interconnected and business becomes more complex and dynamic, work must become more 'learningful,' " writes Senge. "It is no longer sufficient to have one person learning for the organization, a Ford or a Sloan or a Watson. It's just not possible any longer to 'figure it out' from the top, and have everyone else following the orders of the 'grand strategist.' The organizations that will truly excel in the future will be the organizations that discover how to tap people's commitment and capacity to learn at *all* levels in an organization."[2] Senge's disciples went even further. For example, when asked to respond to the question "Why should we want to create a learning organization?" they offered numerous justifications, which are presented in Exhibit 3.1.

EXHIBIT 3.1. Reasons for Creating a Learning Organization

- For superior performance and competitive advantage
- To improve customer relations
- To avoid decline
- To improve quality
- To understand risks and diversity more deeply
- To promote innovation
- For personal and spiritual well-being
- To manage change
- For true understanding
- To create an energized and committed workforce
- To expand our boundaries
- To engage in community
- For independence and liberty
- Because the times demand it
- To make it more fun to work in organizations
- To give people hope that things can be better
- To provide a playground for creative ideas
- To provide people with a safe place to take risks with new ideas and behaviors
- To stretch beyond perceived limits
- To improve our environment
- To help people become active actors, not passive recipients
- To embrace and implement the vision of sustainable communities and organizations
- To be free
- To contribute to human evolution
- To stretch the fabric of our soul
- Because it is only natural, that is, in keeping with human nature
- To increase joy in work
- To raise the overall quality of life
- To provide people with more satisfying lives, so they are happier, do more interesting things with their lives, and are more fun to have lunch with
- To channel, support, and enhance the basic human passion to learn
- To provide a rational explanation of the necessity of caring about each other
- To provide an invitation and rationale for building communities
- Why not?

Source: These are adopted from "Why a Learning Organization?" a compilation of responses from list subscribers to learning-org@world.std.com in February 1995.

Expressed in these ways, the learning organization was simply irresistible. It was the business equivalent of the fountain of youth, and Senge, along with a few other learning organization gurus, turned the CEOs of some of America's best-known companies into would-be Ponce de Leóns searching in vain for the source of eternal corporate renewal.

Most students of the learning organization admit that the discipline is neither easy nor much fun, but we will try to make our discussion as enjoyable as possible. Part of the problem, as we said earlier, is the almost impenetrable jargon learning organization gurus choose to employ. There is also the problem of scope. The learning organization has been described as a "big conceptual catchall" whose tentacles reach into everything from customer service to quality to corporate strategy and change.[3] As a consequence, some writers have compared understanding the learning organization to trying to understand the concept of an elephant while blindfolded. Your perception of the whole is determined by which guru is your guide and which part of the elephant he or she directs you to.[4] So, where should we start? Where is the best place to begin dissecting this elephant known as the learning organization? We will start where many of our gurus start—with the individual learner.

INDIVIDUAL AND ORGANIZATIONAL LEARNING

Our gurus agree that individuals and organizations both learn, but that organizational knowledge is something more than just the sum of what the individuals in an organization know. You can send all of your employees to the Harvard Business School, spend millions on in-house technical training, and still end up with a pretty dumb organization, say our gurus, even though individually your workers might be brilliant. The fact that educated workers don't necessarily make smart organizations doesn't mean, of course, that you can ignore individual learning and create a learning organization. On the contrary, individual learning is a necessary but not sufficient condition for organizational intelligence. The crucial factor is not just what and how much individuals in organizations learn, but how effectively they transfer what they know to the organization as a whole. The linkage between individual learning and organizational learning is a key concept in this chapter, and it is a fitting place for us to start our discussion of the learning organization.

So how do individuals learn and, perhaps more importantly, how do they transfer what they learn to the organization so it can learn also? Each of our learning organization gurus has a theory about individual and organizational learning, but we think one of the best and easiest to understand is Daniel H. Kim's. Kim, cofounder of the Center for Organizational Learning at MIT with Peter Senge, presented his theory in a 1993 article in the *Sloan Management Review* entitled "The Link Between Individual and Organizational Learning."[5]

Kim suggests that we begin with a definition—what does *learning* mean? If you fire up your on-line dictionary as we did, you will probably get a definition that looks something like this:

learn-ing (lɐrn'iŋ) **n.**
the acquiring of knowledge or skill

Notice that learning has two meanings—acquiring knowledge and acquiring skill. Knowledge is the know-why, conceptual part of learning—knowing why something works or happens. Skill is the know-how, application part—having the ability to use the know-why to make something happen. Our gurus argue that in the real world, particularly in the real world of business, know-why and know-how are both important. Consider Kim's example of the sad situation of two carpenters. The first carpenter has developed a vast knowledge of architecture and design—the know-why—but has never acquired the skills to use that knowledge to build anything—the know-how. The second carpenter has mastered the skills of woodworking—the know-how—but has no understanding of what makes a coherent structure—the know-why—so all his tables fall apart and his houses fall down. Obviously, neither carpenter is very effective. In short, says Kim, true learning requires the acquisition of both know-why and know-how.

The path to true learning, however, is often blocked by common misconceptions. Here are some notions many of us have about learning. Which of these statements do you think are true?

A. The most effective learning occurs in a classroom setting away from the distractions of the workplace where learners can be presented with the wisdom of an expert and have the opportunity to demonstrate their mastery of the new material by answering questions on tests.

B. Learning is an individual and largely passive activity for the learner. It is somewhat analogous to information being transferred from one mind to another, similar to files being copied from one computer to another.

C. The most important things for people to learn, from an organizational standpoint, are the explicit rules, operating procedures, and policies of the workplace.

D. All of the above.

E. None of the above.

According to our gurus, the correct answer is

E. None of the above.

Our gurus cite compelling research to show that

- The most important learning occurs on the job and not in the classroom.
- The most effective learning is social and active, not individual and passive.
- The most important things for people to learn aren't the explicit rules, procedures, and policies of the workplace but the tacit stuff found in the rich, nourishing soup of intuition, judgment, expertise, and common sense that is imbedded in the seeming chaos of day-to-day activity.

Our gurus argue that the most effective learning, particularly for adults, results from a continuing cycle of experience in the workplace itself. Real learning, they maintain, occurs something like this:

- We have concrete experiences in the workplace.
- We reflect on those experiences, trying to understand what happened and why.
- We form concepts and generalizations based upon those experiences.
- We test those concepts and generalizations through new experiences.
- Then we repeat the cycle, similar to the turning of a wheel.

The Wheel of Learning

Daniel Kim suggests that we think of this learning process as a wheel that goes around and around like the one illustrated at Exhibit 3.2. Notice in Ex-

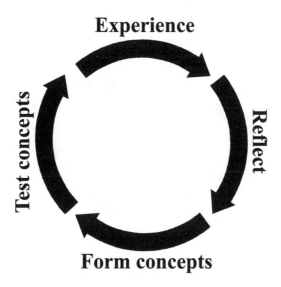

EXHIBIT 3.2.   **The Wheel of Learning**

hibit 3.3 that during half the cycle, when we are testing our concepts and observing what happens in a concrete experience, we are learning know-how. In the other half of the cycle, when we are reflecting on our observations and forming concepts, we are learning know-why.

The Wheel of Learning and Our Mental Models

Of course, the knowledge we gain as the wheel of learning turns around and around isn't lost. We store in our memory the know-how and know-why we pick up through the multiple turns of the wheel as assumptions, notions, and theories about how the world works. Our gurus call these assumptions, notions, and theories our "mental models." These can be simple generalizations, such as "people are untrustworthy," or they can be complex theories about business, politics, economics, consumer behavior, and so on. They represent our unique view of the world and our assessment of the consequences that are likely to flow from any given action we might take. Our mental models are the inner voice that says, "If you do this in this type of situation, then this will happen" (see Exhibit 3.4).

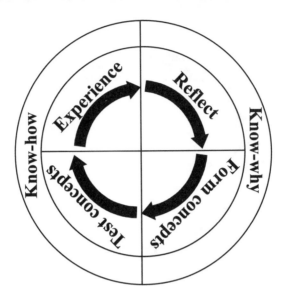

EXHIBIT 3.3. **The Wheel of Learning**

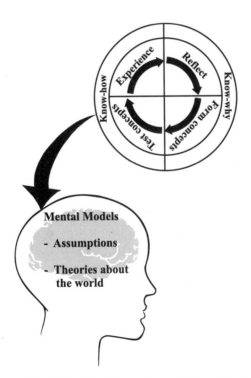

EXHIBIT 3.4. **The Wheel of Learning and Our Mental Models**

Our mental models are deeply held images of how the world works, but they aren't passive images since our minds are far from being static storage devices. Not only are our minds shaped by our experiences in the world, but our minds also shape our experiences (Exhibit 3.5). Our mental models not only are formed by the turns of the wheel of learning but they also shape how and when the wheel turns, and how fast it turns. Kim observes that

mental models represent a person's view of the world, including explicit and implicit understandings. Mental models provide the context in which to view and interpret new material, and they determine how stored information is relevant to a given situation. They represent more than a collection of ideas, memories, and experiences—they are like the source code of a computer's operating system, the manager and arbiter of acquiring, retaining, using and deleting new information. But they are much more than that because they are also like the programmer of that source code with the know-how to design a different code as well as the know-why to choose one over the other.[6]

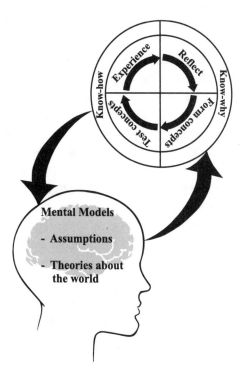

EXHIBIT 3.5. **The Wheel of Learning and Our Mental Models**

Our mental-model source code is extremely powerful, literally controlling and directing what we see, hear, and pay attention to. It affects our interpretation of events and even our physical response to those events. William N. Isaacs, director of the Dialogue Project at MIT's Organizational Learning Center, provides a good example of how mental models work. "Two men are walking down a dark street late at night. Suddenly, a shadow moves rapidly across their path. One man's heart begins to pound and he takes a short quick breath. The other man remains calm." Both men experienced the same event, but their reaction was totally different because of their differing perceptions of reality, caused by their different mental models of what shadows mean on dark streets at night.[7]

Shared Mental Models

Everyone develops mental models. They are a natural part of human life and a natural consequence of the work experience. As our wheel of learning turns at work, we learn how to complete routine tasks, like filling out forms and operating machinery, as well as more complex ideas about what is acceptable and unacceptable, rewarded and punished in the organization. When we begin to share our knowledge of know-why and/or know-how with others, organizational learning begins (Exhibit 3.6).

Kim points out that in the early stages of an organization's existence, individual learning and organizational learning are almost synonymous. Because the organization is usually small, there is frequent sharing of information and ideas. As an organization grows, however, management usually makes an effort to capture some of the knowledge and learning of individual members in the form of paper and computer files, reports, training manuals, operating procedures, strategic plans, memos, letters, and so on. Some of the know-why and know-how in an organization is retained through such devices. However, even in the most bureaucratic organizations much more knowledge and learning go unrecorded than are captured on paper or in computer files. The vast amount of organizational know-why and know-how, accumulated through years of constantly turning wheels of learning and the sharing of mental models, remains a kind of tacit, shadowy, and fragile but necessary collective memory of the community of workers (Exhibit 3.7). This accumulated tacit knowledge is both unique to an organization and critical for its success.

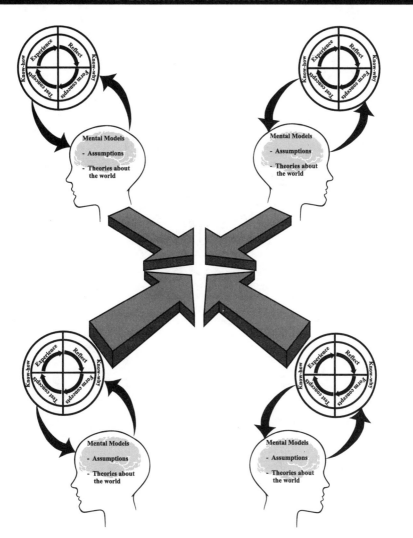

EXHIBIT 3.6.   **Organizational Learning through Shared Mental Models**

The Communities of Practice

When our gurus venture into the workplace to observe how people and organizations really learn, they inevitably find that the organization's unrecorded wisdom is more valuable than its captured knowledge. They also find that this unrecorded asset is developed and enhanced by social exchanges in a community atmosphere. People form what our gurus call

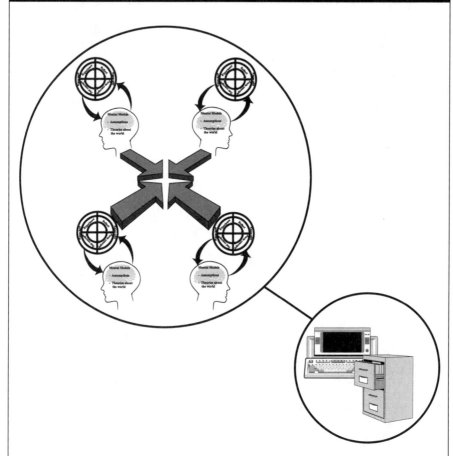

EXHIBIT 3.7.   **Individual and Organizational Learning**

"communities of practice," and it is through these communities that real
learning occurs. What are these communities of practice like? Etienne
Wenger, of the Institute for Research on Learning, describes one, based
upon his experience as a claims processor in a large insurance company.
Wenger took the job for the express purpose of investigating how learning,
understanding, and competence revealed themselves in everyday practices.
His experiences are typical of what our gurus find in the workplace and
provide a good illustration of what is meant by communities of practice.
Wenger recalls:

I found . . . that this supposedly routine job gives rise to a very complex so-cial community. In order to work together, claim processors have estab-lished a versatile web of informal networks. Through exchanging questions, meeting in hallways, telling stories, negotiating the meaning of events, in-venting and sharing new ways of doing things, conspiring, debating and re-calling the past, they complement each other's information and together construct a shared understanding of their environment and work.

In fact, the claim processors' ability to learn and perform their jobs de-pends on their community—its shared memories, routines, improvisations, innovations and connections to the world. The community functions within and without—and sometimes in spite of—the company's official organiza-tional and procedural frameworks.[8]

Our learning organization gurus are most concerned about the health of these social learning communities because their well-being seems to be vital to the survival and renewal of organizations. Daniel Kim presents two scenarios to illustrate just how important the unwritten know-why in the community of practice truly is. He writes:

Imagine an organization in which all the physical records disintegrate overnight. Suddenly, there are no reports, no computer files, no employee record sheets, no operating manuals, no calendars—all that remain are the people, buildings, capital equipment, raw materials, and inventory. Now imagine an organization where all the people simply quit showing up for work. New people, who are similar in many ways to the former em-ployees but who have no familiarity with that particular organization, come to work instead. Which of the two organizations will be easier to rebuild to its former status?[9]

Kim and most of our other learning organization gurus have no doubts about which of these two scenarios they would prefer. They would rather lose the data and keep the people. Their reasoning is simple. In the first scenario, the static memory of the organization is eliminated, but the em-ployees' shared mental repository of know-why and know-how remains intact. The community of practice endures. With their mental models, the people can recreate most of the policies, procedures, manuals, and so on. They can rebuild the organization's static memory. In the second and much worse scenario, the shared mental models are gone. The community of practice is destroyed and the linkages between the minds that form organizational memory are irretrievably severed. "Without these mental models, which include all the subtle interconnections that have been developed among the various members," writes Kim, "an organization will be incapacitated in both learning and action."[10] The organization's mind dies and its body soon follows.

In theory, then
> **If** the individual wheels of learning always turn rapidly and smoothly,
>> **If** individual mental models are constantly shaped, challenged, and reshaped,
>>> **If** the accumulated know-why and know-how of the organization is always shared efficiently and effectively,
>>>> **If** the social communities of practice always remain intact and strong,

Then the organization learns and thrives—at least, according to learning organization theory.

Unfortunately for organizations, if not for our gurus' earning power, that is rarely what happens. Instead, learning wheels begin to wobble or partially revolve. Mental models stagnate. Communication channels break down. Learning slows and sometimes stops. The organization gets sick and needs a remedy. As you might expect, our learning organization gurus just happen to have a few prescriptions in mind.

THREE APPROACHES: HOW TO DIAGNOSE AND CURE LEARNING DEFICIENCIES IN YOUR ORGANIZATION

Each of our gurus has his or her own way of defining learning deficiencies in organizations and his or her own unique prescriptions for a cure. The various approaches, however, can be grouped roughly into three major types.

One approach to organizational learning focuses on mental models and how organizational and individual learning breaks down when mental models aren't made explicit and consequently go unchallenged. This approach is most closely associated with the work of Christopher Argyris, professor of education and organizational behavior at Harvard and author of numerous articles on organizational effectiveness and learning, and Donald A. Schön, professor emeritus and senior lecturer at MIT.

A second approach focuses on learning breakdowns that occur when our if-then mental models are defective for one of two reasons: (1) because they attribute a causal relationship to events when no such relationship exists, or (2) because they fail to recognize such a relationship when it does exist. This approach is most closely associated with the work of Peter Senge, Jay W. Forrester, and the Center for Organizational Learning at MIT.

A third and a broader approach focuses on organizational culture and the conditions that are necessary to sustain and nurture the wheels of learning and the communities of practice we mentioned earlier. This approach is most closely associated with the work of MIT professor Edgar H. Schein.

Let's look at each of these approaches in some depth.

Approach #1: Learning to Reflect and Communicate

Chris Argyris and Donald Schön have been writing about learning organizations since the 1970s. Although their research and writing is often couched in painfully precise technical language, their basic approach is to help people recognize and share with others the mental models that influence their actions. In short, Argyris and Schön are interested in two related problems that inhibit both individual and organizational learning: (1) our failure to recognize and challenge the mental models that control our actions, and (2) our failure to make our assumptions clear to others and to help them do the same. Argyris and Schön propose remedies for both problems in terms of two types of learning skills they say we all need to develop: (1) reflection—slowing down our thinking process to become more aware of our mental models, and (2) inquiry—being more open about the assumptions behind our actions and helping others to do the same.

The Skill of Reflection

Here is a common situation you may have encountered.

> You call a meeting for 9:00 A.M. for your entire staff. Everyone arrives but John. He comes wandering into the room at 9:30. You don't say anything,

but you can't help but think, "You know I'm certain John knew exactly when the meeting was supposed to start. I bet he deliberately came in late. He always seems to come late. John is just unreliable. You can't count on him."

Or you may have experienced something like this.

You overhear your boss talking to Jane, one of your coworkers. The boss is saying, "Jane, your work has really not been up to the kind of performance we expect around here. If you don't start doing better I'm going to have to take some action." You think to yourself, "That's the second time I've seen him calling some woman to task for her performance. Jane seems like a good worker to me. I bet he's just picking on her because she's a woman. If that's the way he is, he shouldn't be a supervisor."[11]

If you haven't had these exact experiences, you have probably have had ones quite similar. We all have. We see or hear something and our mental models kick in, often without our realizing what is happening. We quickly make assumptions and draw conclusions. We may be right, but in many cases we find out later that we were wrong. For instance, John may have come in late because he was delayed helping a key client resolve a problem. Or we may discover that the boss was right about Jane's performance and that she had made a series of critical mistakes lately.

Chris Argyris calls this predisposition for jumping to conclusions "climbing the ladder of inference."[12] The steps of this ladder are shown in Exhibit 3.8, which you should read from the bottom step upward.

Of course, there is nothing wrong with the ladder of inference if we know we are climbing it and we don't climb it too fast. What Argyris and his associates want us to do is slow down and reflect upon what we are doing; and they suggest a simple exercise they call "Exposing the Left-Hand Column" to help us do that.

As detailed in Exhibit 3.9, the exercise helps us examine how we responded to a particular interpersonal problem by looking first at what was said or done (the right-hand column) and then at what we were thinking and feeling at the time (the left-hand column). The exercise then asks us to answer a series of questions that are designed to improve our responses in the future.

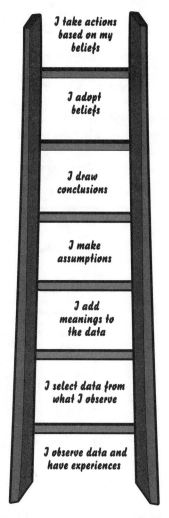

EXHIBIT 3.8. **The Ladder of Inference**

Take a few moments to work through the exercise in Exhibit 3.9; you will develop a better feeling for the left-hand-column concept than if we continued to describe it.

In addition to this self-examination, our gurus suggest that you share the results with a friend and seek his or her help. Some of our gurus also suggest that you rewrite the right-hand column (what was said/done) and change your responses based upon what you learned from the exercise.

EXHIBIT 3.9. **Exposing the Left-Hand Column**

Step 1: Choose a difficult interpersonal problem that you have been involved in lately. For example, you might select a situation where you felt you were being treated unfairly or you felt someone on the team wasn't pulling their weight.

Step 2: Take a piece of paper and divide it into two columns. In the right-hand column, write down what was said in a conversation you recently had about the problem. If you haven't had the conversation yet, write down what you think might be said when you discuss the problem with someone. For example, if your boss has just called and said he wanted to meet with you to discuss your project you might write something like this.

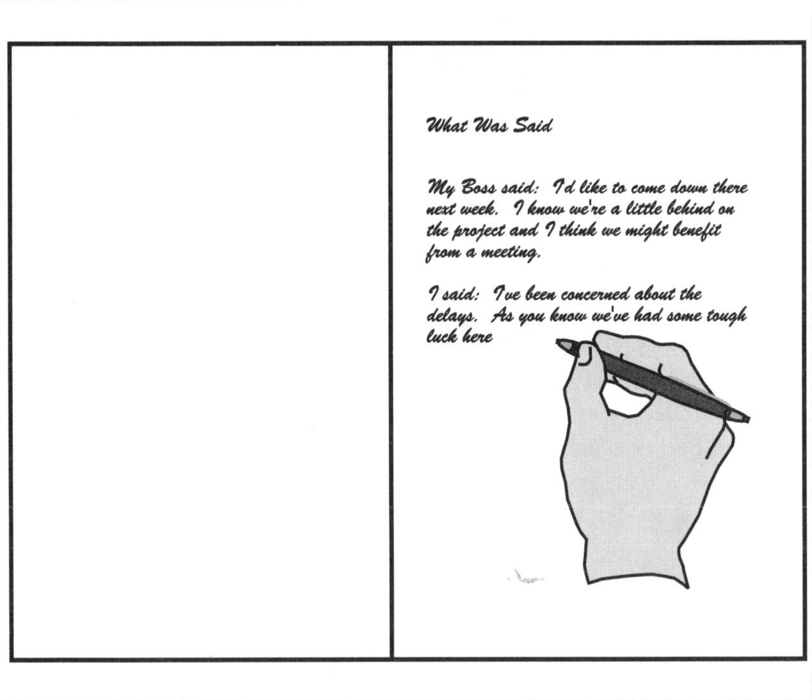

What Was Said

My Boss said: I'd like to come down there next week. I know we're a little behind on the project and I think we might benefit from a meeting.

I said: I've been concerned about the delays. As you know we've had some tough luck here

Step 3: In the left-hand column, write out what you were thinking and feeling.
Step 4: Review what you have written and ask yourself
  What led me to think and feel this way?
  What was I trying to accomplish?
  Why didn't I say what I was thinking?
  What assumptions was I making about how the other person might respond?
  What prevented me from acting differently?
  What were the costs/benefits to me/the organization for the way I acted?
  How can I use what I learned from this exercise to improve my communication?[1]

What I Was Thinking	*What Was Said*
Uh. Oh. We're two months late, not just a little behind. I didn't think he suspected.	*My Boss said: I'd like to come down there next week. I know we're a little behind on the project and I think we might benefit from a meeting.*
I was hoping we could catch up before he realized.	
He never offered to help when we were in the planning stages. Now this meeting will just put us further behind.	*I said: I've been concerned about the delays. As you know, we've had some tough luck here, and we're working around the clock. But, of course, we'll squeeze in a meeting at your convenience.*
I don't want to	*My Boss said: Well, it's occurred to me that we could use better coordination between us. There are probably some ways I could help.*

1. See Rick Ross and Art Kleiner, "The Left-Hand Column," in Peter Senge et al., **The Fifth Discipline Handbook** (New York: Currency Doubleday, 1994), pp. 246–250, for a more complete explanation of this exercise.

The left-hand column exercise is intended to help us slow down the march up the ladder of inference and recognize the underlying mental models that influence what we say and do. That's all fine and good, but how do we make use of what we learn? Even if we know what our underlying assumptions are, how do we express them to others? That, say our gurus, is where the skill of inquiry comes in.

The Skill of Inquiry

Have you ever been in a conversation with someone and found yourself saying things that you didn't really mean? Consider this scenario:

You're working on a big project with a colleague, Bill. Bill has just given a major presentation to your boss on the status of your project. Since you were out of town you had to miss the presentation, but you have been told that the presentation was a disaster. You meet with Bill your first morning back. Your conversation goes something like this.[13]

You say: How did the presentation go?

  You are thinking: Everyone says you bombed.

Bill says: Well, I don't know. It is really too early to tell.

  You are thinking: Can he be that stupid? Doesn't he realize how bad it was.

You say: What do you think we should do? This project is important and there are some real issues we need to resolve.

Bill says: Let's just wait and see what happens. I'm sure everything will be OK.

  You are thinking: He's afraid to face the truth. I can't believe what a bind this puts us in. I've got to find a way to salvage things.

You say: Well, you may be right, but I think we can't afford to just sit and wait.

You lied, didn't you? And so did Bill. Okay, maybe you didn't exactly lie, but you didn't tell the whole truth. Why?

  Argyris says one of the reasons we tell half-truths, and sometimes outright untruths, in the workplace is that most of us carry around in our heads a mental model that governs our behavior in business situations—a mental model he calls "Model I" (see Exhibit 3.10).

EXHIBIT 3.10. **Chris Argyris's Model I**

Model I suggests that in business you should do the following:

- Always try to design and manage your work environment so that, to the maximum extent possible, you stay in control of the factors that affect you.

- Give approval and praise to others. Tell others what you believe will make them feel good about themselves. Reduce their hurt feelings by telling them how much you care and, if possible, agree with them that others acted improperly.

- Never confront others' reasoning or actions.

- Advocate your position in order to win. Hold your position in the face of advocacy. Feeling vulnerable is a weakness.

- Never tell other people all you think and feel.

- Stick to your principles, values, and beliefs.[1]

---

1. See Chris Argyris, "Double-Loop Learning in Organizations," **Harvard Business Review**, September–October 1977, pp. 118–119.

So what is wrong with this model? You are just being nice and being smart. You go along, get along, win as often as you can, and try to take care of yourself. Everybody does it, right? Right, and that's just Argyris's point. Everyone is so busy avoiding conflict and taking care of themselves that they wreak havoc with the organization. People pretend to be candid and straightforward, but they aren't. No one exposes the assumptions behind their reasoning, even to themselves, and consequently, mental models go unexamined and unchallenged. Worse, this kind of behavior becomes routine. We don't even realize what we are doing. Our Model I takes over and we become very skilled at carrying out its instructions. As far as learning is concerned, says Argyris, we have a kind of "skilled incompetence" that can be severely debilitating.

To illustrate their point, Argyris and Schön provide the example of what happened to a hapless Chief Information Officer who held a meeting with his subordinates to discuss a serious problem. The CIO had come under fire from line managers who complained that the CIO's "techies" weren't being responsive to the line's concerns. Senior management was threatening to cut the information systems department's budget, fire people, and even outsource some services. The CIO assembled his staff to discuss the problem. The meeting proceeded as follows:

CIO: The reason for this meeting is that I have just gotten a read-our-lips order from senior management. The line managers say we're not cooperating with them. We keep asking for higher budgets, but frankly, they don't think we are adding much value. I want to discuss with you our ability to react to their needs and why we always seem to be having difficulties with them. After all, they are our customers. We have to be concerned about meeting their needs.

Information Professional #1: We *are* concerned about their needs. The big trouble is they don't know what they want.

Information Professional #2: When they do know what they want, they have no idea how long it will take for us to provide them with what they want. They want everything yesterday.

Information Professional #3: I've had it up to here with their complaining. There wouldn't be any problem if they would just give us the people and money we need.

CIO: I understand. I appreciate what you are saying and I know you are all frustrated with the way things have been going. But I think we have to come up with some credible plan to respond to their concerns.

Information Professional #2: There's no sense in planning. The users don't plan. And even if we had a plan they would just make more demands and complain about what we were failing to do.

CIO: Yes, yes, I know. But since we don't a have solid plan, we can't review the way we are managing our resources. As I see it, we have two choices. The first is to do what we are now doing—and I believe that would be disastrous. The second is to break out of this mold and change the way we do business.

Information Professional #3: There is no way you are going to change the line managers. If you want to try it, good luck, but I think you are just wasting your time.

CIO: Well if planning isn't the answer, how do you propose to solve the problem?

Information Professional #3: It isn't solvable. At least, we can't solve it. The line managers just need to stop making impossible requests.

Information Professional #1: We are already working ourselves to death trying to satisfy them. That's why all our good people are leaving.

Information Professional #3: It's like we have been saying, it's just not fixable.

CIO (losing his patience): Well, it *has* to be fixable. We have to fix it. We have no choice.[14]

Does the CIO's predicament sound familiar? Most of us have participated in similar meetings. There's a lot of wheel spinning. Everyone is defensive. The real problems are never addressed and nothing is accomplished. So what can we do to avoid such situations and improve learning? Two things, say Argyris and Schön.

How to Avoid Sticky Situations and Continue Learning

First, Argyris and Schön argue that we should seek to understand the assumptions we bring to the conversation and how we respond to what others are saying. Perhaps we should begin by completing the left-hand column exercise and trying to understand how Model I is controlling our actions. For example, by exposing his left-hand column, the CIO might have recognized that he was being too diplomatic and letting his subordinates get away with their defensive arguments. He wasn't making his true feelings known, and he was accepting his subordinates' sloppy reasoning and untested claims. Most importantly, the CIO might recognize that he was letting his Model I assumptions make learning and problem solving nearly impossible.

Second, say Argyris and Schön, we should consciously seek to change our conversation to interject more inquiry and to invite inquiry from others. Exhibit 3.11 shows some of our gurus' suggestions on how to do this.[15]

How might following these new rules of conversation have changed our CIO's meeting with his subordinates? Argyris and Schön say that when his subordinates said that the line managers did not trust them or care for them, the CIO should have responded:

Have you tested out your assumptions about their views of us? If so, what did you say to the line [manager]? If not, what led you not to do so?

In response to his subordinates' untested assertions, he could have said:

I ask if you have tested the validity of your assertions about the line [managers].The answer I get is another set of untested assertions.

You state that our customers are inflexible and insensitive. . . .You do not like this behavior, and you use it as evidence that the problems are not correctable.

You may be right, but I do not hear anyone presenting a compelling argument that is also testable. Whenever I have tried to make some suggestions, the responses that I hear from you include "good luck to you" and "trust us, our users are uninfluenceable."

It is difficult for me to trust your diagnosis. If you act toward the line managers the way you are acting toward me, I can see how they would become, in your eyes, uninfluenceable. But I can also see how they may come to a similar conclusion about you.

This leads me to another issue.You may be finding me uninfluenceable. I want to establish conversations that do not require me to distance myself from my responsibility or yours for the problems we are experiencing.[16]

The words are tough, direct and, confrontational, but, in Argyris's opinion, necessary. "The idea," he writes, "is to increase the others' capacity to

EXHIBIT 3.11. How to Inject More Inquiry into Our Conversations

Argyris and Schön suggest that we

- Make our thinking process clear to others by prefacing our comments with such phrases as

  ✔ "Here's what I think and here's how I got there."

  ✔ "I assumed that. . . ."

  ✔ "I came to this position because. . . ."

  ✔ "Here are some examples of the kinds of things I was thinking about when I came to the conclusion that. . . ."

- Encourage others to explore our assumptions and conclusions by asking clarifying questions such as

  ✔ "What do you think about what I just said?"

  ✔ "Do you see any flaws in my reasoning?"

  ✔ "What can you add?"

- Get others to make their thinking process clear with such questions as

  ✔ "What leads you to that conclusion?"

  ✔ "What data do you have that support that conclusion?"

  ✔ "What causes you to say that?"

  ✔ "Can you help me understand your thinking here?"

- Clarify our understanding of what others are proposing with follow-up questions or comments such as

  ✔ "Is this similar to . . .?"

  ✔ "If I understand you correctly, you're saying that. . . ."

  ✔ "Am I correct that you are saying. . . ?"

- Explore, listen, and offer our views in an open way when we disagree with others.

  ✔ "Have you considered. . . ?"

  ✔ "When you say . . . I worry that. . . ."

  ✔ "I have a hard time seeing that because. . . ."

- Look for information that will help people move forward when we have reached an impasse with them.

  ✔ "What do we know for a fact?"

  ✔ "What don't we know?"

  ✔ "What do we agree upon and where do we disagree?"

  ✔ "Are we starting from two different assumptions?"

  ✔ "What would have to happen for you to consider an alternative?"

examine their defensive reasoning and the unrecognized negative consequences. This type of caring is to say, in effect, 'I trust that you have the capacity to face up to any gaps and inconsistencies in the way that you reason.' This is what the CIO was asking his subordinates to do. . . . He showed the deepest type of respect for them. Instead of dodging the root issues, he attributed to them a high capacity for self-reflection and self-examination."[17]

👁 OUR VIEW

Argyris and Schön make a good case, but we suspect that many people will still have difficulty being as open, blunt, and inquisitive as they propose. Model I is just too strong for most of us. Being frank is never easy. Nevertheless, our gurus argue that brutal honesty is the personal and organizational price we have to pay for learning.

That's the first approach to learning, but don't worry if it is not exactly what you hoped for. As we said at the beginning, there are other approaches, such as the one presented in the next section.

Approach #2: Learning Systems Thinking

Whereas Argyris and Schön worry about our ability to recognize our if-then mental models and make them explicit, our next set of gurus, represented most notably by MIT professors Jay W. Forrester and Peter Senge, worry about our mental models themselves. Forrester, who invented random-access magnetic-core memory (RAM) during the first wave of modern digital computing, is an engineer and a pioneer in the field of systems dynamics. His approach to helping us learn more effectively involves having an expert carefully and systematically examine our mental models and then construct an elaborate computer simulation that clearly demonstrates the error of our reasoning.

Senge is somewhat more diplomatic. Instead of bluntly pointing out the error of our thinking, Senge prefers to educate us in the discipline of systems thinking so that we can discover for ourselves the defects in our mental models. Regardless, both Forrester and Senge are confident that most of our if-then interpretations of the world are wrong most of the time and that the benefits of the learning organization would flow to us if we could only grasp our wrongheadedness.

The Loopiness of the World

Forrester's and Senge's approaches to organizational and individual learning are often mired in technical jargon, but at their most basic level they come down to this: Our mental models misrepresent reality, and as a result, we attack the symptoms of our problems rather than identifying and correcting the underlying causes of them. Forrester puts it this way, "Partly, the weaknesses [in our mental models] . . . arise from incompleteness, and internal contradictions. But more serious is our mental inability to draw correct dynamic conclusions."[18] Our mental models draw a picture of a "unidirectional world in which a problem leads to an action that leads to a solution."[19] Our mental models imply a simple structure like this:

Information about problem → Action → Result

"Instead," argues Forrester, "we live in an on-going circular environment . . . in which each action is based on current conditions, such actions affect conditions, and the changed conditions become the basis for future action. There is no beginning or end to the process. People are interconnected. Many such loops are intertwined. Through long cascaded chains of action, each person is continually reacting to the echo of that person's past actions as well as to the past actions of others."[20] The real world, says Forrester, looks more like the structure shown in Exhibit 3.12.

In short, our systems theorists argue that the world is a loopy place where cause and effect go around and around like a long winding spring of causality (Exhibit 3.13). Nothing ever really begins or ends; there is just cause, effect, cause, effect, for eternity.

The spring may unwind in an orderly fashion or it may stretch out haphazardly, with long lapses of time between action and result. When the cycle is inconsistent and unpredictable, we lose our sense of the interconnectedness of the world. We are fooled by the craziness of it all because it isn't what we expect. Forrester explains:

From earliest childhood we learn that cause and effect are closely associated. If one touches a hot stove, the hand is burned here and now. When one stumbles over a threshold, the cause is immediately seen as not picking

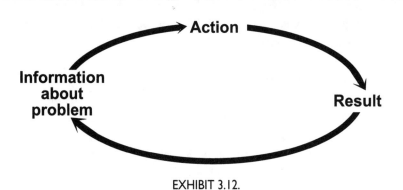

EXHIBIT 3.12.

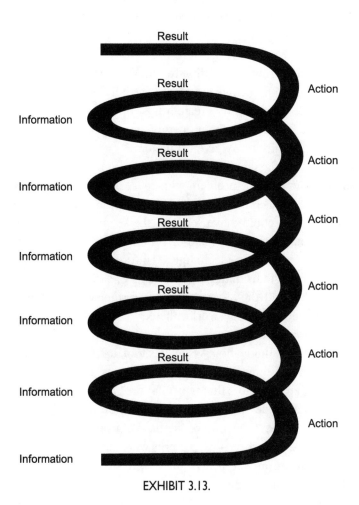

EXHIBIT 3.13.

the foot high enough, and the resulting fall is immediate. All simple feedback processes that we fully understand reinforce the same lesson of close association of cause and effect. However, those lessons are aggressively misleading in more complex systems.

In systems composed of many interacting feedback loops and long time delays, causes of an observed symptom may come from an entirely different part of the system and lie far back in time.

To make matters even more misleading, such systems present the kind of evidence that one has been conditioned to expect. There will be apparent causes that meet the test of being closely associated in time and location.

However, those apparent causes are usually coincident symptoms arising from the distant cause. People are thereby drawn to actions that are not relevant to the problem at hand.[21]

The principal learning disability for most of us, argue Forrester and Senge, is that we fail to recognize, or only partially recognize, the loopiness of the world and consequently create a host of problems for ourselves. In other words, we fail to make the proper connection between the true cause-and-effect relationship in any given situation.

Imagine the limitless number of such situations that might occur in a business environment. The problem with cause and effect, of course, is that there are so many causes and so many effects. Some systems theorists were convinced that they could make sense of the seemingly endless combinations and permutations of cause-and-effect relationships that might exist by applying computer-modeling techniques. Unfortunately for those of us who are not trained in systems thinking, the results of such modeling were often incomprehensible and therefore unusable. Fortunately, there is an easier way to understand our loopy world, thanks largely to Senge's consulting group, Innovation Associates.

In the mid-1980s, Innovation Associates took up the challenge of simplifying the study of systems thinking. Their goal was to document categories of commonly seen behaviors that typify failures of systems thinking and to present them in an understandable manner. This effort resulted in what has been referred to as the "stepchild of the field of systems thinking"[22]—a series of *archetypes,* or archetypical patterns of behavior.

By definition, an archetype is "the original pattern, or model, from which all other things of the same kind are made; prototype," or "a perfect example of a type or group."[23] Senge's group documented a set of such prototypes, or perfect examples, of commonly occurring patterns of behavior that were to be used as diagnostic and problem-solving tools. This set of archetypes has since been expanded and modified but essentially consists of eight patterns of behavior. We summarize the archetypes in Exhibit 3.14, drawing upon explanations provided by Daniel Kim and others. For each archetype, we identify the most clearly relevant business issue the archetype impacts, provide a description and example of the archetype, suggest how you can determine if the archetype is present, and provide some strategies our gurus suggest you employ if the archetype does exist.

Beyond Archetypes to Microworlds

Archetypes are tools that help you think about the interconnectedness of the world. Peter Senge and his cohorts describe archetypes as diagnostics that can help you begin to think in systems terms, but systems thinking is rarely enough for our systems gurus. They want you to go even further. Jay Forrester describes the difference between beginning systems thinking and the ideal approach he prefers:

> Systems thinking appears to be thinking about systems, talking about the characteristics of systems, acknowledging that systems are important, discussing some of the insights from systems archetypes, and relating experiences people have with systems. . . . Systems thinking can be a door opener and a source of incentive to go deeper into the study of systems. But I believe that systems thinking . . . will change very few of the mental models. . . . Systems thinking is not more than five percent of a systems education.
>
> On the other hand, systems dynamic modeling is learning by doing. It is learning through being surprised by the mistakes one makes. Systems . . . modeling is a participative activity in which one learns by trial and error and practice. I believe that immersion in such active learning can change mental models. . . .
>
> To appreciate the nature of systems, students must have extensive personal experience in working with systems. This means creating systems . . . models on a computer, simulating their behavior, exploring how the models respond to changes in structure and policies, and comparing model behavior to the real systems being represented.[24]

EXHIBIT 3.14.   **Eight Archetypes of Systems Thinking**

Archetype #1: Fixes That Fail

Relevant business issue: Problem solving

Description: Applying short-term fixes to the symptoms of a problem may temporarily alleviate the symptoms, but the fix ultimately can exacerbate the underlying problem.

Examples

- Senge tells the story of a rug merchant whose carpet had a large bump in the center. Each time the merchant would step on the bump to flatten out the carpet, the bump would just reappear in another place. Finally, the merchant lifted the edge of the carpet and an angry snake crawled out. The merchant focused on the symptom—the bump—and failed to identify and deal with the real problem—the snake.

- Consider the example of one of our clients who, faced with a shortfall in projected sales in the fourth quarter, offered a significant price cut to customers who booked orders by year-end. The incentive worked better than the company had hoped and fourth-quarter sales exceeded all expectations. Unfortunately, the year-end solution proved to be a disaster for the new year. Having doubled or tripled their normal orders to take advantage of the year-end price cuts, most customers cut their orders to near zero during the first quarter of the new year, and the company experienced the worst sales slump in its history.

Identifying the archetype: To determine whether you are dealing with a Fixes That Fail archetype, ask yourself the following questions:[1]

- Are short-term actions being taken without consideration for their long-term consequences?

- Have similar short-term actions been taken in the past in response to similar situations?

- Do you find yourself saying, "It always worked in the past, so why isn't it working now"?

Strategies for dealing with Fixes That Fail

- Separate symptoms of the problem from the problem itself.

- Acknowledge that the fixes are only alleviating the symptoms.

- Make a commitment to deal with the real problem.

- Consider the long-term consequences for any solution applied to a problem, and select solutions that produce the least harmful consequences.

Archetype #2: The Tragedy of the Commons

Relevant business issue: Allocation of resources

Description: The Tragedy of the Commons is essentially the archetype of greed. When each individual tries to maximize his or her own benefit from a common resource, everyone suffers.

Example
This archetype takes its name from what happened in the Sahel region of sub-Saharan Africa. Once a fertile region supporting 100,000 herdsmen and a half million head of cattle, the region today is a barren desert. Senge described the Tragedy of the Commons this way in *The Fifth Discipline*:

> *The tragedy of the Sahel was rooted in steady growth of population and herd sizes from the 1920s to the 1970s. The growth accelerated from 1955 to 1965 due to unusually heavy rainfalls and assistance from international aid organizations who financed numerous deep wells. Each herdsman on the Sahel had incentives to expand his herd of [cattle], both for economic gain and social status. As long as the common grazing lands were large enough to support these new, larger herds, there were no problems. But in the early 1960s, overgrazing began to occur. Eventually rangeland vegetation grew sparser. The sparser the vegetation, the more overgrazing, until it got to the point where the cattle consumed more foliage than the ranges could generate. The desertification reinforced itself as decreases in plant cover allowed wind and rain to erode the soil. Less vegetation was produced, which got overgrazed more severely to support the herds, leading to further desertification. The vicious spiral continued until disaster struck in the form of a series of droughts in the 1960s and 1970s. By the early 1970s, 50 to 80 percent of the livestock was dead and much of the population of the Sahel was destitute.[2]*

Identifying the archetype: To determine whether you are dealing with a Tragedy of the Commons archetype, ask yourself the following questions:

- Do large numbers of individuals or organizational units have unrestricted access to a common limited resource?
- Is access to the resource self-regulated?
- Do individual incentives outweigh group incentives?
- Do you ever wonder why there used to be plenty of the resource to go around, but there isn't anymore?

Strategies for dealing with the Tragedy of the Commons: Daniel Kim recommends the following approach to the Tragedy of the Commons:[3]

- Identify the common resource(s) that are being shared.
- Determine what motivates individuals to use the resource. These motivators can be personal or they may be incentive systems in the company.
- Make the long-term loss or degradation of the common resource more real to the individual users. Tie the effects of individual actions to overall performance goals.
- Reevaluate the nature of the common resource. Determine if there are other resources that can be used to relieve the stress.
- Identify a final arbiter to limit access to common resources. The arbiter can be a shared vision, a measurement system, or a person who is empowered to allocate resources.

EXHIBIT 3.14. (Continued)

Archetype #3: Escalation

Relevant business issue: Competition

Description: In the Escalation archetype, an individual or organization (party A) takes actions that are perceived by another (party B) as a threat. Party B responds in kind and increases the threat to party A. Party A escalates the action and party B responds with even more threatening actions. This cycle of response and escalated response spins out of control.

Example

- You are in an all-out war to gain market share. You cut prices to grab some customers away from the competition. Not to be outdone, your competitor cuts prices even more. You respond with further cuts. So does your competitor. Your customers and your competitor's customers love it. They run back and forth chasing the next bargain. You and your competitor go bankrupt.

Identifying the archetype: To determine whether you are dealing with an Escalation archetype, ask yourself the following questions:

- Are there two or more entities whose actions can be perceived as a threat by the others?

- Does each entity have the ability to retaliate in kind?

- Have I used logic: "If our competition would just slow down, we could stop this one-upmanship"?

Strategies for dealing with Escalation[4]

- Identify your company's or industry's competitive basis—what differentiates you from your competitors.

- Identify the key players in the Escalation.

- Identify what is actually being threatened and determine whether you are addressing a real threat.

- Determine if the focus of the competition—price, quality, speed, service, and so forth—can be changed.

- Identify larger goals and structure the system to achieve those goals. Are there ways to expand the market rather than cutting it into little pieces?

Archetype #4: Shifting the Burden

Relevant business issue: Organizational gridlock

Description: When seemingly positive results follow a short-term fix to a problem, the fix is likely to be used again and again. As this fix is used more and more, long-term corrective measures are used less and less and become increasingly ineffective.

Examples

- The computer system crashes, and John steps in to save the day by getting it up and running again. He becomes the hero of information systems. The next week, Mary steps in, cuts through the red tape, and salvages the launch of the company's new product just in the nick of time. Now, Mary is the hero. You've seen this happen and maybe even tried it yourself a time or two. It's called "crisis heroism," and it's addictive. When people learn that they can win accolades simply by fixing a symptom, that's what they do. The real fix—the one that may take years and lots of hard work—may never be tried.

- A banking client of ours had statement-processing software that crashed every month, and every month a dedicated crew of programmers and analysts got a call, jumped from their beds in the middle of the night, and rushed in to fix things. They always succeeded in getting the system patched and running again just in time, making them the heroes of the bank. When we asked the department manager why they didn't fix the problem permanently, he just looked at us quizzically and said, "Obviously you don't know anything about what we do. It's our job to fight fires."

Identifying the archetype: To determine whether you are dealing with a Shifting the Burden archetype, ask yourself the following questions:

- Are we tackling the real problem or just the symptoms of the problem?
- Are our actions shifting attention away from fundamental solutions?
- Do people in the organization achieve "hero" status on a regular basis?
- Have you ever heard the lament "This has worked so far, so why should I worry about what could happen in the future?" or "You're just making a mountain out of this molehill"?

Strategies for dealing with Shifting the Burden

- Identify the problem symptom(s).
- Identify any and all of the fixes that have been used to deal with these symptoms.
- Determine how these fixes impact those individuals involved with their implementation.
- Identify a long-term, systemic solution to the problem.
- Communicate long-term visions or goals for implementing the solution.
- Reduce your dependency on the short-term fixes you have identified, and beware of replacing them with other, equally addictive behaviors.

Archetype #5: Limits to Success

Relevant business issue: Planning for limits to growth

Description: "A process feeds on itself to produce a period of accelerating growth or expansion. Then the growth begins to slow . . . and eventually comes to a halt, and may even reverse itself and begin an accelerating collapse. The growth phase is caused by a reinforcing feedback process (or by several reinforcing feedback processes). The slowing arises due to a balancing process brought into play as a 'limit' is approached. The limit can be a resource constraint, or

EXHIBIT 3.14. (Continued)

an external or internal response to growth. The accelerating collapse (when it occurs) arises from the reinforcing process operating in reverse, to generate more and more contraction."[5]

Example

- You implement a quality-improvement program. You establish quality teams and everyone is trained in problem solving and statistical-process control. The first year everything goes well. The teams find hundreds of ways to improve quality and cut costs. By the second year, however, you hit a plateau. The teams have "picked the low hanging fruit"—found the easy and obvious improvements—and further improvements become harder to obtain. You've reached the limits of success. You can't keep improving by doing the same old thing.

Identifying the archetype: To determine whether you are dealing with a Limits to Success archetype, ask yourself the following questions:

- Are once-successful efforts stalling or experiencing reversals?
- Are there resource limits that may be limiting growth or expansion?
- Do you find yourself thinking that the harder you work, the more things stay the same?

Strategies for dealing with Limits to Success

- Identify the process(es) that are reinforcing growth.
- Determine your rate of growth and, consequently, the point at which you will outstrip current capacity.
- Identify potential limits to resources or capacity by examining such categories as the following:
  - ✔ Physical capacity—new plants, capital investments;
  - ✔ Information systems;
  - ✔ Personnel;
  - ✔ Management expertise;
  - ✔ Attitudes.
- Determine ways to deal with each of the limits you have identified and the time frames in which each of these changes should be made.
- Find a balance between anticipated growth and potential limits to resources or capacities. This may require limiting the reinforcing feedback processes in order to restrain growth.
- Reconsider your growth strategy. As Daniel Kim reminds us, "Companies can become so focused on preventing failure that they neglect planning adequately for dealing with success."[6]

Archetype #6: Success to the Successful

Relevant business issue: Resource allocation

Description: Two or more people, groups, projects, and so forth are competing for the same resources. The one receiving more resources or support is more likely to succeed and, because of that success, receive even more resources in the future. At the same time, the people, groups, projects, and so on that receive fewer resources are more likely to fail and, as a result, receive even fewer resources in the future. In other words, success breeds success.

Examples

- A classic example is what can happen with work-family conflicts. You work long hours to be successful and make more money so that your family can enjoy a better life. Your longer hours and dedication pay off. You get a promotion and an increase in pay. You are praised by your boss and coworkers and are happy with your career success. But the more hours you work, the more conflicts you have at home. Your spouse and children complain about your frequent absences. To avoid the situation, you take on extra assignments and spend more time at work, which increases stress at home and makes you want to flee even more.

- You write your first novel, which is doing fairly well. Then Oprah Winfrey picks it as one of her favorites. Suddenly sales triple. Book buyers clamor for more copies and stack your books in the main aisle of their stores. Sales jump even more. Then your publisher comes out with a full-size poster of you, showing the book and Oprah's endorsement. Sales jump again, and your publisher can't print enough copies to stock the shelves. When it hits the *New York Times* best-seller list, sales skyrocket, Hollywood calls, and your publisher starts talking about seven-figure advances on your next work, sight unseen. Success breeds success.

Identifying the archetype: To determine whether you are dealing with a Success to the Successful archetype, ask yourself the following questions:

- Is one interrelated activity, group, or individual doing very well while the others are struggling?
- Is the system set up to create only one "winner"?

Strategies for dealing with Success to the Successful

- Determine whether resources are being allocated on a winner-take-all basis.
- Make your people, groups, teams, projects, and so on collaborators rather than competitors.
- Set the goals and objectives that define success at a level above the individual(s) involved.

Archetype #7: Drifting Goals

Relevant business issue: Focus on goals and objectives

Description: Various pressures—productivity standards, cost control measures, stockholders, and so on—may take attention away from what a group or individual is trying to achieve,

EXHIBIT 3.14. (Continued)

leading to a Drifting Goals archetype. Focus shifts from what is truly important, and standards begin to slip.

Example

- Senge uses the example of a high-tech manufacturer that found itself losing market share, in spite of the fact that it had a good product and ongoing improvements. The company focused so heavily on its development efforts that it never got production scheduling under control. When told that customers were becoming increasingly dissatisfied with late deliveries and turning to their competitors, the company responded by extending the quoted delivery dates rather than fixing its scheduling and delivery problems. Delivery goals were allowed to slip and the quoted delivery times got longer and longer. As a result, customer defections soared.

Identifying the archetype: To determine whether you are dealing with a Drifting Goals archetype, ask yourself the following questions:

- Are your goals and standards eroding?
- Are you focused on achieving your goals, or are you focused on finding short-term relief for problem symptoms?
- Have you ever said or heard someone else in your company say, "We can let that standard slide until this crisis is over"?

Strategies for dealing with Drifting Goals

- Identify performance measures that have deteriorated or fluctuated over time.
- Identify any implicit or explicit goals that conflict with stated goals. For instance, cost-cutting efforts may implicitly conflict with stated goals of quality.
- Determine how reality differs from stated goals.
- Determine whether the goals themselves have been lowered to meet short-term needs.
- Anchor your goals to external reference points like benchmark data.

Archetype #8: Growth and Underinvestment

Relevant business issue: Capital planning

Description: Growth is approaching a limit that can be eliminated or delayed if sufficient investments in capacity are made. Instead, standards are lowered to justify underinvestment, which leads to the justification of further underinvestment.

Example

- Senge gives the example of People Express Airlines, which found itself unable to increase capacity rapidly enough to keep pace with demand. "Rather than putting more resources into training or growing more slowly (for example, through raising prices somewhat), the firm tried to 'outgrow' its problems. The result was deteriorating service quality and increased competition, while morale deteriorated. In order to keep up with the continued stress, the company relied more and more on the 'solution' of underinvesting in service capacity, until customers no longer found flying People Express attractive."[7]

Identifying the Archetype: To determine whether you are dealing with a Growth and Underinvestment archetype, ask yourself the following questions:

- Are decisions about investment made in reaction to growth rather than in anticipation of growth?

- Are decisions about investment made because of problems related to growth rather than on the basis of long-range planning?

- Have you ever heard the excuse, "Someday we will be the market leader again, but right now we have to conserve resources and not overinvest"?

Strategies for dealing with Growth and Underinvestment

- Build capacity in advance of demand.

- Minimize the delay between performance shortfalls and the acquisition of additional capacity.

- Check the validity of your performance standards before using them as the basis for investment decisions.

- Avoid self-fulfilling prophecies. If you declare a product to be a failure without adequate evaluation, that's what it's likely to become.

1.   Daniel H. Kim and Colleen Lannon, **Applying Systems Archetypes** *(Cambridge, Mass.: Pegasus Communications, 1977), p. 3,* and Senge, **The Fifth Discipline,** *p. 388.*

2.   Senge, **The Fifth Discipline,** *p. 294.*

3.   Daniel H. Kim, **Systems Archetypes II** *(Cambridge, Mass.: Pegasus Communications, 1994), pp. 24–25.*

4.   *Ibid., pp. 12–13.*

5.   Senge, **The Fifth Discipline,** *p. 379.*

6.   Kim, **Systems Archetypes II,** *p. 19.*

7.   Senge, **The Fifth Discipline,** *p. 390.*

When these models are used for education, they become an important component of the systems theorist's approach to individual and organizational learning. In our chapter on leadership, we quote Manfred Kets de Vries on the importance of experience in shaping the skills of future leaders. Kets de Vries noted that when he interviewed global business leaders about how they had learned to lead, they all told him similar stories. They told about being sent, in their late twenties or early thirties, on a challenging mission to set up a plant, restructure a sales office, arrange a joint venture, or complete some other assignment that caused them sleepless nights. It was by sweating through those tough assignments that they learned.[25]

Senge uses computer simulations to create what he calls "practice fields" or "learning labs" in which people can test their mental models and see systems dynamics operate in a risk-free environment. These computerized and interactive business games, entitled Microworlds and Simuworlds, allow current and future leaders to practice running businesses the same way pilots use flight simulators to practice maneuvers without worrying about crashing. Today's Microworlds and Simuworlds, some of which are listed in Exhibit 3.15, are so sophisticated and create such lifelike situations that participants describe the experience as being similar to confronting a gyroscope for the first time. The games' time compression enables participants to begin seeing the pushes, pulls, and loops embedded within the system. They develop an appreciation for the interconnectedness of events that is

EXHIBIT 3.15. **Sample Microworlds and Simuworlds**

- Beefeater™ Restaurants
- Boom & Bust Enterprises™ simulator
- Commercial Real Estate Management
- International Oil Tanker Management Flight Simulator
- People Express Management Flight Simulator™
- Service Quality Microworld™

From MicroWorlds, Inc., Cambridge, Mass.

- Copex Management Flight Simulator
- Electronic Beer Game
- Competitive Dynamics Simulator
- Sharebuilder

From Gould-Kreutzer Associates, Cambridge, Mass.

- Maintenance and Service Strategies Explorer
- World3–91 Explorer
- Urban Game

From Ventana Systems, Harvard, Mass.

much more profound than can be conveyed through the system archetypes. Players come away from the experience with insights such as the following:

- There are no right answers. There is just a variety of potential actions, each of which will produce some desired consequences and some unintended consequences.
- There is no way to break a system into parts and fix it. Systems have integrity, and you must treat the whole, not just the individual parts. As Senge says, you can't divide the elephant in half and get two elephants.
- Cause and effect often are not closely related in time and space and, as a result, the real cause of a problem may not be obvious.
- The most obvious solutions may not work at all. If they do work, they may make the situation better in the short term, but worse in the long term.
- Many apparent dilemmas, such as quality versus costs, may not be either-or choices at all. Over time it may be possible to have both if you are willing to be patient. As Senge puts it, "You can have your cake and eat it too—but not at once."[26]
- While people like to blame others for their difficulties, problems in a system are often caused by the people within it and not by some outside force.

OUR VIEW

All of these are useful insights, of course. Participants develop a deep appreciation for the dynamics of the work environment and finally begin to understand the tensions in the uncoiling spring of Information—Action—Result. But what difference does it make if we truly understand the circle of causality? So what if we recognize the complexity of the relationships that exist within our organization and between our organization and the environment? What can we do with our newfound knowledge? It is one thing to realize that we are facing a classic archetype and our problems are the result of the counterproductive dynamics of a complex system. It is quite another for us to have the power to change the system and the underlying culture that created it. Indeed, is it possible to change the system and if it is, how should the system be changed? Is there a learning culture that must exist before we can use our knowledge of systems and mental models to productive advantage? Our last group of learning organization gurus thinks there is such a culture and they are determined to define it.

Approach #3: Creating the Learning Culture

The chief architect—or perhaps the chief excavator—of learning cultures is MIT professor Edgar H. Schein. He defines organizational culture as "the accumulation of prior learning based on prior success"[27] and "a pattern of basic assumptions . . . invented, discovered, or developed by a given group . . . as it learns to cope with its problems . . . that has worked well enough to be considered valid and, therefore . . . is to be taught to new members as the . . . correct way to perceive, think, and feel in relation to those problems."[28] Exhibit 3.16 demonstrates how an organization can develop its own culture.

An organization's culture, says Schein, is grounded in the founders' basic beliefs, values, and assumptions and then elaborated upon and embedded in the organization over time through a variety of mechanisms, such as:

- What the leaders pay attention to, measure, and control;
- How leaders react to critical, emotion-charged events and organizational crises;
- Deliberate role modeling and coaching;
- Criteria used for granting rewards and status;
- Criteria used for recruitment, selection, promotion, retirement, and excommunication;
- The organization's design and structure;
- Organizational systems and procedures;
- The design of physical space, facades, and buildings;
- Stories, legends, myths, and symbols;
- Formal statements of organizational philosophy, creeds, and charters.[29]

So what does organizational culture have to do with organizational learning? What difference does it make what kind of culture your organization has? Just this. Schein says that the necessary conditions for learning don't exist in most organizations because their culture is unsuitable, at least for long-term learning.

EXHIBIT 3.16. **Developing an Organizational Culture**

Ultimately, says Schein, culture can be thought of as the way an organization's members, and particularly its founders, have resolved important issues, such as:

- The organization's relationship to its environment
  Does the organization perceive itself to be dominant, submissive, harmonizing, or searching for a niche?

- The nature of human activity
  Is the correct way for humans to behave to be dominant/proactive, harmonizing, or passive/fatalistic?

- The nature of reality and truth
  How do we define what is true and what is not?
  How is truth ultimately determined both in the physical and social world—by pragmatic test, reliance on wisdom, or social consensus?

- The nature of time
  What is our basic orientation in terms of past, present, and future?
  What kinds of time units are most relevant for the conduct of daily affairs?

- The nature of human nature
  Are humans basically good, neutral, or evil?
  Is human nature perfectible or fixed?

- The nature of human relationships
  What is the correct way for people to relate to each other to distribute power and affection?
  Is life competitive or cooperative?
  Is the best way to organize society on the basis of individualism or groupism?
  Is the best authority system autocratic/paternalistic or collegial/participative?

- Homogeneity versus diversity
  Is the group best off if it is highly diverse or if it is highly homogeneous?
  Should individuals in a group be encouraged to innovate or conform?

---

*Source: Edgar Schein, "Organizational Culture," **American Psychologist,** February 1990, p. 114.*

How different is a culture that enhances learning from one that inhibits learning? Review Exhibit 3.17 and try to determine which culture is most like your own organization.

Well, how did you do? Is your organization one that enhances or inhibits learning? If your organization is like most that Schein and our other gurus encounter, it is probably more similar to the latter than the former. The truth is that very few organizations today have a learning culture, and the transformation to

EXHIBIT 3.17. Cultures That Enhance and Inhibit Learning

✔ A Culture That Enhances Learning	✔ A Culture That Inhibits Learning
• *Balances interests of all stakeholders.* Leaders balance the interests of all stakeholders—customers, employees, suppliers, the community, and stockholders. "No one group dominates the thinking of management because it is recognized that any one of these groups can slow down and destroy the organization."[1]	• *Distinguishes between "hard" and "soft" issues.* Task issues take precedence over relationship issues. Management is sorted into the "hard" things and "soft" things and the "hard" things are considered to be more important. Leaders pay attention to the hard things—data, money, bottom lines, payoffs, production, competition, structure, and so on. Everyone pays lip service to "soft" people things and relationships, but the real work of management is seen as that which can be quantified. People are viewed by managers as another resource to be used and manipulated like capital and raw materials.
• *Focuses on people rather than systems.* Leaders and managers believe that their people can and will learn, and value learning and change. Schein notes that "it takes a certain amount of idealism about human nature to create a learning culture."[2] That idealism exists in full measure.	• *Focuses on systems rather than on people.* Leaders and managers are engineers and technocrats who are preoccupied with creating and maintaining systems that will be free of human foibles and errors. A key theme of the culture is designing humans out of the systems rather into them.
• *Makes people believe they can change their environment.* People hold the shared belief that they have the capacity to change their environment and that ultimately they make their own fate. This may be a necessary assumption for learning. After all, writes Schein, "If we believe that the world around us cannot be changed anyway, what is the point of learning to learn? Relax and make the best of your fate."[3]	• *Allows people to change only when they must.* People in the organization are reactive rather than proactive. They change only in response to outside forces that are seen as threats. People focus on solving problems rather than creating something new.
• *Makes time for learning.* Some "slack" time is not only allowed but desired so that it can be used for learning. "Lean and mean is not a good prescription for organizational learning."[4]	• *Is "lean and mean."* The organization is preoccupied with short-term coping and adapting. Being lean and mean dominates the thinking of leaders and managers. The idea of "slack" is unthinkable.

✔ A Culture That Enhances Learning	✔ A Culture That Inhibits Learning
▪ *Takes a holistic approach to problems.* People in the organization have a shared belief that economic, political, and sociocultural events are interconnected, a condition that is true inside the organization as well as in the environment. There is a shared commitment to learning and thinking systemically and to understanding how things work and especially the consequences of actions over time. *Takes a holistic approach to problems.*	▪ *Compartmentalizes problem solving.* Work roles and tasks are compartmentalized and sepa-rated from family and self-development. "Walls" and "chimneys" separate functions. In solving problems, people believe that the best approach is to break the problem into its components, study and fix each in isolation, and then synthesize the components back into the whole.
▪ *Encourages open communication.* Managers and employees have a shared commitment to open and extensive communication. The organization has spent some time helping people develop a common vocabulary so that communication can occur. People have a shared commitment to tell the truth.	▪ *Restricts flow of information.* Managers are presumed to have a "divine right" to information and prerogatives. Financial and other information is kept from all those who do not have a need to know. Position and access to information confer status and power. People keep relevant information to themselves, put a spin on things to protect their power position, and sometimes actually lie to put themselves in a better light.
▪ *Believes in teamwork.* People share the belief that trust, teamwork, coordination, and cooperation are critical for success. Individualistic competition is *not* viewed as the answer to all problems.	▪ *Believes in individualized competition.* Individual competition is perceived as the natural state and the proper route to power and status. There is a cultural bias toward rugged individualism. The lone problem solver is seen as a hero. Teamwork is viewed as a practical necessity but not something that is intrinsically desirable.
▪ *Has approachable leaders.* Leaders acknowledge their own vulnerability and uncertainty. The leader acts as a teacher and steward of change rather than as a charismatic decision maker.	▪ *Has controlling leaders.* Leaders and followers assume that leaders are supposed to be in control, decisive, certain, and dominant. Leaders are not allowed to acknowledge their vulnerability.

1. Edgar Schein, "Organizational and Managerial Culture as a Facilitator or Inhibitor of Organizational Learning," *MIT Organizational Learning Network Working Paper 10.004* (May 19, 1994): p. 7.

2. Ibid.

3. Ibid.

4. Ibid.

a learning culture is, if anything, highly problematic. The learning culture that Schein and our other gurus describe is so far removed from the cultural reality of most workplaces that getting there seems barely possible. Becoming a learning organization not only requires change, which, as we discuss in our chapter on managing change, is difficult enough, but also requires a great deal of change. The same things that inhibit learning in organizations also inhibit the kind of transformative change that makes learning possible. It seems that you cannot become a learning organization unless you already are one, or as one of our clients quipped, "Only learners learn and only learners learn to learn."

Confused? So are our gurus. And they are frustrated. In a speech in 1995, Schein wondered aloud about the amazing tenacity of organizations to stubbornly resist learning.

Why is it, that organization after organization first exposes itself to new revolutionary ideas like employee empowerment, total quality, visionary leadership, networking, re-engineering, information technology, and all the other concepts that academics and consultants have been touting as the way of the future, then launch crash programs to implement them, yet conclude a year or so later that the ideas did not work out?

Why do so many programs of total quality and re-engineering have such high reported failure rates?

Why is it that the idea of empowerment, of involving people in the changes that will affect them, an idea which has been around at least since the Hawthorne studies of the 1920's, has to resurface about every two or three decades under new kinds of labels and still only take hold here and there?

Or, worse, why do many organizations claim to empower their employees, yet their day to day management practices change hardly at all?

Why is it that McGregor's Theory Y, the assumption that people are willing and able to work and make contributions to organizations, an idea he espoused in 1960 in his classic *The Human Side of Enterprise,* is still overridden in most organizations by the cynical assumptions of Theory X that people are basically lazy and have to be motivated and controlled by management?[30]

Schein offers two possible answers to his rhetorical questions. One is that we adhere to the cynical model of human nature because organizations have been able to function effectively while following it. Of course, Schein notes, any model might have worked just as well in the predictable, stable, slow-moving environment most U.S. businesses have experienced over the last 30 years. Perhaps a better answer, says Schein, is that our negative assumptions about human nature—our human-nature mental models, if you will—have been shaped over a long period of time and are very difficult to change. We have been emotionally conditioned to cling to our outmoded assumptions and behavioral rituals regardless of the cost. Schein uses the following analogy to illustrate the power of this emotional conditioning.

> If you put a dog in a green room, ring a bell, and then give the dog a painful electric shock, it will fairly quickly learn to avoid green rooms, and, if it hears a bell, the dog will run away or cower anxiously. Even if you turn the shocks in the green room off, the dog will not enter it and, therefore, will not discover that the shock is off. If you teach a dog to avoid a green room in this way, allow it to jump into a red room as escape, and then give it shocks in the red room, the dog will jump back and forth between the green and red rooms until totally exhausted, *and this behavior will continue even after you have turned off the shock in both rooms.* Once the pattern has been learned, the anxiety alone is enough to keep the behavior going even if no shocks are ever again administered.[31]

Like the dog, argues Schein, most of us have been conditioned to one way of thinking about human nature in organizations; and when we have experimented with any different set of assumptions, we have usually been punished. Consequently, like the dog, we avoid such situations at all costs, limiting ourselves to very narrow, safe ranges of behavior. We become paralyzed for fear of making mistakes, stick with the tried-and-true, and avoid learning. When learning something new, we need a significant level of reassurance. We need, says Schein, a psychologically safe haven where learning can occur. Then, and only then, will we begin not only to learn, but also to learn to learn.

Safe Havens Encourage Learning

The idea of a haven for learning isn't new. We often use psychological safety nets to make learning palatable. Schein uses the example of teaching a child to cross the street. "We hold the child's hand as we cross, or provide a safety-producing behavioral ritual such as looking both ways before crossing. We provide a path, a direction, and some first steps to get started on the dangerous journey. We provide encouragement, support and coaching. We say that if you look both ways and listen for cars you will be able to tell whether or not it is safe."[32]

Schein proposes that we create psychologically safe havens in organizations to encourage learning. These havens would be "parallel systems" that would exist alongside or within the organization. In these secure environments, people would have "(1) opportunities for training and practice, (2) support and encouragement to overcome the fear and shame associated with making errors, (3) coaching and rewards for efforts in the right direction, [and] (4) norms that reward innovative thinking and experimentation."[33] In such parallel organizations, learners could be exposed to the newest ideas from academics, consultants, and gurus and have the opportunity to test the new concepts and practices in a risk-free environment. People could expose their left-hand column and practice inquiry without being ridiculed or criticized. And the parallel organization could utilize learning experiences, such as Senge's Microworlds and Simuworlds.

In short, all of the things our learning gurus want to do, they would be able to do—in an artificial world, outside the organization or buried deep within it. Schein gives up on the main body of the organization being the birthplace of transformative learning and instead settles for a more malleable parallel system. Of course, the organization will eventually detect this foreign body in its midst and will alert its immune system. The parallel system will therefore have to be placed near the top of the organization so that it can resist attack. Schein sees the CEO as being the initial learner and the parallel system being composed of a group surrounding the CEO. Of course, the learning gurus would advise this senior group, and eventually these parallel organizations would be networked with consultants, research centers, and other parallel organizations to form giant learning consortiums that would be linked to the Organizational Learning Center at MIT, with Schein as the central guru, and so on. Well, we're sure you get the idea. Move over Senge, it's time to share the throne.

KEY POINTS

- An organization must utilize its people's commitment and capacity to learn in order to excel.

- True learning requires the acquisition of both know-why and know-how.

- The most important learning occurs on the job, not in the classroom.

- The most effective learning is social and active, not individual and passive.

- The most important things for people to learn aren't the explicit rules, policies, and procedures of the organization, but the tacit things—intuition, judgment, expertise, and common sense imbedded in day-to-day activity.

- Mental models are deeply held images of how the world works. They are shaped by our experiences and shape our experiences.

- Learning occurs when people within an organization share, examine, and challenge each others' mental models.

- The skill of reflection helps people slow down their thinking process to become more aware of their mental models.

- The skill of inquiry helps people to be more open about the assumptions behind their actions and to encourage other people to do the same.

- A key learning deficiency for most people is their inability to see how information, action, and results form a chain of causality in the world. A relatively small number of archetypes, or patterns of behavior, can illustrate many of the problems people cause themselves and organizations because of their failure to think systemically. Computer simulations of more complex chains of causality can be used to help people obtain an even greater appreciation for the interconnectedness of things.

- Most organizations today have a culture that inhibits learning. Separate parallel organizations must be created in order for real learning to occur.

K. W. (Ken) Bamforth, pioneer in the sociotechnical approach to the redesign of work

Fred Emery, pioneer in the sociotechnical approach to the redesign of work

Jon R. Katzenbach, coauthor of *The Wisdom of Teams*

Edward E. Lawler III, director of the University of Southern California's Center for Effective Organizations

Charles C. Manz, coauthor of *Business without Bosses*

Allan M. Mohrman, Jr., coauthor of *Designing Team-Based Organizations*

Susan Albers Mohrman, coauthor of *Designing Team-Based Organizations*

Linda Moran, coauthor of *Self-Directed Work Teams*

Ed Musselwhite, CEO of Zenger Miller, Inc. and coauthor of *Self-Directed Work Teams*

Glenn M. Parker, author of *Team Players and Team Work*

Peter R. Scholtes, author of *The Team Handbook*

Henry P. Sims, Jr., coauthor of *Business without Bosses*

Douglas K. Smith, coauthor of *The Wisdom of Teams*

Eric Trist, a founder of the Tavistock Institute for Social Research and pioneer in the sociotechnical approach to the redesign of work

John H. Zenger, chair of Times Mirror Training and coauthor of *Self-Directed Work Teams*

4

Creating
High-Performance
Organizations
Through Teamwork

I n 1949, after completing a year of postgraduate work at the Tavistock
Institute for Social Research (the Tavvy) in London, Ken Bamforth, a
trade unionist and former coal miner, returned to his former industry
and reported back to the Tavvy on any new perspectives he could uncover
on the organization of work in mining. What Bamforth discovered at the
newly opened Haighmoor seam in Durham so intrigued Eric Trist, one of
the founders of the Tavistock Institute, and Fred Emery, an Australian social scientist who was visiting the Institute, that they both quickly joined
Bamforth to study mining practices at the Haighmoor and elsewhere.
What had Bamforth discovered? The miners, on their own, with nary a
guru in sight, had created a new paradigm for work organization that was
yielding significant improvements in productivity, costs, cycle times, absenteeism, and worker morale. As elaborated, documented, and refined by

Trist, Bamforth, Emery, and others, this method of workplace design, which became known as the sociotechnical approach, has been described as perhaps one of the most "highly relevant, least understood and rarely applied perspectives" on management and organizational design in history.[1] It is the foundation for just about all of our gurus' pronouncements about new ways of building high-performing companies. As is usually the case, what our high-performance gurus package in their bright new consulting bottles is very old wine indeed.

DOWN IN THE COAL MINES

As we said, the genesis for much of what our gurus preach about designing high-performance organizations comes from observations Bamforth, Trist, and Emery made of developments in the British coal industry in the late 1940s. Considering the timing, it is little wonder that the researchers from the Tavistock were excited about Bamforth's finding. After all, the British mining industry was in trouble at the time. In spite of mechanization, productivity was flat, costs were up, labor disputes were frequent, and worker absenteeism was running about 20%. Any system of arranging work that led to the kind of improvements Bamforth was reporting had to be important. It was. It was also brilliant in its simplicity. Trist described the differences between the conventional work arrangements in British mines and the new composite system that the miners had developed this way:

> The conventional system combines a complex formal structure with simple work roles; the composite system combines a simple formal structure with complex work roles. In the former the miner has a commitment to only a single . . . task and enters into only a very limited number of . . . social relations that are sharply divided between those within his particular task group and those who are outside. With those "outside" he shares no sense of belongingness and he recognizes no responsibility to them for the consequences of his actions. In the composite system the miner has a commitment to the whole group task and consequently finds himself drawn into a variety of tasks in cooperation with different members of the total group;

he may be drawn into any task on the coal-face with any member of the total group and do his share on any shift.[2]

Under the conventional system, work tasks were strictly allocated according to shift. If one shift failed to complete its assigned tasks or did them poorly, the other shift inevitably suffered. Under the new system, the oncoming shift picked up at whatever point the previous shift left off and completed whatever jobs remained. Under the conventional system, miners were assigned specific tasks and developed only those skills associated with that particular task. Under the new system, all of the miners were multiskilled and could perform most of the jobs associated with the mining operation. Under the conventional system, miners were assigned tasks and job locations by management, and the miners were often suspicious that management favored some workers over others when making job assignments. Under the new system, tasks were rotated among miners who worked on autonomous teams, and the team members themselves selected new members. Under the conventional system, there were up to five different methods of payment, ranging from a daily rate to a piece rate tied to tonnage of coal removed. Under the new system, all miners were paid a flat rate plus an incentive bonus tied to the cubic yards of coal produced.

Trist and his associates noted that the new composite system was an obvious improvement for several reasons. First, the mining operation involved the completion of a complex series of tasks, any of which could be made more difficult by changing underground conditions or other occurrences outside the miners' control. Such variances often required changes in the level of effort expended on a task and even the order in which tasks were performed. The rigid division of labor under the old system made it difficult for the miners to respond efficiently to such disruptions. The new system was much more flexible.

Second, as Trist put it, the new system also made "better provision to the personal requirements of the miners."[3] Under the conventional systems, miners were relatively isolated from each other and rarely could count on support from the other miners in times of stress and strain. The new system was more conducive to camaraderie and cooperation.

Third, there was the issue of pay. Under the conventional system, writes Trist, "the distribution of rewards and statuses . . . [reflected] the relative bargaining power of different roles and task groups as much as any true differences in skill and effort."[4] The new system of pay put everyone on an equal footing. It was, in effect, much fairer.

Finally and perhaps most importantly, under the old system miners were in effect slaves to the technology. It was assumed that the requirements of the technology dictated work arrangements and that little concern could or should be given to the impact of those technology-driven arrangements on the social needs of the miners. Under the new composite system, the miners demonstrated that multiple work arrangements were possible, given the same technology, and that a work design that integrated and optimized both social and technical concerns—in other words, a sociotechnical design[5]— would lead to superior performance.

THE BASIC REQUIREMENTS FOR HIGH PERFORMANCE

Over the last 40-plus years countless academicians and gurus have studied, prodded, probed, extended, refined, tested, argued about, proved, and re-proved the basic tenets of what Trist and his associates documented and dissected in the British coal mines. Today our gurus offer up volumes of advice about the dos and don'ts of promoting organizational performance, and our gurus are very certain about their advice. They know what works and doesn't work, or at least claim they do. About the only thing they will readily admit not knowing with any certainty is why so few high-performance organizations exist.

So, exactly what is a high-performance organization? How different is it from the traditional organization? We've constructed a comparison of the traditional organization with the kind of organization our high-performance gurus propose based upon many of their writings. As you read the comparison in Exhibit 4.1, notice the sociotechnical themes. Also notice how much our gurus have expanded upon and added to the basics that Trist and his colleagues discovered in the coal mines.[6]

Notice how prescriptive and specific our gurus are. They know exactly what a high-performance organization must look like. Notice also how different the new high-performance organization they propose is from the traditional organization most of us have known. Can our gurus justify such a radical departure from tradition? They think they can and trot out mounds of statistics and anecdotes to make their case.

EXHIBIT 4.1. Traditional versus High-Performance Organizations

Traditional Organizations	High-Performance Organizations
Support for innovation and risk taking	
New ideas are ignored. The motto is "Don't fix it if it's not broken."	New ideas are constantly sought and tried.
People who take risks and fail are punished.	People who take risks and fail are told to try again.
People who try to change things are not rewarded.	People who try to change things are often promoted.
Emphasis on learning	
There are few opportunities for people to learn new skills.	There are many opportunities for people to learn new skills.
There are few rewards for learning.	Learning is highly prized and rewarded.
The organization makes it difficult to learn much outside the narrow scope of one's own job.	People are encouraged to learn as much as they can about all aspects of the organization.
No time is set aside for learning.	Time is regularly set aside for learning.
Cross-training is viewed as inefficient.	Cross-training is the norm.
Training for nonmanagers focuses primarily on technical skills.	Everyone receives training in a wide variety of skills including interpersonal, administrative, and technical skills.
Job design	
Jobs are designed to require almost no skills to perform.	Jobs are designed to require many skills that take a long time to learn.
People who perform the work make no important decisions about how the work will be performed. They just do the work as they are told.	People are relied upon to make almost all of the important decisions about how their work will be done.
People work alone.	People work in a team where they regularly switch jobs with one another.
People do the same thing all the time.	People do a variety of different things.
People work on only a small piece of an overall task.	People work on a whole and complete task, leading to satisfying an internal or external customer's need.
It is hard for people to see how their efforts contribute directly to the final product or service.	People see a direct connection between what they do and how the final product or service turns out.

EXHIBIT 4.1. (Continued)

Traditional Organizations	High-Performance Organizations
People don't do any of the support work for their jobs (maintenance, setup, quality control, supply, record keeping, and so on).	People frequently do almost all of the support work required by their jobs.
The pace of work is dictated by management.	People control the pace of their own work.
People are told what work to do.	People decide what work they want to do.
People never get involved in problem solving. When a problem occurs, supervisors step in to solve it.	Problem solving is an important part of everyone's job.
Jobs are designed so they don't require people to think.	All jobs require a great deal of thought.

Role of management

Managers tell people exactly how things are to be done and then watch to make sure employees do as they are told.	Managers explain the results that are needed and help their subordinates figure out how to do the work.
Managers view their job as being in charge and giving orders.	Managers view their role as facilitators who help their subordinates succeed. Managers don't give orders.
Managers care only about their own department, shift, or function.	Managers focus a lot of energy on what is happening outside their own part of the organization.
Managers make sure rules are followed.	Managers encourage innovation even when it means breaking the rules.
Managers seldom tell employees how they are doing.	Managers provide regular feedback to employees on how they are doing.
Managers are never evaluated by their subordinates.	Managers are often evaluated by their subordinates.
Managers use meetings for one-way communication from themselves to employees.	Managers facilitate discussions at meetings on how performance can be improved and invite questions from their employees. Meetings are designed to encourage two-way communication.
Managers make assignments, schedule work, provide training, review performance, and decide on work procedures with no input from employees.	Employees make their own work assignments, schedule work, provide training, review performance, and decide on work procedures.

Traditional Organizations	High-Performance Organizations
Managers speak to higher management on behalf of their subordinates. There is a strict chain of command that must be followed.	Managers encourage free and open communication between higher management and employees. Anyone can speak to anyone anytime about anything.
Managers view their presence as essential to the work getting done.	Managers view their presence as helpful but nonessential to the completion of day-to-day work.
Managers are selected primarily for their technical skills.	No one is allowed to be a supervisor or manager who does not have excellent skills for dealing with people.

Organizational structure

Traditional Organizations	High-Performance Organizations
There are many levels of management.	There are only a few levels in the organization from the lowest-level worker to senior management. The organization is very flat.
The basic organizational unit is the functional department.	The basic organizational unit is the work team.
There are clear boundaries between departments and/or functions.	Boundaries between departments or functions are fuzzy.
Boundaries between departments and/or divisions often interfere with cross-functional problem solving.	There is a lot of cross-functional problem solving and interdepartmental communication. The organization seeks to eliminate boundaries.
Meetings seldom occur across levels or between departments or functions.	Cross-functional and interdepartmental meetings occur frequently.
Most people would say that they don't feel as if they are running their own small business within the larger organization.	Everyone feels as if they are working in a small business. People work in units or teams that make a whole product or provide a complete service. Everyone feels a strong identification with the end product or service their unit provides.
Work is divided so that line work (production, customer service, and so on) is separated from staff-support work (maintenance, record keeping, and so on) and the different types of work are assigned to different departments.	Line and staff functions are fully integrated.

EXHIBIT 4.1. (Continued)

Traditional Organizations	High-Performance Organizations
Customer relations	
Only a few people in the organization talk directly to customers to find out what the organization can do to serve them better.	Everyone in the organization is constantly striving to determine what customers want and how to meet customer needs.
People working on one step of an operation do not regard the people working on the next step as their customers.	Everyone has an internal or external customer and is constantly striving to understand and meet that customer's needs.
No one fully understands the standards used by customers to judge the quality of the final product or service.	Everyone knows the standards customers use to judge the quality of the final product or service and what the organization must do to meet those standards.
Flexibility	
The organization is slow to respond to changes in its environment.	The organization anticipates changes in its environment and is quick to adapt itself to new demands.
The organization is slow to adopt new technology or to convert existing technology to new purposes.	The organization quickly exploits technological advances and is adept at finding innovative ways to use existing technology.
The organization is adept at producing only a limited number of products and services and is slow to introduce them.	The organization can produce a wide variety of products and services easily and can readily adapt existing products and services to meet new or changing customer requirements.
Teamwork	
People look out just for themselves. They do not normally go beyond their regular duties to help others.	People help one another without being told to do so, even when the task is not part of their normal duties.
Different parts of the organization work toward different goals. There is often destructive competition.	Different parts of the organization work together well. Everyone has a shared sense of what the organization as a whole is trying to accomplish.
Few people can state the values behind decisions that are made.	Everyone can state the values of the organization and how they are used to make decisions.
Values, if they exist at all, only concern profit.	The organization values teamwork, participation, innovation, quality, and so on, as much as it does profit.

Traditional Organizations	High-Performance Organizations
Dedication	
Only a few people at the very top of the organization feel personally responsible for how well the organization performs.	Everyone has a sense of personal responsibility for the overall performance of the organization.
Few people are willing to put out effort above the minimum required to do their own job.	People frequently expend effort well above the minimum necessary.
People slack off when their supervisors are not present.	Almost everyone performs at a peak level regardless of whether a supervisor is present.
Rewards	
People are rewarded the same financially or otherwise, whether they perform or not.	People are rewarded based upon their performance and/or the performance of their team.
People are rewarded for seniority.	People are rewarded for what they know.
There are large differences in the way managers and their employees are rewarded.	Managers and their employees are rewarded in similar fashions.
Financial gains due to improvements in performance are not shared with employees.	Financial gains due to improvements in performance are shared equitably with all employees.
People are rewarded on an individual basis.	People are rewarded primarily for their teamwork rather than as individuals.
Access to information	
Little information about the state of the business is shared with employees.	A great deal of information about the state of the business is shared with everyone.
Managers and technical experts withhold information.	Managers and technical experts share information freely.
Information is viewed as a source of power and privilege.	Information is viewed as a valuable resource that belongs to the entire organization.
Access to information systems and data is tightly controlled.	Information systems are designed to enable the maximum number of people to communicate electronically across boundaries, access data and analysis tools, and share information readily.
Sociotechnical balance	
Technology is considered to be more important than people.	Technology and people are treated as having equal importance in the organization.

EXHIBIT 4.1. (Continued)

Traditional Organizations	High-Performance Organizations
When new technology is considered, the people who will operate it are not consulted.	When new technology is considered, the people who will operate it are intimately involved in decisions regarding its acquisition and use.
Only a few technical experts understand how the technology works and how to maintain it.	Most people understand the basics about the technology and are sufficiently skilled to perform at least routine maintenance on their own equipment.
There is either too much or too little technology for the demand that must be met.	The technology is well matched to the demand.
The technology in use inhibits teamwork.	The technology is designed to support teamwork throughout the organization.
The technology used by the organization is difficult to change.	The technology used by the organization is easy to change.

THE CASE FOR HIGH-PERFORMANCE ORGANIZATIONS

Jon R. Katzenbach and Douglas K. Smith, consultants with McKinsey & Company and coauthors of *The Wisdom of Teams,* are emphatic in their support of the high-performance organization. They have no doubt that it is needed and that it works. For example, they write that "A 'high-performance organization' consistently outperforms its competition over an extended period of time, for example, ten years or more. It also outperforms the expectations of key constituents: customers, shareholders, and employees."[7]

Our other gurus agree and they back up their agreement with example after example of anecdotal evidence. Here are just a few.

- AT&T Credit Corporation used high-performance cross-functional teams to improve efficiency and customer service. The teams doubled the number of credit applications handled per day and cut loan approval time by 50%.

- High-performance teams at Federal Express reduced costs by $2.1 million in one year while reducing the number of lost packages and billing errors by 13%.
- Production teams at GE Appliance reduced cycle time by over 50%, increased product availability by 6% and cut inventory costs by more than 20% within the first eight months of their operation.
- Kodak's high-performance teams improved productivity so much at one plant that the work of three shifts could be completed in one.
- Eli Lilly used high-performance teams to bring a new product to market. Its rollout was the fastest in the company's history for a medical product.
- Hewlett-Packard designed a business unit using the principles of a high-performance organization. The unit became HP's highest-margin business.
- Knight-Ridder used high-performance organization principles at one of its papers, which became the corporation's top performing paper for three years in row.
- Motorola used high-performance teams to develop a supply management system. The teams improved quality by 50% and reduced late deliveries by 70%.
- Weyerhauser used high-performance teams to improve customer service. Delivery performance jumped from 85% to 95%, with significant increases in quality and productivity.

Impressive? Yes, definitely. Install high-performance teams, say Charles C. Manz and Henry P. Sims, Jr., coauthors of *Business Without Bosses,* and you will:

- Increase productivity
- Improve quality
- Enhance employee quality of work life
- Reduce turnover and absenteeism
- Reduce conflict
- Increase innovation
- Become more flexible
- Realize cost savings from 30% to 70%

It all sounds breathtakingly good. You would think, therefore, that every company in America would be rushing to install high-performance practices. Right? Wrong. In reality, few such organizations exist. In 1993 the Economic Policy Institute reported that "Despite the accumulating evidence that companies investing in [high-performance organization practices such as] work reorganization, involving front-line workers in decision making, and upgrading worker skills realize high payoffs in improving productivity, efficiency, and increasing their ability to get products to market quickly, these changes have been slow to spread in the U.S."[8]

Indeed they have. In fact, in practically every case that our gurus cite as an example of the success of high-performance teams, the company experiencing the success has found it difficult, if not impossible, to expand high-performance practices much beyond a few isolated experiments. It is almost as if the world said to our gurus, "Yes, we know. We understand that what you are saying will make us all richer and happier, but no thank you. We prefer to stay as we are—poor and miserable."

As you might imagine, such irrational resistance to their ideas frustrates our sages, particularly since they are not quite sure why it occurs. They speculate about the cause of the resistance and why successful experiments in high performance are so slow to spread throughout companies. Here are a few of their speculations.

Maybe people resist because "in the United States, we have a strong political and personal tradition of individual freedom that at times runs counter to the collective nature of teamwork," suggest Manz and Sims.[9]

Maybe some people "find the team approach too time-consuming, too uncertain, or too risky . . . [or they] just don't like the idea of having to depend on others, having to listen or agree to contrary points of view, or having to suffer the consequences of other people's mistakes," reason Katzenbach and Smith.[10]

Maybe, suggests John H. Zenger, chairman of Times Mirror Training, Inc., the reason there aren't more high-performance organizations is because managers are threatened by them. "For them, teams are a loss, pure and simple: loss of status, loss of perks, loss of authority, loss of responsibility. [Maybe] they resent having to 'give away the store' to their subordinates."[11]

Or maybe, just maybe, high-performance organizations aren't spreading like wildfire because the transition from the traditional organization is just so hard to accomplish. As we said earlier, the results our gurus point to for their high-performance organization may be breathtakingly good, but it is also true that the organizations they want to create are breathtakingly different. Going from traditional to high performance is not easy by any means.

MAKING THE TRANSITION TO HIGH PERFORMANCE

As you might expect, all our gurus offer their own unique step-by-step guidance for making the transition from a traditional to a high-performance organization. For example, John Zenger and the team from Zenger Miller describe "four pillars of a coherent implementation architecture."[12] Charles Manz and Henry Sims provide a "road map to success."[13] Susan Albers Mohrman and the team from the Center for Effective Organizations offer a five-step "design sequence."[14] And Jon Katzenbach and Douglas Smith provide eight approaches for "moving up the performance curve."[15] Which of these is best? Well, as Katzenbach and Smith admit, there is no single best how-to recipe. There are, however, some common issues that all our gurus agree organizations must face in making the transition to high performance, regardless of the architecture they employ, the road map or design sequence they follow, or the performance curve they seek to scale. The most critical of these are the following:

1. What types of teams will be used and how will technical coordination and decision making across teams be accomplished?
2. What will be the roles and responsibilities of managers, supervisors, team leaders, and team members?
3. What new skills will managers, supervisors, team leaders, and employees need to function effectively in the new organization?

Here is what our gurus have to say about each of these issues.

Types of Teams and Integration across Teams

Teams are the foundation of high-performance organizations. As our gurus say, try as you might, you can't get to high performance without them. Therefore, one of the first things you must do in making the transition to high performance is decide upon the number and types of teams that the new organization will have.

Types of Teams

Choosing the right type of team isn't as simple as it might seem, because our gurus offer a bewildering array of choices:

Work teams	Management teams
Cross-functional teams	Project teams
Problem-solving teams	Guidance teams
Performance-improvement teams	Self-managed teams
Process teams	Semiautonomous teams
Integrating teams	

Every guru has his or her own terminology. Regardless of the names, however, there are really only three basic types of teams: work teams, improvement teams, and integrating teams. All high-performance organizations are built by mixing and matching these three fundamental types.[16]

1. *Work teams.* Work teams design, manufacture, and deliver a product or provide a service to an internal or external customer. These teams are composed of people who are on the front lines of most organizations, doing the research, making the product, selling, servicing customers, and performing most of the direct value-adding jobs in the organization. These teams include manufacturing production teams, new-product development teams, proposal teams, consulting teams, sales and service teams, and so on. In a manufacturing environment, a work team might consist of a group of operators who are cross-trained to perform all the tasks necessary to produce a particular product. In a service industry such as insurance, a work team might consist of claims processors, customer service representatives, and underwriters assigned to handle life, health, and disability insurance products for a specific geographic area.

2. *Improvement teams.* Improvement teams make recommendations for changes in the organization, its processes, and/or its technology in order to improve the quality, cost and/or timeliness of delivery of products and services. Members of improvement teams are normally drawn from one or more work teams. Unlike work teams, improvement teams are often temporary. They are created to work on a specific problem or project and then disband. Project teams, audit groups, quality teams, task forces, process improvement teams, and similar problem-solving groups are examples of improvement teams.

3. *Integrating teams.* Integrating teams make sure that work is coordinated across the organization. These teams link two or more interdependent work teams and/or improvement teams around a shared focus, such as a particular customer, a product line, a technology, or a geographical market or service area. Integrating teams serve as links between work teams and/or improvement teams. They are normally composed of members of the interdependent teams that are being linked. For example, software engineers from development work teams might be members of the integrating team formed between two software development teams. Management teams represent a special form of integrating team that sets overall strategic direction, establishes goals, and monitors the performance of work and improvement teams.

Work teams and improvement teams may be either functional or cross-functional in nature, depending upon the type of work they must perform and how much coordination they require for their success. Functional teams look very much like departments or sections in a traditional organization, with people grouped according to their particular specialty—quality assurance, marketing, manufacturing, purchasing, engineering, and so on. Cross-functional teams group people by project or process, with specialists from many different disciplines on the same team. How do you decide whether a team should be functional or cross-functional? Susan Albers Mohrman, Susan Cohen, and Allan M. Morhman, Jr., coauthors of *Designing Team-Based Organizations* and researchers at the Center for Effective Organizations, suggest that you answer the following key questions:[17]

1. *What are the sets of activities that have to be conducted and integrated with each other to deliver value to the customer?* If you need a high level of coordination between specialties so that the customer will experience integrated, one-stop services, then you should design cross-functional teams.

2. *What are the issues and trade-offs that often hold up work in the organization because of inability to arrive at a shared agreement about how to proceed or because conditions change and agreement falls apart?* When you need frequent ongoing deliberations to ensure timely decisions, say our gurus, then you need cross-functional teams.

3. *Where does the work that is done by different individuals require the greatest amount of on-line technical coordination to fit together?* When you have work that requires complex and reciprocal interdependencies or a lot of on-line technical coordination, say our gurus, then you need cross-functional teams.

Although most high-performance organizations contain both functional and cross-functional teams, the latter are typically the dominant type of team in most true high-performance organizations. There are several reasons, as noted by Glenn M. Parker, author of *Cross-Functional Teams:*

1. *Speed.* Cross-functional teams reduce the time it takes to get things done, especially in the product development process.
2. *Complexity.* Cross-functional teams improve an organization's ability to solve complex problems [because they bring together people with a wide variety of skills and orientations.]
3. *Customer focus.* Cross-functional teams focus the organization's resources on satisfying the customer's needs.
4. *Creativity.* By bringing together people with a variety of experiences and backgrounds, cross-functional teams increase the creative capacity of an organization.
5. *Organizational learning.* Members of cross-functional teams are more easily able to develop new technical and professional skills, learn more about other disciplines, and learn how to work with people who have different team-player styles and cultural backgrounds than those who do not participate in cross-functional teams.
6. *Single point of contact.* The cross-functional team promotes more effective cross-team teamwork by identifying one place to go for information and for decisions about a project or customer.[18]

Here is an example of how our gurus might restructure a company to form a high-performance organization.[19] In this case, the company is a high-tech defense contractor that designs navigational systems. Traditionally, it was organized around functional departments or discipline-specific work groups—software development, electrical engineering, mechanical engineering, and so on. Software development was performed in two separate departments, one for each navigational system under development. The electrical engineering department and mechanical engineering department provided services to both software groups. A technical support group provided technical support and quality control for the entire organization, and a systems integration group was responsible for technical integration across all of the systems under development. The company's organizational chart looked like Exhibit 4.2.

After being redesigned as a high-performance organization, the company had an organizational chart that looked like Exhibit 4.3. The separate functional electrical engineering and mechanical engineering departments were abolished, and the two software development groups were converted to cross-functional work teams containing a full complement of software, electrical, and mechanical engineers. The systems integration group was abolished and replaced with a cross-functional systems integration team composed of software, electrical, and mechanical engineers from the two work teams.

Accomplishing Integration across Teams

Notice that in a true high-performance organization, the traditional hierarchy is dismantled. The work teams and improvement teams take over many of the responsibilities normally performed by traditional managers and supervisors (see our discussion in the next section), including the responsibility

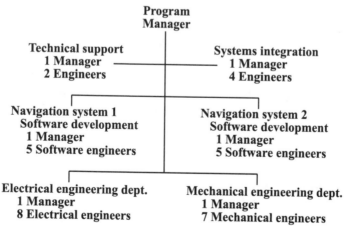

Traditional Organization

Program Manager

Technical support
1 Manager
2 Engineers

Systems integration
1 Manager
4 Engineers

Navigation system 1
Software development
1 Manager
5 Software engineers

Navigation system 2
Software development
1 Manager
5 Software engineers

Electrical engineering dept.
1 Manager
8 Electrical engineers

Mechanical engineering dept.
1 Manager
7 Mechanical engineers

EXHIBIT 4.2. **Traditional Organization**

High-Performance Organization

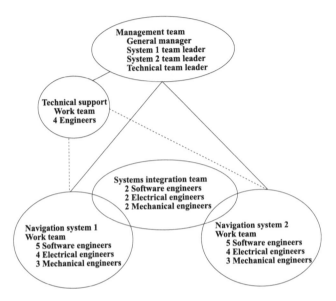

EXHIBIT 4.3. **High-Performance Organization**

for technical coordination and decisions concerning trade-offs between conflicting goals and priorities. Since most of the teams are cross-functional, most of the parties that should be involved in a decision are represented on the team. Consequently, each team can handle most interdependencies that fall within the scope of the team's authority. Some issues, however, will transcend teams and require technical coordination and decision making across team boundaries. Our gurus offer several ways to accomplish this integration.[20]

1. Individual liaison. If the required coordination is relatively simple, a single individual may be able to provide the coordination between two or more teams. For example, a member of the marketing team might be assigned responsibility for attending meetings of a product design team to share marketing information and collect information about the developing design that would be helpful to marketing in planning materials for the product.

2. Integrating team. If the ongoing coordination between two or more teams is more complex, a formal integrating team may be created. For example, in the redesign of the navigation systems company, as we saw earlier, a cross-functional integration team was established to provide technical coordination between the two navigation system work teams.

3. Management team. Ultimately, organizationwide integration in a high-performance organization is the responsibility of the senior management team. Normally, this team consists of the senior manager for the organization and team leaders from the various cross-functional and functional work teams.

Roles and Responsibilities of Team Members and Team Leaders

High-performance organizations permanently alter the relationships among managers, supervisors, and employees. Some traditional organizational roles, such as those of the foreman or supervisor, disappear almost entirely. Other traditional roles, such as those of worker and manager, are totally redefined. How significant are the changes? Exhibit 4.4 contains a brief list of typical supervisory responsibilities that cross-functional, self-managed work teams in one high-performance manufacturing organization perform, as reported by Charles Manz and Henry Sims.[21] Notice the breadth and scope of traditional management responsibilities that the team takes on.

Obviously, this plant delegates a large number of traditional managerial and supervisory roles and responsibilities to work teams, but how much is too much? Are all teams prepared to take on this much responsibility? No, say our gurus, at least not right away. Rather than loading new responsibilities on teams all at once, our gurus typically suggest that team responsibilities be phased in over several months or even years. At first, teams are given only a few traditional managerial/supervisory tasks to perform. Over time, these responsibilities are expanded. Some gurus suggest that you negotiate responsibilities with team members and prepare a responsibility

EXHIBIT 4.4.   Team Roles and Responsibilities

- *Establish relief and break schedules.* Team members establish their own work schedules, including taking breaks when they choose.

- *Select and dismiss the group leader.* Either people are elected to serve as internal team leaders or the job is rotated among team members. Typically, the internal team leader performs many of the organizing, planning, interpersonal, and conflict-resolution tasks of traditional supervisors but serves solely at the discretion of team members. The role of the traditional supervisor is altered almost beyond recognition as the team itself takes on more and more responsibility. (See our discussion of this transition later in this chapter.)

- *Initiate equipment and machinery repair.* Team members themselves perform most of the routine maintenance on their own equipment and make minor repairs. Major repair orders are initiated by the team without prior approval by management.

- *Make specific job assignments within the work group.* Teams develop different methods for making job assignments. Some teams rotate jobs among members. Others make job assignments strictly on the basis of seniority, with the most senior workers having first choice of jobs. In other teams, employees negotiate with each other over assignments and seek ways to allow everyone to perform their favorite job without sacrificing performance.

- *Train new members of the work group.* Team members provide on-the-job training for new members. They also decide the type and extent of training team members need from outside sources and schedule this training.

- *Ensure that needed production materials and spare parts are available.* The elected or rotating internal team leader often has responsibility for monitoring material and parts usage and arranging for replenishment from external suppliers.

- *Keep record of hours worked for each group member.* High-performance organizations normally have no time clocks. Instead, team members keep a record of their hours and turn it in to the internal team leader, who consolidates the information for payroll and other purposes. Manz and Sims note that when they asked a team member if people cheated, the team member replied, "Who do they cheat? Other team members! You may be able to get away with it once or twice, but that's all. You can't fool your team-mates."[1]

- *Perform quality control inspections and compile data.* Many high-performance manufacturing plants have no quality control inspectors. Instead, team members are responsible for their own quality and for compiling quality statistics. A very small quality control department may periodically audit the quality data assembled by the teams, but for the most part, quality control is a responsibility of the teams.

- *Prepare material and labor budgets.* Manz and Sims note that two parallel budgets may be prepared—one by the work team and a second by management or external accountants. Teams then negotiate with management to reconcile any differences and arrive at a final budget.

- *Prepare daily logs of quantity produced and amount of in-process inventory.* Team members maintain their own production records subject to periodic audits by an outside group such as production scheduling.

- *Recommend engineering changes for equipment, process, and product.* Teams conduct their own process analysis and make recommendations to management for new equipment and technology and for changes in work processes and product design. Typically, teams have wide discretion to change internal work methods and processes as they deem necessary to improve team performance.

- *Select new members for the group and dismiss members from the group.* Existing team members typically have final approval on the selection of new members of the team and may exercise most of the disciplinary authority of a traditional supervisor.

- *Evaluate group members for pay raises.* Team members frequently have responsibility for evaluating each others' performance in annual or semiannual peer reviews. If pay is tied to skill or knowledge, as it frequently is in high-performance organizations, team members may help design and/or administer tests that are used to judge mastery of the skills.

- *Shut down the process or assembly if quality is in question.* Typically, teams have the authority to stop production without asking management permission should they encounter a production or quality problem.

- *Conduct weekly group meetings.* Teams hold weekly half-hour meetings on company time and longer problem-solving meetings as needed to work on quality or performance problems.

1. Charles C. Manz and Henry P. Sims, **Business without Bosses** (New York: John Wiley & Sons, 1993), pp. 45–46.

chart, similar to the one in Exhibit 4.5, indicating which responsibilities the teams will take on immediately, which they will undertake at some future date, and which will be reserved indefinitely to management.

Making the Transition in Stages

Most of our gurus suggest that you accomplish the transition from traditional supervision to team leadership in stages. Here is a four-stage approach based upon the writings of several of our gurus.[22]

Stage #1: The Start-up Team (Exhibit 4.6)

Cross-functional work teams are created but retain formal supervisors (designated team leaders) who are appointed by management. The supervisor is

EXHIBIT 4.5. **Sample Responsibility Chart**

Responsibility	Team Now	Team in Six Months	Management
Assign work		X	
Balance workload		X	
Solve problems	X		
Conduct team meetings		X	
Complete time sheets	X		
Schedule vacation	X		
Train new employees	X		
Mentor employees from same discipline	X		
Consult on technical difficulties			X
Enforce technical standards			X
Assign people to future projects			X
Provide career counseling			X
Develop team goals	X		
Review and approve team goals			X
Survey customers about team performance		X	
Provide input for performance appraisals	X		
Conduct performance appraisals		X	
Handle disciplinary problems		X	
Recommend improvements	X		
Develop team budget		X	

*Source: Adapted from Susan Albers Mohrman, Susan G. Cohen, and Allan M. Mohrman, Jr., **Designing Team-Based Organizations: New Forms for Knowledge Work** (San Francisco: Jossey-Bass, 1995), pp. 163–164, ex. 5.1.*

still present in the team's day-to-day activities, but team members are expected to share some of the responsibility for the team's success or failure. Duties formerly performed by the supervisor are delegated first to some and then to all team members. Team members are required to solve their own problems. The supervisor/team leader is available to teach and coach employees in problem-solving techniques, but team members can no longer go to him or her to resolve every problem that arises.

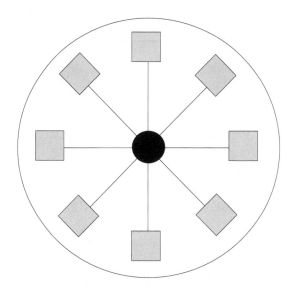

EXHIBIT 4.6. **The Start-up Team—Work teams (boxes) are supervised day-to-day by a team leader (center circle).**

Jon Katzenbach and Douglas Smith spell out several key expectations of team leaders at this stage of team development. Supervisors/team leaders are expected to handle the following responsibilities:

Help the team shape its own common purpose, goals, and approach. Team leaders are expected to be working members of the team, but they are also expected to maintain some distance and perspective that will enable them to help the team clarify and commit to a mission, goals, and approach. Leaders at this stage maintain a delicate balance between providing team members with some guidance and issuing more direct advice.

Build commitment and confidence. A key task of the leader at this stage is to build the confidence and commitment of individuals and the team as a whole by providing large amounts of positive feedback and reinforcement.

Strengthen the mix and level of skills on the team. Team leaders are expected to encourage team members to take risks, learn, grow, and take on new assignments and roles. The most effective team leaders at this stage are vigilant about acquiring and/or developing the technical, functional, problem-solving, decision-making, interpersonal, and teamwork skills the team will need to perform and progress to higher stages of team development.

Manage external relationships and remove obstacles to team performance and development. Team leaders are viewed by those inside and outside the team as principally responsible for managing the team's relationship with the rest of the organization. The team leader is responsible for interceding on the team's behalf, whenever necessary, to remove obstacles to team performance and/or acquire resources the team needs to function effectively.

Create opportunities for team members to excel. Instead of grabbing the best opportunities, assignments, and credit for themselves, team leaders are expected to help team members grow and develop by allowing them to take on additional responsibilities and by ensuring that they receive credit for their accomplishments.

Do real work. Everyone on the team, including the leader, is expected to do roughly the same amount of real work. Team leaders maintain a certain distance from the team because of their position, but they do not use their position to avoid work. Team leaders must contribute, just like any other member, and they do not delegate the unpleasant jobs to others.[23]

Stage #2: The Transitional Team (Exhibit 4.7)
As team members begin taking on more responsibility for day-to-day management of team operations, the team leader's role changes to more coordination than supervision. Team members gradually take on specific tasks for seeking information, developing group consensus, resolving intragroup conflict, making decisions without the supervisor's input, and initiating action to change policies, procedures, and methods of performing day-to-day activities. The team leader manages the group by coordinating individual skills and activities. However, the team leader increasingly spends much of his or her time acquiring team resources and managing relationships with outside groups rather than monitoring day-to-day team activities.

Stage #3: The Experienced Team (Exhibit 4.8)
By this stage, the team leader (who may now be called a coordinator) is removed from the group and no longer has direct control or perhaps even

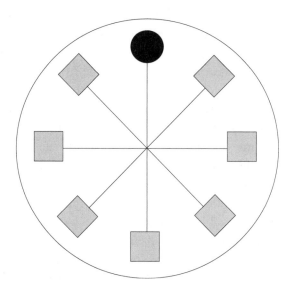

EXHIBIT 4.7. **The Transitional Team—Team leader begins to coordinate more than supervise work teams; leader no longer monitors day-to-day activities.**

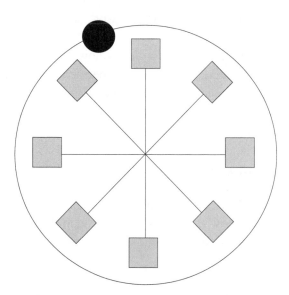

EXHIBIT 4.8. **The Experienced Team—Team leader (or coordinator) is removed from the group and merely oversees team activities.**

knowledge of day-to-day team activities. The team members themselves become solely responsible for day-to-day decisions that, as a result of experience at the previous stages, they have shown they can handle. The team leader/coordinator acts more as a chief executive officer, overseeing a number of teams. He or she collects data on productivity, quality, costs, customer satisfaction, and other critical variables and gives the teams feedback on their performance. At this stage, the coordinator focuses an increasing amount of her/his time and attention on acquiring resources for the teams reporting to her or him and on mediating with other teams and external clients and customers. The teams are largely self-managed on a day-to-day basis, and the team coordinator may not have any direct knowledge of routine problems encountered by the teams or how they responded to those problems. The team members make their own decisions by consensus and are held fully accountable for team performance on critical measures. Days elapse during which the former team leader, now team coordinator, has only fleeting, if any, interaction with the teams.

Stage #4: The Mature Team (Exhibit 4.9)

In this final stage, the team has complete accountability for its own work, and the first-line supervisory role has essentially disappeared. To a large extent, administrative, financial, and personnel matters are handled primarily by team members, who schedule their own work, assign team roles and responsibilities, and resolve their own technical and other problems with little outside intervention. The team coordinator now becomes a true resource person to a group of teams, but the teams themselves decide when they need help with social or technical issues and the level of assistance they need. When requested, the coordinator either furnishes the help directly or acquires it from external sources.

How Fast Should Teams Make the Transition

Susan Mohrman and the team from the Center for Effective Organizations note that how far and how fast teams move through these stages depends upon a number of factors, including those described in the following paragraphs.[24]

Amount of interdependence among team members. If the tasks performed by the various team members are highly interrelated so that the work of one

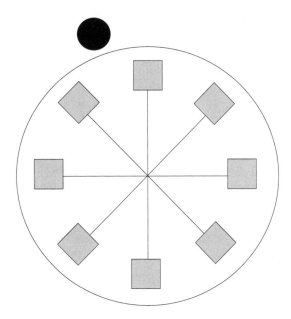

EXHIBIT 4.9. **The Mature Team—Team leader has disappeared; the team has complete accountability for its own work.**

member influences the work of other members in critical ways, then a formal team leader may be needed to keep track of open issues, facilitate meetings, and make sure that the right people are involved in making critical decisions. When the level of interdependence of team members is weak or diffused, then they are much more likely to be able to handle internal coordination informally without the intervention of a formal leader.

Size of the team. As the size of the team grows, the number of interactions, decisions, points of view to be considered, and planning required increases proportionately. Three people can easily coordinate their activities without any formal assistance. It is much more difficult, argue Mohrman and her associates, for a 20-person team to do the same. Larger teams are therefore more likely to continue to need people in formal leadership roles.

Functional/discipline diversity of members. The more disciplines on the team, the more points of view will need to be considered. Team members from different functions or disciplines think and approach problems differently, so integration between members of these disciplines may require the assistance of *translators* who have a broad background as leaders.

Degree of team self-containment. The degree to which a team is self-contained affects the complexity of information processing. If the team has all the resources it needs, then coordination and decision making are internal team processes. If a team is not self-contained—is interdependent with other teams or individuals—then the complexity of information processing increases dramatically. Integration teams are sometimes sufficient to handle such cross-team relationships, but formal team leaders or liaisons may also be needed to handle complex boundary-management functions.

Amount of change. Any number of circumstances, including unanticipated technical difficulties, changes in strategies or resource allocations, and competitive surprises, can alter the team's mission and/or strategy. The greater the disturbance, the more a team may be overwhelmed by the decisions it needs to make. The team's ability to respond quickly and appropriately to such situations can be enhanced by having a person in a leadership or managerial role who can bring crucial information to the team.

Technical experience and skill. The ability of team members to exercise responsibility for training, coaching, and mentoring new team members and for upholding technical standards depends largely on the experience and skill sets of team members. Teams with less seasoned members may require someone in a formal leadership role to provide technical guidance.

Life span of the team. If members of the team have never served on a stage-four self-managed team before and the project is of short duration, it may not make sense to invest the resources and time to fully develop the team. Instead, the team may continue to operate at stage one with a designated leader who can facilitate meetings, plan schedules, insure that work is distributed equitably, and manage interfaces with other teams.

New Skills Required by High-Performance Teams

If people must take on new responsibilities and play new roles in the high-performance organization, it stands to reason that they will need new skills. Our gurus divide the skill requirements of the high-performance teams into four categories: technical skills, administrative skills, interpersonal skills, and decision-making and problem-solving skills.

Technical Skills

Obviously, members of high-performance teams must have the knowledge and skills required to complete their assigned tasks, so a lot of attention must be given to the conceptual and practical knowledge of people being selected for the team. Mohrman and the team from the Center for Effective Organizations (CEO) note that the mix of skills on a high-performance team is as important, if not more important, than the depth of knowledge in specific technical areas. They reason that it is easier to teach team members more about a specific subject within a discipline with which they are already familiar than it is to educate them in an entirely new discipline. As an example, Mohrman and her team note that "a pharmaceutical team charged with the commercialization of a new drug . . . should consist of physicians, marketers, and clinical researchers. It would be a mistake to have only physicians on this team, [and a] product-line marketing team would not be able to compensate for the lack of a technical writer to prepare product marketing documents."[25]

A related technical training issue has to do with the amount of cross-training there will be on the team. Mohrman notes that in the prototypical high-performance work team, such as those found in manufacturing, team members are trained to perform all or most of the jobs required on the team. Such extensive cross-training, however, may not be appropriate for all teams, especially if they are composed of knowledge workers with true professional specialties. "Certainly," writes the CEO team, "the pharmaceutical company should not cross-train its marketers as physicians (and vice versa). . . . On the other hand . . . physicians can get some exposure to the marketing world view by going on customer visits. Teams require members to have, at a minimum, enough understanding of the skills of their teammates to be able to discuss issues and trade-offs as the team goes through the cycle of considering divergent views and arriving at convergence on a direction. Familiarity across disciplines provides a basis for communicating across the thought-worlds of the different disciplines."[26]

Administrative Skills

Most high-performance teams will be expected to take on tasks previously performed by managers and supervisors. For example, see Exhibit 4.4, which lists typical supervisory responsibilities undertaken by one high-performance work team in a manufacturing company. To perform these duties effectively, team members will need at least some formal training in the following skills, among others.

- Conducting effective meetings
- Interviewing prospective team members
- Conducting peer-performance appraisals
- Disciplining team members
- Negotiating for resources
- Reviewing financial reports
- Setting schedules
- Planning
- Measuring performance and setting goals
- Handling grievances
- Managing diversity

Interpersonal Skills

High-performance organizations bring together people from different disciplines who have absorbed different bodies of knowledge, view information in different ways, have different world views, and may frequently use entirely different languages when discussing technical issues. Such differences provide a fertile breeding ground for misunderstanding and interpersonal conflict. Since most people, unless they have previously worked in high-performance team-based organizations, will not come to teams with the requisite communication and conflict-resolution skills, most teams will need at least some interpersonal-skills training to avoid such problems. The two most critical interpersonal skills emphasized by practically all of our gurus are communication skills and conflict-resolution skills. Team members have to be taught to listen, express their ideas and feelings, develop a shared understanding, and work for mutually acceptable solutions. (See chapter 3, "The Learning Organization," for a discussion of some of the skills of communication, inquiry, and testing of mental models that teams may be taught to develop interpersonal skills.)

Decision-Making and Problem-Solving Skills

Finally, most team members will require some training in systematic problem solving. Typically, all of the teams within an organization are taught to follow the same multistep process, for example:

Step 1: prioritize problems
Step 2: collect data
Step 3: analyze data
Step 4: generate alternative solutions
Step 5: evaluate solutions and select solution to implement
Step 6: plan and implement the solutions
Step 7: evaluate results

At each step in the process, teams are provided with tools and techniques to analyze data, solve problems, and improve work processes. Exhibit 4.10 lists some of the most popular of these.

Amount of Training Needed by High-Performance Teams

How much time should you devote to training? A lot, say our gurus, at least a lot compared to the amount of training offered in a traditional organization. Edward E. Lawler, for example, recommends that you free up a minimum of 5% of employee time for training each year. Otherwise, says

EXHIBIT 4.10. **Tools and Techniques Designed to Improve Work Processes**

Benchmarking	Quality-function deployment
Cause-and-effect diagrams	Pareto charts
Nominal group technique	Statistical process control (SPC)
Histograms	Design of experiments
Check sheets	Cost of quality
Input/output analysis	Control charts
Scatter diagrams	Work-flow analysis
Concurrent engineering	

Lawler, you are just not demonstrating a true commitment to meeting your teams' needs.[27]

THE PREDICTABLE PHASES OF TEAM DEVELOPMENT

Okay, so you do just as the gurus advise. You carefully plan your team organization. You answer all of our gurus' questions and work out exactly how many teams you should have and what types they should be. You mix and match work, improvement, and integrating teams perfectly to create the ideal configuration. You carefully phase in the teams' new responsibilities and you conduct a lot of training to ensure that everyone has the skills to succeed. You do everything the gurus want you to do, and what is the result? Everything goes smoothly, right? Wrong. In fact, say our gurus, things are going to get worse before they get better. Charles Manz and Henry Sims, for example, predict that the performance of most teams will actually decline after start-up and not return to preteam levels for as long as a year. True performance gains may not occur for as long as 18 months.[28] In spite of all your planning and our gurus' sage advice, the road to high performance is going to be bumpy. The best help our gurus can give you is to prepare you for the ride. Expect, they say, for your teams to pass through four highly predictable stages: Forming, Storming, Norming, and Performing.

Stage #1: Forming

You should expect a period of nervous excitement when teams are first formed. People who have been picked to be on teams will feel a sense of pride that they have been chosen, but they will have a lot of questions. "What's expected of me?" "Will I fit in?" "What am I supposed to do?" "What are the rules?"

The forming stage is a stage of exploration. Along with the excitement of being involved in something new, people feel insecure, anxious, and confused. Everyone on the team is privately assessing everyone else—sizing up their abilities and attitudes. In *The Team Handbook,* Peter R. Scholtes and his colleagues at Joiner and Associates describe this stage as one in which the team members are all hesitant swimmers, standing by the pool, dabbling their feet in the water. Because no one is quite sure of what is going to happen, productivity is low. Don't expect your teams to accomplish much during the forming stage, warn our gurus.

To lead your team through forming, Scholtes and the team from Joiner suggest that you:

- Help team members get to know each other;
- Provide the team with clear direction and purpose;
- Involve members in developing plans, clarifying roles, and establishing ways of working together;
- Provide the information the team needs to get started.[29]

Stage #2: Storming

In stage two, things appear to go from bad to worse. Team members grow impatient with the lack of progress and want to get down to work, but they don't know how to get anything accomplished. Everyone is beginning to find out that this team business is much more difficult to accomplish than anyone suspected. People feel awkward working together. Everyone is frustrated and frequently angry with themselves and others on the team. This is a period of blaming, defensiveness, confrontation, disunity, tension, and hostility. People become jealous of each other. Subgroups form. Infighting breaks out between opposing factions competing for influence. The team struggles to sort out its mission, goals, roles of team members, and agreements on how to work together. Productivity continues to take a beating. The team passes through its most difficult stage.

To lead your team through storming, Scholtes suggests that you

- Resolve issues of power and authority. For example, don't allow one person's power to squash others' contributions;
- Develop and implement agreements about how decisions are made and who makes them;
- Adapt the leadership role to allow the team to become more independent. Encourage team members to take on more responsibilities.[30]

Stage #3: Norming

Suddenly, things begin to improve in stage three. The team develops some ground rules, or "norms," concerning ways to work together. People finally stop grandstanding and begin to realize that they are all in this team business together. Gradually, people even come to like the team and develop an attachment to one another. Increasingly, people begin to feel that they belong. There is a sense of **WE**. People take pride in being part of something and start cooperating instead of competing. Communication opens up and trust deepens. After the storming phase, life on the team becomes almost tranquil—sometimes too tranquil. The team goes from fighting to almost the opposite extreme. People focus on maintaining team relationships. There is less interest in tangible results than in keeping the peace. Productivity continues to lag as little gets done.

To lead your team through norming, Scholtes and his colleagues advise you to

- Fully utilize team members' skills, knowledge, and experience;
- Encourage and acknowledge members' respect for each other;
- Encourage members to roll up their sleeves and work collaboratively.[31]

Stage #4: Performing

Finally, a breakthrough occurs. The team gains confidence. People reach a consensus on who the team is and what it is trying to accomplish. The team develops and begins to use structured processes and procedures to communicate, resolve conflict, allocate resources, and relate to the rest of the organization. People freely and constructively share information and viewpoints. Conflict is channeled in constructive ways and leads to finding creative solutions to work-related problems. The team starts to develop a strong sense of pride in team accomplishment. Finally, work gets done.

To lead your team through performing, Scholtes and the Joiner Associates team would have you:

- Update the team's methods and procedures to support cooperation;
- Help the team understand how to manage change;
- Represent and advocate for the team with other groups and individuals;
- Monitor work progress and celebrate achievements.[32]

The passage from storming to performing can take a few weeks or many months. Scholtes describes it as a roller-coaster ride of highs and lows in which every team is different, progress is never smooth, and the team's mood swings are usually unpredictable.

TIPS, TRICKS, AND TECHNIQUES FOR TEAM SUCCESS

A team's progress through the stages of forming, storming, norming, and performing may be unpredictable, but you can still do some things to ease the transition. While not a total solution, a number of the things we have already discussed, such as carefully planning the team structure, phasing in team responsibilities over time, paying attention to team skills, and so on, can help make the transformation go more smoothly. And there are other tips, tricks, and techniques you can employ to even out the bumps. Here are some of the success secrets mentioned most frequently by our gurus.

Team Tip #1: Redesign Work—Don't Just Create Teams

Linda Moran and Ed Musselwhite, senior consultant and CEO of Zenger Miller, respectively, along with John Zenger, advise that "although certain residual benefits such as improved communication accumulate simply by switching to teams, generally only after the work has been redesigned is it possible to streamline the processes and remove variances. That's when you begin to see less work in process, reduced cycle times, faster internal feedback, lower rework and scrap."[33]

In accomplishing the work redesign, our gurus have the following recommendations.[34]

1. Focus on a few strategic issues rather than trying to redesign everything at once. For example, if improving customer service is critical, you might focus on redesigning the work processes related to such things as ordering, telephone service, information systems, and training.

2. Organize around whole processes. Give teams responsibility for all aspects of work associated with producing a product or providing a service to a clearly identifiable internal or external customer. Ed Lawler writes:

> The fundamental grouping approach in a high-involvement organization should be toward organizational units that feel responsible for a particular product or customer. The alternative of structuring around function (such

as engineering or accounting) is incongruent with high-involvement management because it creates a situation where individuals are performing their own particular specialty; they have no identification with the product or contact with the customer. This creates the need for hierarchy and extensive control systems to assure that the different functions work together to deliver the product or service that the customer wants. It also limits the degree to which they understand the business and are motivated to produce a high-quality product or service.[35]

3. Expand job responsibilities. Push traditional management tasks and decision-making authority down to the teams.

4. Design for immediate feedback. Design work in such a way that people have frequent opportunities to experience the impact of their actions. Give teams closer links to customers, allow them to check their own quality, and give them direct access to performance reports.

5. Make sure that the teams have ready access to technical and other forms of support. Make it easy for production teams and support teams to communicate, and where possible, place support teams physically close to production teams. For example, move the support team directly onto the production floor.

6. Don't overdesign. Get the basic structure right and then let the teams flesh out the details. The more the teams are involved in the work redesign, the more ownership they will have for the final product.

Team Tip #2: Redesign the Compensation System

Chances are very good that you will need to change your compensation system as you move to a high-performance team-based organization. This is particularly true if your existing compensation system ties pay to jobs and seniority. The problem with such pay systems, writes Ed Lawler, is that they "support [organizational] designs in which large amounts of power, information, knowledge, and rewards are at the top of an organization. Since the best way to make more money is to get promoted, they tend to motivate individuals to develop skills that help them move up the hierarchy rather than other skills that may be critical to the organization's success because they contribute to key organizational [particularly team] capabilities and core competencies."[36]

As an alternative to traditional job-based pay, Lawler and most of our other gurus recommend that you adopt a pay-for-knowledge compensation system that ties base pay to an employee's skill and knowledge, rather than to the position he or she occupies. Lawler argues that you should:

- Tie specific pay raises to learning identified skills.
- Create broad pay bands that allow for significant increases as individuals learn additional skills. Instead of putting people in a pay range that tops out at 50% higher than the bottom, use a range in which the top is double the bottom. This structure allows for pay to rise as employees continue to learn.
- Give employees one-time, lump-sum payments when they develop new skills. This is appropriate if the skills will be used only on a temporary or short-term basis, or if pay is already high and the organization can't afford an ongoing extra cost that would result from an increase in base pay.
- Tie promotions or changes in pay grades to increases in skills.[37]

In addition to moving to a pay-for-knowledge system, our gurus recommend that you adopt incentives that pay teams for performance. The most widely recommended types of incentives are gainsharing, which rewards the entire team for improvements in performance over a target or baseline, profit sharing, and stock ownership. Lawler notes that "there is little or no room for such traditional pay practices as merit pay. The principles of the new logic instead call for team bonuses, gain-sharing plans, stock option plans, and stock ownership plans."[38] For more information on pay systems that support performance teams, see Chapter 6, "Managing and Motivating People."

Team Tip #3: Redesign the Information System

You will probably need to redesign your information system as well. Susan Mohrman and her associates report that team performance is directly related to the team members' access to information technology that links them to people with whom they work and allows them to share common databases. Computer systems that allow team members to communicate within and among teams and with customers, suppliers, and business partners are critical, as is widespread and universal access to databases.[39] Ed

Lawler says that "the information system is the key to effective coordination and feedback in any organization but is particularly crucial in a high-involvement system."[40] He provides a few additional insights about information systems.

> Since many of the levels of hierarchy and staff support are gone, the information system must provide the capability for people to coordinate and manage themselves. Even with the best of intentions, in the absence of an effective information system, employees cannot become self-regulating. . . .
>
> The information system needs to be open to all members of the organization, so that they can get the kind of financial, production, and other information that they need. Mini-enterprises or teams need to get information about how effectively they are performing and how their performance compares to standards and their competitors. It also needs to tell them how they are serving their customers. Feedback from customers is particularly crucial.[41]
>
> The information system should not only include data about financial operating results; it should also include information on the human system. In particular, survey data should be regularly collected and fed back to individuals in the organizations.[42]

Lawler argues for the use of computer terminals throughout the organization to collect on-line, real-time data on employee opinions about management actions and proposed actions and employee job satisfaction. He also favors a decentralized information system that provides individuals and work teams with the information they need to plan, coordinate, manage, and evaluate their own performance. The information system should also provide employees with up-to-the-minute information on financial, planning, and market information so that employees will understand how the company is doing.[43] See Chapter 6 for more ideas on how to share information with teams.

Team Tip #4: Change or Eliminate Individual Performance Appraisals

Most of our gurus agree with W. Edwards Deming's assessment that annual employee performance evaluations, as they are traditionally done, destroy teamwork. Our gurus see individual appraisals as particularly destructive when they are combined with a competitive rating system to allocate a pool of money budgeted for raises. Glenn Parker notes that "although employees are usually not told their ranking, they know they are in competition with their colleagues in the ranking process. The result is that people are more likely to be competitive than collaborative with their teammates."[44]

If you feel you must retain individual appraisals, our gurus suggest that you do the following.

1. Change the performance criteria to emphasize teamwork. For example, include in the appraisal phrases such as "shares information with others," "negotiates differences effectively," "encourages and acknowledges the contributions of others," and "encourages cooperation and teamwork among people in his or her group" to send a message that performance as a team member and/or team leader matters.[45]

2. Involve team members in the appraisal process. As soon as the team reaches the performing stage, consider adding peer appraisals—team members evaluate each other—as part of the team's administrative responsibilities.

3. Keep the appraisal process as simple and informal as possible. Avoid elaborate, multipart forms and complicated rating scales.

Team Tip #5: Set Specific and Demanding Team Performance Goals

Jon Katzenbach and Douglas Smith write that "a demanding performance challenge . . . is far more important to team success than team-building exercises, special incentives, or team leaders with ideal profiles."[46]

Specific goals—like getting a new product to market in less than half the normal time, responding to all customers within twenty-four hours, or achieving a zero defect rate while simultaneously cutting costs by 40 percent—provide clear and tangible footholds for teams for several reasons. First, they define a *team work-product* that is different from both an organizationwide mission and the summation of individual job objectives. . . . Second, the specificity of the performance objectives facilitates clear communication and constructive conflict within the team. . . . When such goals are clear, team discussions can focus on how to pursue them or whether to change them. . . .Third, the attainability of specific performance goals helps teams focus on getting results. . . . Fourth . . . specific objectives have a leveling effect conducive to team behavior. When a small group of people challenge themselves . . . to reduce cycle time by 50 percent [for example,] their respective titles, perks, and other "stripes" fade into the background. Instead, the teams . . . evaluate what and how each individual can best contribute to the team's goal and, more important, do so in terms of the performance objective itself rather than a person's status or personality. Fifth, specific goals . . . allow the team to achieve small wins as it pursues its purpose. *Small wins are invaluable to building members' commitment* and overcoming the inevitable obstacles that get in the way of achieving a meaningful long-term purpose. Last, performance goals are compelling. They challenge people on the team to commit themselves, as a team, to make a difference. Drama, urgency, and a healthy fear of failure combine to drive teams who have their collective eye on an attainable goal.[47]

Team Tip #6: Keep the Team Small

Ed Lawler suggests that the ideal team size is somewhere between 5 and 9 members, but certainly never more than 15. Task considerations, particularly in manufacturing, might dictate teams with 25 to 30 members.[48] Glenn Parker argues that team productivity, member accountability, participation, and trust all decline as the size of the team increases. As a result, he suggests an optimal team size of 4 to 6 members, with 10 to 12 being the maximum for effectiveness.[49]

Katzenbach and Smith say that teams should range in size from 2 to 25 people "because large numbers of people—by virtue of their size—have trouble interacting constructively as a group, much less agreeing on actionable specifics. Ten people are far more likely than fifty to successfully work through their individual, functional, and hierarchical differences toward a common plan and hold themselves jointly accountable for the results."[50]

Team Tip #7: Create the Right Work Environment

Lawler argues that the work environment must be consistent with the philosophical underpinnings of the team-based, high-performance organization.

High-involvement organizations need . . . to be egalitarian and to meet people's needs for a safe, pleasant work environment. . . . Thus, such status symbols as reserved parking spaces, separate entrances, executive dining
rooms, and special offices are not acceptable. . . . The normal dress code, in
which people at different levels of power wear different clothes, is also not
appropriate in high-involvement organizations.[51]

Even the physical layout of the workplace may need to change, says
Lawler.

The correct layout of the physical space in which teams operate can be
critical to their success. Putting team members in the same physical space
tends to promote more cohesive and more effective teams. Organizations
can also use . . . information technology to create virtual teams . . . [but] I
am convinced there is no substitute for face-to-face contact. How much in-
person contact is needed depends upon the type of team. Self-managing
work teams seem to require both interaction time and common physical
space—members may be spread over a large facility, but they definitely
need dedicated meeting and gathering spaces to allow them to operate as a
team.

    Common space and high levels of personal interaction are also critical
for most [improvement] teams, because their members come from quite
different backgrounds and are often together only for a short period of
time. Thus they need activities and structures that cause them to talk to
each other.[52]

Team Tip #8: Intervene When the Team Gets Stuck

Almost all teams will get stuck at some point. Katzenbach and Smith list
eight clear signs of a team that's bogged down:

1. A loss of energy or enthusiasm—"What a waste of time."
2. A sense of helplessness—"There's nothing anyone can do."
3. A lack of purpose or identify—"We have no clue as to what this is all
   about."
4. Listless, unconstructive, and one-sided discussions without candor—
   "Nobody wants to talk about what's really going on."

5. Meetings in which the agenda is more important than the outcome—"It's all show-and-tell for the boss."
6. Cynicism and mistrust—"I knew this teamwork stuff was a load of crap."
7. Interpersonal attacks made behind people's backs and to outsiders—"Dave has never pulled his own weight and never will."
8. Lots of finger-pointing at top management and the rest of the organization—"If this effort's so important, why don't they give us more resources."[53]

When these signs appear, teams need help; it is time for higher management to step in. Katzenbach and Smith suggest these approaches to getting the team unstuck:

1. *Revisit the basics.* Teams benefit from going back to ground zero to uncover the hidden assumptions and differences of opinion that help clarify the team's mission and how to accomplish it.
2. *Go for small wins.* Success breeds success. Just setting a clear and specific goal can get a team moving again. Achieving it is even better.
3. *Inject new information and approaches.* Information from competitive benchmarks, internal case histories, best practices, front-line measures, customer interviews, and so on can provide stuck teams with a fresh perspective that allows them to reshape their purpose, approach, and goal.
4. *Take advantage of facilitators or training.* An experienced facilitator can bring problem-solving, communication, interpersonal, and teamwork skills to teams. The same applies to training. Stuck teams can benefit from training programs that highlight key skills, common team purposes, good teamwork, clear goals, and the role of the leader.
5. *Change the team's membership, including the leader.* Teams can avoid getting or staying stuck by changing their membership, by actually adding or excluding members. In other cases, teams may just circumvent members without actually excluding them formally. Teams may also set rules that require periodic rotation of members, ensuring fresh input and vitality.[54]

CONCLUSION

The good news about a team getting stuck, write Katzenbach and Smith, is that the process of coming to grips with the problem and getting unstuck can make the team stronger. "Each time a . . . team overcomes an obstacle, . . . it develops itself as a team, learns how to work more effectively together, and builds individual and collective skills in the process. . . . Being stuck forces the members to rethink team basics, build confidence in and commit to one another, and develop a renewed source of energy by 'overcoming' and moving on. . . . While valuable momentum and continuity can be lost, the long-term benefits will outweigh the short-term losses so long as the focus on performance prevails."[55]

KEY POINTS

High-performance organizations

Support innovation and risk taking

Emphasize learning

Design jobs to require many skills

Organize around cross-functional process teams

Have facilitators and coaches instead of managers

Provide regular feedback to employees on performance

Have only a few levels of management

Place everyone close to the customer

Promote flexibility and teamwork

Pay for performance

Share information about the business with all employees

Design their information systems to support teams

Achieve a sociotechnical balance

High-performance organizations consistently outperform traditional organizations.

☞ High-performance organizations are built by mixing and matching three types of teams—work teams, improvement teams, and integrating teams.

☞ Work teams design, manufacture, and deliver a product or provide a service to an internal or external customer.

☞ Improvement teams make recommendations for changes in the organization, its processes, and/or its technology in order to improve the quality, cost, and/or timeliness of delivery of products and services.

☞ Integrating teams make sure that work is coordinated between work teams and/or improvement teams.

☞ Work teams and improvement teams may be functional or cross-functional, although most gurus emphasize the latter.

☞ Team members in high-performance organizations take on many traditional managerial and supervisory responsibilities, such as scheduling work, making job assignments, training, making quality inspections, preparing budgets, engineering process changes, selecting and disciplining team members, and conducting team meetings.

☞ Team members in high-performance organizations require training in technical skills, administrative skills, interpersonal skills (such as communication and conflict resolution), and decision-making/problem-solving skills.

☞ Teams normally progress through four predictable stages from start-up to fully functioning team—forming, storming, norming, and performing.

☞ A team's progress through all of these stages may take as long as 18 months.

☞ In addition to creating an organization of functional and cross-functional work, improvement, and integrating teams, most high-performance organizations require:

The redesign of work around business processes

The redesign of compensation systems to pay for skills and team performance

The redesign of information systems to provide universal access to databases and to facilitate communication among teams, customers, suppliers, and business partners

The elimination of individual performance appraisals or their redesign to support teamwork

Specific and demanding performance goals for all teams clearly linked to the organization's mission and strategy

Teams with no more than 20 to 30 members each

The willingness and ability of upper management to intervene when teams get stuck

OUR STRATEGY GURUS

Adam M. Brandenburger, coauthor of *Co-opetition*

Gary P. Hamel, coauthor of *Competing for the Future*

Henry Mintzberg, author of *The Rise and Fall of Strategic Planning*

James F. Moore, author of *The Death of Competition*

Barry J. Nalebuff, coauthor of *Co-opetition*

Michael E. Porter, author of *Competitive Advantage* and *Competitive Strategy*

C. K. Prahalad, coauthor of *Competing for the Future*

Michael Treacy, coauthor of *The Discipline of Market Leaders*

Fred Wiersema, coauthor of *The Discipline of Market Leaders*

5

The Pursuit
of Market Leadership

This chapter is a little different from those preceding it. In previous chapters, we summarized the consensus view of our gurus while pointing out their differences. In this chapter we present a straight-forward summary of five different views of strategy, beginning with the reigning view of the 1980s and ending with the most popular views of the mid-1990s.

Why are we adopting a different approach for this chapter? Well, you see, strategy gurus tend to be rather ornery sorts—intellectual demigods with the hubris to think theirs is the only way. Even when they agree, they don't really agree. Each is sure of being right and equally sure the others, if not wrong, are not as right as they are. Our assessment is that there is a lot of insight in what our strategy gurus have to say, and there is also a lot of junk. We have summarized what our gurus have to say—both the nourishing bits of good advice and the junk. You decide what you think is worthwhile, and at the end of the chapter, we'll compare notes. Let's start back in the late 1970s with the emergence of a guru for the 1980s.

A GURU FOR THE 1980s: MICHAEL PORTER

In the mid-1970s, a young Harvard Business School professor named Michael Porter, who later became the youngest tenured professor at that school, examined various state-of-the-art approaches to competitive strategy and came away decidedly dissatisfied. He knew that competitive strategy was an area of primary concern to managers, because it dealt with fundamental questions that all business leaders had to answer, including the following.

- What is driving competition in my industry or in industries I am thinking of entering?
- What actions are competitors likely to take, and what is the best way to respond?
- How will my industry evolve?
- How can my firm be positioned to compete in the long run?

While these were important questions, Porter found that the strategy gurus of that time provided few, if any, analytical techniques that managers could use to find answers. Instead, the gurus offered what Porter saw as weak and simplistic models that lacked both breadth and comprehensive coverage.[1] Porter was particularly dubious about the value of one of the most popular techniques of competitive analysis then in use—the Growth/Share Matrix.

THE BOSTON CONSULTING GROUP'S GROWTH/SHARE MATRIX

The Growth/Share Matrix was developed and popularized by the Boston Consulting Group in the 1960s. It was simple, elegant, quantitative, colorful, and, most importantly, took the guesswork out of strategy. Consequently, it made the Boston Consulting Group a lot of money.

To use the Growth/Share Matrix to determine his or her strategy, all a manager had to do was to plot his or her business units according to two dimensions—industry growth rate and relative market share (see Exhibit 5.1). Once the business units were plotted in the matrix, decisions could be made easily about how to allocate scarce funds.

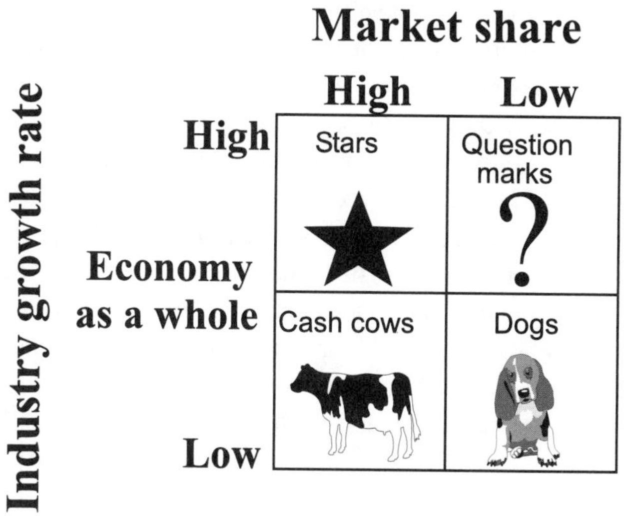

EXHIBIT 5.1. **Growth/Share Matrix**

Business units falling within the upper-left quadrant of the matrix were designated as *Stars.* They enjoyed high market share in high-growth markets. They required cash for their growth, but since they were in a strong competitive position, they presumably had high profit margins and generated plenty of cash. Generally, these Stars were expected to be self-supporting with respect to their cash needs. But if they needed cash, it should be provided, since the return from the investment would be good. Regardless, any temptation to siphon off cash from these units should be re-sisted since the unit's position would be hurt.

Cash Cows, placed in the lower-left quadrant, were units that held highly competitive positions—had high market share—in low-growth markets. Cash Cows were expected to generate large amounts of cash but required little for themselves. They could be milked for dollars to help other business units or to fund research and development.

Question Marks—those units found in the upper-right quadrant of the matrix—were true problem children. They needed lots of cash since they had to fund growth; but they were unlikely to generate lots of cash since they were striving to gain market share and weren't yet benefiting from the economies in producing the product that could be expected to come from experience—the so-called learning curve. The Question Mark was a problem because it could become either a Star at some time in the future or just another cash-hungry Dog as the market matured. Generally, the model suggested that promising Question Marks should be given a short-term influx of cash to see if they could be turned into Stars. But all Question Marks should be watched closely in case they become Dogs.

Dogs were cash losers and even cash traps. They were businesses with low market share in low-growth markets. Their profits could be expected to be weak or nonexistent. There wasn't much one could do for Dogs. It was possible, though not likely, that a Dog could be refocused on a smaller market niche and somehow become a Star or Cash Cow in a redefined market. In general, such turnaround efforts were not likely to succeed and should be avoided. Most often, the model suggested, funds should be withheld from Dogs, and they should be allowed to die. Better still, they should be sold off or liquidated.

Such were the analysis and recommendations at the time. It was all simple, neat, easy, and logical. Once you knew whether you had a Star, Cash Cow, Question Mark, or Dog on your hands, you knew exactly what action to take. You knew which units should get funds, which should be milked for funds, and which should be abandoned. There was just one problem, said Porter. While it all sounded good, in reality the Growth/Share Matrix wasn't all that useful. Why?

CRASH GO THE DOGS AND COWS

Porter found the Growth/Share Matrix lacking in many respects.[2] First, in order to use the model, you had to define the market properly, and that often required a great deal of analysis. But the model gave you no tools for doing such an analysis. You were pretty much left on your own. Second, the model assumed that market share was a good indicator of likely cash generation, and that growth was an equally good indicator of cash requirements. However, neither was as reliable an indicator as the model implied, said Porter. Profits and cash flow depended on a lot of things other than just market share and growth. Finally and most importantly, said Porter, the Growth/Share Matrix by itself was not very useful in determining strategy for a particular business. The simplistic advice to "harvest a Dog" or "grow a Question Mark into a Star" was far from sufficient to guide managerial action. Managers needed to throw away their Stars, Cows, Dogs, Question

Marks, and other childish toys and get down to some actual adult competitive analysis. Managers would, of course, need some analytical tools and techniques and a guru to guide them. Porter was confident what tools and techniques would be most beneficial, and if the mantle of gurudom fell upon his young shoulders, so be it!

MICHAEL PORTER'S COMPETITIVE STRATEGY: THREE CORE CONCEPTS

Porter's first effort to provide the necessary analytical tools came in the form of his book *Competitive Strategy*. Published in 1980, *Competitive Strategy* launched Porter into guru orbit and assured him a six-digit consulting income for the rest of the decade. His second and third books, *Competitive Advantage* (1985) and *The Competitive Advantage of Nations* (1990), solidified his lofty status. Porter became somewhat of a god to strategic planners, and his name was spoken with reverence whenever they discussed strategy, competitiveness, and market leadership in the 1980s and early 1990s. CEOs listened intently to his every word. Would-be gurus gazed on him with envy.

Porter argued that managers needed to understand three core concepts in order to perform the analysis necessary to arrive at valid answers to the critical strategic questions we mentioned earlier.

The first core concept had to do with the relative attractiveness of different industries from the standpoint of long-term profits. Industries varied, said Porter, according to five basic "competitive forces," and understanding these forces was fundamental to developing strategy and securing an advantage.

Porter argued that while the best strategy for any given firm depends upon its particular circumstances, at the broadest level there are only three defensible positions that a firm can take that will allow it to cope successfully with the five competitive forces, secure a superior return on investment for its stockholders, and outperform its competition in the long term.

Finally, said Porter, all the analysis about sources of competitive advantage had to proceed not at the level of the company as a whole, but at the level of the discrete activities a firm performs in designing, producing, marketing, delivering, and supporting its product. In short, every firm could be thought of as having a chain of activities that yielded value to its customers, and it was only through careful analysis of this "value chain" that a company could find sources of sustainable competitive advantage. Let's look at each of these core concepts in more detail.

Core Concept #1: The Basic Competitive Forces

Porter's first core concept identifies five basic competitive forces that he maintains determine the intensity of competition in an industry. "The goal of competitive strategy for a business unit in an industry is to find a position in the industry where the company can best defend itself against these competitive forces or can influence them in its favor."[3] The five competitive forces are:

1. The threat of new entrants
2. The bargaining power of buyers
3. The bargaining power of suppliers
4. The threat of substitute products or services
5. The extent of rivalry among existing competitors in the industry

Each of these competitive forces is described in the following sections.

Competitive Force #1: Threat of Entry

Porter's first competitive force deals with the ease or difficulty a new competitor may experience when beginning to do business in an industry. Obviously, the more difficult entry is, the less the competition and the greater the likelihood of profits in the long term. Porter identifies seven barriers that make it difficult for new competitors to enter a market.

1. Economies of scale. In some industries, large companies have an advantage since the unit cost of producing a product or running an operation declines as the absolute volume of production increases. Therefore, a new entry must spend a lot of money to come in on a large scale or it must accept a significant cost disadvantage as a small start-up. Porter notes that "scale economies in production, research, marketing, and service are probably key barriers to entry in the mainframe computer industry."[4]

2. Product differentiation. Established firms have brand names and have built up customer loyalties over time. A new entry would have to spend heavily to overcome, for example, Coca-Cola's brand name and established customer base.

3. Capital requirements. The greater the financial resources required to start a business, the greater the barrier to entry. This is particularly true if the up-front investment is risky or unrecoverable, such as heavy investment in research and development or advertising. For example, the cost and risk associated with starting a new drug company would be much greater than that associated with starting a small consulting firm.

4. Switching costs. A barrier to entry is created if customers would suffer a substantial cost in switching from one supplier to another. "For example, in intravenous (IV) solutions and kits for use in hospitals, procedures for attaching solutions to patients differ among competitive products and the hardware for hanging the IV bottles are not compatible. Here switching encounters great resistance from nurses responsible for administering the treatments and requires new investments in hardware."[5]

5. Access to distribution channels. Anyone starting a new cable-TV channel would have to fight for viewer attention. Notice, for example, the extensive and expensive advertising from start-up channels to encourage viewers to ask their cable company to provide the History Channel, Romance Channel, or similar new offerings. Manufacturers of new food products have a similar problem fighting for space on the supermarket shelves.

6. Cost disadvantages independent of scale. Established firms may have cost advantages for a host of reasons, including proprietary technology, product know-how, favorable access to raw materials, favorable locations, government subsidies, experienced workforce, and so on.

7. Government policy. The government can limit or stop entry into industries by requiring licenses, by limiting access to raw materials like coal or to public land, and by a host of other regulations. Regulated industries include trucking, railroads, and freight delivery.

Competitive Force #2: Pressure from Substitute Products

Porter's second competitive force relates to the ease with which the buyer can substitute one type of product or service for another. For example, cellulose, rock wool, and Styrofoam insulation are substitutes for fiberglass insulation; high-fructose corn syrup is a substitute for sugar. Porter notes that substitutes become a particular threat when they provide not only an alternative source for the buyer, but also a significant improvement in the price/performance trade-offs. For example, electronic alarm systems had an adverse impact on the security-guard business since they provided equivalent protection at a substantial cost reduction.

Competitive Force #3: The Bargaining Power of Buyers

Third, said Porter, all buyers aren't created equal. Buyers are much more powerful when they do the following:

- *Purchase in large volumes,* which allows them to demand better unit prices. For example, think of the power Wal-Mart has in demanding concessions from a supplier, as opposed to a small mom-and-pop store.
- *Have a significant interest in savings,* because the item they are purchasing represents a significant portion of their total costs. For example, an airline is going to be much more concerned about fuel costs than, say, a retail store that has a single delivery truck.
- *Purchase standard or commodity products.* If the product the buyer is purchasing is commonly available, the buyer is likely to have many alternative suppliers so he/she can play one off against another to get the best deal. For example, the buyer who wishes to purchase a four-door sedan has much more bargaining power with an auto dealership than another buyer who is looking for a popular, custom-designed sport-utility vehicle.
- *Face few switching costs.* Switching from one brand of paper towel to another usually involves little or no switching costs. On the other hand, switching from a Windows-based computer system to an Apple Macintosh system could be quite expensive in terms of replacing hardware and software, and converting data files.
- *Earn low profits.* The tighter the buyers' profit margin, the greater the likelihood that they will seek lower prices. Rich buyers are less likely to be price sensitive.
- *Produce the product themselves.* The major automotive companies often use the threat of self-manufacture as a bargaining chip with their

suppliers. "You don't want to make the brakes at the price we demand? That's okay, we'll just manufacture them ourselves."

- *Are highly concerned about the quality of the product they are buying.* Porter cites the enormous cost associated with a blowout in an oil well. Consequently, purchasers of oil-field equipment are much more concerned about the quality and reliability of blowout-prevention devices than they are about their cost.
- *Have full information.* A customer who negotiates the price of a new car after conducting extensive research on dealer costs and trade-in values for used cars is likely to get a better deal than one who takes the salesperson's word for what constitutes the best deal.

Competitive Force #4: Bargaining Power of Suppliers

Suppliers have bargaining power similar to that of buyers. According to Porter, supplier groups are powerful if the following conditions exist.

- *They are dominated by a few companies and are more concentrated than the industry to which they sell,* so it is unlikely that buyers will gang up to demand better prices, quality, or terms.
- *They don't have to contend with other substitute products sold to the industry.* In other words, the buyer doesn't have a lot of choices.
- *The supplier is not dependent on the buyer for a substantial portion of sales.*
- *The supplier's products are important to the buyer's business.*
- *The supplier's products are unique in some way, or it would be costly or troublesome for the buyer to find a substitute product.*
- *They pose a credible threat of "forward integration"*—the supplier group could become a competitor to the buyer by using the resources/product it currently sells to the buyer to produce the item the buyer currently produces.[6]

Competitive Force #5: Rivalry among Existing Competitors

Finally, said Porter, the level of competition in an industry is shaped by the rivalry that exists among existing competitors. Porter argues that competition is more intense in an industry where the following conditions prevail.

1. There are numerous firms competing, or those firms that compete are relatively equal in size and/or resources. "When the industry is highly concentrated or dominated by one or a few firms . . . then . . . the leader or leaders can impose discipline."[7] When there are many firms competing and/or competitors are roughly equal, then the odds increase that some firm will aggressively cut prices to gain an advantage.

2. The industry is growing slowly. When the industry slows or stops growing, then the only way rivals can improve their results is to take business away from competing firms.

3. Firms have high fixed costs. Fixed costs are those associated with running a business, such as salaries of managers, holiday and vacation pay, insurance, and so on, that don't usually vary based upon the volume of product produced. When fixed costs are high relative to the total value of the product that is produced, firms are under significant pressure to produce to capacity in order to keep unit costs down.

4. Firms have high storage costs. When it costs a lot to carry finished-goods inventory, companies are tempted to cut prices to move the product.

5. Firms are under time restraints within which the product must be sold. For example, airlines can never recover the revenue lost on seats that go unsold. Therefore, they are under pressure to sell all unsold seats, even at a sharp discount.

6. The product or service is perceived as a commodity for which the buyer has many options, and the cost to the buyer of switching from brand or supplier to another is small. In such cases, buyers shop for price and service, and there is stiff competition.

7. Capacity must be added in large increments. In some industries, such as the manufacture of chlorine, vinyl chloride, and ammonium fertilizer, it is not possible or cost effective for companies to add production capacity in small increments. As a result, the industry is likely to experience sharp swings between periods of overcapacity, when firms have the ability to make more product than the market can use, and undercapacity, when there is demand for more product than companies can produce. Undercapacity leads to decisions to expand capacity. Of necessity, capacity is added in large chunks, resulting in overcapacity, which, in turn, leads to price cutting and stiffer competition.

8. Competitors have diverse strategies, origins, personalities, and so on. Porter notes that foreign companies make the competitive environment complex because they approach a business with different goals and objectives than established domestic firms. The same is true of newer, smaller, owner-operated firms that may be more aggressive and willing to take more chances.

9. The stakes are high. For example, competition between long-distance telephone providers in the United States was particularly stiff in the first few years after deregulation, because rivals assumed that they had a limited amount of time to sign up customers and grab market share. They were concerned that once people had picked a long-distance provider it would be much more difficult to get them to switch.

10. Exit barriers are high. It may be expensive from an economic, strategic, and/or emotional standpoint for a firm to give up and get out of the business. Thus, companies may keep competing even though it is not very profitable for them to do so. Porter cites the following examples of barriers:

- Expensive and specialized equipment that would be difficult to liquidate
- A labor agreement that would be expensive to break
- Emotional attachments that managers and owners have to the business
- Restrictions on layoffs and plant closings that are common in foreign countries

Core Concept #2: The Generic Competitive Strategies

"Competitive strategy," writes Porter, "is taking offensive or defensive actions to create a defendable position in an industry, to cope successfully with the five competitive forces and thereby yield a superior return on investment."[8] While Porter admits that companies have found many different ways to accomplish this end, he insists that there are only three internally consistent and successful strategies for outperforming other firms. These generic strategies are

1. Overall cost leadership
2. Differentiation
3. Focus

Generic Strategy #1: Overall Cost Leadership

In some companies, managers devote a great deal of attention to cost control. While they do not neglect quality, service, and other areas, the main theme of these companies' strategy is low cost relative to their competitors. Low cost provides these firms with a defense against the five competitive forces in several ways. Porter explains:

> Its cost position gives the firm a defense against rivalry from competitors because its lower costs mean that it can still earn returns after its competitors have competed away their profits through rivalry. A low-cost position defends the firm against powerful buyers because buyers can exert power only to drive down prices to the level of the next most efficient competitor. Low cost provides a defense against suppliers by providing more flexibility to cope with input cost increases. The factors that lead to a low-cost position usually also provide substantial entry barriers in terms of scale economies or cost advantages. Finally, a low-cost position usually places the firm in a favorable position *vis-à-vis* substitutes relative to its competitors in the industry. Thus, a low-cost position protects the firm against all five competitive forces because bargaining can only continue to erode profits until those of the next most efficient competitor are eliminated, and because the less efficient competitors will suffer first in the face of competitive pressures.[9]

Of course, cost leadership isn't right for every company. Porter maintained that companies that wish to pursue cost leadership as a strategy have to have a high market share relative to their competitors, or they need other advantages, such as favorable access to raw materials. Products have to be designed so that they are easy to manufacture, and a low-cost company would be wise to maintain a wide line of related products so that it could spread costs across the product line and reduce the burden on individual products. Also, the low-cost company has to court a large customer base. It can't go after small, niche markets. Still, once a company achieves cost leadership, it should be able to generate high profit margins; and if it reinvests those profits wisely in modernizing equipment and facilities, it should be able to sustain its low-cost position for some time. Porter cited Briggs & Stratton, Lincoln Electric, Texas Instruments, Black & Decker, and Du Pont as companies that had done just that.

As you might expect, Porter warned that there were some disadvantages and dangers associated with cost leadership. While high volume often leads to lowered costs, the savings are not automatic, and managers of low-cost companies have to be always on guard to ensure that the promised savings are actually obtained. Managers have to be alert to the need to scrap obsolete assets, invest in technology, and constantly run the business with costs in mind. Finally, there is the danger that a newcomer or old rival would imitate the leader's technology or cost-control methods and gain the upper hand. Cost leadership can be an effective response to competitive forces, but nothing is certain.

Generic Strategy #2: Differentiation

Porter suggested differentiation as an alternative to cost leadership. With differentiation, the firm worries less about costs and seeks instead to be perceived in the industry as unique in some way. Caterpillar, for example, emphasizes its product durability, service, spare parts availability, and excellent dealer network to set itself apart from its competition. Jenn-Air does the same thing by providing unique features in its ranges. Coleman does the same with camping equipment. Unlike cost leadership, where there can be only one true cost leader in an industry, there can be many differentiators in the same industry, each emphasizing an attribute that differs from those of their rivals.

Differentiation requires some trade-offs with cost. Of necessity, differentiators have to invest more heavily than cost leaders in research. They have to have better product designs. They have to use higher quality and often more expensive raw materials in their products. They have to invest more in customer service. They also have to be willing to give up some market share. While everyone might recognize the superiority of the differentiator's product and services, many customers are not able or willing to pay for them. A Mercedes, for example, wouldn't be right for everyone.

Still, Porter maintained, differentiation provides a viable strategy. Brand loyalty provides some defense against rivals. The differentiator's uniqueness provides some barrier to entry by newcomers. Its higher profit margins provides it with some protection against suppliers since it has the funds to shop for alternatives. There are few substitutes for what the differentiator offers and, consequently, customers have fewer options and less bargaining power.

On the downside, differentiation carries certain risks just as cost leadership does. If the difference between prices charged by low-cost competitors and the differentiator become too great, customers might abandon the differentiator for a lower-cost, less-differentiated rival. The buyer might decide to sacrifice some of the features, service, and uniqueness the differentiator offers in order to obtain the cost savings. Second, what differentiates a company one day might not do so the next. Buyers' taste could change. The unique feature the differentiator offers could go out of style. Finally, lower-cost rivals might be able to imitate the differentiator sufficiently to lure away customers. For example, Harley-Davidson, a clear brand-name/image differentiator in large motorcycles, might be vulnerable to Kawasaki or other Japanese motorcycle producers that build lower-cost look-alikes.

Generic Strategy #3: Focus

Porter's final generic strategy is focus. In this case a company goes after a particular buyer, product line, or geographic market. "Although the low cost and differentiation strategies are aimed at achieving their objectives industry wide, the entire focus strategy is built around serving a particular target very well."[10] For example, Porter Paint focuses on serving the professional painter and leaves the consumer market to other paint companies. The key difference between focus and the other two strategies is that a company adopting a focus strategy consciously decides to compete only in a narrow segment of the market. Instead of trying to attract all buyers by offering either low-cost or unique features and services, the focused company seeks to serve only a particular type of buyer. In serving that narrow market, a focused company may seek cost leadership or differentiation with the same advantages and disadvantages as the overall cost leaders and differentiators.

The Danger of Being Stuck in the Middle

Ultimately then, a company has three strategic options—cost leadership, differentiation, or focus. The latter is divided into two suboptions—cost focus and differentiation focus (see Exhibit 5.2). According to Porter, these are three eminently viable approaches to dealing with the competitive forces, and he cautioned all managers that they had better adopt only one of them.[11] Fail-

EXHIBIT 5.2. **Michael Porter's Generic Strategies**

ing to do so would leave them and their companies "stuck in the middle" with no defensible strategy. Such a firm would lack "the market share, capital investment and resolve to play the low-cost game, the industry-wide differentiation necessary to obviate the need for a low-cost position, or the focus to create differentiation or a low-cost position in a more limited sphere."[12] Such a firm would lose high-volume customers who demand low prices and would lose high-margin customers who demand unique features and service. The firm that is stuck in the middle would have low profits, a blurred corporate culture, conflicting organizational arrangements, a poor motivational system, and so on. No, argued Porter, rather than risk such dire circumstances, managers would be well advised to choose one of the three strategies. But how? Enter Porter's third and final core concept—the value chain.

Core Concept #3: The Value Chain

"Competitive advantage cannot be understood by looking at a firm as a whole," writes Porter.[13] Real advantages in costs and differentiation must be found in the chain of activities that a firm performs to deliver value to its customers. And it is to the value chain that Porter suggests you turn to conduct detailed strategic analysis and arrive at your strategy choice.

Porter identifies five primary and four secondary activities that constitute the value chain for every firm (see Exhibit 5.3). The five primary activities are:

1. Inbound logistics. Activities associated with receiving, storing, and disseminating inputs to the product, such as material handling, warehousing, inventory control, vehicle scheduling, and return to suppliers.

2. Operations. Activities associated with transforming inputs into the final product, such as machining, packaging, assembly, equipment maintenance, testing, printing, and facility operations.

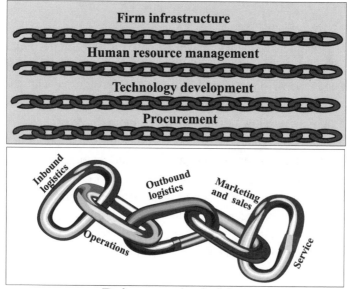

EXHIBIT 5.3. **Michael Porter's Generic Value Chain**

Source: Michael E. Porter, **Competitive Advantage: Creating and Sustaining Superior Performance** (New York: Free Press, 1985), p. 87, Fig. 2–2.

3. Outbound logistics. Activities associated with collecting, storing, and physically distributing the product to buyers, such as finished-goods warehousing, material handling, delivery-vehicle operation, order processing, and scheduling.

4. Marketing and sales. Activities associated with providing a means by which buyers can purchase the product and inducing them to do so, such as advertising, promotion, selling, quoting, channel selection, channel relations, and pricing.

5. Service. Activities associated with providing service to enhance or maintain the value of the product, such as installation, repair, training, parts supply, and product adjustment.[14]

The four secondary or support activities are:

1. Procurement. Activities related to purchasing raw materials, supplies, and other consumable items, in addition to machinery, laboratory equipment, office equipment, and buildings.

2. Technology development. Activities related to improving the product and/or the process, including research and development, product design, media research, process design, design of service procedures, and so on.

3. Human resource management. Activities related to recruitment, hiring, training, developing, and compensating personnel.

4. Firm infrastructure. Activities such as general management, planning, finance, accounting, government affairs, quality management, and so on.[15]

Of course, argued Porter, these are just the activities in the generic value chain. Each generic category could and should be broken down into discrete activities unique to a particular company. For example, the primary activity of marketing and sales could be broken down into marketing management, advertising, sales-force administration, sales-force operations, technical literature preparation, and promotion. And these discrete activities could be broken down even further. The purpose of all of this "disaggregation," as Porter calls it, is to help companies select one of the three generic strategies and to isolate potential areas of competitive advantage a company might have in coping with the five competitive forces that are unique to industries and companies. For example, writes Porter,

> each of the categories may be vital to a competitive advantage depending on the industry. For a distributor, inbound and outbound logistics are the most crucial. . . . For a bank engaged in corporate lending, marketing and sales are a key to competitive advantage through the effectiveness of the calling officers and the way in which loans are packaged and priced. For a high speed copier manufacturer, service represents a key source of competitive advantage. . . . In chocolate manufacturing and electric utilities . . . procurement of cocoa beans and fuel respectively is by far the most important determinant of cost position [and, therefore strategy]. . . . In steel . . . a firm's process technology [development] is the single greatest factor in competitive advantage.[16]

In short, the sources of sustainable competitive advantage for any company are all there, buried in its value chain. All managers have to do is the analysis—step one, step two, step three—draw the charts and analyze the cost figures for their own companies, then do the same for their competitors. In the end, a perfect strategy will emerge. Well, maybe—or maybe not.

CRASH GOES PORTER

The purpose of Porter's detailed analysis was to take the guesswork out of the future and bring order to the world of business. The basic underpinnings of the complicated theory were simple. If every company planned diligently, following Porter's schema, then competition would be stable, with every cost leader, differentiator, and focused firm in its place. No one would get a nasty surprise. Turbulence would disappear from the competitive landscape. Of course, as you might expect, it didn't work.

The main reason Porter's ideas didn't work is that some companies simply refused to play by his ivy-covered rules. Throughout the 1980s, while Porter continued to refine his ideas, many Japanese companies and some American upstarts like Wal-Mart did what Porter had defined as impossible. They were low cost and differentiated at the same time. They got stuck in Porter's middle; but they not only survived, they prospered. It became obvious to corporate America that Porter's theory no longer matched reality. And what about all of the analysis that Porter and his strategic planning devotees seemed to love? Some people were beginning to question how beneficial strategic plans, and even strategic planners, were anyway. Henry Mintzberg, Bronfman Professor of Management at McGill University and two-time winner of the McKinsey Award for the best *Harvard Business Review* article, summarized the criticism of strategic planning in his 1994 obituary for the practice—"The Rise and Fall of Strategic Planning."

The problem, wrote Mintzberg, is that strategic planning is not the same as strategic thinking.[17] In fact, strategic planning sometimes gets in the way of strategic thinking. "Planning," said Mintzberg, "has always been about *analysis*—about breaking down a goal or set of intentions into steps, formalizing those steps so that they can be implemented almost automatically, and articulating the anticipated consequences or results of each step. . . . Strategic thinking, in contrast, is about *synthesis*. It involves intuition and creativity. The outcome of strategic thinking is an integrated perspective of the enterprise, a not-too-precisely articulated vision of direction."[18]

The fallacies of strategic planning, wrote Mintzberg, were threefold. First, strategic planners assumed that the world would hold still during the many months it took them to develop their plan and then stay on the course the plan predicted while it was being implemented. Wrong, said Mintzberg, the world is far from being so accommodating.

Second, the planners assumed that they could be detached and deal with the hard data without ever having to get involved in the hands-on, dirty business of implementation. Thinkers and doers could, and should, be separate. Executives never had to leave their executive suites. Planners could stay comfortably in their offices. The problem with all the hard data the planners relied upon was that the data often took a long time to harden and thus was often out of date by the time the planners got it. Plus, the hard data often missed, if not the point, at least the important nuances. Some of the best data weren't hard at all, but the soft stuff of gossip and hearsay. Anyway, novel strategies often were more the result of serendipitous events than careful analysis. "A salesperson convinces a different kind of customer to try a product. Other sales people follow up with their customers, and the next thing management knows, its products have penetrated a new market."[19]

Finally, said Mintzberg, strategic planning made the fallacious assumption that strategy making should and could be formalized. Planners assumed that their plan should follow a rational and orderly sequence from analysis to eventual action. Mintzberg observed that they missed the point that "strategy making as a learning process can proceed in the other direction too. We think in order to act, to be sure, but we also act in order to think. We try things, and those experiments that work converge gradually into viable patterns that become strategies. . . . Formal procedures will never be able to forecast discontinuities, inform detached managers, or create novel strategies."[20]

Of course, by the time Mintzberg was writing his obituary, strategic planning had already gone bust. Corporate strategy departments in many companies had been shuttered. The thinkers had been pushed aside and the doers had taken over.

By the early 1990s, American CEOs had shelved strategy and become fascinated with downsizing, restructuring, and reengineering. The short-term, quick fix was in. If you couldn't plan your way to competitive nirvana, they reasoned, maybe you could shrink yourself there. Of course, shrinking didn't work either. Most companies that downsized found they weren't that much better off after their crash diet than before. One round of downsizing just led to another and another. Nothing really improved.

By mid-decade, downsizing and reengineering were also on the wane. Growth was once again being discussed. But how could a company grow? What America needed was fresh new ideas about—you guessed it—strategy. And again, as you might expect, there were plenty of Porter wanna-be's with advice. Let's start with two of the most influential—Gary P. Hamel and C. K. Prahalad.

HAMEL AND PRAHALAD GO COMPETING FOR THE FUTURE

Gary Hamel is a professor of strategic and international management at the London Business School. C. K. Prahalad is a professor of business administration, corporate strategy, and international business at the University of Michigan Business School. Hamel and Prahalad first met in 1977 at Michigan, where Hamel was a doctoral student in international business and Prahalad was an associate professor of strategy. They immediately got into an intellectual fencing match in which each, according to their accounts, was determined to administer the coup de grace.[21] Neither succeeded. Instead, they created a partnership. By the mid-1980s, Hamel and Prahalad were publishing articles together. By the late 1980s, they were slowly moving up the guru food chain with a series of most-requested, McKinsey Award-winning *Harvard Business Review* articles.[22] In September 1994 they published their masterwork—*Competing for the Future.* Helped along by a $75,000 marketing blitz from their publisher, serialization in *Fortune,* and a national publicity tour, *Competing for the Future* became a best-seller and launched Hamel and Prahalad into the rarefied Porter-level ranks of guru stardom.

Hamel and Prahalad begin their book with questions others had already raised. Why didn't traditional strategic theory square with reality? Why in the 1980s had so many of America's strategy-savvy behemoths gotten beaten by upstart, resource-poor challengers, mostly from Japan? "What theory could explain how Canon managed to make such a huge dent in Xerox's market share? How could Honda manage to outgun . . . Detroit? And what about Sony versus RCA?"[23] It wasn't just that the challengers had some kind of marginal advantage in operating efficiency or labor costs. No, argued Hamel and Prahalad, there was something much more.

Hamel and Prahalad argued that the real difference was that "the challengers had succeeded in creating entirely new forms of competitive advantage and in dramatically rewriting the rules of engagement."[24] Managers of these upstart challengers were more foresighted than traditional managers. They imagined products, services, and even entire industries that didn't exist and then created them. These managers weren't just benchmarking and analyzing the competition in order to be as good as or better than the best in the marketplace. They were creating a new marketplace in which they could dominate the competition because it was a marketplace of their own design. There were clear strategic lessons to be learned from these upstarts, said our gurus.

The Battle for Intellectual Leadership

The struggle for the future begins not with a battle over market share, said Hamel and Prahalad, but with a battle for intellectual leadership. The trick, they explained, was to develop foresight about the future and, based upon that foresight, to answer the following three critical questions.

- What new types of customer benefits should we seek to provide in 5, 10, or 15 years?
- What new competencies—bundles of skills and technologies—will we need to build or acquire to offer those benefits to customers?
- How will we need to reconfigure our customer interface over the next several years?[25]

They suggest that Motorola is a good example of a company with foresight.[26]

Motorola dreams of a world in which telephone numbers will be assigned to people, rather than places; where small hand-held devices will allow people to stay in touch no matter where they are; and where the new communicators can deliver video images and data as well as voice signals.[27]

And the company uses that foresight to answer the three critical questions.

Motorola knows that it will have to strengthen its competencies in digital compression, flat screen displays, and battery technology. Motorola also knows that to capture a significant share of a burgeoning consumer market, it will have to substantially increase the familiarity of its brand with customers around the world.[28]

How could companies develop foresight such as Motorola did? There are two essentials, our gurus instructed. First, managers have to understand and develop their company's unique core competencies. Second, managers have to focus on the underlying functionalities of their current products and services, and not just on the products and services themselves.

Focusing on Core Competencies

Instead of thinking of the company as a collection of business units, argued Hamel and Prahalad, managers must begin to think of it as a collection of core competencies, that is, skills and technologies that enable the company to provide benefits to customers. Our two gurus observe that "many times what prevents companies from imagining the future and discovering new competitive space is not the unknowability of the future, but the fact that managers tend to look at the future through the narrow aperture of existing served markets."[29] In short, they argue, it makes a significant difference:

- Whether managers at Motorola view their company as a manufacturer of cell phones, mobile radios, and pagers, or a company with unique competencies in digital compression, flat-screen displays, and battery technology;
- Whether managers at Canon view their company as a manufacturer of cameras, copiers, fax machines, and printers, or a company with unique competencies in fine optics, precision mechanics, electronics, and fine chemicals;
- Whether managers at Honda view their company as a manufacturer of motorcycles or a company with unique competencies in engines and power trains.

The first view expressed in each of these examples is confining and leads to future products and services very much like those produced in the past. For example, the view that Honda makes motorcycles leads it to focus on making more and better motorcycles.

The second view is liberating and leads to a wide range of future products and services. For example, the view that Honda is a world leader in engines and power trains leads the company to develop, manufacture, and market cars, lawn mowers, garden tractors, marine engines, and generators in addition to motorcycles.

"When one conceives of a company as a portfolio of competencies," write Hamel and Prahalad, "a whole new range of potential opportunities typically opens up."[30] (See Exhibit 5.4 for other examples of core competencies.)

Underlying Functionality

Second, in order for managers to see the future, Hamel and Prahalad suggest that instead of thinking of existing products and services, they must begin thinking of their underlying functionalities. Instead of asking, "What is our product or service?" managers should ask "What benefits do existing products and services deliver to customers?" Managers would then discover whole new possibilities for their business. For example, if blackboard manufacturers asked themselves, "What is the functionality of the blackboard?" they might have answered, "To share information, in real time,

EXHIBIT 5.4. **Core Competencies**

Definition: A core competency is a bundle of skills and technologies that enables a company to provide a particular benefit to customers.

Company	Competency
Sony	Miniaturization
Federal Express	Logistics management; package routing and delivery
Wal-Mart	Logistics management
Honda	Engines and power trains
Hewlett-Packard	Measurement, computing, and communications
3M	Adhesives, substrates, and advanced materials
EDS	Systems integration
Motorola	Wireless communication, digital compression, flat-screen displays, and battery technology; also, fast cycle-time production
Merck	Drug discovery
Nike	Logistics, quality design, product development, athlete endorsement, distribution, and merchandising
Marriott	Catering and facilities management

Source: Gary Hamel and C. K. Prahalad, *Competing For the Future* (Boston: Harvard Business School Press, 1994), pp. 197–220.

among a small group." That answer might have led them to realize that blackboards cannot be put through a copying machine, and that answer, in turn, might have prompted them to reconceive the blackboard as an electronic board with built-in scanner and copier.[31]

By thinking in terms of their product's functionality, rather than just in terms of the product itself, blackboard manufacturers might have created the electronic whiteboard, instead of allowing the Japanese firm Oki to develop the idea and redefine the industry.

Consulting the Revolutionaries

Such breakthrough thinking wouldn't be easy, said Hamel and Prahalad. Since most executives had developed a kind of myopia about their companies, products, services, and markets, curing or preventing that myopia would require:

- A childlike innocence about what could and should be
- Deep and boundless curiosity
- A willingness to speculate about issues in which one is not an expert
- Eclecticism
- An inherent contrariness
- Being customer led
- Having genuine empathy with human needs[32]

It wasn't a task for which most tradition-bound senior executives were well suited. In fact, argued Hamel, the people at the top had "the least diversity of experience, the largest investment in the past, and the greatest reverence for industrial dogma."[33] They were the last ones likely to develop breakthrough ideas. If you truly wanted innovative thinking about things like core competencies and product/service functionality, he said, you had to reach out to people who were not usually involved in the strategy process.

In particular, said Hamel, you should reach out to three constituencies. First, you should seek the input of young people because they have the biggest stake in the future. You should get your Generation-X employees exchanging ideas with your gray-haired executive committee. Second, Hamel suggested that you reach out to people at the geographic periphery of the organization, since "the capacity for strategic innovation increases proportionately with each mile you move away from headquarters."[34] It was at the geographic periphery that you were most likely to find people who were most exposed to ideas and developments that do not conform to the company's orthodoxies and who were most creative because they had the fewest resources. Finally, Hamel suggested that you should seek to involve as many newcomers to the organization as possible. These people were important because they had "not yet been co-opted by an industry's dogma."[35]

Developing the Strategic Architecture

The result of all of this reaching out to the revolutionaries is consensus, or at least near consensus, about the core competencies you need, the functionality of products and services you can offer, and how you intend to go about delivering value to customers. Of course, you will want to capture all of that information somewhere. Since strategic planning is out of vogue, you can't call this document a strategic plan. Not to worry. Hamel and Prahalad invented a new term. They suggested that you call the document your "strategic architecture."

"Strategic architecture is basically a high-level blueprint of the deployment of new functionalities, the acquisition of new competencies or the migration of existing competencies, and the reconfiguration of the interface with customers," they write.[36] It is equivalent to an architectural blueprint that is sufficiently detailed to show the load-bearing structures, but not the location of every electrical outlet. However, the strategic architecture—or *plan* if you must use that term—is detailed enough to provide some guidance on what your company should be doing right now to prepare itself for the future. Hamel and Prahalad described a strategic architecture this way:

> A strategic architecture . . . shows the organization what competencies it must begin building *right now,* what new customer groups it must begin to understand *right now,* what new channels it should be exploring *right now,* what new development priorities it should be pursuing *right now* to intercept the future. Strategic architecture is a broad *opportunity approach* plan. The question addressed by a strategic architecture is not what we must do to maximize our revenues or share in an existing product market, but what must we do today, in terms of competence acquisition, to prepare ourselves to capture a significant share of the future revenues in an emerging opportunity arena.[37]

Confused? Maybe an example of a strategic architecture will help. Hamel and Prahalad cite as their favorite the strategic architecture developed by the Japanese electronics company NEC in the early 1970s.

> Initially a supplier of telecommunications equipment . . . NEC executives . . . began to sense, in the late 1960s and early 1970s, that the communications industry and computer industry were converging in some important ways. Telecommunications, which had always been a "systems" business (telephones are tied together across the globe), was also becoming a "digital" business (telephone switches were becoming more and more like mainframe computers, based on semiconductors and complex systems software). At the same time the computer business, which had always been dig-

ital, was becoming a complex systems business (companies wanted computers located in offices and factories around the world to be linked together in seamless data networks).

Starting with an understanding of these two industry discontinuities—
systemization and digitalization—NEC built a strategic architecture that
identified the competencies it would need to be able to exploit the opportunities that would emerge at the juncture of the computing and communications industries. . . . NEC's strategic architecture identified three interrelated streams of technological and market evolution. Computing would
evolve from large mainframes to distributed processing (what is now called
"client-server"), components would evolve from simple integrated circuits
(ICs) to ultra large-scale ICs, and communications would evolve from mechanical cross-bar switching to complex digital systems. As this evolution
took place, so NEC's thinking went, the computing, communications, and
components businesses would begin to overlap in important ways (e.g., private corporate networks would need to handle voice, data, and image traffic simultaneously). NEC's ambition was to be a leader in "C&C," computing
and communications. . . .

Consistent with its strategic architecture, NEC worked unceasingly to
strengthen its position in components (semiconductors) and central
processors. Using collaborative arrangements to multiply internal resources, NEC was able to accumulate the necessary core competencies
while investing less in R&D . . . than most of its competitors. . . .

Initially just a telecommunications equipment provider . . . by 1992 NEC
was a global electronics powerhouse.[38]

HAMEL AND PRAHALAD STUMBLE

It all sounded good, or at least new—foresight, functionality, intellectual
leadership, core competency, strategic architecture. Hamel and Prahalad
talked about "standing on the verge of a revolution," "competing to shape the
future," "building gateways to new opportunities," and so on. They found a
willing and enthusiastic audience. They also found critics and cynics.

For example, while John Micklethwait, the business editor of *The Economist,* and Adrian Wooldridge, its management correspondent, praise
Hamel and Prahalad for a book that was "probably as close to required

reading as any management book in the 1990s," they still find much to question in our esteemed gurus' ideas. For example, Micklethwait and Wooldridge write in their 1996 book *Witch Doctors* that being first to reach the future may not be all Hamel and Prahalad crack it up to be. "Visionary companies may earn the applause of management theorists, but it is the plodders who come after them who make the real money. Why not let the leaders make all the investment and take all the risks and then simply copy or buy their product, just as Bill Gates did?"[39] Being first doesn't necessarily mean that you win. Chux, for example, invented disposal diapers and then went defunct while Procter & Gamble cleaned up with Pampers. And it was the American firm Ampex that invented video recorders, not the Japanese who made all the money on them.

What about this idea of visions and strategic architectures? Well, said Micklethwait and Wooldridge, you might have a good vision, but you still had to have the business acumen, luck, or whatever to realize it. After all, hadn't Apple had the vision of the "friendly computer" only to see the vision and the market stolen by Microsoft? And what about Roger Smith's vision of GM as the "car company of the twenty-first century"? Smith's "strategic architecture" led his company from a 46% to 35% market share.

Finally, there was Hamel and Prahalad's notion of core competencies. It sounded good, but, as Jay Stuller put it in a 1992 article in *Across the Board,* saying you should focus on your core competencies was somewhat akin to telling Coca-Cola executives that they should keep selling Coke and not branch out into lawn-care services or other businesses they don't know anything about.[40] So what if you did understand your core competencies? Was that enough to guarantee your success? At least that's what Michael Treacy and Fred Wiersema, two would-be gurus from the consulting firm CSC Index, wondered. Core competence was only part of the story, they said. Sure, Honda had been able to leverage its core competence in small engines to enter a wide variety of businesses. But, they noted, Briggs & Stratton had the same core competence but hadn't been as successful. And what about 3M? Its core competence in nonwoven technology still had not been enough to make it a product leader in tapes and soap pads.[41] Finally, wrote Treacy and Wiersema, "suggesting that Wal-Mart's success stems solely from its logistics competency, or that Intel's success stems solely from its microprocessor design competency, pushes the concept of core competencies too far."[42]

Business success was more multifaceted than Hamel and Prahalad implied. Core competencies were part of the model—but just part of it. They weren't sufficient by themselves. Companies wishing to sail to the head of their markets had to weigh anchor for a better mooring than Hamel and Prahalad had to offer. That better mooring, of course, was the one offered by Treacy and Wiersema. Just a year after Hamel and Prahalad published their esteemed tome, Treacy and Wiersema were producing a slimmer treatise on the art of dominating markets and securing unassailable competitive advantage. In a storm of controversy, they were riding to guru stardom. "Move over Michael Porter!" exclaimed Philip Kotler, distinguished professor of international marketing at Northwestern University, "Treacy and Wiersema have convinced me."[43] Of course they had. Treacy and Wiersema were out to convince everybody, and, as suggested by *Business Week,* they might be willing to go to extraordinary lengths to do so.

TREACY AND WIERSEMA'S DISCIPLINES

Treacy and Wiersema's *The Discipline of Market Leaders* was published in January 1995 with a 120,000-copy first printing. By February the book had made it to number 11 on the *USA Today* best-seller list and was already in its second printing. It was an exceptionally strong start for a business book from first-time authors. Of course, Treacy and Wiersema did have some advantages. Their 1993 article in *Harvard Business Review,* "Customer Intimacy and Other Value Disciplines," had been well received; perhaps more importantly, the authors were closely associated with CSC Index, the consulting firm that had spawned the reengineering craze of the early 1990s. Then, of course, there was one other thing that some felt accounted for the brisk sales of their book.

In August 1995, *Business Week* reported the following in a story entitled "Did Dirty Tricks Create a Best-Seller?"

> Interviews with more than two-dozen bookstores across the nation, as well as over 100 interviews with book industry representatives, indicate that CSC Index and the authors [Treacy and Wiersema] spent at least $250,000 buying more than 10,000 copies of *Discipline.* In addition, CSC funneled bulk purchases by corporate clients of another 30,000 to 40,000 copies through bookstores . . . bookstore sources who talked to Treacy say the purchases were systematically made in relatively small numbers at key locations. They

say the plan, which was based on extensive research by Treacy into how books hit the best-seller lists, was to create the appearance of wide-spread demand for the book.[44]

So, was *Business Week* right? Did Treacy, Wiersema, and CSC Index conspire to fix the best-seller list? The authors, their publisher, and the consulting firm all denied doing anything wrong. Corporate sales were spread out across the U.S. to give retailers a cut of corporate sales, said the publisher. While admitting that they aggressively and energetically marketed the book, Treacy denied doing anything unethical. The numerous multicopy orders at bookstores around the country were simply made to provide books for speaking engagements and to respond to client requests for copies. Anyway, added Treacy, CSC purchased fewer than 10,000 copies and all the purchases were for legitimate reasons. The *New York Times* insisted that its list of bestsellers was valid. "We were on to the bulk purchases of *Discipline* for months," said Michael Kagay, news surveys editor. "We are confident that our list has not been manipulated."[45] *Business Week* stuck by its story and later announced it was building safeguards into its monthly best-seller list to prevent what happened or did not happen, depending upon whom you believed, from ever happening again. The *New York Times* and other list publishers soon made similar adjustments. As for Treacy and Wiersema, they became celebrities on the lecture circuit, commanding speaking fees estimated at somewhere between $20,000 and $30,000 per appearance. *The Discipline of Market Leaders* continued to ride the best-seller list, appearing in the number 11 slot on *Business Week's* revised and "safeguarded" list of top-selling business books for 1996. So what did Treacy and Wiersema have to say that commanded such a following? Not a lot, as it turned out.

The Value Disciplines

Treacy and Wiersema's advice was as succinct as their slim 208-page book. They presented three *value disciplines,* or ways of delivering customer value—operational excellence, product leadership, and customer intimacy. Companies that wanted to dominate their markets had to choose one, and only one, of these disciplines to master. Exhibit 5.5 provides a quick summary of how Treacy and Wiersema describe each value discipline, exam-

EXHIBIT 5.5. **Treacy and Wiersema's Value Disciplines**

Value Discipline #1: Operational Excellence
Description
"Operationally excellent companies deliver a combination of quality, price, and ease of purchase that no one else in their market can match. They are not product or service innovators, nor do they cultivate one-to-one relationships with their customers. They execute extraordinarily well, and their proposition to customers is guaranteed low price and/or hassle-free service."[1]

Examples of Operationally Excellent Companies
- AT&T Universal Card
- Charles Schwab
- Dell Computer
- FedEx
- GE
- Hertz
- McDonald's
- Saturn Corporation
- Southwest Airlines
- Wal-Mart

Chief Characteristics of Companies That Pursue Operational Excellence
- *Focus on efficiency of effort and coordination.* Provide low cost, no-frills products and/or services.
- *Optimize and streamline business processes.* Use standard and efficient operating procedures. Even physical assets are standardized—Wal-Mart's stores all look alike, and Southwest's planes are all the same.
- *Run like the Marine Corps.* Everyone is expected to know the rule book and exactly what he or she is supposed to do. People are expected to fit in. Free spirits are not welcomed. Team play is highly rewarded.
- *Develop close and seamless relationships with suppliers.* For example, Wal-Mart implemented a continuous-replenishment process so that suppliers could assume the responsibility for managing inventories of their products in Wal-Mart stores. The system lowers costs for both Wal-Mart and its suppliers.
- *Develop and maintain integrated, reliable, and high-speed information systems and other technology to achieve better operational efficiency and control.* For example, Hertz, FedEx, and UPS employees all use sophisticated handheld computers that allow them to enter and extract critical information.
- *Abhor waste and reward efficiency.*
- *Deliver standardized, hassle-free, no-frills, basic service.* These companies avoid variety because variety hurts efficiency. For example, Southwest Airlines does not provide food, advance check-in, or baggage handling. In order to get low prices and reliable service, customers adapt their behavior to the efficient standard established by the company.
- *Manage the business in order to secure large, consistent volume throughout the day, week, and/or year.* Peaks and valleys in demand for a product or service are seen as significant operational problems that must be corrected.

EXHIBIT 5.5. (Continued)

Key to Success—Formula

According to Treacy and Wiersema, "A canny weave of unparalleled know-how, technology application, and tight management—that's what makes a leader in operational excellence. The secret of succeeding with this value discipline is summed up in a single word: formula."[2]

Value Discipline #2: Product Leadership

Description

"A company pursuing product leadership continually pushes its products into the realm of the unknown, the untried, or the highly desirable. Its practitioners concentrate on offering customers products or services that expand existing performance boundaries. A product leader's proposition to customers is best product, period."[3]

Examples of Product Leadership Companies

- 3M
- Disney
- Harley-Davidson
- Hewlett-Packard
- Intel
- Johnson & Johnson
- Mercedes-Benz

- Microsoft
- Motorola
- Nike
- Reebok
- Revlon
- Sony
- Swatch

Chief Characteristics of Companies That Pursue Product Leadership

- *Focus on invention, product development, and market exploitation.*
- *Have a loose, ad hoc, and entrepreneurial structure.* Break people up into cross-functional teams or clusters.
- *Are very creative and quick to commercialize ideas.* These companies are very adept at launching new products with the maximum fanfare. Disney, for example, is very good at creating customer excitement in advance of releasing a new movie.
- *Organize work in stages, with clearly defined goals for each stage and tight deadlines.*
- *Engineer their business processes for speed.* Constantly seek to shorten cycle-times.
- *Are known for rapid decision making.*
- *Reward experimenters and out-of-the-box thinkers.*
- *Generate lots of ideas for new products but then find ways to narrow the portfolio of projects to those most likely to hit big.*

Key to Success—Tension

Treacy and Wiersema explain tension this way:

> While a [product leadership] company's left hand prolongs product life with upgrades, en-
> hancements, and other value-adding features, the right hand builds the next generation.

Does this create tension within product leadership companies? You bet! But it's the tension that makes these companies vibrant. It keeps them busy managing the dynamic balance between the defense of existing products and the introduction of new ones; between un- bounded creativity and the concerns of fiscal practicality; between getting the product right and getting it to market; between betting on a few big ideas and nurturing a broader range of maybes. It's this tension that defines product leadership companies.[4]

Value Discipline #3: Customer Intimacy

Description

"A company that delivers value via customer intimacy builds bonds with customers like those between good neighbors. Customer-intimate companies don't deliver what the market wants, but what a specific customer wants. The customer-intimate company makes a business of knowing the people it sells to and the products and services they need. It continually tailors its products and services, and does so at reasonable prices. Its proposition is: 'We take care of you and all your needs,' or 'We get you the best total solution.' The customer-intimate com- pany's greatest asset is, not surprisingly, its customers' loyalty."[5]

Examples of Customer Intimate Companies

- Airborne Express
- Baxter International
- Four Seasons Hotel
- Home Depot
- IBM
- Johnson Controls
- Nordstrom

Chief Characteristics of Companies That Pursue Customer Intimacy

- *Cultivate long-term relationships with customers.* The initial transactions a customer-intimate company has with a new customer may not be profitable by themselves. Rather, they are seen as an investment in establishing a long-term relationship that will be profitable over time.

- *Develop deep knowledge and insights into customers' underlying processes.* Build and maintain systems with detailed information about their customers.

- *Consistently give customers more than they expect.*

- *Focus on customer retention and the lifetime value of the individual customer.* The worst failure in a customer-intimate company is to lose a customer.

- *Customize products and services for customers.* Airborne Express, for example, offers early delivery, special handling, and same-day service.

- *Usually do not sell leading-edge products.* Instead, customer-intimate companies provide their customers with solid, tested products that are tailored to fit the client's specific needs.

- *Work with customers to solve their problems and then manage the implementation of the solu- tion.* Johnson Controls, for example, provides energy-use experts to work with building- management clients to change building designs. The customer-intimate company may not have all of the expertise required to meet the client's needs, but it knows where to locate it and how to coordinate the delivery of solutions.

EXHIBIT 5.5. (Continued)

- *Delegates much decision making to employees who are close to customers.* Their motto is, Do whatever it takes to please the customer.

Key to Success—Solution

Treacy and Wiersema note that, "all in all, the bright glow cast by customer-intimate companies, what draws to them the most loyal customers, is generated by a canny weave of strategies, superior personnel with unparalleled know-how, application of the newest and finest techniques to the customer's vital processes, and an extended network of product and service capabilities. That glow signals one thing: solution. . . . In the customer-intimate company, solution is the foundation of an aggressive and highly successful enterprise."[6]

---

1. Michael Treacy and Fred Wiersema, *The Discipline of Market Leaders* (Reading, Mass.: Addison Wesley, 1995), p. 31.

2. *Ibid.*, p. 60.

3. *Ibid.*, p. 35.

4. *Ibid.*, pp. 95–96.

5. *Ibid.*, p. 38.

6. *Ibid.*, p. 137.

---

ples of companies that practice each discipline, the distinguishing characteristics of these companies, and the key to their success.

Choosing a Value Discipline

Echoing Michael Porter's warning about choosing a strategy (low-cost, differentiated, or focus), Treacy and Wiersema predict dire consequences for those companies that do not choose a value discipline. "Choosing a discipline is the choice of winners," they write. "Not choosing means ending up in a muddle. It means hybrid operating models that are neither here nor there, and that consequently cause confusion, tension, and loss of energy. It means steering a rudderless ship, with no clear way to resolve conflicts or set priorities. Not choosing means setting yourself up to be overtaken by another player that is committed to unmatched value and focused on how to achieve it. Not choosing means letting circumstances control your own destiny."[46] Choosing a value discipline is critical because you are not only choosing a "path to greatness," but also purposefully deemphasizing other possible paths. You should, therefore, choose with care, and that requires three rounds of careful deliberations by the senior management team.

Round #1: Understanding the Status Quo

In this round, the senior management team must discover where the firm currently stands and why it is there by reaching consensus on the following five questions.

- What are the dimensions of value that customers care about?
- For each dimension of value, what proportion of customers focus on it as their primary or dominant decision criterion?
- Which competitors provide the best value in each of these value dimensions?
- How do we measure up against our competition on each dimension of value?
- Why do we fall short of the value leaders in each dimension of value?[47]

Round #2: Realistic Options

In this round, the senior management team switches from discussing the present to discussing the options the company has for a value discipline in the future. The executives identify several options—operational excellence, product leadership, customer intimacy—and some rough ideas concerning the changes that would be required.

Round #3: Detailed Designs and Hard Choices

Finally, the executive team turns over the analysis to tiger teams—small groups of high performers—to flesh out the implications of going with each of the options identified by the senior management. Each tiger team takes one option and thoughtfully answers the following seven questions.

- What does the required operating model look like, that is, what are the design specifications for the core processes, management systems, structure, and other elements of the model?
- How will the model produce superior value?
- What levels of threshold value will the market require in the other dimensions? How will these be attained?
- How large will the potential and captured market be for this value proposition?
- What is the business case—including costs, benefits, and risks—for pursuing this option?

- What are the critical success factors that can make or break this solution?
- How will the company make the transition from its current state to this new operating model over a two- to three-year period?[48]

The tiger teams then submit their reports to the executive committee that makes the hard choice. Treacy and Wiersema don't expect that choice to be easy:

> Executive leadership ultimately comes down to making the hard choice of value discipline—what the company will stand for in its market and how it will operate to back up its promise. The decision to select a value discipline commits a company to a path that it will remain on for years, if not decades. . . .
>
> This third phase of activity . . . challenges [the executive team] to show unprecedented courage. Does the executive team have confidence in its own analysis and the ability to commit to a particular course of action?
>
> Courage in the face of doubt is essential because selecting a value discipline is not just a choice about what to do, it is a choice about what not to do—about what and who to leave behind on the journey toward market leadership. These are painful decisions. . . . But failing to focus, failing to choose one discipline and stick to it, is exactly what leads firms . . . to a state of mediocrity. The courageous will make the decisions to get back on track. The cowardly, shrinking from the task at hand, will forever live with the memories of derailment, of painful journeys never completed.[49]

CRASH GO TREACY AND WIERSEMA

As we said, *The Discipline of Market Leaders* sold well in spite of the miniscandal. Still, questions remained. Were Treacy and Wiersema's disciplines truly breakthrough thinking about strategy or just slick buttered popcorn for the mind? One had to wonder whether their value disciplines were, in reality, all that different from Porter's long discredited generic strategies, and if they were, whether the subtle differences made them any less vulnerable to imitation or obsolescence.

Anyway, Treacy and Wiersema still regarded competition in the old, traditional, head-to-head, I-win-and-you-lose sense. As we reached mid-decade, some of our newer strategy gurus were questioning that time-honored approach. Maybe competing wasn't such a good idea after all. Maybe you were better off cooperating. Consider, for example, the wisdom of James F. Moore.

THE DEATH OF COMPETITION

James Moore is an extremely unlikely management guru. After all, his Ph.D. is in cognitive psychology and he once taught high-school art and photography, which is rather far from a Harvard MBA. Nevertheless, Moore wrote the obligatory *Harvard Business Review* article—all gurus have to produce at least one—and his book, *The Death of Competition*, garnered enough attention and accolades to land him on *Business Week*'s 1996 "hot new strategists" shortlist.[50]

Moore's argument goes something like this. In today's economy, innovation wins. Virtually all businesses, he writes, can obtain significant financial rewards if they create innovative products, services, and processes more efficiently and effectively than others in their industry. But, he adds, there is a trick to making this happen.

> Any given innovation requires customer and supplier partners to be implemented. And the more radical [and frequently more valuable] the innovation, the more deeply and broadly must other players, especially customers, be involved. This places a premium on learning to manage a very wide community or network of organizations, in which all the players share a vision about how to make the innovation happen. Indeed, the major factor today limiting the spread of realized innovation is not a lack of good ideas, technology, or capital. It is the inability to command cooperation across broad, diverse communities of players who must become intimate parts of a far-reaching process.[51]

Today, cooperation is as important, if not more important, than old-style, winner-take-all, head-to-head combat. In fact, Moore says, that old-time ferociousness is dead; and if you don't recognize that fact, you and your company are in trouble. You just can't go it alone any more. The old my-product-versus-your-product kind of competition ignores the context or environment within which both do business; and that context is critical since "even excellent businesses can be destroyed by the conditions around them. . . . A good restaurant in a failing neighborhood is likely to die. A first-rate supplier to a collapsing retail chain . . . had better watch out."[52]

Instead of thinking of yourself as a manager, your company as a company, and the environment you do business in as a market or industry, suggests Moore, adopt a new vocabulary. Start thinking of yourself as a gardener or forester and the environment you do business in as an ecosystem. Moore explains that in biology an ecosystem is a "community of organisms, interacting with one another, plus the environment in which they live and with which they also interact; for example, a lake, a forest, a grassland, tundra."[53] In business, an ecosystem is

an economic community supported by a foundation of interacting organizations and individuals—the organisms of the business world. . . . A business ecosystem is made up of customers, market intermediaries (including agents and channels, and those who sell complementary products and services), suppliers, and, of course, oneself. These might be thought of as the primary species of the ecosystem.

But a business ecosystem also includes the owners and other stakeholders of these primary species, as well as powerful species who may be relevant in a given situation, including government agencies and regulators, and associations and standards bodies representing customers and suppliers. To one extent or another, an ecosystem includes your direct competitors, along with companies that might be able to compete with you or with any other important members of the community.[54]

To succeed, argues Moore, you have to develop an "ecological consciousness." You have to recognize that your company exists in such a business ecosystem and that you should play the role of the grand gardener, shaping and reshaping that ecosystem through your business strategy. Instead of focusing on narrow-minded competition, you should focus your efforts on creating whole new ecosystems in order to bring bold innovations to customers. Instead of trying to win the game, you change the game and generate an entirely new outcome. That, says Moore, is what Intel, Hewlett-Packard, and especially Wal-Mart have done, and that is why they have been so successful. "Competitive advantage in the new world stems from knowing when and how to build ecosystems, and from being able to steer them to lasting growth and continuous improvement."[55]

The Stages of Coevolution

Building business ecosystems and steering them to lasting growth requires that you understand how they develop. In fact, says Moore, there are four predictable and sequential stages through which all business ecosystems pass. Each stage presents its own challenges and raises its own predictable issues. Strategy making is about responding to these issues and challenges and coevolving with others as the ecosystem unfolds. Moore's four stages of coevolution are described in the sections that follow.

Stage #1: Pioneering an Ecosystem

Stage one is the entrepreneurial stage of creation. You are working with customers, suppliers, and business partners to bring to life a new product or service and demonstrate that it is not only viable but also a dramatic improvement over whatever else is available. Ideally, at this stage you will find sponsor/patron customers willing to tolerate a primitive version of your product or service and work with you to make it better over time. Since the main competitive challenge you will face at this stage is from those who would steal your ideas, you should seek out markets that provide room for growth but are relatively isolated and far from the prying eyes of would-be competitors.

Wal-Mart was at this stage in the 1960s and was able to exploit both ideals. First, it located its stores in rural areas far from potential competitors such as Kmart. Second, Wal-Mart built large stores that stocked well-known brands at prices 15% below those of the rural mom-and-pop competition. This allowed Wal-Mart to quickly dominate all the markets it entered. Rural customers soon came to view Wal-Mart as the best-stocked and least expensive store around. It wasn't perfect, but it was so much better than its competition that its customers were more than willing to stick with Wal-Mart while it learned. After all, where else could they go?

Stage #2: Expansion of an Ecosystem

At this stage, you are trying to build a critical mass of business. You are working with your suppliers and other partners to bring your product or service to a larger market. Your major competitive challenge is to protect yourself from alternative providers of the product or service. You do this by seeking to make your version of the product or service the standard in the marketplace. You try to dominate key markets. You tie up critical customers, suppliers, and distribution channels.

By the 1970s, Wal-Mart was at this stage. It continued building stores in rural areas, usually locating them within 10 miles of several small towns so that it could capture business from the entire surrounding area. These were markets Wal-Mart could quickly and safely enter and dominate. Plus, these markets were usually too small for more than one discounter. Once Wal-Mart entered the market, few rivals would dare follow.

As Wal-Mart expanded, it took several steps to shore up its ecosystem:

- Built a set of incentives and measures that would ensure the commitment of employees and managers to local stores, which led to a complex system of training, oversight, bonuses, and stock-purchase plans for employees.
- Managed communication and control of a network of remotely located stores, which required close monitoring of a carefully drawn set of measures that were transmitted daily to Wal-Mart headquarters in Bentonville, Arkansas.
- Set up an efficient distribution system that allowed for joint purchasing, shared facilities, systematic ordering, and store-level distribution of a large number of different goods. (This third "obsession" ultimately became Wal-Mart's trademark hub-and-spoke distribution system: warehouses served constellations of stores located no more than a day's drive from the center.)[56]

Stage #3: Authority in an Established Ecosystem

By the time this stage is reached, the design and structure of the business ecosystem has somewhat stabilized. Growth is continuing and even accelerating, but the ecosystem architecture—the explicit and tacit agreements about how business will be conducted between the various parties—has been established. Simultaneously, the business has matured and customers have become smarter and more demanding. At this stage, companies are under extreme pressure to cut costs. Many turn to restructuring, downsizing, and outsourcing. The stresses and pressures at this stage result in intra-ecosystem competition for leadership.

Clear winners and losers emerge in stage 3, says Moore. The winners who go on to lead the ecosystem they may or may not have created succeed for a combination of three reasons.

1. Innovation. Successful firms at this stage keep improving all the time. They develop what Moore calls an "Innovation Trajectory." Product enhancement follows product enhancement. Winning companies are constantly making their own products obsolete, just as Intel does with its microprocessors, going from the 8086 to the 80286, the 80386, the 80486, the Pentium, the Pentium MMX, and the Pentium II. Each version of the product is better, more powerful, and delivers more value to the end customer.

2. Criticality. Winners at this stage not only continue to innovate, they make sure their innovations are important overall drivers of product and service improvements valued by the ecosystem's customers and partners alike. Intel's faster chips benefit computer users and also the entire Microsoft Windows/Intel personal computer ecosystem because they stimulate demand for new hardware and software.

3. Embeddedness. Finally, successful firms at this stage bond closely with others in the business ecosystem. Intel is "inside" its computer-manufacturing partners' machines in more ways than one, and having "Intel inside" is an advantage. Wal-Mart's electronic data exchange fuses its inventories with its suppliers' manufacturing operations and both benefit.

Innovation, criticality, and embeddedness, argues Moore, solidify the leader's position and yield high gross margins. These three ingredients must be part of a permanent campaign to lead the ecosystem.

The essence of the permanent campaign is to influence the structure of the ecosystem as a whole so that it expresses your core contributions. A link is established between your competencies and the value . . . desired by customers. The campaign starts with customers and with selling your value, and it starts with promoting visions of the future to which you can maximally contribute. The campaign seeks to reinforce this vision—and your importance—by dominating markets and channels.

The permanent campaign goes even further, however, by seeking to influence the evolution of the architecture of the product—that is, how it is offered to customers, what modules and subcomponents are used, and what functions they provide. It involves how business processes are conceived and, if necessary, transformed. It affects organizational relationships, helping to determine what is outsourced and what held dear. The campaign seeks to shape what is produced in large volumes and with economies of scale and scope. And it helps to determine what multiple suppliers provide. . . . Finally, the campaign seeks to secure preferred access to resources of all types and a close alignment to the values and policy apparatus of the society.[57]

Moore concludes that such campaigns are the center of business strategy.

Stage #4: Renewal or Death

Of course, nothing last forever. Eventually all ecosystems will be threatened.

Changes occur in the regulatory and/or economic environment—or in customer preferences and buying patterns.
[The] established business ecosystem becomes less well adapted to its environment and less able to meet the needs of its remaining customers, suppliers, and stakeholders.
New alternative ecosystems and innovations begin to gain acceptance and momentum.
Customers, suppliers, and stakeholders increasingly withdraw from the established ecosystem in favor of alternatives.[58]

It is the ice age. Temperatures change rapidly. Only those who can adapt rapidly, survive.

Of course, you can try to stave off the competition. You can and should work diligently to erect high barriers to entry to prevent innovators from being able to build ecosystems as an alternative to your own. You can and should try to make it expensive for customers to switch from your ecosystem to another. You should do whatever you can to buy time to develop and implement new ideas to renew your ecosystem. Most importantly, says Moore, you must do the following three things.

1. Develop a good understanding of the assumptions behind your ecosystem and why those assumptions are breaking down. What has changed? What isn't valid anymore?
2. Develop a thorough understanding of the alternative ecosystems, including their measures of success, cost drivers, how they create value for customers, and so on.
3. Marshall your stakeholders (customers, suppliers, business partners, etc.) to address simultaneously all of the dimensions of your ecosystem that need to change.[59]

Moore closes with the following admonition about stage 4. "My own work with Stage IV business ecosystems has included a number of ecosystems in high technology and heavy industry, and limited exposure to health care. Without a doubt, I have found that Stage IV situations are among the hardest to influence."[60]

We have no doubt that they are. Fortunately, there are always other gurus who think they can help. We will close this chapter with the ideas of two who are certain they have discovered a way to win the Stage #4 (or 3 or 2 or 1) strategy game. Adam Brandenburger and Barry Nalebuff are sure all you need to know is a little game theory.

HOW TO CHANGE THE GAME OF BUSINESS

Adam M. Brandenburger, a professor of business administration at Harvard, and Barry J. Nalebuff, a professor at the Yale School of Management, are scholars obsessed with applying game theory—the mathematical study of decision making—to business strategy. Their signature work, *Co-opetition,* was published in May 1996. Garnering praise as a "fast-paced read" and "exciting new approach to strategy," it quickly hit the best-seller list and created two new gurus.

Brandenburger and Nalebuff argue that business is a game, just like many think it is. But, they argue, business is a game with a difference. Business isn't a familiar sport or card game like baseball or poker. No, say our gurus, in those games someone must lose in order for you to win; or as Gore Vidal puts it, "It is not enough to succeed. Others must fail."[61] Things are just the opposite in business. "In business," say Brandenburger and Nalebuff, "your success doesn't require others to fail—there can be multiple winners."[62] In short, business is war, but it is also peace. You have to compete, but if you are smart, you will also cooperate. So when should you do which? How do you know when to compete and when to cooperate? Well, say our gurus, you must do both simultaneously.

> Business is cooperation when it comes to creating a pie and competition when it comes to dividing it up. In other words, business is War *and* Peace. But it's not Tolstoy—endless cycles of war followed by peace followed by war. It's simultaneously war and peace. As Ray Noorda, founder of the networking software company Novel, explains: "You have to compete and co-operate at the same time." The combination makes for a more dynamic relationship than the words "competition" and "cooperation" suggest individually.[63]

It certainly does. It also makes for a confusing relationship. But don't worry. Brandenburger and Nalebuff adopt a new word coined by their friend Noorda to make everything clear. Business, the say, isn't about just competition or cooperation. Business is about *co-opetition.*

Understand? No? Well, that's where game theory comes in. "Game theory," say our gurus, "makes it possible to move beyond overly simple ideas of competition and cooperation to reach a vision of co-opetition."[64] Perhaps most importantly, game theory will not only show you how to play the game of business but actually change the game to one closer to your liking. That, say Brandenburger and Nalebuff, is where the big payoff from game theory comes in.

Changing the game of business starts with changing its PARTS. In any game, there are five basic elements:

1. Players—the participants in the game
2. Added values—the value the participants bring to the game
3. Rules—the regulations governing how the game is played
4. Tactics—the moves players can make to gain advantage
5. Scope—the boundaries of the game

"To change the game," explain our gurus, "you need to change one or more of its elements. This means that each of the five elements—**P**layers, **A**dded values, **R**ules, **T**actics, and **S**cope—gives you a way to transform an existing game into an entirely new one. Change one of the **PARTS,** and you change the whole."[65]

Changing the Game by Changing Players

The first way you can change the game, say Brandenburger and Nalebuff, is by changing the players. To determine who the players are, start with your company. Let's say you are Delta Airlines (see Exhibit 5.6). Other players include your suppliers. For example, Boeing supplies all of your 767s and The Peanut Factory supplies your onboard snacks (Exhibit 5.7). Your customers are also players—those full-fare-paying business travelers you love and the vacation travelers you use to fill up your planes (Exhibit 5.8). You also have competitors like American Airlines and low-cost Valu-Jet, now called AirTran. (Exhibit 5.9). Finally, you have *complementors.* These are companies whose products and services complement your products and services. Our gurus explain that companies are complementors "if customers value your product more when they have the other player's product than when they have your product alone."[66] Delta's SkyMiles® partners such as Hertz and MCI might be considered complementors (Exhibit 5.10).

Now, say our gurus, think of the relationships these players have in the great game of business. You have friends and you have foes. Sometimes a

EXHIBIT 5.6.

Your suppliers	Your company
Boeing Peanut Factory	*Delta*

EXHIBIT 5.7.

Your suppliers	Your company	Your customers
Boeing Peanut Factory	*Delta*	*Business travelers Leisure travelers*

EXHIBIT 5.8.

Your competitors
American Airlines AirTran

Your suppliers	Your company	Your customers
Boeing Peanut Factory	*Delta*	*Business travelers Leisure travelers*

EXHIBIT 5.9.

friend can become a foe, or a foe can become a friend, depending upon what is happening at a particular point in the game. For example, your customers and suppliers are your friends when it comes to creating value. After all, you have to cooperate to make the product or service happen. But these friends become foes when it is time to divide the pie. Your customers want to drive prices down, and your suppliers want as much as they can get of the profits.

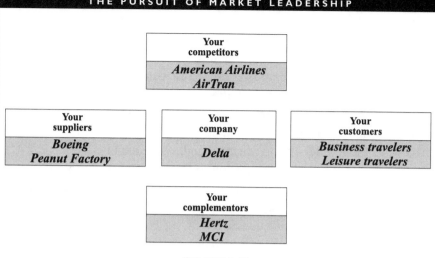

EXHIBIT 5.10.

This mixture of cooperation and competition is pretty clear when it comes to the supplier, company, and customer relationship. What many people miss is that the same kind of mixed relationship exists between competitors and complementors. For example, American Airlines is a competitor (foe) to Delta when it comes to competing for passengers. But what happens when both Delta and American are in the market for new planes? Suddenly, they stop being competitors and become complementors when dealing with Boeing, because it's much cheaper for Boeing to design and build a new a model of aircraft that will meet both airlines' needs than to design a different model for each. The same complementor/competitor relationship is true of many other companies. Take, for example, the relationship of computer companies such as Compaq and Dell when they deal with Intel. "Compaq and Dell . . . compete for the limited supply of Intel's latest chip. But the two companies are complementors as well as competitors with respect to Intel. Between development costs and building a new fabrication plant, Intel will spend over a billion dollars to develop the next-generation chip. Intel will be able to spread that cost among Compaq, Dell, and all the other hardware makers, which means that each one of them will pay less to have Intel inside."[67]

Our gurus remind us that business is both peace and war. Companies are complementors in making markets and they are competitors in dividing up markets. There are both win-win and win-lose elements in all of the relationships you have with customers, suppliers, complementors, and competitors. Don't think just cooperation or just competition, urge Brandenburger and Nalebuff. Think co-opetition.

As you begin to think in terms of co-opetition, you will soon realize that all players in the game are important and that every time a player enters or leaves the game, relationships change, and, consequently, the game itself changes. You can use that information to your advantage. Take a situation in which you are trying to decide whether to play the game at all.

Our gurus ask you to image that you get a call from a prospective customer. He tells you he is not satisfied with his current supplier and wants you to give him a bid. It is a large account and you would like the business. Do you make a bid? No brainer, you say. Of course you make a bid. Not only that, you make an extremely attractive bid—so attractive that you take the business away from your competitor just as you have always wanted. You start dreaming of your win.

But wait, say our gurus. Before you start offering bids, ask yourself "how important is it to the customer that you bid? If your bidding is important, then you should get compensated for playing the game. If it's not important, then you're unlikely to get the business and even less likely to make money. You might want to reconsider bidding at all."[68] Competition is valuable, but remember that when you enter the game, the game itself will change—maybe to the customer's benefit. Now he has two suppliers and can play one off against the other to drive prices down. Competition may be valuable to him, so don't give it away. Maybe you can get him to pay you to play. Of course, you may not be able to get him to pay you cash, but there may be other ways you can get paid. For example, Brandenburger and Nalebuff suggest that

> you can ask for contributions toward bid-preparation expenses. You can ask for help with up-front capital costs, such as the costs involved in building a plant. You can ask for a guaranteed sales contract. Also valuable is a last-look provision: you get the business so long as you match the best price in the market.
>
> In return for bidding, you can ask for better access to information about the business. That gives you a much better chance of winning the account. . . .

Ask to deal with a different person. Make the bidding an opportunity to meet senior management. Ask to meet someone who will appreciate what you bring to the table and not just focus on getting the lowest price. Or in return for bidding on one piece of the business, get access to the customer's other pieces.

Finally, you might try turning the tables. Instead of quoting the customer a price, ask the customer to quote you a price at which he would give you his business. The customer gives you a signed contract complete with price, and you decide whether to sign. If you do, the customer has to switch to you.[69]

The point to remember is that when the players change in a game, the game itself changes. If you are the player who will change the game, think through what impact you will have on it. You may find more options than doing what first comes to mind.

Other ways you can change the game by changing players include bringing in more customers. Instead of fighting your competitors for existing customers and perhaps having to cut prices drastically to do so, you can focus on bringing in more business. With more customers, you have more sales and more profits, and you make yourself less dependent on any given customer. You may even want to bring in customers that you know in advance you will lose to your competitors. That's right. You might actually benefit from your competitor getting more customers. Our gurus explain with an example from the aircraft industry.

Orders for new planes are large and infrequent, and so the airframe manufacturers, Boeing and Airbus, view each one as a must-win. Commercial airlines are able to play Boeing and Airbus off against each other. Anything that either manufacturer could do to bring a few more buyers into the game would make a big difference. It's even okay for Boeing if those new buyers go to Airbus. The reason is that there's limited manufacturing capacity. If Airbus wins several consecutive orders, it starts getting a large backlog. Now Boeing will be able to promise faster delivery and thus be better positioned to win the next few orders. If there are only a few buyers, not enough to create a backlog, then Boeing can't afford to let Airbus win one. Every lost order puts more pressure on Boeing's overhead. Competition heats up until neither Boeing nor Airbus makes money. Just a small shift in the number of customers, one way or the other, can make a big difference to the balance of power in the market.[70]

Second, you can change the game by bringing in more suppliers, even if you have to offer them some inducement to play. With more suppliers, you have more choices, meaning no supplier is essential and you are in a stronger bargaining position. This is the flip side of the bidding example we mentioned earlier. This time you are the buyer seeking a new bidder.

Third, you can bring in new complementors to help make your product or service more valuable to your customers. If you are Apple, the more people producing software for your computers, the better.

Finally, you may even want to bring in competitors. Your customers may want to bring in more suppliers for the reasons we mentioned earlier. Customers may even refuse to do business with you if you are the only source of what they need. That's what happened to Intel in the late 1970s when IBM, Intel's primary customer, refused to adopt Intel's 8086 microprocessor unless Intel agreed to provide a second-source license to other providers, including IBM itself. IBM didn't want to invest in developing hardware around the Intel chip and then find itself with just one supplier.[71]

With regard to changing the players, Brandenburger and Nalebuff have this advice: "Before you enter a game, assess your added value. If you have a high added value, you'll make money in the game; so go ahead and play. But, if you don't have much added value . . . you may still be able to make money by changing the game . . . consider bringing in customers, suppliers, complementors, and even competitors. . . . Anytime the cast of players changes, so do added values."[72] Of course, changing players is not the only way to change the added value and the game. There are more direct ways.

Changing the Game by Changing the Added Value

In the previous section, you changed the game by changing the players. You brought in more suppliers, and as a result, the added value and bargaining power of each supplier went down. You brought in more customers to create a backlog for you and your competitors, and suddenly your added value went up since you were the only one with capacity to meet the increased demand. What other ways can you change the added value and therefore the game? Our gurus suggest three of them.

Limit Supply

Nintendo intentionally limits production of game cartridges to ensure that demand will exceed supply, particularly at peak times like Christmas. The limited supply makes the cartridges that are available even more valuable. Harley-Davidson does the same thing with its motorcycles.

Make Your Product Better

TWA added value when it removed seats from its airplanes in order to create a comfort class with more legroom. Customer satisfaction, employee morale, and passenger traffic all went up. "The trick," write Brandenburger and Nalebuff, "is to spend $1 in such a way that customers value the quality improvement at $2. Then you can raise price by $1.50, and it's a win-win. Likewise, the trick is to save $2 in such a way that customers value your product only $1 less than before. That way, you can cut price by $1.50, and it's a win-win. In both cases, you've engineered an extra dollar of added value and split it with the customer."[73]

Create Customer Loyalty

Reward customers for their repeat business by offering them a frequent-flyer or frequent-buyer program.

Changing the Game by Changing the Rules

Rules determine how the game is played. Of course, some of the rules of the business game, such as laws and customs, are difficult to change and risky to violate. However, there are other rules you can change, such as contractual agreements you have with customers and suppliers. In doing so, our gurus urge that you put yourself in the shoes of the other players. Ask yourself who really benefits from the agreement. Things aren't always as they seem. For example, consider the impact of a common business practice called the most-favored-customer (MFC) clause.

The MFC clause simply guarantees your customer the best price you give to anyone. Customers want it because it ensures that they will never be at a cost disadvantage since they will always get your best price. The question is, who wins with the MFC, the customer or you? Our gurus answer that you win, because the MFC changes the rules of the game.

> When your customers have MFCs, you're more able to withstand pressure to lower price. There's a common ritual in negotiations with customers over price. You say to the customer: "I'd love to give you a better price, but I can't afford to." The customer responds: "You can't afford not to. If you don't, I won't buy from you." Often you lose the argument. But if your other customers have MFCs, your argument becomes a lot more convincing. You can point out that a price concession to one will, by necessity, become a price concession to all. And, that's something you really can't afford. You can just say no.
>
> MFCs are an instance of "strategic inflexibility." . . . This strategic inflexibility is just what you want. It ties your hands when you negotiate, enabling you to stand up to your customers. . . .
>
> [Plus] . . . MFCs, once in place, change the way customers negotiate. MFCs reduce customers' incentive to negotiate . . . the typical customer with an MFC won't push as hard in negotiating with the seller. That makes sense. The customer might as well let others do some of the hard work, secure in the knowledge that he'll benefit from any price breaks. . . .
>
> In sum, MFCs turn sellers into tigers and customers into pussycats. So who do you think gets the lion's share of the pie.[74]

Of course, there is some downside for you. While the inflexibility helps you in negotiations with existing customers, it can make it difficult for you to steal a customer away from a competitor by undercutting its prices. If you lower your price for that one new customer, then you will have to give the same price break to all of your existing customers with MFCs. Likewise, you may have a more difficult time defending yourself against a competitor who is trying to steal your customers by undercutting your price. If you cut your price to keep the customer, you have to cut your price for all your other customers, which may be something you can't afford.

In short, the rule of rules is: Consider how the rule impacts all the players before deciding what to do.

Changing the Game by Changing Tactics

In the game of business, as in the game of life, "perceptions . . . regardless of whether they are accurate drive behavior."[75] Tactics are actions you take to shape perceptions and therefore change behavior. Here are two examples.

In 1990 Gillette was ready to launch its Sensor shaving system. Gillette believed it had a breakthrough product, but how could it convince people of that? To grab attention and convince people that it was serious, Gillette initiated a high-profile and expensive ad campaign to tout the technological advances of its new razor. The message was simple: "Hey, we're spending big to announce this new product because we know we have a winner." Consumers responded by trying the razor just to see what all the fuss was about. They liked it and Gillette's sales jumped 70%. Perception made a difference.[76]

Perception also made a difference with Microsoft's Powerpoint presentation software. At one point, Powerpoint lagged behind Harvard Graphics in sales. Microsoft considered cutting the price of its product to increase sales but quickly rejected the idea, fearing that by heavily discounting Powerpoint it would create the perception that the software wasn't as good as its rival. Instead, Microsoft kept the price of its product high but bundled it with Word and Excel to create Microsoft Office. Buyers of Microsoft Office thought they were getting the expensive Powerpoint software for free and eagerly tried it. Microsoft preserved Powerpoint's high-end image, and it became the leader in presentation software.[77] Again, perception mattered.

Brandenburger and Nalebuff note that "in some sense, everything is a tactic. Everything you do, and everything you don't do, sends a signal. These signals shape people's perceptions of the game. And what people collectively perceive to be the game *is* the game. You need to take account of perceptions to really know what game you're in and to be in control of how you change it."[78]

Changing the Game by Changing Its Scope

Business games, like all games, are played on fields with boundaries, but the boundaries of business games aren't fixed. You can change the boundaries and, sometimes, say our gurus, expanding them to carve out your own little area might be just the thing to do.

Let's say, for example, that you want to get in the game, but there is already a powerful player. Do you challenge him or her on the existing turf, or do you change the game and create some turf of your own? If you are smart, say our gurus, you do the latter. After all, that's what Sega did when it came up against Nintendo in the late 1980s.

At the time, Nintendo owned the video-game market with an 8-bit system and popular games like Mario. Sega, which had been around for a while, had not been able to make headway against the more established player. So Sega changed the game. In October 1988, Sega came out with a 16-bit system that had better sound, more colors, and better images than the 8-bit Nintendo system. It took Nintendo two years to respond with its own 16-bit system. By that time, Sega had come up with a hit, Sonic the Hedgehog, and Nintendo and Sega ended up splitting the market.

Why didn't Nintendo respond sooner? Sega had changed the game, expanded its boundaries, and taken advantage of the market leader's strength. Nintendo was secure and highly profitable in the 8-bit market. Sega's 16-bit system offered it little direct competition since it was more expensive and wouldn't play Nintendo's 8-bit games. Nintendo knew that if it came out with its own 16-bit system, it would devastate the 8-bit market that was still profitable. So Nintendo delayed and left Sega alone. Sega expanded the boundaries of the game and took the advantage. That, say our gurus, is what they mean by changing the scope of the game.

Brandenburger and Nalebuff close with this piece of advice.

Changing the game is not something you'll want to do once and then forget about. It's best viewed as an ongoing process. No matter how successfully you've seized your current opportunities, new ones will appear that can be best utilized by changing the game again. . . . There is no end to the game of changing the game.[79]

There is, of course, an end to this chapter. And this is it.

🔑 KEY POINTS

We promised you a summary of what we consider to be the best overall ideas we gathered from the writings and pronouncements of our strategy gurus. Here are six of their best ideas.

Emphasize Something

Michael Porter wants you to pursue cost leadership, differentiation, or focus. Michael Treacy and Fred Wiersema want you to select operational excellence, product leadership, or customer intimacy. Gary Hamel and C. K. Prahalad want you to focus on a few core competencies. What we think they are all saying is, "Don't try to be everything to everyone," and we think that is good advice.

Be Unique

Of course, your best strategy is not just to emphasize something, but to emphasize something that is unique. The clearest advantage goes to the company that can put together Porter's value chain in a way that delivers value no other company can deliver. Does your company do something unique to add value today? What can it do to add even more value tomorrow?

It's Not Just a Numbers Game

We think Henry Mintzberg has a good point when he says that the world isn't going to stand still while you conduct a detailed analysis and write a strategic plan. You are just not going to have the time to spell out everything in detail. The most you can hope for is a reasonably good definition of the direction you want to take. You and your people have to work out the details day by day. Maybe James Moore had the best idea: Instead of viewing your company as a machine that can be designed, engineered, calibrated, and fine-tuned, think of it as a coevolving, unpredictable organism.

Consult Many Minds

Strategy is a top management job, but it is not a job for top management alone. The more people you involve in thinking about the direction your company should take, the better off you are. Gary Hamel has a good idea about involving the revolutionaries, in particular. After all, these are the people most likely to push the boundaries or change the game in some other way, as Adam Brandenburger and Barry Nalebuff suggest you need to do to win the game.

Commit to the Truth

This is a tough one. You have to be brutally honest with yourself about the present and the past before you can begin preparing for the future. That means admitting what your company is and is not contributing to Porter's value chain. It means not pretending that something is a core competence when deep down you know it really isn't. It means listening to people who disagree with you and to the prevailing wisdom in your company and/or industry, as Gary Hamel urges. It means answering truthfully Michael Treacy and Fred Wiersema's five questions about the status quo. And it means being realistic about your future options even if some of them aren't very pleasant.

Business Is a Team Sport

Finally, we need to reassess the American obsession with competition. Competition may not be dead, as James Moore suggests, but we think he is right that it is not the only or even the best way to achieve market leadership today. You will make it easier on yourself, your employees, your stockholders, and even your customers if you cooperate as much as you compete. Business is a game, but it is a game played best by teams.

Jill Carpenter, coauthor of *The Power of Open-Book Management*

John Case, author of *Open-Book Management*

Aubrey C. Daniels, author of *Performance Management*

Thomas P. Flannery, a managing director of the Hay Group and coauthor of *People, Performance and Pay*

Thomas F. Gilbert, founding father of performance management and author of *Human Competence*

David A. Hofrichter, a managing director of the Hay Group and coauthor of *People, Performance and Pay*

M. Patricia Kane, coauthor of *The Power of Open-Book Management*

Robert S. Kaplan, coauthor of *The Balanced Scorecard*

Edward E. Lawler III, founding director of the University of Southern California's Center for Effective Learning

David P. Norton, coauthor of *The Balanced Scorecard*

Paul E. Platten, coauthor of *People, Performance and Pay*

Jay R. Schuster, coauthor of *The New Pay*

John P. Schuster, coauthor of *The Power of Open-Book Management*

John P. (Jack) Stack, CEO of Springfield Remanufacturing and author of *The Great Game of Business*

Patricia K. Zingheim, coauthor of *The New Pay*

6
—

Managing
and Motivating People

n 1978, Thomas F. Gilbert, a former professor of psychology, published a book entitled *Human Competence: Engineering Worthy Performance.* In the preface, Gilbert said he was writing the book to correct a deficiency. Countless books had been written on different aspects of the topic of human competence, but none, said Gilbert, addressed the issue in a comprehensive and systematic way. Gilbert promised that his book would be different. First, he said, he would define human competence in a precise and unambiguous way. Next, he would provide a method for measuring human competence with precision. Third, he would present a model for finding out why people were incompetent and for engineering human competence. Finally, he intended to translate all the theory about human competence into step-by-step procedures that managers and other performance engineers could use to banish incompetence from the workplace.[1] It was an audacious promise, as Gilbert himself admitted. The fact that his book is still in print today and is considered to be a classic work on human performance is testimony to how well he kept his promise. And so we start this chapter with some words of wisdom from Thomas F. Gilbert. If managing and motivating people is about anything, it is about finding ways for people to be competent and perform at their full potential. There is no better introduction to what it takes to accomplish that than what Gilbert calls his "leisurely look at worthy performance."

GILBERT'S LEISURELY LOOK AT WORTHY PERFORMANCE

Gilbert describes himself as an engineer, behaviorist, and philosopher who pursued the "most desirable and valuable aim of any attempt to improve human competency: . . . *leisure*."[2] By *leisure,* Gilbert doesn't mean the modern notion of laziness or frivolity. His is a more classical definition:

> An opportunity afforded by freedom from occupations.

> OR

> Time allowed before it is too late.[3]

The latter definition is his favorite because, Gilbert notes, "We can reason from it that if we learn to get more leisure, and better use what leisure we have, it will not be too late so soon. . . . In summary, the purpose of performance engineering is to increase [leisure[4]], which can be defined as the product of time and opportunity. Opportunities without time to pursue them mean nothing. And time, dead on our hands, affording no opportunities, has even less value. The beginning point of performance engineering is therefore human potential, its end point is the increase of [leisure.[5]]"

The First Leisurely Theorem

In Gilbert's terms, what we should be pursuing is the ability to accomplish as much as possible with the least amount of effort, thus freeing our time for the leisurely pursuit of other, perhaps more worthwhile, accomplishments. Human competence, or "worthy performance," as Gilbert calls it, is therefore a function of what we accomplish for the behavior we expend. For those of us who enjoy formulas, Exhibit 6.1 provides a handy one.

Gilbert calls this equation his "First Leisurely Theorem" and designates it as the key to engineering human competence. This theorem tells us several things, he writes.[6] Our remarks are in brackets.

1. It tells us that the way to achieve human competence is to increase the value of our accomplishments while reducing the energy we put into the ef-

---

EXHIBIT 6.1. **Gilbert's First Leisurely Theorem**

$$W = f\left(\frac{A}{B}\right)$$

W = Worthy performance or human competence

f = function sign

A = Accomplishment

B = Behavior

---

fort. The true value of competence is derived from accomplishment, not from behavior.

[It's not the hours you work that matter, it's what you accomplish as a result of those hours. Tell that to your boss the next time he or she fusses at you for showing up late for work or leaving too early.]

2. It tells us that great quantities of work, knowledge, and motivation, in the absence of at least equal accomplishment, are unworthy performance. And this says, in turn, that knowledge, motivation, and work, when used competently, are to be husbanded and spent wisely.

[So much for the work ethic and education for its own sake.]

3. It tells us that great accomplishments are not worthy if the cost in human behavior is also very great.

[Gilbert describes the Egyptian pyramids as silent monuments to worthless achievement.]

4. Money, energy, or time invested in reducing the behavior required for performance can pay off splendidly.

[The value of technology is that it allows us not only to reduce costs—decrease the denominator—but also to produce more and/or improve the quality or effectiveness of what we produce—increase the numerator.]

5. A system that rewards people for their behavior (work, motivation, or knowledge) encourages incompetence. And a system that rewards people only for their accomplishments, not for the net worth of their performance, is incomplete because it fails to appreciate human competence.

[So much for paying for hours worked or giving bonuses for production or sales without factoring in their costs.]

6. Human competence is found in overt performance, not in hidden behavior. We have no need to measure behavior until we have measured accomplishment.

[Out go most performance appraisal systems.]

As Gilbert notes, his First Leisurely Theorem provides "the basic 'dimensions' of competence (valuable accomplishments and costly behaviors)."[7] But the theorem doesn't say anything about how competent a person or a group is. We know their worth is $W = f\left(^A/_B\right)$, but we don't know what their worth is worth, that is, how competent they really are. For that we need a comparison and Gilbert's Second Leisurely Theorem.

The Second Leisurely Theorem

In order to determine the competence of any individual, group, or institution, writes Gilbert, you must compare that group's typical performance to that of an exemplary performer. Let's say your team can produce $1000 worth of widgets per hour at a cost of $500, and the best team in your company produces $2000 worth of widgets per hour at a cost of $250. Using the formula from his first theorem, Gilbert would calculate your team's worth index as:

$$W_{your\ team} = f\left(\frac{\$1000}{\$500}\right) = 2$$

He would then calculate the worth index of the best team as:

$$W_{best\ team} = f\left(\frac{\$2000}{\$250}\right) = 8$$

The measure of your team's competence, or your team's performance improvement potential (PIP), says Gilbert, is the ratio of the best team's performance to your team's performance.

$$PIP = \frac{W_{best\ team} = 8}{W_{your\ team} = 2} = 4$$

In short, your team has the potential to perform four times better than it currently is. Put another way, the best team is four times better than your team. So what does this tell you? According to Gilbert, many interesting things. For example, if your team has a PIP of 4, there are probably a lot of things you can learn from the best team to help you get down to a PIP of 2. But if you are already at a PIP of 1.2, getting down to 1.1 may be tricky. The lower the PIP, the more competitive you are and the harder it is going to be to get better. In short, says Gilbert, don't despair if your team has a high PIP and therefore is grossly incompetent. "The more incompetent a person or group of people are, the easier it is to improve their performance."[8]

Knowing your PIP and the PIP of others also can be a big help when you are trying to decide what to do to improve human performance or, more precisely, where to invest your improvement resources to get the most performance bang for your buck. Gilbert illustrates the use of his PIP measure with a fictional tale based on true events. It has to do with Willis Angel, vice president of Surfside Seasonings, Inc.[9]

Angel was concerned about the performance of one of his plants and called in three consulting groups to give him some advice. The three conducted studies and gave Angel their recommendations. To his surprise, Angel discovered that all three groups had the same recommendation. The problem, the reports said, was with the supervisors at the plant—all of whom were middle-aged, non-Hispanic, white males. The workers included young minority women who had been recently hired as part of Surfside's efforts to help the government get people off welfare. What the supervisors needed, said the consultants, was diversity training, and they would be happy to deliver it for just a few hundred thousand dollars. Angel wasn't so sure. He had worked with consultants before. A *few* hundred thousand dollars could turn into *many* hundreds of thousands. Angel decided to get one more opinion.

He had heard of a consultant by the name of Frank Roby from some of the plant and divisional managers, who said Roby was unorthodox but got results; so Angel gave him a call.

Roby took a tour of the facility and proceeded to outline what he felt was causing the performance problem and what Angel could do about it. Roby's plan differed from the other three, but it was the plan that worked. It netted Surfside Seasoning several million dollars from improved productivity, reduced waste, lower employee turnover, and fewer grievances. What had Roby done that the other consultants hadn't? He had calculated the PIPs.

Based upon data he had collected from the few people he interviewed, Roby determined that the average hourly production of employees in the plant was 96.9 units per hour. The best employee was able to produce 194 units per hour. Therefore, the employee PIP was:

$$W_{employee} = f\left(\frac{194}{96.9}\right) = 2$$

However, the PIP was much less significant among supervisors. The best supervisor in the company only had 99.8 units per employee hour, compared to the average of 96.9. The supervisor PIP was therefore:

$$W_{supervisor} = f\left(\frac{99.8}{96.9}\right) = 1.03$$

Based upon these PIPs and other information he had picked up during his visit, Roby had a good idea about what the problem was, what was causing it, and what Angel should do to correct it. Gilbert describes Roby's reasoning this way:

> Roby looked at these variances and then noticed that the job the employees had to do was to operate complex low-tolerance equipment. A lot of learning is required to master it. He also heard people say that it simply took a lot of experience to get maximum production. And he learned that the hourly employees got no formal training—mostly because production managers didn't think that formal training was as good as on-the-job experience. He considered this nonsense, of course, and he advised Angel that $150,000 invested in proper training in the theory and troubleshooting of the equipment could get any new employee producing at about 150 units an hour, reducing the employee PIP to less than 1.3. Roby proved to be right—and the most important information he had was the PIP measures.[10]

Knowing the PIPs helped Roby isolate a problem in human performance and helped him solve it. The solution was training, albeit different training from what the high priced, PIP-less consultants had proposed.

While, training worked in this case, it isn't always the answer. In fact, argues Gilbert, there are many ways to improve human performance that have nothing to do with training and are often much more effective. This is where Gilbert's third and last leisurely theorem comes into play.

The Third Leisurely Theorem

Gilbert notes that his first two leisurely theorems help you

1. measure human competence

$$W_{\text{your team}} = f\left(\frac{\$1000}{\$500}\right) = 2$$

2. determine the potential for improvement

$$PIP = \frac{W_{\text{best team}} = 8}{W_{\text{your team}} = 2} = 4$$

So far, so good. But you still don't know how to improve performance. How do you reduce the PIP to something like 1.3, as Roby did? According to Gilbert, you use the Third Leisurely Theorem. Of the three theorems, it may be the most important, and it goes like this:

For any given accomplishment, a deficiency in performance always has as its immediate cause a deficiency in a *behavior repertory* . . . or in the *environment that supports* the repertory, or in both.[11]

Gilbert says that everyone brings to the job their own personal behavioral repertory, which consists of three parts—knowledge, capacity, and motives.

Knowledge—the know-how and know-why that we discussed in Chapter 3 on learning—is what people bring to the job as a result of their education, training, and experience. *Capacity* is the physical and mental abilities people have. *Motives* are an individual's values, beliefs, preferences, likes, dislikes, and so on.

Gilbert maintains that employees require certain environmental supports in order to function effectively. As in the case of a person's repertory of behavior, Gilbert identifies three environmental supports: information, instruments, and incentives.

First, Gilbert says, people need *information* about such matters as the goals and objectives of the business and their work group, what is expected of them, and how well they are doing. Second, people need *instruments*—

tools, techniques, technology, processes, procedures, work methods, organizational structure, and so on—to help them perform their work efficiently
and effectively. Finally, people need some monetary and/or nonmonetary
incentives to perform the work.

So there you have it, says Gilbert. If you put together the right repertory
of behavior and the right environmental supports, you would get competent, even exemplary performance (see Exhibit 6.2). Take away some or all
of the environmental supports or ignore the person's repertory of behavior,
and you would create incompetence. Gilbert even offers a "behavioral
model for creating incompetence," which is summarized in Exhibit 6.3. As
you review Gilbert's list of tactics for engineering incompetence, ask yourself how many you have encountered in your own workplace. You will
probably agree with his comment that anyone who examines this list and
"doesn't see that most of these tactics are the rule, not the exception—and
that *at least* one of them is vigorously employed by almost every place of
work or by every school—simply hasn't had much experience."[12] Today,
we would add that if you don't see the parallels with real life in most workplaces, then you probably don't get Dilbert either.

EXHIBIT 6.2.　Gilbert's Behavior Engineering Model

Environmental supports

Information	Instruments	Incentives
Business strategies	Tools	Nonmonetary
Goals/objectives	Techniques	Monetary
Expected performance	Technology	
Current performance	Work methods	
Their worth index	Processes	
Their team's PIP	Procedures	
	Organization	

Person's repertory of behavior

Knowledge	Capacity	Motives
Education	Physical ability	Likes, preferences
Skills	Mental ability	Needs, values

*Source: Adapted from Tables 3–1 through 3–4 in Thomas F. Gilbert, **Human Competence: Engineering
Worthy Performance** (New York: McGraw-Hill, 1978), pp. 82–89.*

EXHIBIT 6.3. Behavioral Model for Creating Incompetence

A. Withhold information.
   Don't let people know how well they are performing.
   Give people misleading information about how well they are performing.
   Hide from people what is expected from them.
   Give people little or no guidance about how to perform well.

B. Don't involve people in selecting the instruments of work.
   Design the tools of work without ever consulting the people who will use them.
   Keep the engineers away from the people who will use the tools.

C. Don't provide incentives for good performance.
   Make sure that poor performers get paid as well as good ones.
   See that good performance gets punished in some way.
   Don't make use of non-monetary incentives.

D. Don't help people improve their skills.
   Leave training to chance.
   Put training in the hands of supervisors who are not trained instructors.
   Make training unnecessarily difficult.
   Make training irrelevant to the student's purposes.

E. Ignore the individual's capacity.
   Schedule performance for times when people are not at their sharpest.
   Select people for tasks they have intrinsic difficulties in performing.
   Do not provide response aids (e.g., magnification of difficult visual stimuli).

F. Ignore the individual's motives.
   Design the job so that it has no future.
   Avoid arranging working conditions that employees would find more pleasant.
   Give pep talks rather than incentives to promote performance in punishing situations.

Source: Adapted from Table 3-3. A Behavioral Model for Creating Incompetence in Thomas F. Gilbert, **Human Competence: Engineering Worthy Performance** (McGraw-Hill, 1978), p. 87.

Diagnosing and Treating Performance Deficiencies

Of course, Gilbert intends his behavior engineering model to serve as a diagnostic tool. Presumably, you would first determine how to measure worth performance.

$$W_{\text{your team}} = f\left(\frac{\$1000}{\$500}\right) = 2$$

Then you would identify an exemplary performer and calculate your PIP.

$$PIP = \frac{W_{best\ team} = 8}{W_{your\ team} = 2} = 4$$

Once you determined your PIP, you would refer to the behavior engineering model (Exhibit 6.2) for guidance on where to look for performance improvement.

As you might expect, Gilbert has some definite ideas about how to use his model as a diagnostic tool. First, he says, we should recognize that no person or environment is ever perfectly suited for the job we wish to have performed. There is always room for improvement in at least one of the six elements of the model. "The question," writes Gilbert, "is not *if* we can improve this or that aspect of behavior, but which strategies will yield the most worthy results: the greatest improvement in accomplishment with the least cost of behavior. The question is, Where is the greatest leverage?"[13] But, he continues, the greatest leverage isn't where most people think it is. In what some would call Gilbert's most controversial pronouncement, but one with which we totally agree, he maintains that

the two causes of poor performance most commonly espoused are motives ("they don't care") and capacity ("they're too dumb"). But these are usually the last two places one should look for causes of incompetence, simply because they rarely are the substantial problem. I make this assertion without hesitation. Except for a few strange individuals, people generally care a great deal about how they perform on the job, or in school; and defects in capacity—mental or physical—are the exception, not the rule. . . . I am saying that most people have both sufficient motive and capacity for exemplary performance in almost all circumstances of work and school. So, we should look to these variables [capacity and motives] only when we have exhausted other remedies. If you have done a good job in correcting defects of information, tools, incentives, and training and you still have not achieved exemplary performance—and if the PIP is still economically significant—then you can sensibly worry about the selection of people who have greater motives or capacity.[14]

Gilbert argues that if you truly want to help people improve their performance, forget about most of what they bring to the job (their repertory of behavior) and focus instead on the environment you create for them. Exhibit 6.4 shows the steps Gilbert believes you should take to create a good work environment.

First, says Gilbert, you should ask yourself whether people have sufficient and reliable information to tell them how they should perform and how well they are performing. "Improper guidance and feedback," he writes, "are the single largest contributors to incompetence in the world of work, and a principal culprit at school."[15]

Next, you should examine the tools, techniques, methods, and technology people must use to perform the work. For example, have the people who must use the instruments been involved in their design and development?

Third, check out the monetary and nonmonetary incentives that you are offering. Are the incentives sufficient to encourage superior performance, and are they directly contingent on performance? What is in it for the people who must perform?

Finally, check to see if people lack some skills and need training. Gilbert notes that training is often a powerful but expensive strategy for improving performance. For that reason, he leaves training for last. By correcting deficiencies in information, instruments, and incentives first, you make sure you don't end up "training people to use tools that could be redesigned, or to memorize data they don't need to remember, or to perform to standards

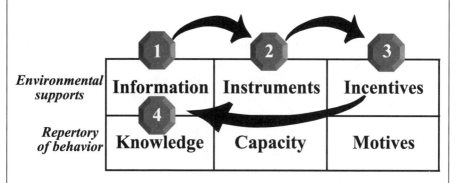

EXHIBIT 6.4.

they are already capable of meeting and would meet if they knew what these standards are."[16]

Following Gilbert

As we said in the beginning, we think what Thomas F. Gilbert calls his "leisurely look at worthy performance" is one of the best introductions to the issue of managing and motivating people you can find. Obviously, in the 20 years since Gilbert wrote his masterpiece, many other gurus have also made significant contributions to the topic of human competence. Most of them address the same themes that Gilbert incorporates into his model (information, instruments, incentives, and knowledge). In the remainder of this chapter, we will review some of the latest guru wisdom concerning two of these topics:

1. Information. Who needs to know what and when do they need to know it?
2. Incentives. How can you use monetary and nonmonetary incentives to promote superior performance?

After looking at some more of Gilbert's ideas about information, we'll look at Jack Stack's style of open-book management (a style that is also supported by gurus John Case, John P. Schuster, Jill Carpenter, and M. Patricia Kane). These gurus provide additional answers to the questions about information. Next we'll discuss the topics of finance and incentives and look at the ideas of David Norton and Robert Kaplan. Finally, we'll examine Aubrey Daniels's beliefs on the power of performance management and other gurus' ideas about compensation.

You will notice, of course, that we are leaving out the topics of instruments and knowledge. The reason is that we have covered these topics in other chapters. Gilbert and most of our other gurus urge you to involve the people who actually have to use the technology, tools, work methods, processes, and so on in their design. For a discussion of how to do that, see Chapter 4 on building high-performance teams, particularly the sections on the design and operation of work teams and improvement teams. Check out Chapter 2 for some of the latest thinking about how individuals and organizations learn.

INFORMATION—WHO NEEDS TO KNOW WHAT?

If you truly want to improve human performance, writes Gilbert, then start by improving information. His reasoning is simple: "improved information has more potential than anything else . . . for creating more competence in day-to-day management of performance."[17] How much improvement is possible from providing people with better and more timely information? Gilbert states categorically that

1. Inadequate information is the major cause of more than half of all the problems of human competence.
2. A properly engineered information system can reduce the PIP of any group of people from whatever it is to 1.2 or less.
3. Improvements from better and more timely information are "never less that 20 percent, often a 50-percent change, and sometimes . . . as high as six fold."[18]

While such improvement sounds dramatic, even astounding, Gilbert argues that we should not be surprised at the power of information. Consider, he writes, how important a small bit of information can be.

You are driving down a road you have never traveled before on your way to an important meeting with a new client. You glance nervously at your watch wondering just how far you have to go to reach your destination in Bentonville, Arkansas. Suddenly, you top a hill and see a small green road sign.

EXHIBIT 6.5.

What has the small bit of information in Exhibit 6.5 done for you? Two things, says Gilbert.

1. It has given you direction—you know what to do: Turn right and proceed 12 miles.
2. It has given you confirmation—you know how well you are performing: Relax, you're on the right road and almost there.

According to Gilbert, direction and confirmation are two powerful and necessary ingredients for performance, but in most workplaces they are inadequate or almost totally absent. People often don't understand the mission of their company or its business strategy because they are never told. They don't have good measures, goals, and objectives they can use to monitor their performance. They don't understand how their day-to-day behavior makes a difference. No wonder they don't perform. They don't have adequate information.

The tragedy is that the requirements of an effective information system are simple. Gilbert enumerates eight steps, which are listed in Exhibit 6.6. As you read, you can almost hear Gilbert's plea: "It is all so simple. Just

---

EXHIBIT 6.6. How to Set Up an Effective Information System

1. Identify the expected accomplishments: mission, responsibilities, and duties.
2. State the requirements of each accomplishment. If there is any doubt that people understand the reason why an accomplishment and its requirements are important, clarify this.
3. Describe how performance will be measured and why.
4. Set exemplary standards, preferably in measurement terms.
5. Identify exemplary performers and any available resources that others can use to become exemplary.
6. Provide frequent and unequivocal feedback about how well each person is performing. This confirmation should be expressed as a comparison with an exemplary standard. Consequences of good and bad performance should also be made clear.
7. Supply as much backup information as needed to help people troubleshoot their own performance and that of the people for whom they are responsible.
8. Relate various aspects of poor performance to specific remedial actions.

Source: Thomas F. Gilbert, Human Competence: Engineering Worthy Performance (New York: McGraw-Hill, 1978), p. 179.

provide the information. Is anybody listening?" But remember that Gilbert was writing this in 1978 and hardly anyone was listening. In the late 1970s, America was in denial. We hadn't faced the productivity crisis, the quality crisis, the Japanese onslaught, the layoffs, downsizing, and restructuring of the 1980s and 1990s. Share information with employees? Why should we? We never had, and we saw no reason to start, regardless of what Gilbert or anyone else said. Thanks, Gilbert, but no thanks. We'll just keep on keeping secrets.

Now, skip forward a few years. It's February 1983 in Springfield, Missouri. Jack Stack, the manager of a small-engine plant, is about to start playing "the great game of business." A decade later, Stack will become a full-fledged guru, sitting on top of a new guru trade. In the mid-90s, we will call this sphere of gurudom "open-book management," and it will have much to teach us about how to provide the information Gilbert said people needed. Back in the mid-80s, Jack Stack just called it an act of desperation.

Playing the Great Game of Business with Jack Stack

Jack Stack wrote that "it's amazing what you can come up with when you have no money, zero outside resources, and 119 people all depending on you for their jobs, their homes, even their prospects of dinner for the foreseeable future."[19] That was exactly the situation he faced in February 1983, a predicament he never expected to find himself in.

Stack's father, who was a foreman at the International Harvester tractor manufacturing plant in Melrose Park, Illinois, got Stack a job in the plant's mail room. Stack writes that the plant was a tough place to work in the 1970s.

> We had racial incidents, death threats, burning effigies, bombings, shootings, aggravated assaults—you name it. Workers and managers were constantly at each other's throats. There were two or three walkouts a year—when things were going well, that is. In a bad month, there might be two or three work slowdowns as well. Every time we turned around, we heard another rumor that the factory was going to be shut down because of labor problems.[20]

For reasons Stack says he still doesn't understand, the plant turned out to be the ideal place for him. Over the next 10 years, he moved up the supervisory ranks and got a reputation for solving problems and cleaning up messes. "People came up with a slogan for me," he writes, "Have Shovel, Will Travel. Whenever there was a mess that had to be cleaned up, they would put me in the middle of it and let me dig my way out."[21] And dig his way out he did, often in the most unorthodox manner. Take, for example, his solution for getting steel deliveries to the plant during a truckers' strike. Stack explains what happened:

> The truckers went out on strike and shut down the highways. We couldn't get steel delivered from the U.S. Steel plant in Gary, Indiana, because snipers were shooting at the trucks. . . .
>
> So I brought five of my guys together, and I told them this one really had me in a bind. How were we going to transport two tons of steel from Indiana to Illinois without getting our heads blown off? Someone said, "School buses. They wouldn't shoot at school buses, would they?" Another guy said, "It depends who's driving the buses." Someone else said, "They wouldn't shoot at nuns driving school buses." That's exactly what we did: we rented a school bus and dressed guys up as nuns. They pulled into the steel mill, loaded the steel bars into the school bus and drove the bus back to Melrose Park.[22]

It was a little crazy, but it worked. That episode and others like it got Stack noticed by upper management. When International Harvester needed someone to take over and clean up a troubled small-engine plant in Springfield, Missouri, in the late 1970s, Stack seemed like the perfect choice for the job.

The plant, called the Springfield ReNew Center, had been created in the late 1960s to service and repair used Harvester engines. By the late 1970s, when Stack arrived as the new plant manger, the plant was losing tons of money and the workers were demoralized. The plant itself was cluttered and run-down. Workers sometimes stood idle all day because they either ran out of parts or didn't have the tools they needed. Employees hated management and were actively courting a union. The whole situation looked hopeless.

Stack recalled spending the first few months just trying to restore trust.

> I met with every single one of the hundred or so employees. I brought them into the conference room in little groups, three, four, five at a time. I

asked them what they wanted, what they felt, where they wanted to go, what they wanted to do. We talked about life. We talked about dreams. We talked about winning. I asked them what tools they needed to do their jobs. People talked very freely, and they had harsh things to say about management. I asked them just to give us a chance.[23]

Stack tried to instill some pride in the workers, reasoning that if they weren't proud of their company or their plant, they would never try to make things better. He held fishing tournaments, baseball tournaments, and relay races with people from other plants in the area to let the workers have some fun and possibly boost morale. He handed out hats, caps, and jackets with the company emblem, and he initiated attendance games and housekeeping games in which workers could win prizes. He even had an open house where workers could bring their families to see where they worked and what they did.

In preparation for the open house, we gave people buckets of paint and allowed them to decorate their machines and their work areas. Some of the guys got their wives, who were generally more artistic, to paint bold statements on the walls. We had American flags, Hell's Angels insignias, everything you can imagine. Some departments put up slogans, like "Machining—We Make It Work." There were signs and symbols everywhere, and none of it was color coordinated. It looked awful, but it was theirs. They were putting their own identities out there for everyone to see. When they brought their families in, they could say, "Here's where I work—this is my environment."[24]

Stack's efforts to revitalize the plant worked—but not well enough or fast enough. By the early 1980s, International Harvester itself was in trouble and looking to shed its unprofitable plants and divisions. Eventually the company laid off 90,000 of its 100,000 workers, sold off most of its operations, and reorganized as Navistar. Stack's employees were worried. Rumors were circulating that Harvester would close or sell off the plant. Workers had a lot of questions. Should I go ahead and buy a new car or hold off? Should I buy the house? Should I get married or wait to see if I'll have a job? What's going to happen to the plant? What's going to happen to us? Stack and the other senior managers were also worried. They even approached Harvester with a proposal to buy the plant themselves if that's what it would take to keep it open. Harvester declined.

In fall 1982, Harvester announced that it was in final negotiations to sell the Springfield plant to another truck and earth-moving-equipment manufacturer. But suddenly, just before Christmas, the whole deal fell through. Harvester was stuck with a plant it didn't want. It could close the plant, but there was one other option. If Stack and his managers still wanted to buy the plant and could quickly come up with $9 million, Harvester would sell it to them. Stack scurried to get the money. He and 12 other managers at the plant came up with $100,000 from personal savings and loans from their relatives and friends. After being turned down by 50 banks, Stack finally found a loan officer who agreed to loan the rest of the money. In early February 1983, Stack and his team closed the deal. It was the highest leveraged buyout in history. The debt-to-equity ratio was 89 to 1, which is equivalent to buying a $90,000 house with only $1,000 down. The deal was so bad that the loan officer who agreed to it got fired for making the loan. The plant that was in trouble to begin with was now awash in debt as well. That's how Stack found himself with no money, no resources, and 119 dependents.

Stack and his fellow managers/owners had jumped at the chance to buy the plant and save their jobs, but said Stack, "it was like jumping into a leaky raft in the middle of a hurricane. Our new company was loaded down with so much debt that the smallest wave could capsize us."[25] The new owners were desperate to make money and generate cash fast. To do that, they needed the help of everyone in the plant. There was just one problem. The people in the plant didn't know how serious the problems were or what they could do to help solve them.

Stack admits that while he had spent time in the years prior to the buyout trying to build employees' trust and get them to take pride in the company and plant, most of the workers at Springfield knew little about how the business was run or what was necessary to make it successful. Stack notes that the workers, like those in most companies, had been told what to do during the workday but never how they fit into the bigger picture. No one had ever explained to them how one worker's actions affected another, how the various departments depended upon each other, or how the actions of each worker impacted the company as a whole. Most importantly, writes Stack, no one had ever told the people at Springfield how to make money and generate cash, or the difference between the two for that matter. Stack and his managers decided to share information with their workers—to open the books, so to speak—and the information, as Gilbert predicted, provided direction and confirmation that made all the difference.

Between 1983 and 1986, Stack's newly independent company, called Springfield Remanufacturing, increased its sales 30% per year. By 1987, it had pretax earnings of $2.7 million, or 7% of sales. By 1994, the company that Stack and his managers had bought for a down payment of $100,000 in 1983 was worth an estimated $25 million, and Stack and his people had accomplished all of this in a decidedly unglamorous industry with no new technology. Their accomplishment sparked a new guru trade and turned Jack Stack into a kind of sorcerer with the secret formula for success.

Open-Book Management

Since Stack and his comanagers/owners first launched the idea of open-book management in 1983, a host of gurus, semigurus, and interpreters have come forward to ply the trade. In explaining the concept, we are going to rely upon four of them, in addition to Stack himself.

John Case, a writer for *Inc.* magazine, coined the phrase *open-book management* in a 1989 article and has done much to popularize the concept. Case edits the *Open-Book Management Bulletin,* a biweekly newsletter, and is the author of *Open-Book Management: The Coming Business Revolution.* John P. Schuster, Jill Carpenter, and M. Patricia Kane are principals in Capital Connections, a consulting firm specializing in open-book management. They are also coauthors of *The Power of Open-Book Management: Releasing the True Potential of People's Minds, Hearts and Hands.*

While Stack, Case, Schuster, Carpenter, and Kane define open-book management in slightly different ways, they all agree that it involves two practices that are not typically found in most organizations:

1. Business and financial education. Training employees to understand the critical numbers, particularly the financial numbers that managers use to measure and monitor the performance of the business.

2. Information sharing. An intensive system of meetings, called huddles, to keep employees informed about the status of the business, particularly its performance on critical financial measures.

Business and Financial Education

Companies that practice open-book management make a concerted effort to educate their employees about the business. This usually involves mandatory classroom training for everyone in the company. For example, Wabash National, a trailer manufacturer and open-book company, has its employees take six hours of training, covering topics such as how to read financial statements and balance sheets, how the company makes money, and the meaning of terms such as *gross profit, net profit, depreciation,* and so on. Other companies have employees play games to learn common financial concepts, such as assets, liabilities, and equity. The idea is to make everyone in the company business literate. Why?

Well, says John Case, open-book companies recognize that "to most people, which is to say 99 percent of those who don't sport the letters CPA or MBA after their name, financial statements—the fundamental data that show how a company is doing—might as well be written in Sanskrit."[26] Open-book companies reason, says Case, that relations between managers and workers will improve if everyone can understand and operate from the same set of numbers. It's easy for workers who don't know anything about how their company's finances actually work just to assume that their employer has tons of money piling up in a bank account somewhere. On the other hand, if employees could understand financial statements, they could see for themselves where the money was going. If profits were up and revenue per employee was rising, then they could expect a raise or other benefits. If profits were down and labor costs were up, they could understand why budgets had to be tightened and raises had to be postponed.

Second, open-book companies reason that employees will be less wasteful if they know what things costs. "If you assume your employer is rich," writes Case, "then you figure that the issues the boss gets all bent out of shape over can't really matter that much. . . . What if expenses are up a little? Lighten up, for Pete's sake. It's human nature: If we don't know the impact of spending a little extra money, we don't give it a second thought. Hey, the company's paying for it. Don't worry about it."[27] Open-book companies educate employees to help them understand the numbers and how a dollar here and a dollar there impact the profits of the whole business. To make their point, some open-book companies actually walk employees line by line through financial statements to show how one line item affects another, and so on.

Third, says Case, open-book companies reason that employees will make better decisions if they know the stakes. Line employees make decisions every day that impact the finances of a business. Do I throw out a part or try to remachine it to make it work? Do I report the funny noise the truck is making or just wait until it breaks? Do I give that customer a refund? Do I stay in the budget hotel or go for the Ritz? The right decision, notes Case, always has financial consequences, and employees can't make the right decision unless they understand the business's finances.

Case's final point involves fun. As Jack Stack said, business is a great game if you know how to play it and, most importantly, know how to keep score. When employees know how to read the financial reports, they know when the company is growing and when it isn't. They know when the company is building value or destroying it. They understand how the game is played because they know how to keep score. "Watching a business grow is exciting," writes Case. "People get caught up in the enterprise, become committed, work hard, work smart."[28]

Of course, to know the score and get excited, you not only have to know how to read the financial reports, you also have to have access to them. That's where the second major open-book management practice comes into play.

Sharing Information

By definition, open-book management means just that—opening the books, sharing information, giving every employee access to the financial data. Stack notes that the very idea of opening up the company's books strikes terror in the hearts of many CEOs. They are terrified that a competitor will get hold of the numbers. Relax, says Stack, your fears about sharing the numbers may not be totally unfounded, but they are almost certainly exaggerated. So what if your competitors get some of the numbers? If yours is a publicly traded company, they probably have access to a lot of numbers anyway, and if you are privately held, the amount of information you can hide may be a lot less than you think. Even if competitors find out something new about you from your open books, that doesn't necessarily mean they will be able to use that information to their advantage. At best, anything your competitors can learn from your open books gives them only a short-term tactical advantage, and that, according to Stack, "pales alongside the benefits that come from educating your employees about the numbers."[29] Quit worrying so much about what your competition might find out, he argues, and start worrying about how much your employees don't know. Their ignorance is going to do you a lot more harm than what your competition has learned about you. Just get the numbers out.

Of course, Stack's definition of getting the numbers out involves more that just posting printouts in the company cafeteria. Our gurus agree that getting the numbers out requires a series of meetings, or in the game vernacular of open-book management, a series of "huddles." John Schuster and the Capital Connections team identify three types of huddles that are usually found in open-book companies: prehuddles, main huddles, and posthuddles.[30]

Prehuddles

Prehuddles are meetings in which teams or departments gather information about their own performance to pass upward to the main huddle. First, they look at what happened over the last week or month and compare their team's or department's performance to its planned or budgeted performance. Are we over or under budget, and why? Next they develop forecasts for the coming week or month. What will the future hold, and why will we perform better or worse than we planned?

The Main Huddle

Once the teams and departments have assembled their numbers in the prehuddles, they send their reports up to a cross-functional meeting where all of the numbers are assembled into one big picture for the entire organization. Schuster, Carpenter, and Kane note that the main huddle is quite different from what happens in most traditional organizations where departments and units report their numbers to the finance department and then wait for it to get them the cost and margin data. Open-book companies cut out that time-consuming step. Instead, the final numbers are computed on the fly in the main huddle as they are being reported by the representatives from the various departments and teams. Jack Stack describes what happens in the main huddle at Springfield Remanufacturing this way:

> They start at 9:00 A.M. every Wednesday in the conference room of our building on Division Street in Springfield. There are usually about fifty managers, supervisors, and other people from around the company in attendance, as well as an assortment of curious outsiders—customers, auditors,

bankers, suppliers, visitors from other companies, and so on. As the group gathers, people stand around joking with one another, exchanging news, sharing fishing tips. Everybody seems relaxed. But there is a certain buzz in the air, the sound you hear in a theater before the lights go down and the curtain goes up, or in a ballpark as the pitcher finishes his warm-ups and the lead-off batter steps to the plate. . . .

People come to the meeting with the latest numbers from their departments. For every entry in the income statement, someone has a number representing the most accurate, up-to-date assessment his or her team can make as to what the entry will be when the month closes. After a brief introduction by me (or whoever is chairing the meeting in my absence), we go around the room, and people announce their numbers, while everybody else scribbles them down on the scorekeeping forms—really blank income statements. There are "oohs" and "aahs" and good natured digs. We can all see how the reported numbers differ from the ones in the . . . plan, which are printed on one side of the form, and from those given in the last meeting, which we've written down on the previous week's form.[31]

Stack provides the following tips for making the main huddle effective.

Keep it regular and on time.   Springfield Remanufacturing first held its main huddles weekly and then moved to a biweekly schedule. The ideal frequency will vary from company to company. The meetings should be spaced far enough apart in time for the numbers to change enough so that people don't get bored, but the meetings should not be so far apart that people lose track of what is going on.

Put a name and a face on every line in the income statement.   Stack emphasizes that you should divide responsibilities for the financial information so that each line item is assigned to a specific person. That way, the good news or bad news doesn't come from some faceless entity such as accounting, but from a real person. Typically, the person reporting a number should be the leader of the team that has the most impact on the number. Sales numbers should be reported from someone in sales, production numbers from someone in production, and so on.

Invite anyone with something to contribute.   Stack writes that most of the participants in the main huddle at his company were middle or top managers but that other people were included. "There should not be any mystery about the meeting. It should be a familiar part of the landscape. So we make a point of inviting a lot of people in the course of a year. Occasionally they wish we hadn't. From time to time, a manager will bring a front-line supervisor into the meeting—say, the head of the cylinder head department. Whenever we see that, we know there's a bad number to report, and the manager has decided to let the person responsible come in and explain it himself. It creates a little incentive not to have a bad number again."[32]

Have a fixed format, but don't be boring. Stack notes that main huddles at Springfield lasted about an hour and a half. Typically, the meeting began with some brief opening remarks from Stack. In his remarks, he tried to establish a theme or focus for the meeting by mentioning some national or local event, such as the state of the economy or a big local employer going out of business. He might review a recent success Springfield had or bring up a trend the group had been watching from previous meetings. After the opening remarks, he then went around the room and had each person with responsibility for a line item report their results. When bad numbers were reported, the person reporting the results was asked for an explanation. Good numbers brought cheers. Good or bad, the group wanted to hear the stories behind the numbers. They wanted to know what happened and why. After the first round, the chief financial officer (CFO) began to pull together a cash-flow statement based upon the information the group had shared. While he did so, Stack went around the room a second time asking participants to share any stories or information that might be of interest to the whole group. When he was finished, the CFO then reviewed the cash-flow statement, and Stack closed the meeting by summarizing the results and emphasizing any themes that had emerged from the discussion.

Posthuddle

Once the main huddle is finished, the participants return to their respective departments or teams and share the information with those who did not attend the main huddle. The purpose of the posthuddle is to make sure everyone in the company has the same information and to educate them about the business.

Are Financial Measures Sufficient?

Open-book management places heavy emphasis on financial information. The principal idea behind this approach is that such data will get everyone in the business focused on generating cash and producing strong balance sheets. While none of our gurus fault managers for trying to make as much money as they can, some have begun to question whether the summary financial measures are a sufficient or even very reliable gauge of future company performance. By far, the most vocal critics of performance measurement based primarily on financial accounting measures are Robert S. Kaplan and David P. Norton.

Kaplan, a professor of accounting at Harvard, and Norton, president of an information-technology consulting firm, presented their arguments in a series of *Harvard Business Review* articles and the best-selling book *The Balanced Scorecard*. Essentially, their argument boils down to this. Financial accounting measures, which are the chief indicators top executives use for information on corporate performance, are no longer sufficient. Most of these measures, argue Kaplan and Norton, were developed for an industrial economy in which the success of a business was largely contingent upon how well executives invested in and managed physical, tangible resources. Today, we have an information economy in which intangible assets such as customer loyalty and employee skills are as important, if not more so, as tangible resources. In an ideal world, we might expect to enhance financial measures to account for the true value of these intangible assets but, write Kaplan and Norton, that is not likely to happen. After all, no one has found a way to place a reliable price on the intangibles, and Kaplan and Norton aren't about to try. The solution, they say, is to create a "balanced scorecard," covering both financial and nonfinancial measures, that could be used at all levels.

The Balanced Scorecard

Kaplan and Norton admit that there is nothing new about their call for companies to monitor both financial and nonfinancial measures. After all, most companies already do that. The problem, they argue, is one of balance. In the typical company, senior managers tend to focus heavily on aggregate financial measures and give less attention to nonfinancial measures. They explain that "aggregate financial measures are used by senior managers as if these measures could summarize adequately the results of operations performed by lower and mid-level employees."[33] At lower levels, nonfinancial measures are used almost exclusively, and employees rarely receive information about the financial consequences of their actions.

Kaplan and Norton want to set things right. To do so, they propose a balanced scorecard to expose senior managers to the nonfinancial measures that drive long-term financial success and expose line employees to aggregate financial measures so that they can see the financial consequences of their actions.

The Four Key Perspectives

Kaplan and Norton are certain they know the types of measures the scorecard needs to have for balance. They maintain that it must contain measures covering four perspectives: financial, customer, internal process, and learning-and-growth. Here is how they define each.

Financial Perspective

Measures covering the financial perspective indicate whether the company's strategy, implementation, and execution are contributing to bottom-line improvement.[34] These measures include:

- Operating income
- Return on capital employed
- Return on investment
- Economic value-added (after-tax net operating profit minus cost of capital)
- Sales growth
- Revenue growth
- Percent of revenue from new products/services
- Profitability by product/service/customer
- Net revenue per ton/price per call/price per unit
- Revenue per employee
- Unit costs of performing work or producing output (cost per gallon, cost per pound, cost per transaction)

- Selling, general, administrative expenses as a percent of total costs or revenues

Customer Perspective

The customer perspective represents the people whose interests often get lost in all the planning and positioning that go on in most organizations.

This perspective contains core outcome measures of such things as customer satisfaction, customer retention, and new customer acquisition, in addition to more specific measures such as:

- Market share with target customers
- Percent growth of business with existing customers
- Customer profitability
- Lead time for product development

The perspective also includes measures of things customers truly care about, such as:

- On-time delivery
- Response time
- Defect rates
- Returns by customers
- Warranty claims
- Success in handling field-service requests

Internal Process Perspective

Internal process measures indicate how successful the company is at developing and deploying key business processes for identifying markets, creating product/service offerings, building and delivering products/services, and providing effective postsale service to customers. These are the measures that engineers and reengineerers care about. Tom Gilbert would regard this perspective as including tools or instruments. It includes such measures as:

- Percent of sales from new products
- The rate of new product introduction versus plan
- Elapsed time to develop next generation of products
- Break-even time for new products

This perspective also includes traditional manufacturing measures, such as labor efficiency, machine efficiency, quality—waste, scrap, rework—and cycle time

Learning-and-Growth Perspective

Learning-and-growth measures reflect the success the company is having in retraining employees, enhancing technology and systems, and aligning organizational procedures and routines to develop capabilities in people, systems, and procedures the company will need in the future. These measures could be called the employee perspective, but that wouldn't be trendy. Nevertheless, they deal mostly with things workers are concerned about—knowing what to do, how to do it, and getting some recognition. The learning-and-growth perspective includes such measures as:

- Employee satisfaction
- Turnover and employee retention
- Revenue per employee
- Value-added per employee
- Strategic job-coverage ratio (number of employees qualified for specific jobs versus anticipated needs)
- Retraining cycle time (length of time required to take existing employees to new skill level)
- Suggestions per employee
- Suggestions implemented
- Percent of employees with personal performance goals linked to business strategy
- Strategic information coverage (current availability of information relative to anticipated needs)
- Percent of processes with real-time quality, cycle time, and cost feedback
- Percent of customer-facing employees with on-line access to information about customers

Linking Measures to Business Strategy

Building the scorecard involves more than just picking some measures and sorting them into four categories. Good scorecards need some linkage, say Kaplan and Norton. The measures have to fit together, but how? Our gurus identify three important principles that govern the design of a good score-card.

First, there is cause and effect—the measures must relate to each other. They must tell a story such as this:

> If we improve employee access to customer information and provide our employees with more training (learning-and-growth perspective), then our employees will have a better understanding of customer needs and be able to offer customized products and services to meet those needs (internal process perspective). As a result, customers will be more satisfied and purchase a wider range of services from us (customer perspective), which will broaden our revenue base and make us more profitable (financial perspective).

Second, you need two types of measures in addition to the four categories. Kaplan and Norton explain that some measures should lag while others should lead. Let's say you have a measure like customer satisfaction. That's a laggard, they say. It's an after-the-fact measure that doesn't really tell you how to get better. To back up your lagging outcome measures, you need some leading indicators—measures that tell you the why that caused the what. For example, in the case of customer satisfaction, you would need some leading measures like cycle time, quality, and low prices—the things that lead, cause, or predict customer satisfaction.

Finally, say Kaplan and Norton, you need to tie everything back to money. Training employees, installing information systems, reengineering processes, satisfying customers, and so on, are all good things to do, but they don't mean anything unless they make a buck.

How Many Scorecards Do You Need?

Kaplan and Norton argue that all companies should have at least one balanced scorecard. Ideally, you would build multiple scorecards and hook the whole organization together from top to bottom. The corporate scorecard would be connected to the business unit scorecard, which would be connected to the department scorecard. The department scorecard would be connected to the team scorecard. And the team scorecard would be connected to the employees' scorecard.

Unfortunately, admit Kaplan and Norton, this is not likely to happen. Corporations may be too complex and teams too simple to fit their scheme. This condition is just another example of reality stubbornly refusing to live up to theory, but don't despair. Kaplan and Norton say the business unit scorecards will do just fine, provided of course that they meet some simple standards.

> An ideal strategic business unit (SBU) for a Balanced Scorecard conducts activities across an entire value chain: innovation, operations, marketing, distribution, selling, and service. Such an SBU has its own products and customers, marketing and distribution channels, and production facilities. And, most important, it has a well-defined strategy.
>
> Once a Balanced Scorecard has been developed for an SBU, . . . the relevant question for whether a department or functional unit should have a Balanced Scorecard is whether that organizational unit has (or should have) a mission, a strategy, customers (internal or external), and internal processes that enable it to accomplish its mission and strategy. If it does, then the unit is a valid candidate for a Balanced Scorecard.[35]

OUR VIEW

It all sounds good, but we have some questions. For example, why must there be only four categories and particularly these four categories? What about a supplier perspective, or business partner perspective, or the perspective of regulatory agencies, or the communities in which you do business? Shouldn't their concerns be included on the scorecard? We think so.

Also, there is the whole linkage issue. We agree that every measure should tell a story and that whenever several measures coalesce we should have the makings of a fairly good documentary—or, at worst, some interesting fiction. But in the real world, the cause-and-effect linkage is seldom so clear. Most of the time, we would be happy just to get most of the right measures on the card, much less figure out exactly how they all relate.

So, is the scorecard a bust? No. Kaplan and Norton have some good ideas. Everyone does need to look at the financial and nonfinancial measures, and it helps if they can look at the same numbers. We should also try to make some sense out of how everything relates, regardless of how imperfect that sense might be. We need to push information down and out into the organization, as Gilbert prescribed, because the people who do the work need to know what needs to be done and how they are doing. And, finally, we must reward their efforts—the next key leverage point for human competence that Tom Gilbert mentioned. Let's turn to it now.

INCENTIVES

In his book *Human Competence,* Gilbert offers the opinion that "there is more nonsense, superstition, and plain self-deception about the subject of motivation (and incentives) than about any other topic."[36] We agree. In fact, we would add that the amount of junk published annually about the topic would fill several of the largest landfills—and should do so. Most of these worthless tomes carry titles like "Light the Fire In Your Belly" or "Be the Genius You Know You Are." We aren't going to cover such trash here, even if it is written by so-called presidential advisors. Instead, we are going to focus on a backwater area of the guru trade called performance management since, in our opinion, you must understand at least the basics of that subject to make intelligent and effective use of incentives.

The Power of Performance Management

Performance management was extremely popular during the 1970s and early 1980s and then was overtaken by the quality and reengineering fads of the late 1980s and early 1990s. Although it is less popular today, there are still gurus who practice the trade and preach the gospel of performance management. None preaches it better or has practiced it longer than Aubrey C. Daniels, the publisher of *Performance Management* magazine and author of *Performance Management* and *Bringing Out the Best in People.*[37] We will rely heavily on Daniels's approach in our discussion of the subject, since his treatment of it is typical of the field.

Business is Behavior

According to Daniels, all management ultimately comes down to managing behavior, since it is through the behavior of people that all things get done. In fact, managing behavior is so important to the success of any organization that it is the one thing executives, managers, and supervisors must know the most about. That's where performance management comes in. It teaches managers how to manage behavior and use performance incentives, and the first lesson that it teaches is that there are two ways to influence someone's behavior.

Two Ways to Influence Behavior

Daniels suggests that most people try to manage performance by telling other people what to do or not to do. We tell others to work harder, to show more initiative, and to be creative. We order, command, issue memos, circulate policy statements, conduct meetings, develop and circulate balanced scorecards, and so on. In the technical jargon of performance management gurus, including Daniels, this is called providing people with antecedents.

an·te·ced·ent (an'tə sēd'nt), *n.*
a trigger or signal such as a request, command, or prompt that says "do this." Anything that gets behavior started.

The problem with antecedents, Daniels warns, is that they don't work very well or for very long. People may change their behavior temporarily, but when we aren't around, they just go back to their old ways.

Daniels explains that if we understood performance management we would realize that there is a second and better way to influence behavior. In addition to providing an antecedent to get behavior started, we can also provide something after the behavior occurs to increase or decrease the probability that it will be repeated. For example, in addition to asking people to get their work done on time, we can provide them with a reward, recognition, or praise when they submit their reports on time, and we can fine them, fire them, or otherwise punish them when they are late. The technical jargon for what comes after the behavior is a consequence.

con·se·quence (kon'si kwens', -kwəns), *n.*
what happens to a person as a result of the behavior.

Antecedents Get Behavior Started but Can't Sustain It

Antecedents and consequences are important tools for managing behavior, but as Daniels argues, lasting changes in behavior are influenced much more by what comes after the behavior (the consequence) than what comes before (the antecedent). He writes that "antecedents have limited control over behavior. *It is the role of an antecedent to get a behavior to occur once or, at best, a few times.* It is the role of a consequence to get it to occur again."[38] Daniels cites the health warnings on cigarette packages as an example of an antecedent's limited power to produce lasting change.

> How many smokers do you know who pulled out their cigarettes to light up, looked at the warning and said, "Whoa! Do you know these things are dangerous? I'm gonna stop." There is no evidence that any of these printed warnings had any effect on smokers whatsoever.[39]

But haven't many people stopped smoking? you may ask. Yes, responds Daniels, but not because of the warnings alone. Most people stopped because the consequences of smoking changed. They couldn't smoke in airplanes, so flying became uncomfortable. They couldn't smoke in restaurants, or if they did, they were relegated to the worst seating. They couldn't smoke in public buildings so they had to huddle outside in the cold and heat with all of the other addicts. Smoking went from being a smart and attractive thing to do to being a smelly, dirty, and dangerous addiction. The cigarette-pack warning antecedents may have caused some smokers to think about stopping, but as Daniels points out, it was the negative social consequences of smoking that got people to change their behavior. Just remember his words:

Antecedents get behavior started.
Consequences keep behavior going or make it stop.

The Four Types of Consequences

Daniels describes four types of consequences. Two increase the likelihood that the behavior will be repeated, and the other two decrease that likelihood. Let's start with the two forms of consequences with which you are probably most familiar.

Consequence Type #1: Positive Reinforcement—The Carrot
Popularly called the "carrot," this type of consequences causes behavior to increase, as illustrated in Exhibit 6.7 and exemplified in Exhibit 6.8.

EXHIBIT 6.7. **Positive Reinforcement**

Behavior	Consequence	Result	This is
A person does or says something.	The person gets what he or she wants.	The behavior will increase.	Positive reinforcement

EXHIBIT 6.8. **Example of Positive Reinforcement**

Behavior	Consequence	Result	This is
You are having trouble doing a report and ask your boss for information.	The boss provides you with the information.	The next time you need information you will ask your boss.	Positive reinforcement

Consequence Type #2: Punishment—The Stick

You probably know this type of consequence as the "stick." If the consequence of a behavior is that the person gets something he or she does not want, the person will avoid that behavior in the future (Exhibits 6.9 and 6.10).

Consequence Type #3: Extinction—"Ignore It and Maybe It Will Go Away"

You've heard the saying, "Ignore it and maybe it will go away." That's what extinction is all about (see Exhibits 6.11 and 6.12).

Consequence Type #4: Negative Reinforcement—"Do It or Else"

The "do it or else" consequence is common but can sometimes be confusing. We provide an illustration of negative reinforcement in Exhibit 6.13 and an example in Exhibit 6.14. Exhibit 6.15 provides an additional example with an antecedent added.

Daniels says all four types of consequences are useful tools for managing behavior, but he points out that positive reinforcement is much more useful than the others. Here's why.

The Problem with Negative Reinforcement

Negative reinforcement ("do it or else") is probably the most common type of consequence found in most organizations. You are told to have the report

EXHIBIT 6.9 **Punishment**

Behavior	Consequence	Result	This is
A person does or says something.	He or she gets what the person doesn't want.	The behavior will decrease.	Punishment

EXHIBIT 6.10 **Example of Punishment**

Behavior	Consequence	Result	This is
You are having trouble doing a report and ask your boss for information.	Your boss says, "Do I have to do all the work around here myself? Get your own . . . information."	The next time you need information you will think twice before asking your boss.	Punishment

EXHIBIT 6.11. **Extinction**

Behavior	Consequence	Result	This is
A person does or says something.	He or she gets a neutral or no response.	The behavior will increase at first and then gradually decrease over time.	Extinction

EXHIBIT 6.12. **Example of Extinction**

Behavior	Consequence	Result	This is
You are having trouble doing a report and ask your boss for information.	Your boss says, "I don't have time to answer that question right now."	You will ask your boss a few more times for the information. If you still get no response, you will eventually quit asking.	Extinction

EXHIBIT 6.13. **Negative Reinforcement**

Behavior	Consequence	Result	This is
A person does or says something.	The person escapes from or avoids something he or she doesn't want.	The behavior will increase.	Negative reinforcement

EXHIBIT 6.14. **Example of Negative Reinforcement**

Behavior	Consequence	Result	This is
You are having trouble doing a report and ask your boss for information.	Your boss says, "I've been thinking about that report. It's repetitive. You don't need to do it."	The next time you have trouble with an assignment or question its usefulness, you'll ask your boss about it.	Negative reinforcement

EXHIBIT 6.15. **Example of Negative Reinforcement**

Antecedent	Behavior	Consequence	Result	This is
Your boss threatens to fire you if you don't meet your sales quota.	You meet your sales quota.	You avoid being fired.	You will meet, or at least try to meet, your sales quota in the future.	Negative reinforcement

on your boss's desk by Friday or you'll be fired. You get the report to your boss by Friday. Your sales force is given a sales quota to meet by the end of the quarter and they meet it. It's the same with practically every other instance of negative reinforcement. People are given a do-it-or-else threat and they respond. They change their behavior.

So, you might ask, what's wrong with that? The problem is that people respond to negative reinforcement just to the extent necessary to avoid the negative consequence. You get the report to your boss by Friday, not Thursday, Wednesday, or Tuesday. The sales force meets its quota, but just barely.

If all you want is compliance or minimum performance, then use negative reinforcement. You'll get just what you ask for—but nothing more.

The Problem with Punishment

Punishment is really the flip side of negative reinforcement. With negative reinforcement, you are using negative consequences to encourage a behavior you want. With punishment, you are using negative consequences to discourage a behavior you don't want. Like negative reinforcement, say our gurus, punishment may work in the short term but will only get you compliance or minimum performance. People will work to only the level necessary to avoid punishment. Plus, punishment typically produces a number of negative and sometimes serious side effects. The people being punished usually will try to avoid or escape from the punishment and the individual doing the punishing. They will complain, lie, make excuses for what happened, sneak around, hide from those in authority, and refuse to accept responsibility for their actions. Retaliation, sabotage, and even physical attacks are possible. If you punish your employees too severely, you could end up getting shot. It has happened.

The Problem with Extinction

Extinction is an alternative to punishment. Instead of providing negative consequences to stop undesirable behavior, you simply ignore the behavior in the hope that it will go away eventually. Our gurus argue that the advantage of extinction is that it does work eventually. The problem is that "eventually" can seem like a very long time; and even after the undesirable behavior stops, it may resume or be replaced by another undesirable behavior. Here's how Aubrey Daniels describes what typically happens when you use extinction to get people to stop doing something.

> *Extinction Burst:* The first thing that happens when a well-developed behavior is ignored is an increase in the behavior. In other words, the behavior that is being extinguished will actually occur more often. We witness this in our everyday affairs. If we push the button for an elevator and it is slow to arrive, we will push the button several times in succession, although this has no effect on the elevator. . . .
>
> *Emotional Behavior:* Following the extinction burst, you will usually see negative emotional behavior. The child flails about in his crib, . . . an individual kicks the elevator when it doesn't arrive. . . .

Erratic Behavior: After the emotional behavior has run its course, the behavior will continue to occur at various, irregular intervals until it stops altogether. . . . Sometimes the behavior will be replaced by a similar . . . undesired behavior. . . .

Resurgence: When the old behavior has stopped for a period of time, it is not unusual for it to occur again, seemingly out of nowhere. This has led us to believe that people don't really change. You see someone try to eliminate a habit, quit for a while, but eventually go back to the old ways.[40]

Extinction takes time and perseverance. The problem most people have with using it, warn the gurus, is that they tend to give in during the stages of extinction burst or emotional behavior and respond either with punishment or sometimes a reward. Even if extinction works, it only works to eliminate the undesirable behavior. People learn what not to do, but they don't learn what they should do. Like negative reinforcement and punishment, extinction is not a very effective way to manage behavior. Fortunately, note the gurus, there is something better.

The Power of Positive Reinforcement

Positive reinforcement is our gurus' favorite tool for managing behavior for two primary reasons:

1. Unlike extinction and punishment, positive reinforcement teaches people what to do and not just what not to do. As a result, people learn and get better, which is the goal of performance management.

2. Unlike negative reinforcement, where people perform at the minimum to avoid the negative consequence, people who receive positive reinforcement perform to their full potential. They go far above and beyond the minimum.

Of course, to use positive reinforcement, you have to understand it. Here's a short quiz. Ask yourself which of the following represents instances of positive reinforcement.

1. You walk into your office and flip on the light switch. The light comes on.
2. You pull on your desk drawer to retrieve a file you need and the drawer opens.

3. You call somebody's name and she responds.
4. You type on your computer keypad and words appear on the screen.
5. You win an award for perfect attendance.
6. All of the above.
7. None of the above.

Answer: All of the above

Daniels notes that when he asks people for examples of positive reinforcement, most cite things such as attaboys, pats on the back, service plaques, applause, or some kind of public recognition for a job well done. They fail to mention things such as the light coming on, or the pen working the way it should, and so on, which are also examples of positive reinforcement. Here's the definition of positive reinforcement:

pos·i·tive re·in·force·ment (poz´i tiv rē′in fôrs´mənt), *n.*
any consequence that follows behavior and increases its frequency
in the future.

The light coming on and the pen working are reinforcing. They follow behavior and increase its frequency in the future. You expect the light to come on when you flip the switch, so when you want light, you flip the switch. You expect the pen to write, so you use it when you want to write a note. In fact, the reinforcement is so powerful that you think something is wrong if you don't get reinforced.

These types of reinforcers are so powerful because they are naturally occurring—they are automatically connected to the behavior. You flip the switch (behavior) and the light comes on (positive reinforcement). You push the keys on the keyboard (behavior) and the computer responds with letters on the screen (positive reinforcement). There is no delay between the behavior and the reinforcement, and best of all, notes Daniels, no one has to intervene to make the reinforcement happen.

Daniels warns that the mistake most people make with positive reinforcement is to assume that it applies only to such things as praise, a congratulatory note, an award, or a trophy that are added after the fact. They fail to recognize that the most powerful way to manage behavior is to build performance reinforcement into the job by reengineering work along the lines we discuss in Chapter 4 on creating high-performance organizations. Awards and pats on the back should be used when you haven't or can't build reinforcement into the job or when you want to supplement the naturally occurring reinforcement.

Tips and Tricks in Using Positive Reinforcement

Aubrey Daniels and most of our other motivation gurus strongly believe in the power of positive reinforcement, particularly when it is done right and ideally made a natural part of the job itself. Daniels cites performance gains of as much as 300% when positive reinforcement is used effectively, but there are some tricks associated with getting such results. Here are a few of the most important.

Individualize the Reinforcement

You have heard the saying that beauty is in the eye of the beholder. Well, say our gurus, positive reinforcement is in the mind of the person being reinforced. Nothing pleases everyone. Some people like sports and some don't. Some people like to go to the opera while others hate it. You have to match the reinforcer to the desires, needs, and preferences of the person you want to reinforce. How do you find out what people want? Our gurus suggest that you start with observation. Notice what people talk about and how they spend their free time. If someone talks excitedly about baseball, you have a clue to their interest. Once you have made a few observations, try something as a reinforcer. Don't be too concerned if you pick the wrong thing. Daniels notes that in most cases people are so starved for reinforcement that just about anything you pick will work, at least the first few times. If you find that this approach isn't giving you the results you want, our gurus suggest that you use a very straightforward method—ask people what they would find reinforcing. However, don't be surprised if they don't know or are reluctant to tell you.

Make Reinforcement Contingent

There is a big difference between positive reinforcement and gift giving. You may be pleased when you get a birthday present, but the only thing it reinforces you to do is live another year. Similarly, Christmas bonuses for everyone, company picnics, and other such unconditional gifts may be nice, but they are not positive reinforcers. They aren't contingent upon any behavior. To make sure that your reinforcers are contingent, Daniels suggests that you try to state them in the following way:

You can get _____ if and only if you do this _____ .
　　　　　　　(reinforcer)　　　　　　　　　　　　　　　　(behavior)

If you can't complete the sentence, you don't have a positive reinforcer.

Make Reinforcement Immediate

The longer you wait after the behavior to give the reinforcement, the weaker the reinforcement. You also run the risk of the performer misinterpreting what is actually being reinforced. When time elapses between the behavior you want to reinforce and the reinforcement, the person you are reinforcing may become confused about which behavior you are trying to reinforce. Daniels cites research that shows that the most effective managers and supervisors aren't necessarily those who reinforce more, but rather those who reinforce people while they are performing. In short, the immediacy of the reinforcement seems to be as important, if not more important, that its frequency.

Reinforce Often

Positive reinforcement is powerful, but only in the aggregate. As Daniels says, one positive reinforcer won't change a life. How much does it take? A lot. For example, the famous psychologist B. F. Skinner once estimated that it could take as many as 50,000 reinforcers to teach a student basic math. That's more than one reinforcer per minute for every minute a student is in school during the first four grades. Contrast that with the average of six reinforcers per hour that most students actually receive and with the annual performance appraisals, annual recognition dinners, and quarterly bonuses that most employees receive, and you can see why performance suffers.

Don't Make People Compete for Reinforcement

Competition may be good in many spheres of life, but it can be counterproductive to performance improvement efforts. This is particularly true for modern organizations that are trying to encourage teamwork and cooperation. You should therefore eliminate all Employee of the Month awards or any other awards that only one person can win. Our gurus suggest that you replace these winner-take-all awards with award and recognition programs in which everyone competes against a standard or against their own previous performance. Anyone and everyone who achieves the standard or beats their previous performance wins.

Never Pair Reinforcement with Instruction

Don't say something like, "That was a great job you did on that report, but you could have. . . ." The "but you could have," says Daniels, is a verbal eraser. It wipes out all the reinforcement that has gone before. People remember only what they did wrong, not what they did well. In short, say our gurus, save the "but you could have" for later.

Don't Forget Compensation

There is much debate about whether and to what extent money motivates. Some of our gurus say that while the lack of money will make most people dissatisfied, the promise of riches will not necessarily make them do what they wouldn't do otherwise. Others insist that money makes the world go around. Regardless of the position they take about money as a reinforcer, our gurus agree that your compensation system can have a big impact on your efforts to manage and motivate people.

Compensation

In *Human Competence,* Tom Gilbert wrote that while money was a powerful incentive, he had seldom had the opportunity to experiment with it in all of his years as a performance engineer. The primary reason, Gilbert explained, was that even his most enlightened clients—those who were very willing to take his advice about changing their information systems, reengineering work tools, or completely revising their training programs—shrank from any mention of changing the way people were paid. In the 1970s, pay was sacrosanct. It no longer is.

The Problem with Traditional Pay

Our attitudes about pay practices began to change in the 1980s when American business was seriously challenged by global competitors for the first time. Until that time, most American workers, 95% in major U.S. corporations, were paid a base salary established as a result of a *point-factor* job evaluation. The point-factor approach worked like this:

1. Managers prepared detailed job descriptions for all positions in the company.

2. Each job description was then rated according to common factors, such as working conditions, problem-solving requirements, knowledge required to perform the job, and accountability for performance.

3. Each job accumulated points based upon how much of each factor the job contained.

4. The resulting total point score was then used as a basis for establishing a salary level for each job. Jobs with high point scores were paid more than jobs with low point scores.

5. The point-factor base pay was then coupled with an annual merit increase that itself was linked to individual performance appraisals. The company would budget for an annual increase at least equal to what other companies were paying. Supervisors would then evaluate employees and assign performance ratings. The ratings in turn would determine the percentage increase each employee received.

Edward E. Lawler, director of the University of Southern California's Center for Effective Organizations and author of *Strategic Pay,* notes that American businesses liked the point-factor system for several reasons:[41]

1. It promised high levels of fairness and internal equity. With a point-factor system, every job in the company was paid on the basis of a single system. Thus, the company was assured of pay comparability across organizational boundaries. A person could move from job to job and even from business unit to business unit and find consistent pay practices. A job with higher responsibilities would always bring higher pay, regardless of its location.

2. Not only did the point-factor system promise comparability across a single organization, it promised comparability between companies. Since most companies used the point-factor approach, it was relatively easy to compare jobs across companies and even entire industries. A company could quickly determine if it was paying higher or lower wages than its competitors for jobs with comparable point scores.

3. Point-factor systems ensured centralized control. Corporate staff could easily audit divisions to see if they were paying people properly. All they had to do was review job descriptions and calculate point scores. Corporate staffers could then compare their calculations with the division's and could check the division's pay rates with those of its competitors. The whole system enabled senior management to control pay tightly across the entire corporation, regardless of its size.

4. The point-factor system was so well established that consulting firms, most notably the Hay Group, offered large databases and complex, off-the-shelf quantitative models that provided what Lawler described as "an aura of science and objectivity" to the whole messy issue of pay and that took some of the conflict out of the subject. Executives could use the excuse that it wasn't their fault that you got paid what you did; the system made them do it.

5. Finally, the linkage of base pay to individual performance appraisals provided the illusion, if not the reality, of paying for performance. Outstanding performers would receive high scores and thus would receive large increases. Mediocre performers would receive low ratings and, consequently, minimum or no increases.

The point-factor system was perfectly suited for the bureaucratic organization in which the top executives made all of the decisions, middle and lower managers were responsible for implementing those decisions, and workers were expected to keep their mouths shut and do what they were told. And that was the problem with it.

Beginning in the mid-1980s, bureaucracy became anathema. American companies began to realize that to compete globally they had to become fast, flexible, responsive, innovative, and creative. They had to become decidedly unbureaucratic. But, as Lawler and other gurus pointed out, traditional pay practices, particularly point-factor systems, made that almost impossible for several reasons:

1. A point-factor system based upon rigid job descriptions encouraged people to do only what was in their job description. This attitude didn't fit very well with the idea that flexibility was critical and that everyone should be willing to do whatever was needed to satisfy customers.

2. Point-factor systems reinforced the outdated idea of a hierarchy. At a time when American companies were downsizing and reducing layers of management to become flat and lean, the point system rewarded people for building up layers and levels. It even encouraged people to lie when creating job descriptions designed to get the points they needed for higher pay.

3. Point-factor systems seemed out of step with the values most companies were beginning to espouse. Most executives were proclaiming that people were their companies' most important asset. But, argued Lawler, point-factor systems "depersonalize people, equating them with a set of duties rather than with who they are and what they can do. It tends to de-emphasize paying people for the skills that they have and for the performance that they demonstrate."[42]

4. At a time when change was critical, point-factor systems made reengineering and restructuring all the more difficult. Rewriting job descriptions was time consuming and often led to costly infighting, as everyone tried to preserve responsibilities, accountabilities, and as many points as they could.

5. The widespread practice of linking base-pay increases to individual performance appraisals was a demotivating disaster. After all, most performance appraisals were nothing more than the highly subjective judgments of supervisors. Companies then compounded the problem by insisting that ratings across the organization had to be "normally" distributed so that most people were rated as neither outstanding nor poor. This approach guaranteed that the only way one person could get a large increase was for another to get a small increase or nothing at all. The whole system was demoralizing for employees and managers alike and ensured that most workers, regardless of their actual talents, would be rated as average. Aubrey Daniels reflected the view of most motivation gurus when he wrote that the annual performance appraisal was a "masochistic and sadistic ritual" and "a total waste of time."[43]

By the mid-1990s, the point-factor system was dead or dying in most American companies. Even the Hay Group was forced to agree that the time for such systems may have passed. Hay vice presidents Thomas P. Flannery, David A. Hofrichter, and Paul E. Platten, for example, admitted in their 1996 book *People, Performance and Pay* that there is a "growing chasm between organization change and compensation" and that, while some organizations might only need to modify their current Hay-type program, others might require creating entirely new nonpoint-factor systems.[44] Coming from executives of the nation's premier point-factor consulting firm, it was an extraordinary statement. It was also recognition that a consensus had emerged among compensation gurus. The consensus was that point-factor systems should be not only abandoned by most, if not all, companies, but also replaced with a compensation system consisting of two essential components: (1) base pay tied to the skills a person possesses rather than the job he or she holds and (2) incentive pay tied to group and/or company performance, rather than to individual performance. Here are some of the key features of each of these components and the issues involved in their implementation.

Pay-for-Skill Systems

Pay-for-skill compensation systems tie base pay to the skills an employee possesses, rather than to the position the employee occupies. In general, there are two types of pay-for-skill systems:

1. Increased-knowledge-based systems. Tie pay to the depth of skills a person possesses in a particular specialty. This type of system is similar to the entry-to-journeyman progressions found in many skilled trades and to professional pay progressions found in law offices, universities, and R & D labs.

2. Multiskilled systems. Tie pay to the breadth of skills people have and/or the range of jobs they can perform across the entire organization. Multiskilled systems are often found in manufacturing environments where employees are paid based upon the number of jobs they can perform upstream and downstream in the manufacturing process.

Advantages of Skill-Based Pay

Our gurus cite several key advantages that skill-based pay has over more traditional job-based pay:

1. Flexibility. Skill-based pay systems, particularly multiskilled systems, encourage employees to learn and perform a wide variety of tasks rather than just those listed in their job description. Companies benefit from this increased flexibility by having the ability to move employees from one work assignment to another when absenteeism, turnover, or work backlogs occur.

2. Better problem solving. Ed Lawler notes that "when employees learn both horizontal and vertical skills (breadth and depth of knowledge) they gain an entirely different perspective on the organization's operations, the way it is managed, and the information system that supports it. Thus . . . [they are able] to solve systemic problems more effectively. Their broader perspective helps employees to be more innovative in improving operations . . . [and] . . . more effective in . . . problem-solving."[45]

3. Lessened resistance to change. Jay R. Schuster and Patricia K. Zingheim, authors of *The New Pay,* note that a skill-based pay system can be of significant help to organizations in overcoming resistance to change. For example, when an organization is planning a major change, such as a significant reengineering of work methods and/or the introduction of new technology, a pay-for-skill system can be modified easily to reward people for acquiring the new skills.[46]

4. Improved customer service. Schuster and Zingheim also note that service organizations, particularly insurance companies and financial institutions, can benefit from having more well-rounded, multiskilled employees. These employees are able to deal with a customer on a variety of issues without having to send him or her from specialist to specialist for answers. The organization is more efficient and the customer is better served.[47]

5. Promotes commitment and a learning culture. Finally, say our gurus, pay-for-skill is consistent with the kind of participative, open-book, learning culture that most organizations should be trying to create.

Disadvantages of Skill-Based Pay

Of course, our gurus admit, skill-based pay does have some disadvantages. It can be expensive and time consuming to identify the skills you truly need. Keeping track of who has the needed skills and who needs to learn them can become an administrative headache. Also, most companies that have adopted pay-for-skill have found that their payroll costs rose since they were paying more for the increased skills. Finally, there is the cost of training and retraining, as well as the expense associated with lost production while people are learning. Still, argue our gurus, when you consider the advantages that result from flexibility, better problem solving, improved customer service, and faster adoption of new technology, pay-for-skill seems well worth it. Plus, what alternative do you have? The traditional point-factor system clearly doesn't work anymore, and if you don't pay for skills, what's left?

Implementing Pay-for-Skill

As you might expect, each of our gurus has his or her own method for implementing pay-for-skill. Most, however, cover the design issues outlined in Exhibit 6.16.

Pay for Competencies

Skill-based pay systems compensate employees for learning observable and testable skills. For example, employees in a manufacturing plant might earn extra pay for learning to perform tasks that occur earlier or later in the manufacturing process than their normal job. Equipment operators might

---

EXHIBIT 6.16. How to Compensate Employees for Their Skills

- *Identifying skills and skill levels.* Typically, an employee design team is assigned the task of identifying skills to be included in the pay-for-skill system. Existing jobs are audited to identify essential tasks, which are then broken down into required skills. The challenge at this stage, say Jay Schuster and Patricia Zingheim, is "to select from the skills the employees have those skills that are needed to perform the required work. This means that not all existing employee skills may be necessary. It also means that skills the employees do not have may be needed to get the work done. Not only must specific skills be described, but if a skill exists in varying levels of complexity and application, these levels must be clearly differentiated."[1] As you might expect, the number of skills that are identified can vary greatly and in some cases can range into the hundreds.

- *Skill blocks.* Once skills are identified, they are normally grouped into blocks. Schuster and Zingheim note that "skills may be combined based upon technical depth—as, for example, with telecommunications field technicians and field engineers. Alternatively, skills may be combined logically based on the work performed, with each skill block being of equal or varying complexity."

- *Maximum skills to learn.* If a large number of skills are identified and/or if the skills are difficult to learn and retain, most gurus recommend that companies place some restrictions on the maximum number of skills employees can learn. This ensures that employees remain proficient in the skills for which they are being compensated.

- *Minimum skills to learn.* In addition to establishing an upper limit on the number of skills employees can learn, companies may also establish a lower limit. For example, Au Bon Pain requires all employees to master at least three skill blocks within their first year on the job.

- *Sequencing.* Some companies also require employees to learn skill blocks in a specific sequence.

- *Length of time in one skill block.* A related issue is whether there will be a minimum time period during which an employee must perform a skill before he or she can learn the next skill block. Companies typically require a minimum payback period to recoup their investment in training before an employee is allowed to learn a new skill.

- *Determining proficiency in a skill.* An individual's proficiency in a skill can be determined through formal testing, peer evaluations, and/or supervisor ratings. In addition to initial testing, there is also usually some provision for periodic retesting, refresher training, and certification. Employees who fail to pass retesting may lose their pay for the skill or be placed on probationary status while they relearn the skill.

- *Compensating employees for learning new skills.* Ed Lawler lists four basic approaches companies can use to compensate employees for learning additional skills:

1. They can tie specific pay raises to learning identified skills.

2. They can create broad pay bands that allow individuals to receive significant pay increases as they learn additional skills. That is, instead of putting people in a pay range in which the top is about 50% higher than the bottom, they can use a range in which the top is almost double the bottom. This leaves a great deal of room for pay to rise as employees continue to learn. (In this case, employees progress from the bottom to the top of the pay range by completing training and demonstrating proficiency in skill blocks.)

3. They can give employees one-time lump-sum payments when they develop new skills. This is particularly appropriate where the use of the skills is temporary or short-term, or where pay is already high and it is difficult for the organization to afford an ongoing extra cost.

4. They can tie promotions or changes in pay grades to increases in skills. This is the approach taken with technical ladders and some competency-based plans for managers.[3]

---

1. Jay R. Schuster and Patricia K. Zingheim, *The New Pay* (San Francisco: Jossey-Bass, 1992), p. 98.

2. *Ibid.*

3. Edward E. Lawler, *From the Ground Up* (San Francisco: Jossey-Bass, 1996), p. 204.

be awarded pay supplements for learning to perform routine maintenance on their equipment. In these cases, the skill is highly observable and/or can be easily tested. There is a clear and objective way to determine if the person has learned the skill and therefore is entitled to the skill-based pay. Competency-based pay takes this concept one step further.

Those who support competency-based pay argue that the highly testable technical skills and knowledge normally rewarded in skill-based pay are merely the most visible predictors of superior performance. They are the tip of the iceberg. Beneath the surface are deeper competencies that are as important as, if not more important than, the visible skills. These deeper competencies include such things as a person's self-concept, traits (tenacity, flexibility, etc.), and internal motives such as the need for achievement. Competency-based pay seeks to recognize and reward these additional inner traits.

Thomas Flannery, David Hofrichter, and Paul Platten of the Hay Group describe a three-step process for developing a competency-based compensation program in their 1996 book *People, Performance, and Pay.*

Step #1: Identify the Competencies That Create Value for the Organization

Our three gurus say there is more to this step than just drawing up a wish list of attributes you would like your employees to possess, such as being self-motivated, achievement oriented, and customer focused. Instead, you must carefully and systematically identify the competencies that you require to support your business strategy and create added value to your product or service. A company seeking to provide a high-level personalized service to its customers, they note, might seek employee competencies such as:

- Customer service orientation
- Listening and responding
- Flexibility
- Interpersonal understanding
- Teamwork and cooperation[48]

Step #2: Interview Superior Performers

For each job, role, or family of jobs in your organization, the Hay Group consultants suggest that you identify your superior performers and interview them to determine what they do most often in most situations to achieve outstanding results. Flannery, Hofrichter, and Platten suggest that

> by asking questions about how they approach their jobs or how they solve problems, an experienced interviewer can begin to draw out the key competencies. Take, for example, the issue of customer service: In answering questions about how customer complaints are handled, the superior-performing employee will probably talk about proactively addressing complaints, going beyond the normal expectations, if necessary, to answer them satisfactorily. The average employee, on the other hand, may talk about following established procedures and maintaining company policy—nothing

more, nothing less—while the lower-performing employee may place all responsibility and blame with others.[49]

Step #3: Define and Test Competencies

Based upon your interviews with superior performers, you develop a list of the behavioral characteristics that supposedly predict outstanding performance. For example, Flannery and his coauthors say you might come up with the following lists of characteristics for the teamwork and cooperation competencies mentioned in step one:

- Outstanding performers
  Bring conflict (personal and professional) within the team into the open
  Encourage or facilitate a beneficial resolution that promotes teamwork
  Do not hide conflicts or avoid the issue, but try to resolve conflicts as quickly as possible
- Acceptable performers
  Express positive expectations of the capabilities of other team members
  Speak of team members and to others within or outside the team in a supportive manner
  Appeal to reason in situations of conflict rather than taking an argumentative position
- Less than acceptable performers
  Cooperate
  Participate willingly in teams
  Support team decisions
  Perform as good team players
  Do their share of the work

After identifying the competencies, Flannery and the others emphasize that you must test them to determine whether they actually make a difference in performance, since you want to utilize only distinguishing competencies that truly separate the best from the rest.

The Hay Group consultants warn that ferreting out competencies will not be an easy task.

Determining these behaviors—most of which are not readily visible—requires careful, thoughtful, disciplined analysis. It is one thing to test an individual to determine his or her knowledge about a particular subject or skill on a particular job. It is quite another challenge to determine what makes one individual more responsive to customers, more driven to succeed, and more consistently a top performer. The process of assessing competencies is more than making a simple albeit subjective laundry list. It requires a certain level of training and expertise.[50]

OUR VIEW

If the whole idea of basing compensation on below-the-waterline, barely discernible, and highly elusive trait competencies makes you a little queasy, it does the same to us. We aren't reassured by the explanation that the assessment of such competencies requires "a certain level of training and expertise" that most people presumably don't possess. The statement conjures up images of hordes of high-priced consultants descending upon a company. We think that skill-based pay plans that tie an individual's compensation to his or her ability to learn and to perform specific tasks of value to the organization is a good idea. When the concept is extended to compensate people for underlying psychological traits or vaguely defined characteristics, such as leadership, adaptability, innovation, team orientation, communication, or customer focus, we think the idea is being pushed too far and is actually taking us back to the discredited 1960s and 1970s practice of trait ratings. Maybe Ed Lawler put it best in a 1996 article when he wrote:

> You should pay individuals for what they can do that is related to task performance, not for their "potential." Once an individual has performed a job, we can identify and measure the person's task-related skills and knowledge. . . . [T]he task-related skills and knowledge, not underlying competencies, are the most useful basis for setting pay because they most directly determine what work an individual can do. . . . [T]hese skills and knowledge are also likely to be the key determinant of market value.[51]

We believe Lawler is right. When it comes to pay, stick with knowledge and skill that you can observe and objectively measure.

Incentive Pay

Pay-for-skill or pay-for-competencies is a method for setting base compensation that encourages learning and skill development. The second component of the new pay system provides the incentive for people to apply their knowledge and skill to the benefit of the organization. There is nothing new about providing employees with financial incentives for performance. What is new, however, is an emerging consensus among our gurus about the keys to success of such plans. Here are some of the most important success factors cited by our gurus.[52]

Incentives Should Provide a Clear "Line of Sight"

Most of our gurus cite evidence that incentive awards must be in the range of 10 to 15% in order to be motivating.

Incentives Should Be Clear

Employees must be able to see a direct connection between their day-to-day performance and the amount and probability of receiving the desired reward.

Incentives Should Be Tied to Organizational Results

While incentives must be clear, the performance measures used to determine whether bonuses are earned should not be so narrowly defined that they allow employees to receive large payouts when the organization is not financially successful.

Incentives Should Be Based on Relevant and Simple Measures

Schuster and Zingheim establish two criteria for effective measures in an incentive plan. First, they must be relevant to the organization and the employees. Employees must be able to directly influence performance on the measures, and the organization must win if performance goals are met. Second, the measures must be simple enough for employees to understand. "It makes no sense," write Schuster and Zingheim, "to spend time developing complex measures that employees do not understand or measures that are not important to evaluating the performance of both employees and the organization."[53]

Incentives Should Be Timely

The award must be made as close as possible to the performance of the behavior. In short, monthly awards are better than quarterly bonuses, and quarterly bonuses are better than annual ones.

Incentives Should Be Public

Obviously, the award can't be motivating if no one knows that it exists. While this point would seem obvious, Ed Lawler recalls one organization that offered large amounts of money—as much as $100,000 in some instances—to people for outstanding performance. The problem was that only a few senior executives and those fortunate enough to receive the award knew that it existed. The company made the award even less motivating by stipulating that a person could win the award only once, regardless of how well he or she performed in the future.[54]

Incentives Should Be Attainable

People must think that they have a realistic possibility of receiving the award. Lawler notes that "the Nobel Prize, for example, is motivating only to the small number of leading research scientists and authors who feel that they can in fact win it. It is not motivating to most people—even, for example, to most research scientists—even though they would very much like to receive it."[55]

Incentives Should Be Coupled with Employee Involvement

Ideally, say our gurus, any incentive program should be part of an overall effort to create a partnership with employees and involve them in efforts to improve performance. If there is no systematic way for employees to influence how work is performed and how technology is used, then they have no meaningful way to influence performance on the measures except by working harder. The goal for employees should be to find ways to work smarter and not just harder. This requires employee participation and structured involvement. (See Chapter 4 on high-performance organizations for our gurus' ideas about what employee involvement really means.)

Incentives Should Reward Group Rather Than Individual Performance

Ed Lawler writes that "an individual pay-for-performance system does not fit an organization that is designed around processes and teams and that emphasizes the importance of lateral relationships and cooperation. . . . [I]ndividuals who need to cooperate and help each other should not be put in a position of competing for the same rewards."[56]

OUR VIEW

What then is the best approach to incentive pay, given our gurus' key success factors? First, let us say that we agree with Thomas Flannery, David Hofrichter, and Paul Platten that:

1. Pay is first and foremost a people issue. It is about motivating them. It is about reshaping and refocusing their behaviors and accepting new values.
2. Pay is a major organizational communication tool. It is perhaps the most direct way that an organization has of communicating with its employees.
3. No single pay strategy is right for everyone. Different organizations, as well as different employee groups in the same organization, may require different strategies.
4. Pay must support—not lead—the organization's vision, values, and business strategies.
5. To achieve points 1 through 4, pay must be aligned with the organization's work cultures.[57]

That said, we suggest, as Ed Lawler does, that the best incentive pay system for most companies probably would involve some combination of corporatewide profit sharing and stock ownership, coupled with gain sharing plans in major operating units that award groups for cost saving and/or improvements in productivity or quality over specified targets. Such a combination seems ideal. First of all, gain sharing, profit sharing, and stock ownership all tie incentive pay to team and/or organization performance, rather than to individual performance, an approach that we believe is critical today. Second, while gain sharing typically provides clear line of sight and timely payouts, profit sharing and stock ownership provide a complementary long-term focus and organizationwide perspective. As the Hay Group consultants argue, there is no single compensation solution that fits the needs of all organizations, but we think the intelligent mixture of gain sharing, profit sharing, stock ownership, and base pay tied to the acquisition of skills comes closest. At least it represents a good model from which most organizations can start to build their own unique compensation system.

KEY POINTS

- Human competence is a function of the value of accomplishment divided by the cost of the behavior required to produce that accomplishment. Thus, there are only three ways to improve human performance: (1) increase the value of accomplishment, (2) reduce the cost of behavior, or (3) do both.

○━┳ In order to determine the competence of any individual, group, or institution, you must compare its typical performance to that of an exemplary performer. You can determine the improvement potential of any individual, group, or institution from that comparison.

○━┳ For any given accomplishment, a deficiency in performance always has as its immediate cause a deficiency in a behavior repertory or in the environment that supports the repertory. A person's behavior repertory consists of motives (likes, preferences, needs, values), capacity (mental and physical abilities), and knowledge (education and skills). Environmental supports, provided by the organization, consist of information about strategies, goals, and current performance; instruments (tools, techniques, technology, work method); and incentives (nonmonetary and monetary).

○━┳ The best way to improve human performance is to

1. Provide people with better, more timely, and more complete information about the organization's strategies, goals, and current performance;
2. Involve the employees who must use tools, techniques, methods, and technology in their design, development, and selection;
3. Provide strong financial and nonfinancial incentives that are directly contingent upon superior performance and/or performance improvement;
4. Provide people with just-in-time training targeted to their specific needs.

○━┳ Inadequate information is the major cause of more than half of all problems with human performance. By improving the quality and timeliness of the information people receive, you can improve performance by as much as 20 to 50%.

○━┳ People need two types of information in order to perform well. First, they need information to give them direction. They must understand the mission of their company, its business strategy, and what constitutes good performance. Second, they need information for confirmation. They need measures, goals, and objectives they can use to monitor and get feedback on their day-to-day performance.

○━┳ Companies should train employees to understand the critical numbers, particularly the financial numbers, that managers use to measure and monitor the performance of the business, and should hold regular meetings to keep all employees informed about the status of the business, particularly its performance on critical financial measures.

○━┳ In addition to monitoring such financial measures, everyone in the company should constantly monitor nonfinancial measures that are useful in predicting future financial performance. These measures should reflect the concerns of customers, suppliers, business partners, regulatory agencies, communities in which the business operates, and all other affected parties. In addition, everyone should regularly monitor measures of the efficiency and effectiveness of internal processes, the satisfaction of employees, and the rate of ongoing individual and organizational learning.

○━┳ All of the measures monitored throughout the organization should be linked in a series of cause-and-effect relationships back to the company's overall business strategy and financial performance. It should be easy to determine how the performance on any measure being tracked at any level of the organization contributes to the implementation of the business strategy and financial success of the company.

○━┳ All organizations should make extensive use of positive reinforcement to encourage good performance. Positive reinforcement is preferable to all other consequences organizations can provide to influence employee behavior.

○━┳ Whenever possible, positive reinforcement should be built into the performance of the task as a natural and immediate by-product, rather than added on as a reward, recognition, or praise after the behavior has occurred.

○━┳ The most effective positive reinforcers are immediate, individualized, contingent on the behavior, and occur frequently. Ideally, people should never have to compete with others for reinforcement, and the reinforcement should never be paired with instruction, as in "That was a good job, but you should have. . . ."

Traditional point-factor compensation systems that tie pay to the jobs people perform should be replaced with compensation systems that (1) tie base pay to skills and skill acquisition, and (2) provide incentive pay tied to group and/or company rather than individual performance. The ideal model for such a compensation system is one that provides corporatewide profit sharing and stock ownership, coupled with gain sharing in major operating units.

Peter F. Drucker, professor of social science and management at the Clairmont Graduate School and author of *Concept of the Corporation*

Charles Handy, author of *The Age of Paradox* and *The Age of Unreason*

Thomas J. (Tom) Peters, founder of the Tom Peters Group and coauthor of *In Search of Excellence*

7

Business, Work, and Society

I n his 1993 book, *The Post-Capitalist Society,* Peter Drucker wrote, "The same forces which destroyed Marxism as an ideology and Communism as a social system are . . . also making Capitalism obsolescent."[1] Drucker's pronouncement carries extraordinary implications. It also represents a fitting end to this book, because in many respects the destruction of communism and the obsolescence of capitalism are both the causes and results of just about everything we have discussed so far.

It is supremely ironic that Drucker, the guru of all business gurus and the ultimate chronicler and proponent of capitalism, has declared capitalism obsolete. Here is what he had to say about the end of capitalism as we know it.

For two hundred and fifty years, from the second half of the eighteenth century on, Capitalism was the dominant social reality. For the last hundred years, Marxism was the dominant social ideology. Both are rapidly being superseded by a new and very different society.

> The new society—and it is already here—is a post-capitalist society. . . .
> The center of gravity in the post-capitalist society—its structure, its social
> and economic dynamics, its social classes, and its social problems—is differ-
> ent from the one that dominated the last two hundred and fifty years.[2]

How significant is this transformation from capitalist to postcapitalist society? Very significant. "Every few hundred years," writes Drucker, "there
occurs [such] a sharp transformation. We cross . . . a 'divide.' Within a few
short decades, society rearranges itself—its worldview; its basic values; its
social and political structure; its arts; its key institutions. Fifty years later,
there is a new world. And the people born then cannot even imagine the
world in which their grandparents lived and into which their own parents
were born. We are currently living through just such a transformation."[3]

In Exhibit 7.1, Drucker compares the significance and magnitude of the
current transformation to several that have occurred before. These were
hardly subtle changes. They were all great watersheds that fundamentally
and permanently changed the world. Now, writes Drucker, we are in the
midst of another, yet greater transformation. It began at the end of World
War II and will be fully completed by 2010, certainly no later than 2020,
he writes. The basic outlines of this new world, however, are already in
place.

PETER DRUCKER'S POSTCAPITALIST SOCIETY

Drucker argues that we are fast becoming a society of new classes.[4] Capitalist society, he reminds us, was a society of two dominant social classes. Capitalists owned and controlled the means of production. Blue-collar workers—
what Karl Marx called proletarians—labored for the capitalists and were
alienated, exploited, and dependent. Today, both the capitalist and the proletarian have largely disappeared. Blue-collar workers reached their peak in
numbers and influence in the 1950s and have been in steady decline ever
since. "By the year 2000," predicts Drucker, "there will be no developed
country where traditional workers making and moving goods account for
more than one sixth or one eighth of the work force."[5] Capitalists reached
their peak in numbers and economic importance, says Drucker, around the
turn of the century and certainly no later than the end of World War I. "Since

---

EXHIBIT 7.1. **Great Watersheds that Changed the World**

Thirteenth Century

- The European world becomes centered in the city.
- City guilds emerge as the dominant social groups.
- Long-distance trade is revived.
- Gothic architecture develops.
- Aristotle emerges as the fountainhead of wisdom.
- Urban universities replace monasteries as the centers of culture.
- New urban religious orders, the Dominicans and Franciscans, emerge as transmitters of religion, learning, and spirituality.
- Dante becomes the wellspring of European literature.

1455 to 1517

- Johannes Gutenberg invents moveable type.
- The Renaissance blossoms in Florence and Venice.
- America is discovered by Europeans.
- The Spanish infantry, the first standing army since Rome, is created.
- The science of anatomy is rediscovered and, with it, scientific inquiry.
- The West adopts Arabic numerals.
- Martin Luther sparks the Protestant Reformation.

1776 to 1820

- James Watt perfects the steam engine.
- Adam Smith writes *The Wealth of Nations*.
- Capitalism and communism emerge.
- The industrial revolution occurs.
- The modern university is created.
- Nations begin offering universal schooling.
- The Rothschilds become a great European economic power.

Source: Peter F. Drucker, **Post-Capitalist Society** *(New York: HarperCollins, 1993), pp. 1–8.*

---

then, no one has matched in power and visibility the likes of Morgan, Rockefeller, Carnegie, or Ford in the United States; Siemens, Thyssen, Rathenau, Krupp in Germany; Mond, Cunnard, Lever, Vickers, Armstrong in Great Britain; de Wendel and Schneider in France; or the families that owned the great *zaibatsu* of Japan: Mitsubishi, Mitsui, and Sumitomo. By World War II they had all been replaced. . . ."[6] Drucker explains that "pension funds increasingly control the supply and allocation of money. In the United States, these funds in 1992 owned half of the share capital of the country's large businesses and held almost as much of these companies' fixed debts."[7]

So how and why has this strange new world with no capitalists and no proletariat emerged? What led to the fall of communism and the obsolescence of capitalism? Knowledge, says Drucker. "Knowledge is fast becoming the sole factor in production, sidelining both capital and labor."[8] Notice that he writes that knowledge is becoming *the* sole factor in production, not just *a* factor. Of course, the knowledge that is the foundation of the new society is a different kind of knowledge.

The New Meaning of Knowledge

Drucker reminds us that knowledge has meant different things throughout history. For hundreds of years, knowledge was applied to a person's "being," and two theories dominated in both the West and East. One theory, associated with Plato and Socrates in the West and the Taoist and Zen monks in the East, held that the purpose and function of knowledge was to enable self-knowledge through intellectual, moral, and spiritual growth. A competing theory, associated with Protagoras in the West and Confucius in the East, held that the purpose and function of knowledge was the acquisition of logic, grammar, and rhetoric to enable the holder of knowledge to know what to say and how to say it.

Somewhere around 1700, the meaning of knowledge changed radically. Knowledge began to be applied to "doing," not just to "being." That change in the meaning and purpose of knowledge, writes Drucker, initiated the first of three revolutions in the application of knowledge that created and then destroyed both communism and capitalism and ultimately led to the creation of a postcapitalist knowledge society.

Phase #1: The Industrial Revolution (1700–1880)

The first phase of applying knowledge to doing, says Drucker, began around 1700 and lasted roughly 180 years. During this period, the first engineering, agricultural, and mining schools were founded, and the first technical university (École Polytechnique) was created in 1794. Also during this period, Denis Diderot and Jean d'Alembert edited the *Encyclopédie,* which Drucker calls "one of the most important books in history."[9] "The underlying thesis of the *Encyclopédie* was that effective results in the material universe—in tools, processes, and product—are produced by systematic analysis, and by the systematic, purposeful application of knowledge.... The early technical schools and the *Encyclopédie* ... brought together, codified, and published the *techné,* the craft mystery.... They converted experience into knowledge, apprenticeship into textbook, secrecy into methodology, doing into applied knowledge."[10] In the process, there evolved the two big *C*s of the nineteenth and twentieth centuries—Capitalism and Communism.

First, the application of knowledge to tools, processes, and product required concentration of production since, as Drucker notes, the new knowledge and technology could not be effectively applied in thousands of small craft workshops in rural villages. Concentration meant large factories, and large factories demanded capital—ergo capitalists.

Second, the large factories required workers—Marx's proletarians. He argued that since the workers did not own the means of production—the steam engines, factories, raw materials, tools, and technology—they would become dependent on the capitalists for their living. Consequently, the new system was one-sided in favor of the capitalist and ripe for the alienation and exploitation of workers. Over time the means of production would be concentrated in the hands of fewer and fewer people. This concentration of power and the inherent inequities that it would engender would lead inevitably to class conflict. The proletariat would be increasingly impoverished, and the system would come to a violent end. One day the masses, with "nothing to lose but their chains," would rise up and overthrow the few remaining capitalists in a great revolution. Of course, it didn't quite work out that way. Workers didn't rise up to overthrow their capitalist bosses as Marx had predicted. Why not? Why did Marx become a false prophet? Because, writes Drucker, neither Marx nor anyone else foresaw the impact of the second revolution in the application of knowledge—the productivity revolution.

Phase #2: The Productivity Revolution (1881–Post World War II)

According to Drucker, the second knowledge revolution began in 1881, just two years before Marx's death, when the American Fredrick Winslow Taylor began using knowledge to improve work methods. Taylor's scientific

management eventually turned Marx's exploited proletariat into the afflu-
ent bourgeoisie.

Yes, you read that right. Drucker argues that Frederick Taylor's scientific
management—the same "one best way," "worker as eminently interchange-
able cog in the capitalist factory machine" way of organizing work that was
hated by labor unions and intellectuals alike—actually benefited workers as
much as, if not more than, it benefited owners. And it did so by dramatically
increasing their productivity. Drucker writes that

> within a few years after Taylor began to apply knowledge to work, produc-
> tivity began to rise at a rate of 3.5 to 4 percent compound a year—which
> means doubling every eighteen years or so. Since Taylor began, productivity
> has increased some fifty fold in all advanced countries. On this unprece-
> dented expansion rest all the increases in both standard of living and qual-
> ity of life in the developed countries. . . . Most of this increase—just as Tay-
> lor predicted—has been taken by workers, that is, by Marx's proletarian.[11]

Marx's prediction of the overthrow of capitalists by the proletariat never
happened for a very simple reason, says Drucker. "The blue-collar worker
in manufacturing industry, the 'proletarian' rather than the 'Capitalist,' became the true beneficiary of Capitalism and the Industrial Revolution."[12] It
was the productivity revolution that ultimately defeated communism, not
Ronald Reagan, as some believe (an opinion that is the authors', not
Drucker's). Ironically, the productivity revolution also ushered in a new
phase in the application of knowledge that would lead to the obsolescence
of capitalism itself. Drucker calls that third and current phase of the knowledge revolution the management revolution.

Phase #3: The Management Revolution (Post World War II–2020)

Drucker dates the start of the third knowledge revolution from the signing
of the GI Bill in the late 1940s, although he admits that it might not have really started until 1960 or even later. Regardless, he maintains that we are in
the middle of this third phase, and it is already having a tremendous impact.

Knowledge work is rapidly replacing manual labor. Drucker notes that in
1881, when Taylor first started applying knowledge to work, 9 out of 10
workers made or moved things. They were engaged in manual labor. By the
1950s, the majority of the workforce in most developed countries still made

or moved things. The quickest way to the middle-class for these workers was not via college. The route was through working from their late teens until retirement in a blue-collar, unionized, mass production manufacturing job. By 1990, that had all changed. Only 1 worker in 5 was employed in manual labor, and the percentage of workers who were so engaged was expected to decline steadily and reach a ratio of no more than 1 in 10 by 2010. The productivity revolution had worked so well that it made manual labor less and less critical.

The Impact of the Postcapitalist Society

The productivity revolution changed the route to the middle class. By the mid-1990s, wrote Drucker, there was "practically no access to a middle-class income without a formal degree, which certifies to the acquisition of knowledge that can only be obtained systematically and in a school."[13] Knowledge was key to personal and economic success. Knowledge had become the only meaningful resource. The traditional factors of production—natural resources, capital, and labor—had not disappeared, but they had become secondary. Knowledge was king but, Drucker cautioned, it wasn't just any knowledge.

The reigning knowledge was the knowledge of Frederick Taylor, not Socrates or Protagoras. The knowledge that was valued in the new world was knowledge that could be applied for results and, most especially, knowledge that could be applied systematically and purposefully to define what new knowledge was needed and to accomplish systematic innovation. This new knowledge was specialized. We no longer have *knowledge,* writes Drucker. We have many *knowledges*—disciplines, each converting a craft into a methodology; ad hoc experiences into a system; anecdotes into information; or skill into something that can be taught and learned. He concludes that

> this is as great a change in intellectual history as any ever recorded. . . . The shift from knowledge to knowledges has given knowledge the power to create a new society. But this society has to be structured on the basis of knowledge as something specialized and of knowledge people as specialists. This is what gives them their power. But it also raises basic questions—of

values, of vision, of beliefs, of all the things that hold society together and give meaning to our lives.[14]

In Exhibit 7.2, Drucker outlines seven ways our organizations and lives change with the shift to the postcapitalist knowledge society.

TOM PETERS AND CHARLES HANDY INTRODUCE A "FEDERAL" ORGANIZATION

Of course, this is all interesting and thought provoking, but it is not very specific. For example, what does this new, decentralized, constantly innovative, knowledge worker organization look like? Are there any examples of such organizations we can look to as models? How does the leadership of such an organization guide it? If all of the knowledge worker specialists are equal, who pulls their talent together toward a common goal? And what about the people? When everything is impermanent and competitive, how does one survive? What is the secret to a successful career in such a world? Drucker lets others flesh out such details, so we have to go elsewhere for answers.

We will turn to two gurus who have written extensively on many of the same themes as Drucker. We warn you, however, that these two are quite different in style. One is shrill and exuberant. He screams about "nanosecond nineties," "topsy-turvey times," and "crazy organizations." The other is calm, reasoned, and lectures about "*subsidiarity,*" "shamrock organizations," and federalism. One is optimistic and certain about the future. The other is often doubtful and certain only that these are uncertain times. One is decidedly practical. The other is more philosophical and speculative. Yet both gurus seek to convey many of the same ideas. Their audiences differ only in their preferences for the teacher. Style is the issue here, not substance. The two gurus, so alike in message but so different in style, are Tom Peters and Charles Handy.

Peters is the screamer. He is a self-described "gadfly, curmudgeon, champion of bold failures, prince of disorder, maestro of zest, professional loudmouth!"[15] He burst onto the guru scene in 1982 with the phenomenally successful book *In Search of Excellence,* which he coauthored with Robert H. Waterman, Jr. Throughout the 1980s and into the 1990s, he produced a

EXHIBIT 7.2. **How Organizations Can Work in a Knowledge-Based Society**

1. *The purpose of organizations in a knowledge society is to make knowledge productive.* "The organization's function [in a knowledge society] is to put knowledge to work—on tools, products, and processes; on the design of work; on knowledge itself."[1]

   The more specialized knowledges are, the more effective they will be. The best radiologists are not the ones who know the most about medicine; they are the specialists who know how to obtain images of the body's inside through X-ray, ultrasound, body scanner, magnetic resonance. The best market researchers are not those who know the most about business, but the ones who know the most about market research. Yet neither radiologists nor market researchers achieve results by themselves; their work is "input" only. It does not become results unless put together with the work of other specialists. Knowledges by themselves are sterile. They become productive only if welded together into a single, unified knowledge. To make this possible is the task of organization, the reason for its existence, its function.[2]

2. *In a society of knowledge worker specialists, organizations will focus on the work their specialists do well.* They will contract out the rest. Drucker predicts that organizations will outsource all work that is "support" in nature rather than "revenue producing." Additionally, all activities that do not offer career opportunities to senior management will be outsourced.[3]

3. *An organization of knowledge specialists is an organization of equals.* There can be no boss or subordinate. "Knowledge employees cannot, in effect, be supervised. Unless they know more [about their specialty] than anybody else in the organization, they are to all intents and purposes useless."[4] And there can be no higher or lower specialty in knowledge organizations, except in the context of a particular situation. Drucker notes that "philosophy is the queen of the sciences, ... But to remove a kidney stone, you want a urologist rather than a logician."[5] He adds that the prototype of such an organization of equals may be the symphony orchestra: "The first violin may be the most important instrument in the orchestra. But the first violinist is not the 'superior' of the harp player. He is a colleague. And the harp part is the harp player's part and not delegated to her by either the conductor or the first violinist."[6]

4. *Since the goal of postcapitalist organizations is innovation in tools, processes, products, work, and knowledge itself, they must be designed for constant change.* Innovation demands "systematic abandonment of the established, the customary, the familiar, the comfortable—whether products, services, processes, human and social relationships, skills, or organizations themselves."[7]

5. *In order to innovate successfully, the postcapitalist organization will have to be decentralized.* Such organizations are positioned to recognize the often fleeting opportunities for innovation. They will have be decentralized in order to be close "to performance, to the market, to technology, and to all the many changes in society, the environment, demographics, and knowledge that provide opportunities of innovation if they are seen and utilized."[8]

EXHIBIT 7.2. (Continued)

6. *A knowledge society is a mobile society.* "This very mobility means that in the knowledge society, social challenges and social tasks multiply. People no longer have 'roots.' People no longer have a 'neighborhood' that controls where they live, what they do, and indeed, what their 'problems' are allowed to be."[9]

7. *A knowledge society is a competitive society.* "Knowledge [is] accessible to everyone, everyone is expected to place himself or herself, to improve himself or herself, and to have aspirations. It is a society in which many more people than ever before can be successful. But it is therefore, by definition, also a society in which many more people than ever before can fail, or at least come in second."[10]

1. Peter F. Drucker, *Managing in a Time of Great Change* (New York: Dutton, Truman Talley Books, 1995), p. 77.
2. Peter F. Drucker, *The Post-Capitalist Society* (New York: HarperBusiness, 1993), p. 50.
3. Drucker, *Managing in a Time*, p. 68.
4. Drucker, *Post-Capitalist Society*, p. 65.
5. Ibid., p. 56.
6. Drucker, *Managing in a Time*, p. 248.
7. Drucker, *Post-Capitalist Society*, p. 57.
8. Drucker, *Managing in a Time*, p. 81.
9. Ibid., p. 251.
10. Ibid.

string of books and articles, each becoming more outrageous both in title and content—*A Passion for Excellence* (1985, with Nancy Austin); *Thriving on Chaos* (1987); *Liberation Management* (1992); *The Tom Peters Seminar: Crazy Times for Crazy Organizations* (1994, with Peters in his boxer shorts on the cover); and *The Pursuit of WOW!: Every Person's Guide to Topsy-Turvey Times* (1994).

Handy, the more stately guru, is a former corporate executive, economist, and professor. He bills himself as a management philosopher and is the author of numerous books and articles, most notably *The Age of Unreason* (1989), *The Age of Paradox* (1994), and *Beyond Certainty* (1996).

Here are three of the most important themes our disparate gurus emphasize as the natural, indeed inevitable, outgrowth of the postcapitalist knowledge society. We will discuss each theme in more detail later.

1. Peters and Handy agree that knowledge organizations will be forced to decentralize radically. In fact, the decentralization will be so radical that the word *decentralize* doesn't quite work. Handy suggests that a better term might be *federalize.*

2. Our gurus expect organizations in the knowledge society to go beyond federalism and essentially become networks of specialists. Peters calls this "the corporation as a Rolodex."[16] Handy uses the shamrock, the Irish national emblem, as his model.

3. Finally, our gurus see new challenges and opportunities for workers. In this new postcapitalist society, every person will have to be a businessperson. If one is smart, loyalty to oneself will have to take precedence over loyalty to an organization, and the most success will flow to those who build what Handy calls a "portfolio life."

The "Federal Organization"

As we move to a knowledge society, Peters and Handy predict that organizations will increasingly adopt a federal structure. Handy points out that *federalism* is not just a classy word for *decentralization.*

> Decentralization implies that the center delegates certain tasks or duties to the outlying bits, while remaining in overall control. The center does the delegating, and initiates and directs. Thus it is that we have that most consistent of organizational findings: The more an organization decentralizes its operations, the greater the flow of information to and from the center. The center may not be *doing* the work in a decentralized organization, but it makes sure that it knows how the work is going. . . .
>
> Federalism is different. In federal countries, states are the original founding groups, coming together because there are some things which they can do better jointly (defense is the obvious example) than individually. The center's powers are given to it by the outlying groups, in a sort of reverse delegation. The center, therefore, does not direct or control so much as coordinate, advise, influence, and suggest. . . .
>
> Federal organizations, therefore, are reverse thrust organizations; the initiative, the drive, and the energy come mostly from the parts, with the center an influencing force, relatively low in profile.[17]

This move to a structure that obviously decimates the power of the center will not occur voluntarily, says Handy. Postcapitalist knowledge organizations will be forced, as Drucker predicted, to decentralize in order to innovate. As Peters puts it, "you can't do brain work in groups of a thousand, or probably even hundreds. You do it in quartets, octets, groups of ten, fifteen, twenty-five. Or duos."[18] Consequently, organizations will increasingly be broken up into clusters of small units that can be close to markets and react rapidly to societal, demographic, technological, and other changes that provide opportunities for innovation. These small units will pursue a wide range of projects and be in a constant state of change.

Handy predicts that initially the center will attempt to closely monitor all of this activity and control its direction. New information technologies will be employed to process the data that will flow into the center from the remote operating units, but the effort to exercise central control will eventually fail. Without enough people to interpret the information, says Handy, much of it will "lie unused in piles of printout or in the unseen memories of computers."[19] In the end, the center will be forced to stop trying to run everything and will have to begin letting go or, as Peters puts it, the entire formal organization will have to "dis-organize" and self-destruct.[20] At that point, decentralization will end and federalism will begin.

Tom Peters offers the following three highly different examples of what it is like when a traditional organization dis-organizes, self-destructs, and becomes a federation.[21]

1. 1980. Percy Barnevik takes over as head of the Swedish firm Asea. He cuts the headquarters staff from 1,700 to 200 in the first 100 days. In 1987, he merges Asea with the Swiss firm of Brown Boveri to create ABB (Asea Brown Boveri). He cuts Brown Boveri's headquarters staff from 4,000 to 200 and breaks the company into 5,000 40-person profit centers. He ends up running a 200,000-person company with a corporate staff of just 150 and only three layers of management.

2. 1991. August 8, 8:00 A.M. in Copenhagen, Denmark. Lars Kolind, president of Oticon, a leading manufacturer of hearing aids, makes a dramatic change in how the 87-year-old business is run. He orders workers to tear down the walls between offices, eliminates secretaries, and throws out job descriptions. He creates a 100% project-oriented organization in which employees are required to decide for themselves what needs to be done and then arrange themselves in teams as they deem necessary. A month later, Kolind auctions off all of the company's office furniture. Instead of desks, people are provided with mobile carts or caddies in which to store their personal effects as they move from team to team. Oticon soon makes record profits and recovers market share it had been losing before the change.

3. 1991. IBM sells its unprofitable typewriter and printer business, Lexmark, to its managers. In the first 16 months, the new owners cut the number of managers by 60%, dramatically increase the authority of line managers, create autonomous business units, simplify business procedures, particularly those having to do with financial approvals, eliminate most of the central office staff, significantly increase outsourcing, and totally reorganize manufacturing. The first year the new Lexmark, sans IBM, pulls in $100 million in pretax profits on $2 billion in sales.

The Basic Principles and Assumptions of Federalism

Handy lists a number of principles and assumptions that underlie the concept of federalism and make it work.

The Organization Has a Small Center

In a federation, what would normally be the top of the organization becomes the center. The center is kept small, like the 150-person center in ABB's 200,000-person organization, and the responsibilities of the center are different. The center is more than just a banker to the rest of the organization. Indeed, says Handy, "to see the center only as a banker, pulling in surplus profits and dispensing funds for worthwhile projects, is to throw away most of the advantages of federalism."[22] The center's job is to think beyond the next annual report and construct global strategies that link the various autonomous units. But, cautions Handy, it is not a matter of the center dictating long-term strategy and leaving short-term implementation to the business units. The center doesn't dictate anything. Instead, it is a place of persuasion and representation. The center may not have a single formal leader. It may instead be run by a triumvirate or committee composed of representatives from the various units. The small staff servicing the center will concern itself with researching and constructing future plans, possibilities, scenarios, and options that the leadership committee can consider. Because of its broad scope and future orientation, says Handy, the center will become a training ground for future unit chiefs. It is there that they will be exposed to the whole of the organization before committing themselves to the advancement of one of its parts.

The Organization Believes in Subsidiarity

Handy explains that one of the reasons a small center can function as it does in a federation is the widespread and necessary acceptance of the philosophy of subsidiarity. Most simply stated, subsidiarity is the philosophical and moral position that the power in an organization rightfully belongs to the units, not to the center, and that it is the individual parts that cede power to the center—not the center that delegates to the units. The Tenth Amendment to the U.S. Constitution is a formal expression of subsidiarity. The powers that are not delegated to the United States by the Constitution or prohibited by it to the states are reserved to the states respectively or to the people. Another expression of subsidiarity can be found in the papal encyclical *Quadragesimo Anno:* "It is an injustice, a grave evil and a disturbance of right order for a large and higher organization to arrogate to itself functions which can be performed efficiently by smaller and lower bodies."[23]

Handy notes that subsidiarity is not the same thing as empowerment. "Empowerment implies that someone on high is giving away power. Subsid[i]arity, on the other hand, implies that the power properly belongs, in the first place, lower down or further out. You take it away as a last resort. Those in the center are the servants of the parts. The task of the center, and of any leader, is to help the individual or the group to live up to their responsibilities, to enable them to deserve their subsid[i]arity."[24]

The Organization Has Twin Citizenship

A central idea behind federalism is that it is possible to be big and small at the same time. Borrowing from author and consultant Rosabeth Moss Kanter, Handy notes that small units have some real advantages. Compared to big organizations, they are faster, more focused, more flexible, more friendly, and more fun (Kanter's five fs). Plus, small business units can get closer to the customer. They are less bureaucratic and more personal. Also, as Peters notes, they are more conducive to thinking. Perhaps more importantly, writes Handy, "most of us frogs prefer a small pond, if the truth be told. In smaller groups there is more chance to be yourself, less likelihood of being anonymous."[25]

That's all true, but it's also true that large organizations have some advantages, such as economies of scale. Large companies also generally offer better job security to their people and can invest more in training and research. A 200,000-person ABB can do some things that a 200-person ABB could not.

The federalized organization finds a way to balance big and small and gain the advantages of both. The units within the organization are small, while the federation can be as large as it wants. Handy cites research that favors units with a maximum of 120 to 200 people. The point, he says, is to keep the unit small enough so that everyone knows everyone else but big enough so that it is competent.[26] Peters tends to favor units of 50 or so people but argues that the ideal number might be a lot less. For example, he cites one hospital in the U.S. that has broken up its teams into "care pairs" of two (a registered nurse and a technician). Peters asks that you imagine your organization, regardless of its overall size, broken up into virtually self-sufficient quartets, trios, or even pairs. That's right. He wants you to imagine a gigantic organization composed of essentially independent two-person units. That's the small/big concept behind federalism.

The Organization Is Composed of "Gotta Units"

One reason such organizations work so well, says Peters, is that they are composed of "gotta units." "A gotta unit," he writes, "is one of modest size, which may be living in a larger body . . . but which routinely does the impossible, not because its members read books . . . or get close to the customer, but for precisely the reason that a mom-and-pop grocery store will do almost anything (and then some) to serve its neighbors in the surrounding seven-block area. Without that effort, it goes out of business. Kaput. In other words, they do it 'cause they gotta." "Implementing the gotta unit concept," he goes on, "almost amounts to automating spunk—making it absolutely necessary for the unit to deliver a spirited response to every customer."[27] Handy speaks of this concept as the implicit assumption of subsidiarity that people have both the right and responsibility to sign their own work. In the federal organization people are expected to take responsibility—personal responsibility—for their own and their group's work.

The Organization Contains Large Doughnuts

The units and individuals working within the operating units of such federal organizations have much more discretion than those in typical companies. One way to visualize this difference, says Handy, is to think of the responsibilities inherent in a job, whether team responsibilities or individual responsibilities, as an inverted doughnut, like the one in Exhibit 7.3. The center of this strange doughnut is filled; the space on the outside is empty. In other words, the dough is where the hole used to be, and the hole is where the dough once was. Now, says Handy, assume that the filled-in hole of the doughnut represents the core responsibilities of a job. These are the things the team or individual has to do or they will fail and be fired. The surrounding empty space represents all of the other tasks and duties that the team or individual could do if they choose. That's the discretionary stuff.

In any job, writes Handy, there are always some core tasks. These are the things that used to be written down in job descriptions. There were also discretionary tasks, the things you could do that went beyond your job description, but that you weren't specifically required to do. Of course, there were always some limits on the discretionary stuff, although they were frequently ill defined and had to be learned by trial and error.

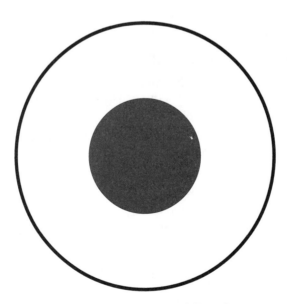

EXHIBIT 7.3. **The Inverted Doughnut**

In the traditional organization, the doughnut looked somewhat like Exhibit 7.4 for most people. There was a lot of core stuff and little discretionary stuff. You were basically told what to do, and you did it. You could not venture much beyond the core without exceeding your authority.

In contrast, the situation is reversed in the federal organization. You and your team have very few core requirements spelled out and have a lot of discretion in your activities. The federal doughnut then looks like Exhibit 7.5.

The point, says Handy, is that federal organizations require large, and largely empty, doughnuts. They have to be managed by results and not by activities. While that concept sounds simple, it is a major departure from past practices.

Most managers feel more comfortable when the cores are large as well as closely defined, when they control the methods and therefore the results, the means and not the ends. To let go, to specify success criteria, to trust people to use their own methods to achieve your ends—this can be uncomfortable. It is particularly uncomfortable when we realize that

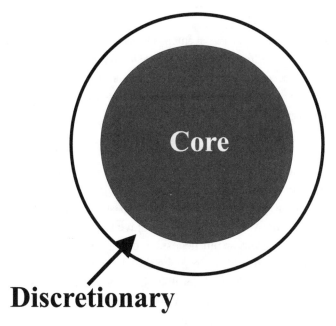

EXHIBIT 7.4. **The Traditional Doughnut**

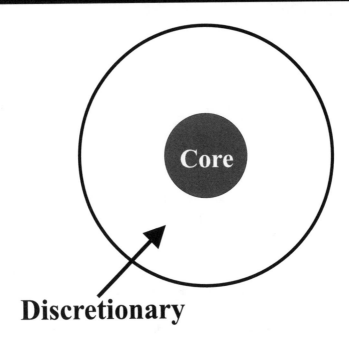

Discretionary

EXHIBIT 7.5. **The Federal Doughnut**

after-the-event controls, or management-by-results, means that mistakes can and will be made. It may be true that we learn more from our mistakes than from our successes, but organizations have in the past been reluctant to put this theory into practice. Now they will have to, *and* they will have to learn to forgive mistakes.[28]

Such forgiving organizations, he continues, will require different kinds of leaders. The new leader will have to learn to be a teacher, counselor, and friend, rather than a commander, inspector, or judge. The new manager will have to be adept at specifying the measures of success and at spotting the signs of failure. In between, he or she will have to give employees space to succeed or fail. It is a major but necessary change in the way we manage, but the consequences of failing to make the change are severe. "If we can not do it," writes Handy, "then federalism becomes anarchy, control reverts to the center, the center becomes too big and too expensive, the organization is crippled, withers, and can die."[29]

The Organization Has "Businessed" Jobs

A final key feature of the federal organization, as described by Peters, is that every job is what he calls "businessed." In short, every employee is turned into a businessperson, which is quite different from what the traditional organization does to employees. Peters finds mostly "slot fillers" and "box servers" in traditional organizations. "The average employee in the average organization still fills a slot or serves a box on the organization chart. Most people pass their days following the strictures of some absurdly narrow job description. Boxed in. It's time to break the box."[30] All employees, that's 100% according to Peters, can become entrepreneurs "with the flair and commitment of mom or pop of Mom & Pop, Inc."[31] All employees can become businesspeople who are willing to go anywhere and do anything inside or outside their organization box to get the job done. The federal organization creates a "businesses" job, according to Peters, by incorporating key elements such as cross-training, budgeting, spending authority, autonomy, access to financial and nonfinancial information, and so on into every job in the company (see Exhibit 7.6).[32]

CHARLES HANDY'S "SHAMROCK" ORGANIZATION

Peters notes that the federal organization smashes the traditional company into small, self-sufficient, "atomized" units with distinctive personalities and with almost all of the superstructure above them removed. In the process, everyone is forced to become a de facto businessperson and create their own job. What Charles Handy calls a "shamrock organization" is a way of putting all of these disparate pieces back together again. If the federal organization is the "loose" in the "loose but tight" nature of the new postcapitalist knowledge society, then the shamrock organization is the "tight."

Handy first used the shamrock symbolically to represent an interesting facet of the new organization in his 1989 book *The Age of Unreason*.[33] The shamrock is the small, cloverlike, three-leafed plant that is the Irish national emblem. Handy uses the shamrock's three leaves to symbolize the three very different groups of people in the new organization (see Exhibit 7.7).

EXHIBIT 7.6. Elements of a Job in a "Federal" Organization

- *Extensive cross-training.* Employees are trained in all or nearly all of the skills needed to perform 80 or 90% of the tasks that used to require numerous steps, multiple departments, and authority from several levels of management. Employees are able to produce a complete product or provide a complete service to customers.
- *Budgeting.* Employees form, track, and amend their own budgets.
- *Spending authority.* Employees can purchase just about anything they think they need to perform their jobs without seeking prior approval from management.
- *Quality assurance.* All employees do their own quality measurement, monitoring, and undertake their own quality improvement efforts.
- *Requirement to act.* Employees are required to act on their own initiative and to involve anyone else they deem necessary to get the job done without seeking prior approval or enduring second-guessing from management.
- *Autonomy.* Employees have the authority to make decisions, including the authority to commit substantial resources without recourse to higher-ups.
- *Responsibility for customers.* Employees are held responsible either for personally performing all of the tasks required to meet a customer's need or for handling the "case" (i.e., arranging for and overseeing the services provided by others) until the customer is satisfied.
- *Access to financial information.* All employees have real-time access to financial information from all functions.
- *Access to nonfinancial information.* All employees have complete access to nonfinancial information, such as schedules, and the ability to alter others' databases, for example, to update schedules in other parts of the business.
- *Access to experts.* Internal staff experts and subject matter specialists work at the beck and call of the front line. Employees can call on them or on outside consultants and experts as needed for advice and support. The front line also has access to global electronic bulletin boards and databases for information and support.
- *A limitless travel budget.* In respect to the latter, Peters writes:

Employees don't expect to be able to sign off on an expenditure of millions. (I can't, and I own the majority of shares in my company.) But the businessperson does expect to be able to do what's necessary to move projects forward. You've told Tom and Joe that their project is important to the company. But when they need to travel, say, with another team member to a distributor on the other side of the country, or to visit a global expert who will be in Osaka only for the next two weeks, you stymie them with a corporate rule that requires four signatures on a travel voucher. You just gang-tackled them. The ball is not in their hands after all. Upshot: Kiss their psychological ownership of the project goodbye.[1]

The bottom line of "businessed" jobs, says Peters, is trust. And it has to be full trust, not half trust or somewhat trust or sometime trust. "The instructor pilot can't 'half' sit next to you during your first solo. Put another way, people either 'own' a task or they don't. Yes or no."[2]

1. Tom Peters, **The Tom Peters Seminar** *(New York: Vintage, 1994), p. 74.*
2. *Ibid., p. 80.*

EXHIBIT 7.7. **The Shamrock Organization**

The First Leaf: The Professional Core

The first leaf, says Handy, represents the core workers of the new organization. They are the professionals, technicians, knowledge workers, and managers that are considered to be critical to the future of the organization, because they are the carriers of the knowledge that distinguishes the organization from all others. These people get the high salaries, the fringe benefits, and all of the other perks that the company can offer. In return, these people are supposed to work 70-hour weeks and dedicate themselves to the company. They get their identity and purpose from the work they perform. They think in terms of careers and advancement, can't be ordered around, and want their names to be known. They act like partners in a professional-service organization, such as a consulting firm, advertising agency, or law office. The core is small, critical, and paid very well, although a substantial portion of its pay, perhaps as much as 40%, will be tied to the group's and/or company's performance. Since the core is small, it needs help. That's where the second leaf comes in.

The Second Leaf: Outsource Contractors

These are the consultants, contractors, and other assorted specialists that are hired from the outside to work on specific projects or to perform work that is not crucial to the organization—not part of the core staff's particular expertise or routine work the core professionals don't want to do. Employees of outsourcing firms and self-employed professionals or technicians fall into this category. They may be former full-time employees of the company that now contracts with them. They are paid for results, not for their time, and the organization exercises only minimum supervision over their daily activities. Handy notes that there is a temptation to exploit these workers by paying minimal fees for maximum work. He advises organizations to resist that temptation. "The shamrock organization has to remember that in the contract fringe, it is money paid for work done. There is no longer a residual loyalty to be relied on, no longer any implied promise of security in return for obedient labor. Good work must, in the long run, receive good rewards, or it will cease to be good work."[34]

The Third Leaf: Temps and Part-Timers

Handy's third leaf represents the flexible labor force, the part-time and temporary workers who are called in to keep the shop or service counter open at night and on the weekend, and/or to staff for peak workloads. "In crude terms," he writes, "these people are the labor market, a market into which employers dip as they like and when they need, for as little money as they have to pay."[35] Some of the people in this category want to get out of it as fast as possible and find full-time jobs, either as core employees or full-time, self-employed contractors. Some just want to make some extra money. Some work two or more part-time jobs to patch together a living. Some of the people use these jobs as a kind of apprenticeship in preparation for later full-time work. Handy notes that most of the flexible labor force probably will never demonstrate the commitment and/or ambition of the core, but he argues, a lot depends on how they are treated. "Treated as casual labor such people respond casually. . . . If the flexible labor force is . . . to be a valuable part of the organization, then the organization [must] be prepared to invest in them, to provide training, even training leading to qualifications [for other jobs with other firms], to give them some status and some privileges (including paid holidays and sick leave entitlement). Then, and only then, will the organization get the temporary or part-time help that it needs to the standard it requires."[36]

Doubts about the Shamrock

Handy and Peters admit that shamrock organizations will make some people nervous, particularly due to their heavy reliance on subcontractors and temporaries to get the work done. Here is a brief summary of Peter's rejoinders to four of the main objections people raise.

Objection #1: In a shamrock organization, you'll end up using so many subcontractors that you'll get dependent on them. They'll have you by the throat.

Peters's Rejoinder: "Sure, if there is truly one and only one vendor available, you've got a dependence problem. (Although that doesn't necessarily mean you should do the job inside: Who's to say that you can do it better, dependence or not, than the sole source supplier?) In part, though, increased dependence . . . is precisely the point; in return for accepting mutual dependence, the yield is presumably more innovativeness, more flexibility, more efficiency."[37]

Objection #2: The subcontractors will learn your secrets and then expand into your business. You'll just end up training your future competitors and giving away the store.

Peters's Rejoinder: "When a sub encroaches, it's usually because (1) you were casual about initial selection; (2) you subjected the sub to constant niggling of a sort which would erode any relationship; and/or (3) you didn't make a real investment in partnership—and the development of mutual trust—from the start. Lesson: If you don't want subs to screw you, quit screwing them. Another part of the answer is to work only with 'the best.' The best are invariably preoccupied with doing their own thing ever better—and getting into your business would usually be a distraction. Moreover, 'the best' at anything usually have great integrity."[38]

Objection #3: If subs are far away, then the "soft" but essential intimacy and learning that comes from day-to-day contact will be absent.

Peters's Rejoinder: "First, familiarity often breeds contempt. The accounting department on your payroll typically has the accountant's contempt for non-accountants. If accounting is subcontracted, on the other hand, the outside provider will at least hide the contempt beneath a serious effort to satisfy the customer in order to retain the business. More important, interesting stuff is going on all over the plant—in any discipline you can name. While there may be some loss from the absence of geographic proximity, you must presume that it will be repaid by the cleverness of the very special sub you worked so hard . . . to ferret out."[39]

Objection #4: Doesn't a shamrock organization run the risk of outsourcing its very soul unless it is very careful?

Peters's Rejoinder: "I agree. But what is soul? Where do you find it? Will you know it when you see it?"[40] He continues:

> Though there are no short and easy answers [to your concern], here are a few soul tips:
> 1. The site of soul is changing. Increasingly, soul does not reside in ownership or a technology or functional skill. Soul can be in such skills as alliance management . . . the ability to leverage knowledge . . . logistics and distribution . . . information systems. . . . More and more, soul is "horizontal," a key process skill linked back to suppliers and forward to distributors and ultimate users.
> 2. Soul *can* be outsourced. . . . [Peters points to the example of Optus Communications, an Australian telecommunications company. Although information technology is a core competence of telecommunications, Optus uses a "staff" of 220 independent contractors for information systems work.]
> 3. Soul today, soup tomorrow. Today's valuable soul is tomorrow's millstone. Soul ages, sours, gets copied, and needs changing, too. . . .
> 4. It is true that, at some point, there is no "there" (critical mass around anything) anymore. On the other hand, critical mass no longer demands ownership of people or assets. How about "virtual soul"? . . . Isn't that the secret of Hollywood productions? And isn't Hollywood a pretty good virtual model for tomorrow's everything? I think so.[41]

We agree. Hollywood is a pretty good model of the shamrock organization. Consider what happens in a movie production or video shoot.[42]

Strangers with a variety of different backgrounds have to show up at the right time and immediately begin working together as a team. There is a clear task to be accomplished and a common goal everyone is trying to achieve. Everyone is expected to understand the part they play in the production and to get busy playing it with a minimum of fuss. Each member of the production team is an independent professional and is expected to behave as one. There is little room for error because there are no backups. In that sense, the whole system is brittle and can be easily shattered. A lot of money is at stake and easily can be lost if just one person fails to perform. Formal performance evaluations aren't necessary because everyone gets instant and constant feedback on their performance. And everyone knows that they had better perform. Their professional reputation is on the line all of the time. Everyone understands that their future employment depends on how they perform and who they impress or fail to impress. It's a different way of working. Indeed, it is a completely different lifestyle from the one most of us have known. Handy calls it "portfolio living."

PORTFOLIO LIVING: CHARLES HANDY'S PRESCRIPTION FOR ORGANIZING YOUR PROFESSIONAL LIFE

If we are going to reinvent work, says Handy, we need a new term for what it is we are creating. He proposes the term "portfolio."

port·fo·li·o (pôrt fō′ lē ō′, pōrt-), *n., pl.* **-li·os.**
a collection of different items with a theme such that the whole
is greater than the sum of its parts. Example: artist's portfolio,
architect's portfolio, stock portfolio.

Why not have a work portfolio? asks Handy. In it we might stuff a wide variety of work we perform throughout our lives, and not just the full-time, permanent, for-salary work that most males have known. In addition to our normal work, we could add a lot of different kinds of experiences. Handy suggests at least five:

1. Wage work—money for time
2. Fee work—money for results

3. Home work—cooking, cleaning, fixing, shopping, and so on
4. Gift work—volunteer work
5. Study work—education, training, learning.

Handy suggests that we start to think of our work experience as portfolios—collections of bits and pieces of different kinds of work we performed throughout our lives. At different stages of our life and depending on which leaf of the shamrock we occupied at a particular moment, our work portfolio might look quite different. Those in the core of the shamrock might have portfolios that are so bulging with wage work that they have little time left for anything else. People outside the core, on one of the other two leaves of the shamrock, would have quite different portfolios. Some might work two or more part-time jobs. Some might perform home work to save money, rather than make it. Others might perform fee work as self-employed contractors for different periods of time. Throughout one's life, the work portfolio changes.

Handy maintains that there is nothing new about work portfolios. Small businesses have always had them. Self-employed professionals have always made their living by building portfolios of customers and activities. For most of us, however, our portfolio has been fairly limited—mostly wage work if we are a man or mostly home work or gift work if we are female—and it has accumulated experiences mostly by chance. The difference now, says Handy, is that most of us will have a richer and more varied work portfolio in federal and shamrock organizations; and if we are lucky and accumulate the right skills, we can construct our work portfolio any way we want to. Of course, if we want to take charge of our work portfolios, we will need to prepare.

The first thing we will need to do is compile a portfolio of certificates of competency in a wide a variety of subjects. Handy argues that education will be "the single most important investment that any person can make in their own destiny,"[43] and that each of us will need to determine which of nine kinds of intelligence we possess (see Exhibit 7.8).

All of us are intelligent in at least one of these nine ways, says Handy, and discovering and developing our special form of intelligence is the first step in preparing for a portfolio life.

The second step we need to take is to find an "agent," says Handy, because most of us will spend at least some of our lives on one of the two leaves of the shamrock other than the professional core. We will all need

---

EXHIBIT 7.8.   Self-Quiz: What Kind of Intelligence Do We Have?

---

1. *Factual.* The intelligence demonstrated by people we call "human encyclopedias." Who can answer all of the questions in Trivial Pursuit?
2. *Analytical.* Intelligence that thrives on solving problems, crosswords, and puzzles. "People who score high on this intelligence delight in reducing complex data to more simple formulations. Strategic consultants, scientists, and academics are . . . strong in this type of intelligence."
3. *Linguistic.* Exhibited in people who speak several languages and can learn a new one easily within a short period of time.
4. *Spatial.* "Intelligence that sees patterns in things. Artists have it, as do mathematicians and systems designers."
5. *Musical.* The kind of intelligence that made Mozart a genius—along with the Beatles, James Taylor, and Carole King.
6. *Practical.* "The intelligence that allows your kids to take a motor bike apart and put it together again, although they might not be able to explain why in works."
7. *Physical.* "Intelligence, or talent, that we can see in sport stars, which enables some to hit balls much better than others, to ski better, dance better, and generally coordinate mind and muscle."
8. *Intuitive.* "The gift that some have of seeing things that others can't, even if they cannot explain why or wherefore."
9. *Interpersonal.* "The wit and the ability to get things done with and through people."

---

*Source: Charles Handy, **The Age of Paradox** (Boston: Harvard Business School Press, 1994), pp. 204–205.*

---

agents for the same reason that actors, models, writers, and professional athletes need them. Handy explains.

> It is hard enough to market and price yourself when you are a star; it is impossible when no one knows you and when you are unsure of what you can offer. A good agent will not only find buyers for your talents and negotiate the deal, he or she will be a coach or mentor, helping you review your experience and guiding you to appropriate educational opportunities. Good agents will prod your creativity by floating ideas in front of you: "Have you ever considered . . .?" or "Would this sort of thing interest you . . .?" They will suggest what you need to do or where you need to go to improve your skills or enlarge your experience.[44]

Executive-leasing agencies are already functioning as agents to some degree for the upper end of the market, notes Handy. Trade unions and employment agencies may do the same in the future. Until then, he reasons, you may have to look to a friend or mentor. While you are looking, you'll have to perform many of the agent's tasks yourself. The most important of these, says Peters, is that you "resume."

Okay, Peters admits that he is turning the noun *resume* into a verb, but he explains that he is doing it for a point: to get your attention. You must *t-h-i-n-k r-e-s-u-m-e.*

If you don't want to be a pawn in the new board game of business, writes Peters, then you had better forget about being loyal to a corporation and start thinking about building up your loyalty to a network. You need the mind and behavior of an independent contractor, and independent contractors think and behave "resume." Peters explains that "to resume" means you frequently ask yourself the following questions and answer them with good, solid, practical answers:

1. What the hell do I do?
2. What have I actually done?
3. Who among my customers will testify to it?
4. What evidence is there that my skills are state-of-the-art?
5. Who new do I know, far beyond the company's walls, who will help me deal with an ever-chillier world?
6. Will my year-end resume look different from last year's?[45]

Peters argues that you should put every job and every assignment you are offered through the resume test. Ask yourself whether it will help you answer those six questions. "If you can't imagine adding what you're working on right now—today—to your year-end, updated resume, then let it go."[46] Peters admits that his advice sounds crude and even selfish, but it's realistic. Your prospects are what is on your resume, plus one other thing.

In addition to maintaining and enhancing your resume, advises Peters, you had better get busy fleshing out your Rolodex. A marketable skill isn't enough. You have to know people—lots of people. Peters offers some higher math. "Security is proportional to (1) the thickness of your Rolodex, (2) the rate of Rolodex expansion, (3) the share of Rolodex entries from beyond the corporate walls, and (4) the time devoted to Rolodex maintenance."[47] It's a brave and bold new world we live in, writes Peters. Forget the old social contract that promised job security. It has been torn up and thrown away.

A CONCLUDING THOUGHT

At the very end of his book *The Age of Paradox,* Charles Handy summed up his assessment of the age we live in this way.

> It is . . . the end of the age of the mass organization, the age when we could all confidently expect to be employed for most of our lives if we so wanted, and over 90% did so want. Work will still be central to our lives but we shall now have to rethink what we mean by work and how it might be organized. At first sight, the challenge is daunting, but work in those mass organizations has never been unalloyed bliss for all. . . . Maybe we shall be better off without it.
>
> The hope lies in the unknown, in that second curve if we can find it. The world is up for re-invention in so many ways. Creativity is born in chaos. What we do, what we belong to, why we do it, when we do it, where we do it—these may all be different and they could be better. . . . Change comes from small initiatives which work, initiatives which, imitated, become the fashion. We cannot wait for great visions from great people, for they are in short supply at the end of history. It is up to us to light our own small fires in the darkness.[48]

So it is, and we hope that by condensing some of the best thinking about management and organizations, this book will help you do just that.

KEY POINTS

- We are in the midst of a great watershed change in which we are moving from an industrial to a knowledge economy—from a capitalist to a postcapitalist society. This change will completely alter the society's structure, social and economic dynamics, social classes, and social problems.

- The new postcapitalist society is the result of applying knowledge first to improving tools, processes, and products; then to improving labor productivity; and finally to innovation and improving knowledge itself.

- Knowledge work is replacing manual labor. By 2010, no more than 1 in 10 workers will be engaged in making or moving things.

- Knowledge is now the key to personal and economic success. There is practically no access to a middle-class income without a formal degree certifying the acquisition of knowledge that can only be obtained systematically in a school.

- While the traditional factors of production—natural resources, capital, and labor—have not disappeared, they have become secondary to knowledge.

- The most valued knowledge today is knowledge that can be applied to results, particularly knowledge that can be applied systematically and purposefully to define what new knowledge is needed and to accomplish systematic innovation.

- As knowledge has become more important, it has become more specialized. We no longer have one knowledge; rather we have many knowledges.

- The purpose of organizations in a knowledge society is to bring people with a wide range of specialized knowledges together in an atmosphere where they can be productive.

- In a society of knowledge worker specialists, organizations will focus on the work their specialists do well and contract out the rest of the work.

- An organization of knowledge specialists is an organization of equals. There can be no boss or subordinate.

- Since the goal of postcapitalist organizations is innovation, by definition they are designed for constant change.

- In order to be constantly innovative, postcapitalist organizations will have to be decentralized.

- People in the knowledge society will be highly mobile and highly competitive.

- As we move to a knowledge society, organizations will be forced to decentralize radically and adopt a federal structure with the following characteristics:

  A small center. A corporate headquarters with a few hundred people for a 1,000-person organization.

Subsidiarity. The philosophical and moral position that power in the organization rightfully belongs to the operating units and not the center, and that it is the units that cede power to the center and not the center that delegates to the units.

Twin citizenship. Employees belong both to individual operating units and to the larger organization.

"Gotta units." People in the operating units are responsible for their own fate and function with an entrepreneurial intensity.

Large doughnuts. People in the operating units and the units themselves have a large amount of discretionary authority over what they do and don't do.

"Businessed" jobs. Every employee is a businessperson with responsibility for budgets, spending, training, customers, quality assurance, and complete and unlimited access to financial and nonfinancial information.

- Individual operating units are shamrock organizations with three types of employees: professional, full-time core workers; self-employed consultants and outsource contractors; and part-time or temporary workers.

- Federal and shamrock organizations will force all of us into living portfolio lives in which we will mix five different forms of work: wage work, fee work, home work, gift work, and study work.

- To be successful at living a portfolio life, we will need

  A good education with certificates of competencies in a variety of subjects

  A good understanding of our unique form of intelligence (factual, analytical, linguistic, spatial, musical, practical, physical, intuitive, or interpersonal) and how we can exploit it to add value to organizations

  An agent to help us get work, negotiate contracts, and manage our career

  A solid resume

  A thick Rolodex with the names of lots of contacts

Notes

Chapter 1

1 John Gardner, *On Leadership* (New York: Free Press, 1990), p. 53.
2 Manfred Kets de Vries, *Life and Death in the Executive Fast Lane* (San Francisco: Jossey-Bass, 1995), p. 6.
3 Peter Drucker, quoted in Glenn Rifkin, "Leadership: Can It Be Learned?" *Forbes ASAP,* April 8, 1996, p. 104.
4 Warren Blank, *The Nine Natural Laws of Leadership* (New York: AMACOM, 1995), p. 11.
5 Ibid., p. 33.
6 Laurie Beth Jones, author of *Jesus CEO,* interview in "Jesus CEO?" *Industry Week,* March 6, 1995, p. 20.
7 Blank, *Laws of Leadership,* p. 31.
8 Ibid.
9 Ibid., p. 32.
10 Ibid., p. 14.
11 Ibid., p. 36.
12 Christopher A. Bartlett and Sumantra Ghoshal, "Changing the Role of Top Management: Beyond Strategy to Purpose," *Harvard Business Review,* November–December 1994, p. 80.
13 Ibid., p. 81.
14 Ibid.
15 Karl Albrecht, *The Northbound Train: Finding the Purpose, Setting the Direction, Shaping the Destiny of Your Organization* (New York: AMACOM, 1994), p. 22.
16 Ibid., p. 65.
17 Burt Nanus, *Visionary Leadership: Creating a Compelling Sense of Direction for Your Organization* (San Francisco: Jossey-Bass, 1992), p. 8.
18 Jay A. Conger, *The Charismatic Leader: Behind the Mystique of Exceptional Leadership* (San Francisco: Jossey-Bass, 1989), p. 38.
19 Blank, *Laws of Leadership,* p. 99.
20 Margaret J. Wheatley, *Leadership and the New Science: Learning about Organizations from an Orderly Universe* (San Francisco: Berrett-Koehler, 1994), p. 56.
21 All but the Girl Scout vision is taken from James C. Collins and Jerry I. Porras, "Building Your Company's Vision," *Harvard Business Review,* September–October 1996, p. 69.

[22] Collins and Porras, "Your Company's Vision," p. 74.

[23] Nanus, *Visionary Leadership,* p. 288.

[24] Collins and Porras, "Your Company's Vision," p. 74.

[25] William Safire, *Lend Me Your Ears: Great Speeches in History* (New York: Norton, 1992), p. 498–499.

[26] Collins and Porras, "Your Company's Vision," p. 75.

[27] Conger, *Charismatic Leader,* p. 65.

[28] Nanus, *Visionary Leadership,* p. 34.

[29] Ibid., p. 126.

[30] Collins and Porras, "Your Company's Vision," p. 70.

[31] Jon R. Katzenbach et al., *Real Change Leaders* (New York: Times Business, 1998), p. 97.

[32] Warren Bennis, *On Becoming a Leader* (New York: Addison Wesley, 1989/1994), p. 178.

[33] Juana Bordas, "Power and Passion: Finding Personal Purpose," in *Reflections on Leadership,* ed. Larry C. Spears (New York: John Wiley & Sons, 1995), pp. 184–192.

[34] Bennis, *Becoming a Leader,* p. 49.

[35] Howard Gardner, *Leading Minds: An Anatomy of Leadership* (New York: Basic Books, 1995), p. 62.

[36] Ibid., p. 39.

[37] Ibid., p. 43.

[38] Ibid., p. 37.

[39] Ibid., p. 14.

[40] Ibid., p. 12.

[41] Ibid., p. 43.

[42] Ibid., p. 44.

[43] Conger, *Charismatic Leader,* p. 69.

[44] Ibid.

[45] Sumantra Ghoshal and Christopher A. Bartlett, "Changing the Role of Top Management: Beyond Structure to Processes," *Harvard Business Review,* January–February 1995, p. 87.

[46] Ibid., p. 88.

[47] Christopher Bartlett and Sumantra Ghoshal, "Changing the Role of Top Management: Beyond Systems to People," *Harvard Business Review,* May–June 1995, p. 134.

[48] James Champy, *Reengineering Management: The Mandate for New Leadership* (New York: Harper Business, 1995), p. 76.

[49] Ghoshal and Bartlett, "Beyond Structure," p. 95.

[50] Bartlett and Ghoshal, "Beyond Systems," p. 133.

[51] Robert K. Greenleaf, "Life's Choices and Markers," in Spears, *Reflections on Leadership,* p. 20.

[52] Isabel O. Lopez, "Becoming a Servant-Leader: The Personal Development Path," in Spears, *Reflections on Leadership,* p. 153.

[53] Anne T. Fraker, "Robert K. Greenleaf and Business Ethics: There is No Code," in Spears, *Reflections on Leadership,* p. 46.

[54] Ibid.

[55] Ibid., p. 47.

[56] Ibid., p. 48.

[57] Ann McGee-Cooper, with Duane Trammell, "Servant-Leadership: Is There Really Time for It?" in Spears, *Reflections on Leadership,* p. 119.

[58] Ibid., pp. 119–120.

[59] Peter M. Senge, "Robert Greenleaf's Legacy: A New Foundation for Twenty-First Century Institutions," in Spears, *Reflections on Leadership,* p. 229.

[60] Carl Rieser, "Claiming Servant-Leadership as Your Heritage," in Spears, *Reflections on Leadership,* p. 59.

[61] McGee-Cooper, "Servant-Leadership," p. 117.

[62] Warren Bennis, quoted in Rifkin, "Leadership," p. 103.

[63] Drucker, quoted in Rifkin, "Leadership," p. 104.

[64] Kets de Vries, *Life and Death,* pp. 222–223.

[65] Richard Farson, *Management of the Absurd: Paradoxes in Leadership* (New York: Simon & Schuster, 1996), pp. 154–155.

[66] Lee G. Bowlman and Terrence E. Deal, *Leading with Soul: An Uncommon Journey of Spirit* (San Francisco: Jossey-Bass, 1995), p. 168.

[67] Gardner, *On Leadership,* p. 165.

[68] John P. Kotter, *A Force for Change: How Leadership Differs from Change* (New York: The Free Press, 1990), p. 114.

[69] Ibid.

[70] Kets de Vries, *Life and Death,* p. 88.

[71] Bennis, *Becoming a Leader,* p. 146.

[72] Warren Bennis and Robert Townsend, *Reinventing Leadership: Strategies to Empower the Organization* (New York: William Morrow, 1995), p. 116.

Chapter 2

[1] William Pasmore, *Creating Strategic Change: Designing the Flexible High-Performing Organization* (New York: John Wiley & Sons, Inc., 1994), p. 15.

[2] Robert Jacobs, *Real Time Strategic Change* (San Francisco: Berrett-Koehler, 1994), p. 3.

[3] Ibid.

[4] Bob Filipczak, "Weathering Change: Enough Already," *Training,* September 1994, p. 25.

[5] Nicholas Horney and Richard Koonce, "Using Competency Alignment to Shape, Drive, and Sustain Change Efforts," *National Productivity Review,* Summer 1996, p. 42.

[6] Paul Strebel, "Why Do Employees Resist Change?" *Harvard Business Review,* May–June 1996, p. 86.

[7] Douglas May and Michael C. Kettelhut, "Managing Human Issues in Reengineering Projects," *Journal of Systems Management,* January–February 1996, p. 6.

[8] James O'Toole, *Leading Change: The Argument for Values-Based Leadership* (New York: Ballantine Books, 1996), p. 13.

[9] Ibid., p. 23.

[10] Barry K. Spiker and Eric Lesser, "Change Management: We Have Met the Enemy . . ." *Journal of Business Strategy,* March–April 1995, p. 17.

[11] Ann B. Fisher, "Making Change Stick," *Fortune,* April 17, 1995, p. 122.

[12] Kets de Vries, *Life and Death,* p. 26.

[13] Strebel, "Why Do Employees Resist Change?" p. 87.

[14] Ibid., p. 88.

[15] Ibid., pp. 87–88.

[16] John P. Kotter, *Leading Change* (Boston: Harvard Business School Press, 1996), p. 112.

[17] Ibid.

[18] Ibid., p. 9.

[19] Pasmore, *Creating Strategic Change,* p. 12.

[20] Ibid.

[21] Ibid., p. 18.

[22] Daryl Conner, *Managing at the Speed of Change* (New York: Villard Books, 1992), p. 126.

[23] Pasmore, *Creating Strategic Change,* p. 11.

[24] This version of the formula was provided by F. Robert Jacobs in *Real Time Strategic Change* (pp. 122–123). For another and earlier version see Richard Bechhard and Reuben T. Harris, *Organizational Transitions,* 2nd ed. (Reading, Mass.: Addison-Wesley, 1987), p. 98.

[25] Noel M. Tichy and Stratford Sherman, *Control Your Destiny or Someone Else Will* (New York: Doubleday, 1993), p. 331.

[26] Conner, *Managing at the Speed of Change,* p. 92.

[27] Kotter, *Leading Change,* p. 48.

[28] Ibid., p. 7.

[29] Tichy and Sherman, *Control Your Destiny,* p. 339.

[30] Katzenbach et al., *Real Change Leaders,* p. 167.

[31] Ibid., p. 166.

[32] Pasmore, *Creating Strategic Change,* p. 15.

[33] Kotter, *Leading Change,* p. 11.

[34] Ibid., pp. 123–124.

[35] Ibid., p. 122.

[36] T. J. Larkin and Sandra Larkin, "Reaching and Changing Frontline Employees," *Harvard Business Review,* May–June 1996, p. 95.

[37] Champy, *Reengineering Management,* p. xx.

[38] Pasmore, *Creating Strategic Change,* pp. 11–12.

[39] Kotter, *Leading Change,* p. 135.

[40] Champy, *Reengineering Management,* p. 68.

[41] Pasmore, *Creating Strategic Change,* p. 44.

[42] Jacobs, *Real Time Strategic Change,* p. 4.

[43] Pasmore, *Creating Strategic Change,* p. 45.

[44] Marvin R. Weisbord and Sandra Janoff, *Future Search: An Action Guide to Finding Common Ground in Organizations and Communities* (San Francisco: Berrett-Koehler, 1995), p. ix.

[45] Marvin R. Weisbord, *Discovering Common Ground* (San Francisco: Berrett-Koehler, 1993), pp. 101–103.

Chapter 3

[1] Peter Senge, interview in "The Learning Organization Made Plain," *Training and Development,* October 1991, pp. 37–38.

[2] Peter Senge, *The Fifth Discipline: The Art and Science of the Learning Organization* (New York: Currency Doubleday, 1990), p. 4.

[3] Dave Ulrich, Todd Jick, and Mary Ann Von Glinow, "High Impact Learning: Building and Diffusing Learning Capability," *Organizational Dynamics,* Autumn 1993, p. 57.

[4] Gene Calvert, Sandra Mobley, and Lisa Marshall, "Grasping the Learning Organization," *Training and Development,* June 1994, p. 39.

[5] Daniel H. Kim, "The Link between Individual and Organizational Learning," *Sloan Management Review,* Fall 1993, pp. 37–50.

[6] Ibid., p. 39.

[7] William N. Isaacs, "Taking Flight: Dialogue, Collective Thinking, and Organizational Learning," *Organizational Dynamics,* Autumn 1993, p. 29.

[8] Etienne Wenger, "Communities of Practice: Where Learning Happens," *Benchmark,* Fall 1991, p. 7. Note: The social groups Wenger refers to are called "Communities of Practice." For a more lengthy discussion of Communities of Practice, including another researcher's experience with them, see John Seely Brown and Paul Duguid, "Organizational Learning and Communities-of-Practice: Toward a Unified View of Working, Learning, and Innovation," *Organization Science* 2 (February 1991): pp. 40–57.

[9] Kim, "Individual and Organizational Learning," p. 44.

[10] Ibid., p. 45.

[11] See Peter Senge et al., *The Fifth Discipline Fieldbook* (New York: Currency Doubleday, 1994), pp. 245–246, for these and other examples of ladders of inference.

[12] Chris Argyris, *Overcoming Organizational Defenses* (Allyn and Bacon, 1990), p. 87.

[13] This example is based upon a similar one in Senge, *The Fifth Discipline,* pp. 195–196.

[14] This story and the dialogue are based upon Chris Argyris, "Education for Leading-Learning," *Organizational Dynamics,* Winter 1993, pp. 8–9.

[15] See Rick Ross and Charlotte Roberts, "Balancing Inquiry and Advocacy," in Senge, *The Fifth Discipline Fieldbook,* pp. 253–262, and Philip McArthur, "Opening Lines," in the same volume, p. 263.

[16] Chris Argyris and Donald Schön, *Organizational Learning II* (Reading, Mass: Addison-Wesley, 1996), pp. 114–115.

[17] Argyris, "Education for Leading-Learning," p. 13.

[18] Jay W. Forrester, "Learning through Systems Dynamics as Preparation for the Twenty-first Century" (keynote address for Systems Thinking and Dynamic Modeling Conference for K-12 Education, June 27–29), 1994.

[19] Jay W. Forrester, "Systems Dynamics and the Lessons of 35 Years," in Kenyon B. De-Greene, ed., *The Systemic Basis of Policy Making in the 1990s,* p. 8.

[20] Ibid., p. 8.

[21] Forrester, "Learning through Systems Dynamics."

[22] Senge et al., *The Fifth Discipline Fieldbook,* p. 121.

[23] *Webster's New World Dictionary,* Third College Edition, s.v. "archetype."

[24] Forrester, "Learning through Systems Dynamics."

[25] Kets de Vries, *Life and Death,* p. 88.

[26] Peter Senge, *The Fifth Discipline,* p. 65.

[27] Edgar Schein, "How Can Organizations Learn Faster? The Challenge of Entering the Green Room," *Sloan Management Review,* Winter 1995, p. 87.

[28] Edgar Schein, "Organizational Culture," *American Psychologist,* February 1990, p. 111.

[29] Ibid., p. 115.

[30] Edgar Schein, "Building the Learning Consortium," (speech presented at the MIT Sloan School of Management, Cambridge, Mass., March 30, 1995).

[31] Edgar Schein, "How Can Organizations Learn Faster?" p. 87.

[32] Ibid., p. 89.

[33] Ibid.

Chapter 4

[1] H. Scarbrough, review of "The Social Engagement of Social Science: A Tavistock Anthology," *Human Relations* 48, no. 1 (1995): 23–33.

[2] E.L. Trist, "On Socio-Technical Systems" (lecture presented to the departments of engineering and psychology, University of Cambridge, November 18, 1959).

[3] Ibid.

[4] Ibid.

[5] Our gurus use a wide variety of terms to refer to the type of organization we are discussing in this chapter—"socio-technical designs," "high-performance organizations,"

"high-involvement management," "team-based organizations," "teams," "groups that work," "great groups," "businesses without bosses," and so on. While each guru gives his or her own particular twist to the concept, some common themes can be found in each. These have to do with creating employee teams, moving more responsibility to employees, opening up the flow of information, reducing the hierarchy, and organizing around processes rather than functions. It is this generic high-performance organization that we discuss in this chapter.

6 This comparison is based upon a survey instrument designed by William Pasmore. See his *Designing Effective Organizations: The Sociotechnical Systems Perspective* (New York: John Wiley & Sons, 1988), pp. 157–186. Additional items have been added based upon ideas from the Center for Effective Organizations. See Susan Albers Mohrman, Susan G. Cohen, and Allan M. Mohrman, Jr., *Designing Team-Based Organizations: New Forms for Knowledge Work* (San Francisco: Jossey-Bass, 1995), pp. 350–361.

7 Jon R. Katzenbach and Douglas K. Smith, *The Wisdom of Teams* (Boston: Harvard Business School Press, 1993), p. 16.

8 Eileen Appelbaum and Rosemary Batt, *High-Performance Work Systems: American Models of Workplace Transformation* (Washington, D.C.: Economic Policy Institute, 1993), p. 41.

9 Charles Manz and Henry P. Sims, *Business without Bosses* (New York: John Wiley & Sons, 1993), pp. 17–18.

10 Katzenbach and Smith, *Wisdom of Teams*, pp. 22–23.

11 John Zenger et al., *Leading Teams* (Homewood, Ill.: Business One Irwin, 1994), p. 86.

12 Ibid., pp. 156–170.

13 Manz and Sims, *Business without Bosses*, p. 215.

14 Mohrman, Cohen, and Mohrman, *Designing Team-Based Organizations*, pp. 69–240.

15 Katzenbach and Smith, *Wisdom of Teams*, pp. 119–127.

16 Mohrman, Cohen, and Mohrman, *Designing Team-Based Organizations*, pp. 40–43.

17 Ibid., pp. 82–85.

18 Glenn M. Parker, Cross-Functional Teams (San Francisco: Jossey-Bass, 1994), p. 6.

19 Mohrman, Cohen, and Mohrman, *Designing Team-Based Organizations*, pp. 89–98.

20 Ibid., pp. 116–130.

21 Manz and Sims, *Business without Bosses*, pp. 44–48.

22 See Zenger et al., *Leading Teams*, pp. 15–19, 29–34; Manz and Sims, *Business without Bosses*, p. 68; Carl A. Barmlett, "Free to Change," *Training and Development Journal* (March 1984): pp. 32–40; and Pasmore, *Designing Effective Organizations*, p. 148.

23 Katzenbach and Smith, *Wisdom of Teams*, pp. 139–144.

24 Mohrman, Cohen, and Mohrman, *Designing Team-Based Organizations*, pp. 141–144.

25 Ibid., p. 249.

26 Ibid., pp. 249–250.

27 Edward E. Lawler, *From the Ground Up* (San Francisco; Jossey-Bass, 1996), p. 183.

28 Manz and Sims, *Business without Bosses*, p. 200.

[29] Peter R. Scholtes, Brian L. Joiner, and Barbara J. Streibel, *The Team Handbook,* 2nd ed. (Madison, Wis.: Joiner associates, Inc., 1996), p. 6–4.

[30] Ibid., p. 6–5.

[31] Ibid., p. 6–6.

[32] Ibid., p. 6–7.

[33] Linda Moran, Ed Musselwhite, and John Zenger, *Keeping Teams on Track* (Chicago: Irwin Professional Publishing, 1996), p. 43.

[34] Adapted from Geary Rummler and Alan P. Bache, *Improving Performance: How to Manage the White Space on the Organization Chart* (San Francisco: Jossey-Bass, 1990), and from Moran, Musselwhite, and Zenger, *Keeping Teams on Track,* pp. 46–48.

[35] Edward E. Lawler, *High-Involvement Management* (San Francisco: Jossey-Bass, 1986), p. 195.

[36] Lawler, *From the Ground Up,* p. 197.

[37] Ibid., p. 204.

[38] Ibid., p. 218.

[39] Mohrman, Cohen, and Mohrman, *Designing Team-Based Organizations,* p. 300.

[40] Lawler, *High-Involvement Management,* p. 198.

[41] Ibid., pp. 198–199.

[42] Ibid., p. 199.

[43] Ibid.

[44] Parker, *Cross-Functional Teams,* p. 104.

[45] Ibid., p. 107.

[46] Katzenbach and Smith, *Wisdom of Teams,* p. 3.

[47] Ibid., pp. 53–55.

[48] Lawler, *From the Ground Up,* p. 154.

[49] Parker, *Cross-Functional Teams,* p. 156.

[50] Katzenbach and Smith, *Wisdom of Teams,* p. 46.

[51] Lawler, *High-Involvement Management,* pp. 200–201.

[52] Lawler, *From the Ground Up,* p. 166.

[53] Katzenbach and Smith, *Wisdom of Teams,* p. 151.

[54] Ibid., pp. 160–164.

[55] Ibid., p. 167.

Chapter 5

[1] Michael E. Porter, *Competitive Strategy: Techniques for Analyzing Industries and Competitors* (New York: Free Press, 1980), p. ix.

[2] Ibid., pp. 363–364.

[3] Ibid., p. 4.

[4] Ibid., p. 7.

[5] Ibid., p. 10.

[6] Ibid., 27–28.

7 Ibid., p. 18.

8 Ibid., p. 34.

9 Ibid., pp. 35–36.

10 Ibid., p. 38.

11 Generally, Porter argued that firms had to be pursue only one generic strategy, because a firm could not, in most circumstances, be both low-cost and unique and/or optimize its operations to meet the needs of a target segment (focus) while simultaneously serving a broad range of customers (cost leadership and differentiation). In *Competitive Advantage,* Porter suggests that a firm might be able to create two largely separate business units that could pursue different strategies, but the firm would have to keep the units strictly separated or risk losing the competitive advantage. On the whole, Porter finds the three generic approaches incompatible. See Michael E. Porter, *Competitive Advantage: Creating and Sustaining Superior Performance* (New York: Free Press, 1985), pp. 17–20.

12 Porter, *Competitive Strategy,* p. 41.

13 Porter, *Competitive Advantage,* p. 33.

14 Ibid., pp. 39–40.

15 Ibid., pp. 41–42.

16 Ibid., pp. 42–43.

17 Henry Mintzberg, "The Fall and Rise of Strategic Planning," *Harvard Business Review,* January–February 1994, p. 107. See also Henry Mintzberg, *The Rise and Fall of Strategic Planning* (New York: Free Press, 1994).

18 Mintzberg, "Fall and Rise," p. 108.

19 Ibid., p. 111.

20 Ibid.

21 Gary Hamel and C. K. Prahalad, *Competing for the Future* (Boston: Harvard Business School Press, 1994), p. ix.

22 Gary Hamel and C. K. Prahalad, "Do You Really Have a Global Strategy?" *Harvard Business Review* 63, no. 4 (1985): pp. 139–148; "Strategic Intent," *Harvard Business Review* 67, no. 3 (1989): pp. 63–76 (McKinsey Award-winning article); "The Core Competence of the Corporation," *Harvard Business Review* 68, no. 3 (1990): pp. 79–91 (McKinsey Award-winning article and the most requested reprinted article in *Harvard Business Review* history); "Corporate Imagination and Expeditionary Marketing," *Harvard Business Review* 69, no. 4 (1991): pp. 81–92; and "Strategy as Stretch and Leverage," *Harvard Business Review* 71, no. 2 (1993): pp. 75–84.

23 Hamel and Prahalad, *Competing for the Future,* p. x.

24 Ibid.

25 Ibid., p. 73.

26 Hamel and Prahalad actually use the term *foresight* rather than *vision.* They explain: "For a variety of reasons we prefer the word *foresight* to *vision.* Vision connotes a dream or an apparition, but there is more to industry foresight than a single blinding flash of in-

sight. Industry foresight is based on deep insights into the trends in technology, demographics, regulation, and lifestyles that can be harnessed to rewrite industry rules and create new competitive space. While understanding the potential *implications* of such trends requires creativity and imagination, any 'vision' that is not based on solid factual foundations is likely to be fantastical" (*Competing for the Future,* p. 76).

[27] Ibid., p. 73.

[28] Ibid., pp. 73–74.

[29] Ibid., p. 83.

[30] Ibid., p. 84.

[31] Ibid., p. 86.

[32] Ibid., p. 83.

[33] Gary Hamel, "Strategy as Revolution," *Harvard Business Review,* July–August 1996, p. 74.

[34] Ibid., p. 77.

[35] Ibid.

[36] Hamel and Prahalad, *Competing for the Future,* p. 108.

[37] Ibid., pp. 110–111.

[38] Ibid., pp. 112–114.

[39] John Micklethwait and Adrian Wooldridge, *The Witch Doctors* (New York: Times Books, 1996), p. 153.

[40] Jay Stuller, "The Guru Game," *Across the Board,* December 1992, p. 21.

[41] Michael Treacy and Fred Wiersema, *The Discipline of Market Leaders* (Reading, Mass.: Addison-Wesley, 1995), p. 26.

[42] Ibid.

[43] From the book jacket of *The Discipline of Market Leaders.*

[44] Willy Stern, "Did Dirty Tricks Create a Best Seller?" *Business Week,* August 7, 1995, p. 23.

[45] Ibid., p. 24.

[46] Treacy and Wiersema, *The Discipline of Market Leaders,* pp. 42–43.

[47] Ibid., p. 165.

[48] Ibid., p. 171.

[49] Ibid., p. 172.

[50] See John A. Byrne, "Three of the Busiest New Strategists," *Business Week,* August 26, 1996, p. 50.

[51] James F. Moore, *The Death of Competition* (New York: Harper Business, 1996), pp. 60–61.

[52] Ibid., p. 3.

[53] Ibid., p. 26.

[54] Ibid., pp. 26–27.

[55] Ibid., p. 55.

[56] Ibid., pp. 174–175.

[57] Ibid., pp. 206–207.

[58] Adapted from Figure 10.1 in Moore, *The Death of Competition,* p. 232.

[59] Ibid., p. 239.

[60] Ibid., p. 238.

[61] Adam M. Brandenburger and Barry J. Nalebuff, *Co-opetition* (New York: Doubleday, 1996), p. 3.

[62] Ibid., p. 5.

[63] Ibid., p. 4.

[64] Ibid., p. 6.

[65] Ibid., p. 70.

[66] Ibid., p. 18.

[67] Ibid., p. 20.

[68] Ibid., p. 84.

[69] Ibid., p. 85.

[70] Ibid., p. 94.

[71] Intel was eventually able to stop granting second-source licenses on its later chips. See Brandenburger and Nalebuff, *Co-opetition,* p. 105.

[72] Ibid., pp. 108–109.

[73] Ibid., p. 123.

[74] Ibid., p. 167.

[75] Ibid., p. 198.

[76] Ibid., p. 208.

[77] Ibid., p. 225.

[78] Ibid., p. 223.

[79] Ibid., p. 262.

Chapter 6

[1] Thomas F. Gilbert, *Human Competence: Engineering Worthy Performance* (New York: McGraw-Hill, 1978), p. v.

[2] Ibid., p. 11.

[3] Ibid.

[4] Gilbert uses the phrase *human capital* rather than *leisure* in this quote because of his fear that readers would associate the latter term with idleness. We have chosen to stick with the more complex but precise term *leisure.*

[5] Ibid.,

[6] Ibid., pp. 18–19.

[7] Ibid., p. 30.

[8] Ibid., p. 32.

[9] We have taken some liberties with the retelling of this story. To read the original Gilbert version, go to pages 32–35 of *Human Competence.*

[10] Ibid., p. 34.

[11] Ibid., p. 76.

[12] Ibid., p. 86.

[13] Ibid., p. 89.

[14] Ibid., pp. 89–90.

[15] Ibid., p. 90.

[16] Ibid., p. 91.

[17] Ibid., p. 175.

[18] Ibid., pp. 177–180. The one substantial exception to this dramatic improvement, says Gilbert, is when people have not been adequately trained. In such cases, providing information is not sufficient. He notes, however, that even people who are adequately trained need information on how they are performing in order to perform in an exemplary manner.

[19] Jack Stack, *The Great Game of Business* (New York: Currency Doubleday, 1992), p. 1.

[20] Ibid., pp. 21–22.

[21] Ibid., p. 22.

[22] Ibid., p. 28.

[23] Ibid., p. 40.

[24] Ibid., pp. 41–42.

[25] Ibid., p. 1.

[26] John Case, *Open-Book Management* (New York: Harper Business, 1995), p. 73.

[27] Ibid., p. 76.

[28] Ibid., p. 78.

[29] Stack, *The Great Game of Business,* p. 83.

[30] John P. Schuster and Jill Carpenter, with M. Patricia Kane, *The Power of Open-Book Management* (New York: John Wiley & Sons, 1996), p. 232.

[31] Stack, *The Great Game of Business,* pp. 176–177. Stack notes that they now work with a computer-generated spreadsheet that is projected on a screen at the front of the room. The spreadsheet is updated as people call out their numbers. At the end of the meeting, copies of the revised spreadsheet are printed out for people to take back to their posthuddles that Springfield calls Chalk Talks.

[32] Ibid., p. 192.

[33] Robert S. Kaplan and David P. Norton, *The Balanced Scorecard* (Boston: Harvard Business School Press, 1996), p. 8.

[34] Ibid., p. 25.

[35] Ibid., p. 36.

[36] Gilbert, *Human Competence,* p. 308.

[37] See Aubrey C. Daniels, *Performance Management: Improving Quality Productivity through Positive Reinforcement* (Tucker, Ga.: Performance Management Publications, 1989), and Aubrey C. Daniels, *Bringing Out the Best in People: How to Apply the As-*

tonishing Power of Positive Reinforcement (New York: McGraw-Hill, 1994). Also see Joseph H. Boyett and Henry P. Conn, *Maximum Performance Management: How to Manage and Compensate People to Meet World Competition,* 2nd ed. (Lakewood, Colo.: Glenbridge Publishing Ltd., 1988, 1993), pp. 135–250, for a more complete discussion of how to manage and motivate people using tangible and intangible incentives.

[38] Daniels, *Bringing Out the Best in People,* p. 19.

[39] Ibid., pp. 20–21.

[40] Ibid., pp. 63–64.

[41] Edward E. Lawler, *Strategic Pay* (San Francisco: Jossey-Bass, 1990), pp. 136–139.

[42] Ibid., p. 142.

[43] Daniels, *Bringing Out the Best,* p. 151.

[44] Thomas P. Flannery, David A. Hofrichter, and Paul E. Platten, *People, Performance and Pay* (New York: Free Press, 1996), p. xv.

[45] Lawler, *Strategic Pay,* p. 163.

[46] Jay R. Schuster and Patricia K. Zingheim, *The New Pay* (San Francisco: Jossey-Bass, 1992), p. 108.

[47] Ibid.

[48] Flannery, Hofrichter, and Platten, *People, Performance and Pay,* p. 95.

[49] Ibid., pp. 96–97.

[50] Ibid., pp. 94–95.

[51] Edward E. Lawler, "Competencies: A Poor Performance for the New Pay," *Compensation and Benefits Review,* November 21, 1996, pp. 12–18. For a response to Lawler's criticism, see David A. Hofrichter and Lyle M. Spencer, Jr., "Competencies: The Right Foundation for Effective Human Resource Management," *Compensation and Benefits Review,* November 21, 1996, pp. 26–34. Hofrichter and Spencer write that the Hay Group does not recommend or endorse the use of generic compentencies, that below-the-waterline characteristics are important because they provide the "push" that causes people to display high-performance behaviors and are predictive of how people will apply their knowledge and skill, that valid and reliable techniques for measuring job-related behaviors are available, and that problems with using competencies result from "sloppy practice in some quarters" and don't occur when a rigorous approach to identifying the competencies is followed.

[52] See Edward E. Lawler, *From the Ground Up* (San Francisco: Jossey-Bass, 1996), pp. 206–211; Lawler, *Strategic Pay,* pp. 13–22; and Schuster and Zingheim, *The New Pay,* pp. 193–197.

[53] Schuster and Zingheim, *The New Pay,* p. 194.

[54] Lawler, *Strategic Pay,* p. 18.

[55] Ibid., p. 20.

[56] Lawler, *From the Ground Up,* p. 211.

[57] Flannery, Hofrichter, and Platten, *People, Performance and Pay,* pp. 121–122.

Chapter 7

1 Peter Drucker, *The Post-Capitalist Society* (New York: HarperBusiness, 1993), p. 7.
2 Ibid., p. 8.
3 Ibid., p. 1.
4 Ibid., p. 5.
5 Ibid.
6 Ibid.
7 Ibid., p. 6.
8 Ibid., p. 20.
9 Ibid., p. 28.
10 Ibid., pp. 28–29.
11 Ibid., p. 38.
12 Ibid., p. 39.
13 Ibid., p. 42.
14 Ibid., pp. 46–47.
15 From a speaker's bureau's description.
16 Tom Peters, *The Tom Peters Seminar* (New York: Vintage Books, 1994), p. 121.
17 Charles Handy, *The Age of Unreason* (Boston: Harvard Business School Press, 1989), pp. 118–119.
18 Peters, *Tom Peters Seminar,* p. 39.
19 Handy, *Age of Unreason,* p. 120.
20 Peters, *Tom Peters Seminar,* p. 27.
21 These are all taken from Peters, *Tom Peters Seminar,* pp. 29–63.
22 Handy, *Age of Unreason,* p. 122.
23 Charles Handy, *The Age of Paradox* (Boston: Harvard Business School Press, 1994), p. 134.
24 Ibid., p. 146.
25 Ibid., p. 116.
26 Ibid., p. 141.
27 Peters, *Tom Peters Seminar,* p. 45.
28 Handy, *Age of Unreason,* p. 131.
29 Ibid., p. 132.
30 Peters, *Tom Peters Seminar,* p. 69.
31 Ibid.
32 These elements are summarized from Peters, *Tom Peters Seminar,* pp. 73–74, and Tom Peters, *Liberation Management* (New York: Knopf, 1992), pp. 235–236.
33 This discussion of the shamrock organization is adapted from Handy, *Age of Unreason,* pp. 87–115.
34 Ibid., pp. 98–99.
35 Ibid., p. 99.

[36] Ibid., p. 100.

[37] Peters, *Liberation Management,* p. 314.

[38] Ibid., p. 315.

[39] Ibid.

[40] Peters, *Tom Peters Seminar,* p. 148.

[41] Ibid., pp. 148–149.

[42] Peters provides an excellent and entertaining description of one such video production that he calls the Dallas Organization in *Liberation Management,* pp. 190–200.

[43] Handy, *Age of Unreason,* p. 211.

[44] Handy, *Age of Paradox,* p. 217.

[45] Peters, *Tom Peters Seminar,* pp. 94–95.

[46] Ibid., p. 96.

[47] Ibid., p. 109.

[48] Handy, *Age of Paradox,* p. 286.

Bibliography

Adams, Guy B. "Blindsided by the Elephant." *Public Administration Review* 54 (January 1994): 77–78.

Albrecht, Karl. *The Northbound Train: Finding the Purpose, Setting the Direction, Shaping the Destiny of Your Organization.* New York: AMACOM, 1994.

Angehrn, Albert A., and Jean François Manzone. "A High-Tech Spin on Organizational Learning." *Chief Executive* (April 1996): 66–67.

Appelbaum, Eileen, and Rosemary Batt. *High-Performance Work Systems: American Models of Workplace Transformation.* Washington, D.C.: Economic Policy Institute, 1993.

Arendt, Carl, Russ Landis, and Toni Meister. "The Human Side of Change." *IIE Solutions* (May 1995): 22–26.

Argyris, Chris. "Double Loop Learning in Organizations." *Harvard Business Review* (September–October 1977): 115–125.

———. "Education for Leading-Learning." *Organizational Dynamics* (Winter 1993): 5–17.

———. "Good Communication That Blocks Learning." *Harvard Business Review* (July–August 1994): 77–85.

———. *Overcoming Organizational Defenses.* Needham, Mass.: Allyn & Bacon, 1990.

———. "Teaching Smart People How to Learn." *Harvard Business Review* (May–June 1991): 99–109.

Agyris, Chris, and Donald Schön. *Organizational Learning II.* Reading, Mass.: Addison-Wesley, 1996.

Barmlett, Carl A. "Free to Change." *Training and Development Journal* (March 1984): 32–40.

Barney, Jay. "Firm Resources and Sustained Competitive Advantage." *Journal of Management* 17, no. 1 (1991): 99–120.

Barrett, Michael, and Barbara Luedecke. "What Management Says It Wants in Communicating Change." *Communication World* (June–July 1996): 29–32.

Bartlett, Christopher A., and Sumantra Ghoshal. "Changing the Role of Top Management: Beyond Strategy to Purpose." *Harvard Business Review* (November–December 1994): 80–87.

———. "Changing the Role of Top Management: Beyond Systems to People." *Harvard Business Review* (May–June 1995): 133–134.

———. "Rebuilding Behavioral Context: Turn Process Reengineering into People Rejuvenation." *Sloan Management Review* (Fall 1995): 11–23.

Beckhard, Richard. "Strategies for Large System Change." *Sloan Management Review* (Winter 1975): 43–55.

Beckhard, Richard, and Reuben T. Harris. *Organizational Transitions,* 2d ed. Reading, Mass.: Addison-Wesley, 1987.

Beer, Michael, and Russell A. Eisenstat. "Developing an Organization Capable of Implementing Strategy and Learning." *Human Relations* 49, no. 5 (1996): 597–619.

Belasco, James A., and Ralph C. Stayer. "Why Empowerment Doesn't Empower: The Bankruptcy of Current Paradigms." *Business Horizons* (March–April 1994): 29–41.

Bennett, Joan Kremer, and Michael J. O'Brien. "The Twelve Building Blocks of the Learning Organization." *Training* (June 1994): 41–49.

Bennis, Warren. "The Leader as Storyteller." *Harvard Business Review* (January–February 1996): 154–160.

———. "Lessons in Leadership from Superconsultant Warren Bennis." *Bottom Line Personal* (July 1, 1996): 13–14.

———. *On Becoming a Leader.* New York: Addison-Wesley, 1989.

Bennis, Warren, and Burt Nanus. *Leaders: The Strategies for Taking Charge.* HarperBusiness, 1997.

Bennis, Warren, and Robert Townsend. *Reinventing Leadership: Strategies to Empower the Organization.* New York: William Morrow, 1995.

Benson, Tracy E. "Learning Organization: Heading toward Places Unimaginable." *Industry Week* (January 4, 1993): 35–78

Blanchard, Ken, Don Carew, and Eunice Parisi-Carew. "How to Get Your Group to Perform Like a Team." *Training and Development* (September 1996): 34–37.

Blank, Warren, *The Nine Natural Laws of Leadership.* New York: AMACOM, 1995.

Bolman, Lee G. Interview with Lee Bolman. http://www. spiritlead.com/cr.htm.

Bolman, Lee G., and Terrence E. Deal. *Leading with Soul: An Uncommon Journey of Spirit.* San Francisco: Jossey-Bass, 1995.

Bordas, Juana. "Power and Passion: Finding Personal Purpose." In *Reflections on Leadership,* ed. Larry C. Spears, 184–192. New York: John Wiley & Sons, 1995.

Bowen, David E., and Edward E. Lawler. "The Empowerment of Service Workers: What, Why, How, and When." *Sloan Management Review* (Spring 1992): 31–39.

Boyett, Joseph H., and Henry P. Conn. *Maximum Performance Management: How to Manage and Compensate People to Meet World Competition.* Lakewood, Colo.: Glenbridge Publishing Ltd., 1988. 2d ed., 1993.

Brandenburger, Adam M., and Barry J. Nalebuff. *Co-opetition.* New York: Doubleday, 1996.

———. "The Right Game: Use Game Theory to Shape Strategy." *Harvard Business Review.* (July–August 1995): 57–71.

Brown, John Seely, and Paul Duguid. "Organizational Learning and Communities-of-Practice: Toward a Unified View of Working, Learning, and Innovation." *Organization Science* 2 (February 1991): 40–57.

Buck, J. Thomas. "The Rocky Road to Team-Based Management." *Training and Development* (April 1995): 35–38.

Byrne, John A. "Strategic Planning." *Fortune* (August 26, 1996): 46–52.

———. "Three of the Busiest New Strategists." *Business Week* (August 26, 1996): 50.

Calvert, Gene, Sandra Mobley, and Lisa Marshall. "Grasping the Learning Organization." *Training and Development* (June 1994): 39–43.

Caminiti, Susan. "What Team Leaders Need to Know." *Fortune* (February 20, 1995): 93–100.

Carr, Clay. "Empowered Organizations, Empowering Leaders." *Training and Development* (March 1994): 39–44.

———. "Seven Keys to Successful Change." *Training* (February 1994): 55–60.

Case, John. *Open-Book Management.* New York: HarperBusiness, 1995.

Cerny, Keith. "Making Local Knowledge Global." *Harvard Business Review* (May–June 1996): 22–38.

Champy, James. *Reengineering Management: The Mandate for New Leadership.* New York: HarperBusiness, 1995.

Collins, James C., and Jerry I. Porras. "Building a Visionary Company." *California Management Review* 37 (Winter 1995): 80–100.

———. "Building Your Company's Vision." *Harvard Business Review* (September–October 1996): 74.

———. *Built to Last: Successful Habits of Visionary Companies.* New York: HarperBusiness, 1997.

Collis, David J., and Cynthia A. Montgomery. "Competing on Resources: Strategy in the 1990s." *Harvard Business Review* (July–August 1995): 118–128.

Conger, Jay A. *The Charismatic Leader: Behind the Mystique of Exceptional Leadership.* San Francisco: Jossey-Bass, 1989.

Conner, Daryl. *Managing at the Speed of Change.* New York: Villard Books, 1992.

Conner, Kathleen. "A Historical Comparison of Resource-Based Theory and Five Schools of Thought within Industrial Organization Economics: Do We Have a New Theory of the Firm?" *Journal of Management* 17 (1991): 121–154.

Corey, Stephen R. *Principle-Centered Leadership.* New York: Summit Books, 1991.

———. *The Seven Habits of Highly Effective People.* New York: Simon & Schuster, 1989.

Daniels, A. C. *Bringing Out the Best in People: How to Apply the Astonishing Power of Positive Reinforcement.* New York: McGraw-Hill, 1994.

———. *Performance Management: Improving Quality Productivity through Positive Reinforcement.* Tucker, Ga.: Performance Management Publications, 1989.

Davenport, Thomas H. "Will Participative Makeovers of Business Processes Succeed Where Reengineering Failed?" *Planning Review* (January–February 1995): 24–29.

Davenport, Thomas H., Sirkka L. Jarvenpaa, and Michael C. Beers. "Improving Knowledge Work Processes." *Sloan Management Review* (Summer 1996): 53–65.

Davidow, William H., and Michael S. Malone. "The Virtual Corporation." *California Business* (November 1992): 34–42.

Davids, Meryl. "Where Style Meets Substance." *Journal of Business Strategy* 16 (January–February 1996): 49–60.

De Geus, Arie P. "Planning As Learning." *Harvard Business Review* (March–April 1988): 70–74.

De Pree, Max. *Leadership Is An Art.* New York: Doubleday, 1989.

———. *Leadership Jazz.* New York: Doubleday, 1992.

DiBella, Anthony J., Edwin C. Nevis, and Janet Gould. "Understanding Organizational Learning Capability." *Journal of Management Studies* 33 (May 1996): 361–370.

Dodgson, Mark. "Organizational Learning: A Review of Some Literature." *Organizational Studies* 14, no. 3 (1993): 375–394.

Drucker, Peter F. *The Age of Discontinuity: Guidelines to Our Changing Society.* New York: Harper & Row, 1968.

———. *Concept of the Corporation.* Rev. ed. New York: The John Day Company, 1972.

———. *Landmarks of Tomorrow.* New York: Harper & Brothers, 1957.

———. *Managing for the Future: The 1990s and Beyond.* New York: Truman Talley Books, 1993.

———. *Managing in a Time of Great Change.* New York: Truman Talley Books/Dutton, 1995.

———. *Managing in Turbulent Times.* New York: Harper & Row, 1980.

———. *The New Realities: In Government and Politics/In Economics and Business/In Society and World View,* New York: Harper & Row, 1989.

———. *The New Society: The Anatomy of Industrial Order.* New York: Harper Torchbooks, 1962.

———. *The Post-Capitalist Society.* New York: HarperBusiness, 1993.

———. *The Practice of Management.* New York: Harper & Brothers, 1954.

Duck, Jeanie Daniel. "Managing Change: The Art of Balancing." *Harvard Business Review* (November–December 1993): 109–118.

Dumaine, Brian. "Mr. Learning Organization." *Fortune* (October 17, 1994): 147–157.

Edmondson, Amy C. "Three Faces of Eden: The Persistence of Competing Theories and Multiple Diagnoses in Organizational Intervention Research." *Human Relations* 49, no. 5 (1996): 571–595.

Eisler, Riane. "From Domination to Partnership: The Hidden Subtext of Organization Change." *Training and Development* (February 1995): 32–40.

Epple, Dennis, Linda Argote, and Rukmini Devadas. "Organization Learning Curves." *Organization Science* 2 (February 1991): 58–70.

Farkas, Charles M., and Suzy Wetlaufer. "The Ways Chief Executive Officers Lead." *Harvard Business Review* (May–June 1996): 110–122.

Farnham, Alan. "How to Nurture Creative Sparks." *Fortune* (January 10, 1994): 94–110.

Farson, Richard. *Management of the Absurd.* New York: Simon & Schuster, 1996.

Fetzinger, Edward, and Hau L. Lee. "Mass Customization at Hewlett-Packard: The Power of Postponement." *Harvard Business Review* (January–February 1997): 116–121.

Fiedler, Fred E. "Research on Leadership Selection and Training: One View of the Future." *Administrative Science Quarterly* 41 (June 1996): 241–250.

Filipczak, Bob. "Weathering Change: Enough Already." *Training* (September 1994): 23–29.

Fiol, C. Marlene. "Managing Culture As a Competitive Resource: An Identity-Based View of Sustainable Competitive Advantage." *Journal of Management* 17, no. 1 (1991): 191–211.

Fiol, C. Marlene, and Marjorie A. Lyles. "Organizational Learning." *Academy of Management Review* 10, no. 4 (1985): 803–813.

Fisher, Anne B. "Making Change Stick." *Fortune* (April 17, 1995): 121–130.

Flanagan, Patrick. "The ABCs of Changing Corporate Culture." *Management Review* (July 1995): 57–62.

Flannery, Thomas P., David A. Hofrichter, and Paul E. Platten. *People, Performance and Pay.* New York: Free Press, 1996.

Flynn, Gillian. "Do You Have the Right Approach to Diversity?" *Personnel Journal* (October 1995): 68–75.

Foreman, Peter. "Learning to Avoid the Winner's Curse." *Organizational Behavior* 67 (August 1996): 170–180.

Forrester, Jay W. "Beginning of Systems Dynamics." Speech at the international meeting of the System Dynamics Society, Stuttgart, Germany, July 13, 1989.

———. "Learning through Systems Dynamics as Preparation for the Twenty-First Century." Keynote address at the Systems Thinking and Dynamic Modeling Conference for K-12 Education, Concord Academy, Concord, Mass., June 27–29, 1994.

———. "Systems Dynamics and the Lessons of 35 Years." Unpublished chapter prepared for *The Systemic Basis of Policy Making in the 1990s,* edited by Kenyon B. DeGreene, April 29, 1991. Available online at http://sysdyn.mit.edu/people/jay-forrester.html.

Fox, William M. "Sociotechnical System Principles and Guidelines: Past and Present." *The Journal of Applied Behavioral Science* (March 1995): 91–105.

Fraker, Anne T. "Robert K. Greenleaf and Business Ethics: There is No Code." In *Reflections on Leadership,* ed. Larry C. Spears, 37–48. New York: John Wiley & Sons, 1995.

Frohman, Mark A. "Do Teams . . . but Do Them Right." *Industry Week* (April 3, 1995): 21–24.

Fulmer, Robert M. "A Model for Changing the Way Organizations Learn." *Planning* (May–June 1994): 20–24.

Galagan, Patricia A. "Helping Groups Learn." *Training and Development* (October 1993): 57–61.

———. "Search for the Poetry of Work." *Training and Development* (October 1993): 33–37.

Galpin, Timothy. "Changing the Change Leader." *Employment Relations Today* (Autumn 1995): 83–90.

———. "Connecting Culture to Organizational Change." *HRMagazine* (March 1996): 84–90.

———. *The Human Side of Change: A Practical Guide to Organization Redesign.* San Francisco: Jossey-Bass, 1996.

———. "Pruning Grapevine." *Training and Development* (April 1995): 28–33.

Gardner, Howard. *Leading Minds: An Anatomy of Leadership.* New York: Basic Books, 1995.

Gardner, John. *On Leadership.* New York: Free Press, 1990.

Garvin, David A. "Building a Learning Organization." *Business Credit* (January 1994): 19–28.

Geber, Beverly. "The Bugaboo of Team Pay." *Training* (August 1995): 25–34.

———. "Virtual Teams." *Training* (April 1995): 36–40.

Gephart, Martha A. "Learning Organizations Come Alive." *Training and Development* (December 1996): 35–45.

Ghoshal, Sumantra. "Using People As a Force for Change." *People Management* (October 19, 1995): 34–37.

Ghoshal, Sumantra, and Christopher A. Bartlett. "Changing the Role of Top Management: Beyond Structure to Processes." *Harvard Business Review* (January–February 1995): 87.

———. "Rebuilding Behavioral Context: A Blueprint for Corporate Renewal." *Sloan Management Review* (Winter 1996): 23–36.

Gilbert, Thomas F. *Human Competence: Engineering Worthy Performance.* New York: McGraw-Hill, 1978.

Gilmore, James H., and B. Joseph Pine II. "The Four Faces of Mass Customization." *Harvard Business Review* (January–February 1997): 91–101.

Grant, Robert M. "The Resource-Based Theory of Competitive Advantage: Implications for Strategy Formulation." *California Management Review* (Spring 1991): 114–135.

Grant, Robert M., and Renato Cibin. "The Chief Executive As Change Agent." *Planning Review* (January–February 1996): 9–11.

Gray, Shelia D. "Measuring, Assessing, and Evaluating: The Business Impact of Diversity." *Employment Relations Today* (Winter 1994/1995): 431–437.

Greenleaf, Robert K. "Life's Choices and Markers." In *Reflections on Leadership,* ed. Larry C. Spears, 17–21. New York: John Wiley & Sons, 1995.

Griggs, Lewis Brown, and Lente-Louise Louw. "Diverse Teams: Breakdown or Breakthrough." *Training and Development* (October 1995): 22–28.

Hamel, Gary. "Strategy as Revolution." *Harvard Business Review* 74, no. 4 (1996): 74–84.

Hamel, Gary, and C. K. Prahalad. *Competing for the Future.* Boston: Harvard Business School Press, 1994.

———. "The Core Competence of the Corporation." *Harvard Business Review* 68, no. 3 (1990): 79–91.

———. "Corporate Imagination and Expeditionary Marketing." *Harvard Business Review* 69, no. 4 (1991): 81–92.

———. "Do You Really Have a Global Strategy?" *Harvard Business Review* 68, no. 4 (1985): 139–148.

———. "Strategic Intent." *Harvard Business Review* 67, no. 3 (1989): 63–76.

———. "Strategy As Stretch and Leverage." *Harvard Business Review* 71, no. 2 (1993): 75–84.

Handy, Charles. *The Age of Paradox.* Boston: Harvard Business School Press, 1994.

———. *The Age of Unreason.* Boston: Harvard Business School Press, 1989.

———. *Beyond Certainty: The Changing Worlds of Organizations.* Boston: Harvard Business School Press, 1996.

———. *Gods of Management.* New York: Oxford University Press, 1995.

———. "The Paradox Paradigm." *Chief Executive* (January–February 1995): 32–35.

Harari, Oren. "Good/Bad News About Strategy." *Management Review* (July 1995): 29–31.

Hayes, Cassandra. "The New Spin on Corporate Work Teams." *Black Enterprise* (June 1995): 299–234.

Hendry, Chris. "Understanding and Creating Whole Organizational Change through Learning Theory." *Human Relations* 49, no. 5 (1996): 621–641.

Hirsch, Marcie Schorr. "Learning Organizations: The Latest Management Craze." *Working Woman* (June 1995): 21–22.

Hofrichter, David, A., and Lyle M. Spencer, Jr. "Competencies: The Right Foundation for Effective Human Resource Management." *Compensation and Benefits Review* (November 21, 1996): 26–34.

Holpp, Lawrence. "Applied Empowerment." *Training* (February 1994): 39–44.

Holpp, Lawrence, and Robert Phillips. "When Is a Team Its Own Worst Enemy?" *Training* (September 1995): 71–82.

Horney, Nicholas F., and Richard Koonce. "The Missing Piece in Reengineering." *Training and Development* (December 1995): 37–43.

———. "Using Competency Alignment To Shape, Drive, and Sustain Change Efforts." *National Productivity Review* (Summer 1996): 41–53.

Hout, Thomas, and John C. Carter. "Getting It Done: New Roles for Senior Executives." *Harvard Business Review* (November–December 1995): 134–145.

Huber, George P. "Organizational Learning: The Contributing Processes and the Literatures." *Organization Science* 2 (February 1991): 88–115.

Huey, John "The Leadership Industry." *Fortune* (February 21, 1994): 54–50.

Hutt, Michael D., Beth A. Walker, and Gary L. Frankwick. "Hurdle the Cross-Functional Barriers to Strategic Change." *Sloan Management Review* (Spring 1995): 22–30.

Iacovini, John. "The Human Side of Organization Change." *Training and Development* (January 1993): 65–68.

Isaacs, William N. "Taking Flight: Dialogue, Collective Thinking, and Organizational Learning." *Organizational Dynamics* (Autumn 1993): 24–39.

Jacob, Rahul. "The Struggle to Create an Organization for the Twenty-First Century." *Fortune* (April 3, 1995): 90–99.

Jacobs, Robert F. *Real Time Strategic Change.* San Francisco: Berrett-Koehler, 1994.

Jones, Robert. "The Challenge of World Class Training." *Vital Speeches* (December 1, 1996): 115–125.

Kaplan, Robert S., ed. *Measuring for Manufacturing Excellence.* Boston: Harvard Business School Press, 1990.

Kaplan, Robert S., and David P. Norton. *The Balanced Scorecard.* Boston, MA: Harvard Business School Press, 1996.

Katzenbach, Jon R., and Douglas K. Smith. "The Discipline of Teams." *Harvard Business Review* (March–April 1993): 111–120.

———. "Teams at the Top." *The McKinsey Quarterly* 1 (1994): 71–79.

———. *The Wisdom of Teams.* Boston: Harvard Business School Press, 1993.

Katzenbach, Jon R., Frederick Beckett, Steven Dichter, Marc Feigen, Christopher Gagnon, Quentin Hope, and Timothy Ling. *Real Change Leaders.* New York: Times Business, 1995.

Kets de Vries, Manfred F. R. *Life and Death in the Executive Fast Lane.* San Francisco: Jossey-Bass, 1995.

Keys, J. Bernard, Robert M. Fulmer, and Stephen A. Stumpf. "Microworlds and Simuworlds: Practice Fields for the Learning Organization." *Organizational Dynamics* (Spring 1996): 36–49.

Kiechel, Walter, III. "The Organization That Learns." *Fortune* (March 20, 1990): 133–136.

Kim, Daniel H. "The Link between Individual and Organizational Learning." *Sloan Management Review* (Fall 1993): 37–50.

———. *Systems Archetypes II.* Cambridge, Mass.: Pegasus Communications, 1994.

Kim, Daniel H., and Colleen Lannon. *Applying Systems Archetypes.* Cambridge, Mass.: Pegasus Communications, 1997.

Kirkpatrick, Donald L. "Riding the Winds of Change." *Training and Development* (February 1993): 29–32.

Kling, Jeffrey. "High Performance Work Systems and Firm Performance." *Monthly Labor Review* (May 1995): 29–36.

Kofman, Fred, and Peter M. Senge. "Communities of Commitment: The Heart of Learning Organizations." *Organizational Dynamics* (September 1, 1993): 4–22.

Kotter, John P. *A Force for Change.* New York: Free Press, 1990.

———. *The Leadership Factor.* New York: Free Press, 1988.

———. *Leading Change.* Boston: Harvard Business School Press, 1996.

———. "Leading Change: Why Transformation Efforts Fail." *Harvard Business Review* (March–April 1995): 59–67.

Labich, Kenneth. "Elite Teams Get the Job Done." *Fortune* (February 19, 1996): 90–99.

Lado, Augustine, Nancy C. Boyd, and Peter Wright. "A Competency-Based Model of Sustainable Competitive Advantage: Toward a Conceptual Integration." *Journal of Management* 18, no. 1 (1992): 77–91.

Larkin, T. J., and Sandra Larkin. "Reaching and Changing Frontline Employees." *Harvard Business Review* (May–June 1996): 95–104.

Lawler, Edward E. "Competencies: A Poor Performance for the New Pay." *Compensation and Benefits Review* (November 21, 1996): 12–18.

———. *From the Ground Up.* San Francisco: Jossey-Bass, 1996.

———. *High-Involvement Management.* San Francisco: Jossey-Bass, 1986.

———. *Strategic Pay.* San Francisco: Jossey-Bass, 1990.

Ledford, Gerald E., Jr. "Paying for the Skills, Knowledge, and Competencies of Knowledge Workers." *Compensation and Benefits Review* (July 17, 1995): 18–29.

Leonard-Barton, Dorthy. "Core Capabilities and Core Rigidities: A Paradox in Managing New Product Development." *Strategic Management Journal* 13 (1992): 111–125.

Levitt, Barbara, and James G. March. "Organizational Learning." *Annual Review of Sociology* 14 (1988): 319–340.

Lipshitz, Raanan. "Building Learning Organizations." *Journal of Applied Behavioral Science* 32 (September 1, 1996): 292–302.

Lipton, Mark. "Demystifying the Development of an Organizational Vision." *Sloan Management Review* (Summer 1996): 83–92.

Loden, Marilyn, and Judy B. Rosener. *Workforce America!* Homewood, Ill.: Business One Irwin, 1991.

Lopez, Isabel O. "Becoming a Servant-Leader: The Personal Development Path." In *Reflections on Leadership,* ed. Larry C. Spears, 149–160. New York: John Wiley & Sons, 1995.

Lynch, Robert F., and Thomas J. Werner. "A League of Their Own." *Small Business Reports* (April 1994): 35–42.

Mahoney, Joseph T., and J. Rajendran Pandian. "The Resource-Based View within the Conversation of Strategic Management." *Strategic Management Journal* 13 (1992): 363–380.

Manz, Charles, and Henry P. Sims. *Business without Bosses.* New York: John Wiley & Sons, 1993.

———. *SuperLeadership.* New York: Berkley Books, 1989.

March, James G. "Exploration and Exploitation in Organizational Learning." *Organization Science* 2 (February 1991): 71–87.

Marshak, Robert. "Managing the Metaphors of Change . . ." *Organizational Dynamics* (June 1, 1993): 44–56.

May, Douglas, and Michael C. Kettelhut. "Managing Human Issues in Reengineering Projects: A Case Review of Implementation Issues." *Journal of Systems Management* (January–February 1996): 6–14.

McGee-Cooper, Ann, and Duane Trammell. "Servant-Leadership: Is There Really Time for It?" In *Reflections on Leadership,* ed. Larry C. Spears, 113–120. New York: John Wiley & Sons, 1995.

McGill, Michael, and John W. Slocum, Jr. "Unlearning the Organization." *Organizational Dynamics* (Autumn 1993): 67–79.

Micklethwait, John, and Adrian Wooldridge. *The Witch Doctors.* New York: Times Books, 1996.

Miles, Raymond E., and Charles C. Snow. "Fit, Failure and The Hall of Fame." *California Management Review* 3 (Spring 1984): 10–28.

Miller, Danny. "A Preliminary Typology of Organizational Learning: Synthesizing the Literature." *Journal of Management* 22, no. 3 (1996): 485–505.

Mintzberg, Henry. "The Fall and Rise of Strategic Planning." *Harvard Business Review* (January–February 1994): 107–114.

———. "The Pitfalls of Strategic Planning." *California Management Review* (Fall 1993): 33–44.

———. *The Rise and Fall of Strategic Planning.* New York: Free Press, 1994.

Mohrman, Susan Albers, Susan G. Cohen, and Allan M. Mohrman. *Designing Team-Based Organizations: New Forms for Knowledge Work.* San Francisco: Jossey-Bass, 1995.

Moore, James F. *The Death of Competition.* New York: HarperBusiness, 1996.

———. "Predators and Prey: A New Ecology of Competition." *Harvard Business Review* (May–June 1993): 75–86.

Moran, Linda, Ed Musselwhite, and John Zenger. *Keeping Teams on Track.* Chicago: Irwin Professional Publishing, 1996.

Nadler, David A. "Collaborative Strategic Thinking." *Planning Review* (September–October 1994): 30–31.

Nanus, Burt. *The Leader's Edge: The Seven Keys to Leadership in A Turbulent World.* Chicago: Contemporary Books, 1989.

Nanus, Burt. *Visionary Leadership: Creating a Compelling Sense of Direction for Your Organization.* San Francisco: Jossey-Bass, 1992.

Neal, Judith A., and Cheryl L. Tromley. "From Incremental Change to Retrofit: Creating High-Performance Work Systems." *Academy of Management Executive* 9, no. 1 (1995): 42–54.

Nevis, Edwin C., Anthony J. DiBella, and Janet M. Gould. "Understanding Organizations as Learning Systems." *Sloan Management Review* (Winter (1995): 73–85.

Nichols, Martha. "Does New Age Business Have a Message for Managers?" *Harvard Business Review* 72, no. 2 (1994): 52–60.

Nicolini, Davide, and Martin B. Meznar. "The Social Construction of Organizational Learning." *Human Relations* 48, no. 7 (1995): 727–746.

Nohiria, Nitin, and James D. Berkley. "Whatever Happened to the Take Charge Manager?" *Harvard Business Review* 72, no. 1 (1994): 128–137.

Nonaka, Ikujiro. "The Knowledge-Creating Company." *Harvard Business Review* 69, no. 6 (1991): 96–104.

Normann, Richard, and Rafael Ramírez. "From Value Chain to Value Constellation: Designing Interactive Strategy." *Harvard Business Review* 71, no. 4 (1993): 65–77.

O'Toole, James. "Leadership: The One Thing Missing." *Across the Board* (September 1995): 21–26.

———. *Leading Change: The Argument for Values-Based Leadership.* New York: Ballantine Books, 1996.

Parker, Glenn M. *Cross-Functional Teams.* San Francisco: Jossey-Bass, 1994.

Pasmore, William A. *Creating Strategic Change: Designing the Flexible High-Performing Organization.* New York: John Wiley & Sons, 1994.

———. *Designing Effective Organizations: The Sociotechnical Systems Perspective.* New York: John Wiley & Sons, 1988.

Pasmore, William A., and Mary R. Fagans. "Participation, Individual Development, and Organizational Change: A Review and Synthesis." *Journal of Management* 18, no. 2 (1992): 375–397.

Pava, Calvin. "Redesigning Sociotechnical Systems Design: Concepts and Methods for the 1990s." *The Journal of Applied Behavioral Science* 22, no. 3 (1996): 201–221.

Pennar, Karen. "How Many Smarts Do You Have?" *Business Week* (September 16, 1996): 104–108.

Peters, Tom. *Liberation Management.* New York: Knopf, 1992.

———. *The Pursuit of WOW!* New York: Vintage Books, 1994.

———. *The Tom Peters Seminar.* New York: Vintage Books, 1994.

Pfeffer, Jeffrey. "Competitive Advantage through People." *California Management Review* (Winter 1994): 9–28.

Pine, B. Joseph, II. "Making Mass Customization Happen: Strategies for the New Competitive Realities." *Planning Review* (September–October 1993): 23–24.

Pine, B. Joseph, II, Don Peppers, and Martha Rogers. "Do You Want to Keep Your Customers Forever?" *Harvard Business Review* 73, no. 2 (1995): 104–114.

Podsakoff, Philip M., Scott B. MacKenzie, Mike Ahearne, and William H. Bommer. "Searching for a Needle in a Haystack: Trying to Identify the Illusive Moderators of Leadership Behaviors." *Journal of Management* 21, no. 3 (1995): 423–470.

Porter, Michael E. *Competitive Advantage: Creating and Sustaining Superior Performance.* New York: Free Press, 1985.

———. *Competitive Strategy: Techniques for Analyzing Industries and Competitors.* New York: Free Press, 1980.

————. "What is Strategy?" *Harvard Business Review* 74, no. 6 (1996): 61–78.

Prahalad, C. K. "An Interview with C. K. Prahalad." *Training* (November 1994): 33–38.

Prewitt, Edward. "Know-How and Know-Why: Two Levers for Improving Learning in the Factory." *Harvard Business Review* 74, no. 3 (1996): 9–10.

Quinn, James Brian. "Appraising Intellectual Assets." *The McKinsey Quarterly*, no. 2 (1994): 90–95.

Quinn, James Brian, and Frederick G. Hilmer. "Strategic Outsourcing." *Sloan Management Review* (Summer 1994): 43–55.

Recardo, Ronald J. "Overcoming Resistance to Change." *National Productivity Review* (Spring 1995): 5–12.

Recardo, Ronald J., Kathleen Molloy, and James Pellegrino. "How the Learning Organization Manages Change." *National Productivity Review* (Winter 1995/1996) : 7–13.

Reimann, Bernard C. "Gary Hamel: How to Compete for the Future." *Planning Review* (September-October 1994): 39–45.

————. "Leading Strategic Change: Innovation, Value, Growth." *Planning Review* (July–August 1995): 6–36.

Reimann, Bernard C., and Vasudevan Ramanujam. "Acting versus Thinking: A Debate between Tom Peters and Michael Porter." *Planning Review* (March–April 1992): 36–43.

Rieser, Carl. "Claiming Servant-Leadership As Your Heritage." In *Reflections on Leadership*, ed. Larry C. Spears, 49–60. New York: John Wiley & Sons, 1995.

Rifkin, Glenn. "Leadership: Can It Be Learned?" *Forbes ASAP* (April 8, 1996): 100–112.

Rummler, Geary, and Alan P. Bache. *Improving Performance: How to Manage the White Space on the Organization Chart.* San Francisco: Jossey-Bass, 1990.

Safire, William. *Lend Me Your Ears: Great Speeches in History.* New York: Norton, 1992.

Scarbrough, H. Review of *The Social Engagement of Social Science: A Tavistock Anthology,* vol 2, ed. Eric Trist and Hugh Murray. *Human Relations* 48, no. 1 (1995): 23–33.

Schein, Edgar H. "Building the Learning Consortium." Speech given at the MIT Sloan School of Management, Cambridge, Mass., March 30, 1995.

————. "Career Anchors Revisited: Implications for Career Development in the Twenty-First Century." Working paper for the MIT Sloan School of Management, February 1996. Revised March 1996.

————. "How Can Organizations Learn Faster: The Challenge of Entering the Green Room." *Sloan Management Review* (Winter 1993): 85–92.

————. "On Dialogue, Culture, and Organizational Learning." *Organizational Dynamics* (Autumn 1993): 40–51.

————. "Organizational and Managerial Culture As a Facilitator or Inhibitor of Organizational Learning." Working paper for the MIT Organizational Learning Network, May 19, 1994.

————. "Organizational Culture." *American Psychologist* (February 1990): 109–119.

Schoemaker, Paul J. H. "How to Link Strategic Vision to Core Capabilities." *Sloan Management Review* (Fall 1992): 67–81.

Scholtes, Peter R., Brian L. Joiner, and Barbara J. Streibel. *The Team Handbook,* 2nd ed. Madison, Wis.: Joiner Associates, 1996.

Schuster, Jay R., and Patricia K. Zingheim. *The New Pay.* San Francisco: Jossey-Bass, 1992.

Schuster, John P., and Jill Carpenter, with M. Patricia Kane. *The Power of Open-Book Management.* New York: John Wiley & Sons, 1996.

Sellers, Patricia. "What Exactly Is Charisma?" *Fortune* (January 15, 1996): 68–75.

Senge, Peter. *The Fifth Discipline: The Art and Science of the Learning Organization.* New York: Currency Doubleday, 1990.

———. "The Learning Organization Made Plain (Interview with Peter Senge)." *Training and Development* (October 1991): 37–44.

———. "The Leader's New Work: Building Learning Organizations." *Sloan Management Review* (Fall 1990): 7–23.

———. "Leading Learning Organizations." *Training and Development* (December 1996): 36–37.

———. "Mental Models." *Planning Review* (March–April 1992): 4–44.

———. "Rethinking Leadership in the Learning Organization." *Navran Associates Newsletter* 7 (February 1996): 1–9.

———. "Robert Greenleaf's Legacy: A New Foundation for Twenty-First Century Institutions." In *Reflections on Leadership,* ed. Larry C. Spears, 217–240. New York: John Wiley & Sons, 1995.

Senge, Peter, Charlotte Roberts, Richard B. Ross, Bryan J. Smith, and Art Kleiner. *The Fifth Discipline Fieldbook.* New York: Currency Doubleday, 1994.

Sherman, Stratford. "How Tomorrow's Best Leaders Are Learning Their Stuff." *Fortune* (November 27, 1995): 90–102.

Simon, Herbert A. "Bounded Rationality and Organizational Learning." *Organization Science* 2 (February 1991): 125–134.

Slocum, John W., Jr., Michael McGill, and David T. Lei. "The New Learning Strategy." *Organizational Dynamics* 23, no. 2 (1994): 33–47.

Smith, Patricia L., and Stanley J. Smits. "The Feminization of Leadership." *Training and Development* (February 1994): 43–46.

Solomon, Charlene Marmer. "What You Need to Know." *Personnel Journal* (August 1995): 57–67.

Sorohan, Erica Gordon. "We Do; Therefore, We Learn." *Training and Development* (October 1993): 47–55.

Spears, Larry C., ed. *Reflections on Leadership: How Robert K. Greenleaf's* Theory of Servant Leadership *Influenced Today's Top Management Thinkers.* New York: John Wiley & Sons, 1995.

Spiker, Barry K., and Eric L. Lesser. "Change Management: We Have Met the Enemy . . ." *Journal of Business Strategy* (March-April 1995): 17–21.

———. "Making Change Work." *IABC Communication World* (January–February 1995): 23–26.

Stack, Jack. *The Great Game of Business.* New York: Currency Doubleday, 1992.

Stalk, George. "Time-Based Competition and Beyond: Competing on Capabilities." *Conference Executive Summary* (September–October 1992): 27–29.

———. "What is Strategy?" *Harvard Business Review* (January–February 1997): 152.

Stalk, George, Phillip Evans, and Lawrence E. Shulman. "Competing on Capabilities: The New Rules of Corporate Strategy." *Harvard Business Review* (March–April 1992): 57–69.

Stata, Ray. "Organizational Learning: The Key to Management Innovation." *Sloan Management Review* (Spring 1989): 63–74.

Sterbenz, Kathleen B. "The Historical Roots of Participative Management: Part I—1915 to 1930." Originally appeared in *The Northeast Ohio Center for Labor/Management Cooperation UPDATE* 5 (Fall 1991). Draft provided by Mark Erenburg, Director, Labor/Management Relations Center, Cleveland State University.

———. "The Historical Roots of Participative Management: Part II—1929 to 1946." Originally appeared in *The Northeast Ohio Center for Labor/Management Cooperation UPDATE* 6 (Winter 1992). Draft provided by Mark Erenburg, Director, Labor/Management Relations Center, Cleveland State University.

———. "The Historical Roots of Participative Management: Part III—1947 to 1970." Originally appeared in *The Northeast Ohio Center for Labor/Management Cooperation UPDATE* 6 (Spring 1992). Draft provided by Mark Erenburg, Director, Labor/Management Relations Center, Cleveland State University.

———. "The Historical Roots of Participative Management: Part IV—1970s to Present." Originally appeared in *The Northeast Ohio Center for Labor/Management Cooperation UPDATE* 6 (Summer 1992). Draft provided by Mark Erenburg, Director, Labor/Management Relations Center, Cleveland State University.

Stern, Willy. "Did Dirty Tricks Create a Best Seller?" *Business Week* (August 7, 1995): 23.

———. "A Refreshing Change: Vision Statements That Make Sense." *Fortune* (September 30, 1996): 195–196.

Stewart, Thomas A. "Company Values That Add Value." *Fortune* (July 8, 1996): 145–148.

———. "The Invisible Key to Success." *Fortune* (August 5, 1996): 173–176.

———. "Rate Your Readiness To Change." *Fortune* (February 7, 1994): 106–110.

———. "Why Value Statements Don't Work." *Fortune* (June 10, 1996): 137–138.

Strebel, Paul. "Choosing the Right Change Path." *California Management Review* (Winter 1994): 29–51.

———. "Why Do Employees Resist Change?" *Harvard Business Review* (May–June 1996): 86–104.

Stuller, Jay. "The Guru Game." *Across the Board* (December 1992): 21–23.

Thurow, Lester C. "Surviving in a Turbulent Environment." *Planning Review* (September–October 1995): 24–29.

Tichy, Noel M., and Ram Charan. "The CEO As Coach: An Interview with Allied Signal's Lawrence A. Bossidey." *Harvard Business Review* (March–April 1995): 69–78.

Tichy, Noel M., and Stratford Sherman. *Control Your Destiny or Someone Else Will.* New York: Doubleday, 1993.

Treacy, Michael, and Fred Wiersema. "Customer Intimacy and Other Value Disciplines." *Harvard Business Review* (January–February 1993): 84–93.

———. *The Discipline of Market Leaders.* Reading, Mass.: Addison-Wesley, 1995.

Trist, E. L. "On Socio-Technical Systems." Lecture presented to the departments of engineering and psychology, University of Cambridge, November 18, 1959.

Trist, E. L. and K. W. Bamforth. "Some Social and Psychological Consequences of the Longwall Method of Coal-Getting." *Human Relations* 4 (1951): 3–38.

Ulrich, Dave, Todd Jick, and Mary Ann Von Glinow. "High Impact Learning: Building and Diffusing Learning Capability." *Organizational Dynamics* (Autumn 1993): 57.

Wack, Pierre. "Scenarios: Shooting the Rapids." *Harvard Business Review* (November–December 1985): 139–150.

———. "Scenarios: Uncharted Waters Ahead." *Harvard Business Review* (September–October 1985): 73–89.

Want, Jerome H. "Managing Radical Change." *Journal of Business Strategy* (May–June 1993): 21–28.

Weick, Karl E. "The Nontraditional Quality of Organizational Learning." *Organization Science* 2 (February 1991): 116–124.

Weisbord, Marvin R. *Discovering Common Ground.* San Francisco: Berrett-Koehler, 1993.

Weisbord, Marvin R., and Sandra Janoff. *Future Search: An Action Guide to Finding Common Ground in Organizations and Communities.* San Francisco: Berrett-Koehler, 1995.

Wenger, Etienne. "Communities of Practice: Where Learning Happens." *Benchmark* (Fall 1991): 6–8.

Wernerfelt, Birger. "A Resource-Based View of the Firm." *Strategic Management Journal* 5 (1984): 171–180.

Wheatley, Margaret J. *Leadership and the New Science: Learning about Organization from an Orderly Universe.* San Francisco: Berrett-Koehler, 1994.

———. *A Simpler Way.* San Francisco: Berrett-Koehler, 1996.

Wick, Calhoun W. *The Learning Edge: How Smart Managers and Smart Companies Stay Ahead.* Wilmington, Del.: Wick and Company, 1993.

Wishart, Nicole A., Joyce J. Elam, and Daniel Robey. "Redrawing the Portrait of a Learning Organization: Inside Knight-Ridder, Inc." *Academy of Management Executive* 10, no. 1 (1996): 7–20.

Womack, James P., and Daniel T. Jones. "If You Cut Waste, You Win." *Fortune* (December 9, 1996): 213–216.

Young, Mary, and James Post. "Managing to Communicate, Communicating to Manage: How Leading Companies Communicate with Employees." *Organizational Dynamics* (June 1, 1993): 31–43.

Zemke, Ron. "Creating Customer Value." *Training* (September 1993): 45–50.

Zemke, Ron, and Susan Zemke. "Adult Learning: What Do We Know For Sure?" *Training* (June 1995): 31–40.

Zenger, John, Ed Musselwhite, Kathleen Hurson, and Craig Perrin. *Leading Teams.* Homewood, Ill.: Business One Irwin, 1994.

Zingheim, Patricia K., and Jay R. Schuster. "First Findings: The Team Pay Research Study." *Compensation and Benefits Review* (November–December 1995): 6–10.

The Gurus

Karl Albrecht is chairman of the TQS group, a Chicago-based consulting firm that specializes in the concept of total quality service. Dr. Albrecht is the author of 18 books on management and organizational effectiveness, including *Northbound Train; Service Within;* and *Service America! Doing Business in the New Economy.*

Christopher Argyris is the James Bryant Conant Professor of Education and Organizational Behavior at Harvard University. Over the decades, his research has focused on organizational consequences for individuals and how individuals adapt to change those consequences, ways to change organizations, the role of the social scientist as a researcher and agent of change, and individual and organizational learning in which human reasoning becomes the basis for diagnosis and action. Mr. Argyris was awarded the Judge William B. Grant Alumni Award for scholarly contribution by Cornell University's School of Industrial and Labor Relations.

Some of the titles he has authored and coauthored are *Organizational Learning II: Theory, Method, and Practice; Knowledge for Action; On Organizational Learning;* and *Organizational Learning: A Theory of Action Perspective.*

For additional information, see the following sites on the Internet: http://www.hbs.edu/bios/cargyris.html and http://enhanced-designs.com/actnet/argbib.htm.

K. W. (Ken) Bamforth, through his association with London's Tavistock Institute for Social Research, was the catalyst for the emergence of the sociotechnical approach to the redesign of work. He began his career as a coal miner and trade unionist in South Yorkshire and later received a scholarship to Leeds University. Bamforth graduated from Leeds with a degree in economics and industrial relations and continued his postgraduate studies as an Industrial Fellow at "the Tavvy." As part of his studies, Bamforth returned to the colliery where he had worked to observe any changes in work organization that had taken place since his departure. Eric Trist, a founder of the institute, joined Bamforth in his studies and coauthored the classic 1951 article "Some Social and Psychological Consequences of the Longwall Method of Coal-Getting" with him. The third member to join the team, Fred Emery, was an Australian social scientist on sabbatical at the Tavvy. Emery and Trist's work began their decades-long collaboration. Bamforth later left the institute for a position with an English firm.

Christopher A. Bartlett has been a professor at the Harvard Business School since 1979, where he has focused on general management issues, particularly those relating to multinational corporations. His current research involves the impact of organizational structures and management processes on the core roles and responsibilities of managers. He served as chairman of the school's International Senior Management Program from 1990 through 1993. Prior to his association with Harvard, Professor Bartlett was a marketing manager, a management consultant at McKinsey & Company's London office, and a general manager at a Baxter Laboratory subsidiary in France. He continues to maintain relationships with large corporations, both as a board member and consultant.

Professor Bartlett is the author or coauthor of five books, including *Transnational Management: Text, Cases, and Readings in Cross Border Management* and *Managing across Borders: The Transnational Solution,* which has been translated into nine languages and produced as a video (Harvard Business School Press, 1989).

Additional biographical information is available at http://www.hbs.edu/bios/cbartlett.html.

Warren Bennis is distinguished professor of business and professor of finance and business economics at the University of Southern California. His areas of expertise include leadership and power, the psychology of superleaders, management practice and theory, and the changing corporate culture. He is also the founding chairman of USC's Leadership Institute.

Dr. Bennis received his Ph.D. in economics and social science from MIT. He subsequently served on the school's faculty and was chair of the Organization Studies Department. He was also on the faculties of Boston and Harvard Universities, was provost and executive vice president of the State University of New York at Buffalo, was president of the University of Cincinnati, and has served in an advisory position to four U.S. presidents. He served on the White

House Task Force on Science Policy and was named one of the nation's top 10 leaders in organizational behavior.

Dr. Bennis is the author or coauthor of more than 25 books, including *Leaders: The Strategies for Taking Charge; An Invented Life: Reflections on Leadership and Change;* and *On Becoming a Leader.*

Dr. Bennis lives in Santa Monica, California, and can be reached through USC's Business School at (213)740–0728; fax: (213)740–9725; e-mail: wbennis@sba.usc.edu.

Warren Blank is president of the Leadership Group, a consulting and training firm based in Chapel Hill, North Carolina. In addition to his consulting activities, Mr. Blank has also taught management and leadership courses at the University of Houston and other institutions and is the author of *The Nine Natural Laws of Leadership* (AMACOM, 1995).

Lee G. Bolman holds the Marion Bloch Chair in Leadership at the University of Missouri-Kansas City. In addition to his academic responsibilities, Professor Bolman is an independent consultant and coauthor of *Leading with Soul* and *Reframing Organizations.* He can be contacted by e-mail at lbolman@cctr.umkc.edu.

Juana Bordas is a senior program associate at the Center for Creative Leadership in Colorado Springs, Colorado. She is also the founding president and CEO of the National Hispana Leadership Institute (NHLI) and a founder and executive director of Mi Casa Women's Center in Denver, Colorado. Ms. Bordas was selected as a "Wise Woman" by the National Center for Women and Policy Studies and as a "Wonderwoman" by the Wonderwoman Foundation.

During her 15-plus years of work managing nonprofit corporations, Bordas has written several books and articles on the subjects of diversity and pluralism in America, including *Follow the Leader: Women's Ways of Mentoring.*

Adam M. Brandenburger is professor of business administration at the Harvard Business School and a consultant. He is a pioneer in the application of the science of game theory to business management. Professor Brandenburger is the author of numerous academic papers and articles on game theory. He is best known for his best-selling book *Co-opetition,* which he coauthored with Barry Nalebuff.

For additional information, see http://www.hbs.edu/bios/abrandenburger. html, or you can contact Dr. Brandenburger at Morgan 233, Harvard Business School, Soldiers Field, Boston, MA 02163; telephone: (617)495–6615; fax: (617)496–5859; e-mail: abrandenburger@hbs.edu.

Jill Carpenter is a trainer and consultant with Capital Connections, Inc., a firm that specializes in the concept of open-book management. Ms. Carpenter consults in the areas of systems theory and its practical application to business and of integrating the new processes of open-book management into organizations. She is a coauthor of *The Power of Open-Book Management* (John Wiley & Sons, 1996).

John Case is a senior writer at *Inc.* magazine and editor of *Open-Book Management Bulletin,* a biweekly newsletter. He is also the author of four books, including *Open-Book Management: The Coming Business Revolution.* Mr. Case can be reached at 37A Prentiss Street; Cambridge, MA 02140; voice-mail: (617)248–8457; fax: (617)492–3607; e-mail: john_case@incmag.com.

James Champy is chair and CEO of CSC Index, a management consulting firm that specializes in the practice of reengineering. Champy is the author of the best-selling book *Reengineering Management: The Mandate for New Leadership* and coauthor of *Reengineering the Corporation: A Manifesto for Business Revolution.* Mr. Champy has been featured in such publications as *Fortune,* the *New York Times,* the *Boston Globe,* and the *Wall Street Journal.*

Jay A. Conger is chair of the Leadership Institute at the University of Southern California. He joined the USC staff after 10 years as a professor at McGill University. Mr. Conger is the author or coauthor of several books, including *Learning to Lead* (Jossey-Bass, 1992); *The Charismatic Leader: Behind the Mystique of Exceptional Leadership* (Jossey-Bass, 1989); and *Charismatic Leadership: The Elusive Factor in Organizational Effectiveness* (Jossey-Bass, 1988). He can be reached by e-mail at conger@bus.usc.edu.

Daryl Connor is president and founder of Organizational Development Resources (ODR), a consulting firm in the area of organizational change. Mr. Connor is the author of the best-selling book *Managing at the Speed of Change.* He can be reached through his Atlanta offices at ODR, Inc., 2900 Chamblee Tucker Road, Atlanta, GA 30341; telephone: (770)455–7145.

Stephen R. Covey is the founder and was chair of the Covey Leadership Center and the nonprofit Institute for Principle-Centered Leadership. The Covey Leadership Center recently merged with the training company Franklin Quest to form Franklin Covey, of which he is the cochair. Mr. Covey, who was given the 1991 McFeely Award from the International Management Council for significant contribution to the field of management and management education, has written several books and articles. They include *First Things First: A Principle-Centered Approach to Time and Life Management; Principle-Centered Leadership;* and his best-selling *The Seven Habits of Highly Effective People.*

Aubrey C. Daniels is president of Aubrey Daniels & Associates, Inc. an Atlanta-based international consulting firm that specializes in the application of performance management principles. He is also president of Precision Learning Systems, Inc., and founder and publisher of *Performance Management Magazine.* Mr. Daniels is the author of *Bringing Out the Best in People* and *Performance Management: Improving Quality through Positive Reinforcement.* He can be reached through his Atlanta offices at Aubrey Daniels & Associates, Inc., 3531 Habersham at Northlake, Tucker, GA 30084; telephone: (770)493–5080; fax: (770)493–5095; toll-free: (800)223–6191.

Terrence E. Deal, a specialist in organizational theory and management, is professor of education and human development at Vanderbilt University's Peabody College. He joined the Vanderbilt faculty in 1983 after leaving his teaching position at Harvard. In 1997, he was awarded the Madison Sarratt Prize for Excellence in Undergraduate Teaching. Deal's publications include *Leading with Soul; Managing the Hidden Organization;* and *Corporate Cultures.*

Max DePree is chair of the board of directors of Herman Miller, Inc., manufacturer of office furniture. DePree, who was elected by *Fortune* to the National Business Hall of Fame, is author of *Leadership Jazz* and *Leadership Is an Art.*

Peter F. Drucker is the Marie Rankin Clarke Professor of Social Science and Management at The Claremont Graduate School. He has served as a consultant to government, public sector organizations, and corporations, and his 20-plus books have been translated into more than 20 languages.

Professor Drucker's extensive publication list includes two novels, an autobiography, several volumes of essays, numerous magazine and journal articles, in addition to his well-known books. They include *Management: Tasks, Responsibilities, Practices; The Practice of Management;* and *Concept of the Corporation.*

Professor Drucker can be reached by e-mail at druckerp@cgs.edu.

Fred Emery is a senior research fellow at the Centre for Continuing Education at Australian National University in Canberra. During his long career he has been a psychologist, sociologist, and system theorist. While on sabbatical at the Tavistock Institute for Social Research in London, he collaborated for the first—though certainly not the last—time with Eric Trist on the research that ultimately became known as the sociotechnical systems approach and on the development of a new paradigm of work that was based on democratic participation. Emery joined the staff of the Tavistock Institute in 1958 and, along with Trist, conducted the first Search Conference in 1960. From 1962 through 1969, he worked with Einar Thorsrud on the Norwegian Industrial Democracy Project to test sociotechnical systems methods in manufacturing plants. In 1970 he moved back to Australia to work with the Australian Royal Airforce and ICI, using the participative design methodology. Dr. Emery has been a visiting professor at the Wharton School's Department of Social Systems Sciences and at the Center for Advanced Studies in Palo Alto, California.

His many articles and books include "Sociotechnical Foundations for a New Social Order," in *The Quality of Working Life in the 1980s,* edited by Harvey Koldny and Hans van Beinum; *Systems Thinking,* Volumes 1 and 2; *The Emergence of a New Paradigm of Work; Democracy at Work,* with Einar Thorsrud; and *Futures We Are In.*

Richard Farson is a psychologist, educator, and author of *Management of the Absurd.* He is the cofounder and was president of Western Behavioral Sciences Institute, a founding dean of the California Institute of Arts' School of Environmental Design, president of Esalen Institute, and president of the International Design Conference in Aspen.

Thomas P. Flannery is vice president and managing director of the consulting firm The Hay Group. He is the author of *The Hay Guide to Executive Compensation in Health Care* and a coauthor of *People, Performance and Pay.* Mr. Flannery holds a Ph.D. from Northwestern University.

Jay W. Forrester is the Germeshausen Professor Emeritus of Management and senior lecturer at MIT's Sloan School of Management. He began his career as an electrical engineer working on large digital computers, and he is credited with inventing random-access magnetic-core memory (RAM). While director of the MIT Digital Computer Laboratory from 1946 to 1951, he was responsible for the design and development of one of the first high-speed computers. In 1956 Professor Forrester started the System Dynamics Group at the Sloan School, establishing the field of system dynamics.

In addition to his teaching, writing, and speaking engagements, he is working on the National Model Project, a large computer model of the U.S. economy. He is also director of the System Dynamics in Education Project (SDEP), which is developing ways to use system dynamics and computer modeling as the foundation for a new type of K-12 education. Professor Forrester's books include *Principles of Systems; Industrial Dynamics; World Dynamics;* and *Urban Dynamics.*

For additional information about Professor Forrester and on-line access to some of his papers, see http://web.mit.edu/sloan/www/faculty/forester.html and http://sysdyn.mit.edu/people/jay-forrester.html. He can be contacted through his MIT offices at (617) 253–1571; fax: (617)252–1998; e-mail: jforestr@mit.edu.

Timothy J. Galpin is a principal with the consulting firm Pritchett & Associates, Inc., and a former consultant with Booze-Allen & Hamilton. He specializes in organizational change and merger integration. Mr. Galpin's articles have appeared in such publications as *HRMagazine, Training and Development Journal,* and *Employment Relations Today,* and he is the author of *The Human Side of Change: A Practical Guide to Organization Redesign* (Jossey-Bass, 1996).

Howard Gardner is a professor of education at the Harvard Graduate School of Education and an adjunct professor of neurology at the Boston University School of Medicine. He is the author of 14 books, including *Extraordinary Minds; Leading Minds: An Anatomy of Leadership; Creating Minds: An Anatomy of Creativity Seen through the Lives of Freud, Einstein, Picasso, Stravinsky, Eliot, Graham, and Gandhi; The Unschooled Mind;* and *The Mind's New Science: A History of the Cognitive Revolution.* Mr. Gardner can be contacted at Harvard at (617)496–4929; e-mail: gardneho@hugsel. harvard.edu.

John W. Gardner is a consulting professor at Stanford University's Graduate School of Business. Previously, he served as a vice president (1946–1955) and president (1955–1965) of the Carnegie Foundation for the Advancement of Teaching; secretary of the U.S. Department of Health, Education and Welfare (1965–1968); chair of the National Urban Coalition (1968–1970); founding chair of Common Cause (1970–1977); cofounder/chair of Independent Sector (1980–1983); director of Leadership Studies (1984–1989); and chair of the National Civic League (1994 to the present).

Among his many honors and awards, Mr. Gardner received the Presidential Medal of Freedom in 1964, the U.S. Air Force Exceptional Service Award, and the Distinguished Achievement Medal of Stanford University's Athletic Board. He also served on President Kennedy's Task Force on Education, was chair of President Johnson's Task Force on Education, served on President Carter's Commission on an Agenda for the '80s, chaired the Commission on White House Fellowships, and served on President Reagan's Task Force on Private Sector Initiatives.

Mr. Gardner's list of publications include *On Leadership; In Common Cause,* and *Excellence.*

Sumantra Ghoshal, who is on leave from the European Institute of Business Administration (INSEAD) in Fontainebleau, France, holds the Robert P. Bauman Chair in Strategic Leadership at the London Business School.

Mr. Ghoshal's research interests include the strategic and organizational aspects of managing large corporations, the roles and tasks of top management, the management of change, and the managerial theory of the firm. He serves on the editorial boards of *Strategic Management Journal, The European Management Journal, Journal of International Business;* and he is a consultant to several large U.S. and European companies.

He is coauthor, with Christopher A. Bartlett, of *Managing across Borders: The Transnational Solution,* which has been translated into nine languages and produced as a video by Harvard Business School Management Productions. Other publications include *The Individualized Corporation: A New Doctrine for Managing People,* with Christopher Bartlett; *Transnational Management, International: Text, Cases and Readings in Cross Border Management,* also with Christopher Bartlett; and *Transnational Management: Text, Cases and Readings.*

Thomas F. Gilbert has been hailed as the founding father of performance technology. He is the author of the classic text on performance analysis and instructional design, *Human Competence* (1978), which is still in publication and widely used both in education and in business.

Mr. Gilbert, who died in 1995, taught psychology for 10 years at the University of Georgia, University of Alabama, Emory University, and Harvard University, before joining the staff of B. F. Skinner's research lab at Harvard. He became an early expert on teaching-machine technology, which he used to develop the concept of programmed instruction.

Between 1964 and 1979, Mr. Gilbert founded three consulting firms, including the TOR Corporation and Praxis Corporation. TOR was later purchased by Bell and Howell, and Praxis was purchased by Kepner-Tregoe.

In 1962, Gilbert was named the first honorary member of the National Society for Performance and Instruction. He was inducted into *Training* magazine's Hall of Fame and received the Lifetime Achievement Award from the Association for Behavior Analysis. The International Society for Performance Improvement named its award for achievement in the field of human performance technology the Tom Gilbert Distinguished Professional Achievement Award.

In addition to *Human Competence,* Gilbert coauthored *Dramatic Improvements in Human Performance* with his wife and long-time collaborator, Marilyn Gilbert.

Robert K. Greenleaf (1904–1990) is most well known for his 1970 essay *The Servant As Leader,* in which he introduced the term *servant-leadership.* However, Mr. Greenleaf spent most of his working life in the field of management research, development, and education at AT&T. Before retiring as director of management research for AT&T, he held a joint appointment as a visiting lecturer at MIT's Sloan School of Management and at the Harvard Business School. He also taught at Dartmouth College and the University of Virginia, and he acted as consultant to Ohio University, MIT, the Ford Foundation, the R.K. Mellon Foundation, the Lilly Endowment, and the American Foundation for Management Research.

Greenleaf was a lifelong student of the concept of the organization, and he published his observations in a series of essays, starting with *The Servant As Leader.* In 1972, he published *The Institution As Servant,* based on the concept that institutions could be servants, too. He also wrote *Servant Leadership: A Journey into the Nature of Legitimate Power and Greatness.*

The Greenleaf Center for Servant-Leadership, a not-for-profit organization that propounds the benefits of servant-leadership, released two previously unpublished writings by Greenleaf, *On Becoming a Servant-Leader* and *The Seeker and Servant.* The Greenleaf Center also offers an anthology of Greenleaf's works in *Reflections on Leadership: How Robert K. Greenleaf's Theory of Servant-Leadership Influenced Today's Top Management Thinkers.*

Inquiries about The Greenleaf Center for Servant-Leadership can be sent to 921 East 86th Street, Suite 200, Indianapolis, IN 46240; telephone: (317)259–1241; fax: (317)259–0560; Internet site: http://greenleaf.org.

Gary P. Hamel is professor of strategic and international management at the London Business School and an independent consultant. His research interests include the value-added of senior management in global companies, strategic development, and competition for world leadership.

Mr. Hamel is perhaps best known for two *Harvard Business Review* articles he coauthored with C. K. Prahalad, "The Core Competence of the Corporation" (1989) and "Strategic Intent" (1989). Both won McKinsey Awards and are among *HBR*'s best-selling reprints. The two writers also coauthored *Harvard Business Review* articles "Do You Really Have a Global Strategy" (1985), "Collaborate with Your Competitors—and Win" (1989), "Corporate Imagination and Expeditionary Marketing" (1991), "Strategy As Stretch and Leverage" (1993), and "Competing for the Future" (1994). Mr. Hamel authored *Competition for Competence* and coauthored *Competing for the Future* with C. K. Prahalad.

Michael Hammer is president of Hammer and Company, a management education and consulting firm, and former professor of computer science at MIT. He is considered the originator of the concepts of reengineering and process-centering.

In 1992, Mr. Hammer was named by *Business Week* as one of the four preeminent management thinkers of the 1990s, and *Time* magazine named him as one of America's 25 most influential individuals in 1996. His works include the *Harvard Business Review* article "Reengineering Work: Don't Automate, Obliterate," and three books—*Beyond Reengineering: How the Process-Centered Organization Is Changing Our Work and Our Lives; The Reengineering Revolution: A Handbook;* and *Reeingineering the Corporation: A Manifesto for Business Revolution.*

Mr. Hammer can be contacted through his office: Hammer and Company, One Cambridge Center, Cambridge, MA 02142; telephone: (617)354-5555; fax (617)354–1046; Internet site: http://www.hammerandco.com.

Charles Handy has been a corporate executive, economist, and professor at the London Business School. His books on organizations and the future have sold over one million copies worldwide. They include *Beyond Certainty: The Changing Worlds of Organizations; The Age of Paradox;* and *The Age of Unreason.*

David A. Hofrichter is the managing director of the Hay Group's Global Accounts, Client Relationship Development program. He specializes in compensation and leadership and the role both play in change management. Mr. Hofrichter holds a Ph.D. from Duquesne University and is a coauthor of *People, Performance and Pay.*

William N. Isaacs is a senior lecturer at MIT's Sloan School of Management and the director of the Dialogue Project in the Center for Organizational Learning. The Dialogue Project and the associated Dia-Logos Institute explore the role of conversation and collective thought in addressing issues.

F. Robert Jacobs is professor of operations management at Indiana University. His research involves the design of manufacturing systems using both simulation and mathematical modes. He specializes in the development and application of group technology and cellular manufacturing concepts.

Professor Jacobs is the author of *Real Time Strategic Change.* He can be contacted through the School of Business, Indiana University, Bloomington, IN 47405; telephone: (812)855–2676; Internet site: jacobs@indiana.edu.

Laurie Beth Jones is president and founder of the Jones Group, a marketing, business, and leadership development firm. She is the author of *Jesus in Blue Jeans; The Path;* and the best-seller *Jesus, CEO.* Ms. Jones can be contacted at her San Diego offices at (760)753–7251 or by e-mail at jnsgroup@aol.com.

M. Patricia Kane is a senior consultant with the consulting firm Capital Connections, Inc., and coauthor of *The Power of Open-Book Management.*

Robert S. Kaplan is the Marvin Bower Professor of Leadership Development at the Harvard Business School and an independent consultant. His research and consulting focus on new cost and performance measurement systems, particularly activity-based costing and the balanced scorecard. He has authored or coauthored more than 100 papers and articles and nine books, including *The Balanced Scorecard: Translating Strategy into Action; Implementing Activity-Based Cost Management: Moving from Analysis to Action;* and *Relevance Lost: The Rise and Fall of Management Accounting.*

Mr. Kaplan serves on the board of Renaissance Solutions, a consulting firm that specializes in performance measurement, and on the Academic Committee of the Board of Trustees of the Techron (Israel Institute of Technology). For additional information on Professor Kaplan and his publications, refer to the Internet site at http://www.people.hbs.edu/rkaplan. He can be contacted by telephone: (617)495–6150; fax: (617)496–7363; e-mail: rkaplan@hbs.edu.

Jon R. Katzenbach is a director with the consulting firm McKinsey & Company and coauthor of *Real Change Leaders* and *The Wisdom of Teams.*

Manfred F. R. Kets de Vries is the Raoul de Vitry d'Avaucourt Professor in Human Resource Management at the European Institute of Business Administration (INSEAD) in Fontainbleu, France, and an independent consultant. His area of expertise and research is the interface between psychoanalysis/dynamic psychiatry and management, specifically in the areas of leadership, organizational stress, career dynamics, entrepreneurship and family business, cross-cultural management, and the process of organizational transformation and change.

Prior to joining the faculty at INSEAD, Kets de Vries practiced as a psychoanalyst and taught at McGill University, Harvard University, and HEC, Montreal. He received the Best Teacher Award for the MBA program at INSEAD in 1987, 1989, 1990, 1991, and 1993. He was also awarded The Critics Choice Award for the most acclaimed business book of 1995 for *Life and Death in the Executive Fast Lane.* His extensive list of publications include *Leaders, Fools and Imposters; The Neurotic Organization,* with Danny Miller; and *Power of the Corporate Mind,* with Abraham Zalenik.

For a complete biography and list of publications, refer to the Internet site: http://www.insead.fr. Professor Kets de Vries can be contacted at INSEAD, Boulevard de Constance, 77305 France; telephone: (+33) (0) 1 60 72 41 55; fax: (+33) (0) 1 60 72 42 42; e-mail: ketsdevries@insead.fr.

Daniel H. Kim is an organizational consultant and cofounder with Peter Senge of the Organizational Learning Center at MIT. His current work focuses on helping management teams articulate a shared vision and identify the mental assumptions and systemic structures needed to implement that vision by using his Vision Deployment Matrix as a framework for large-scale change. He has also been working to integrate systems thinking with TQM under the umbrella of organizational learning.

Mr. Kim has a degree in electrical engineering from MIT and a Ph.D. in management from MIT's Sloan School of Management. He is the publisher of *The Systems Thinker,* a newsletter about systems thinking, and the coauthor of *Applying Systems Archetypes* and *Systems Archetypes II.*

John P. Kotter is Konosuke Matsushita Professor of Leadership at the Harvard Business School. Professor Kotter has been given two McKinsey Awards for best *Harvard Business Review* articles, an Exxon Award for Innovation in Graduate Business School Curriculum Design, and a Johnson, Smith & Knisely Award for New Perspectives in Business Leadership. His publications include *Leading Change; A Force For Change: How Leadership Differs from Management;* and *The Leadership Factor.* He also created two videotapes, *Corporate Culture* (1993) and *Leadership* (1991).

For additional information, refer to the Internet site: http://www.hbs.edu/bios/jkotter. Mr. Kotter can be contacted at (617)495–6529; fax: (617)496–6568; e-mail: jkotter@hbs.edu.

Edward E. Lawler III is professor of management and organization at the University of Southern California. He is a founding director of USC's Center for Effective Organizations. Professor Lawler was named by *Business Week* as one of the country's leading management experts and by *Human Resource Executive Magazine* as one of the most influential people in the field of human resources. He lists his areas of expertise as worker motivation and rewards, strategic pay, achieving maximum organizational effectiveness through employee involvement, involving labor unions in organizations, managing the change toward a high-involvement organization, and large-scale organizational change.

Professor Lawler was program director in the Survey Research Center at the Institute for Social Research before joining the faculty of USC in 1978. He is the author or coauthor of more than 200 articles and 25 books, including *From the Ground Up: Six Principles for Creating the New Logic Corporation; Strategic Pay: Aligning Organizational Strategies and Pay Systems;* and *High-Involvement Management.*

Professor Lawler can be contacted at (213)740–9814; e-mail: elawler@ceo.usc.edu.

Charles C. Manz is associate professor of management at Arizona State University. He is coauthor, with Henry P. Sims, of *Businesses Without Bosses* and *SuperLeadership: Leading Others to Lead Themselves.* He also coauthored *For Team Members Only* with James Mancuso, Christopher Neck, and Karen Manz.

Mr. Manz can be contacted at (602)965–8218; fax: (602)965–8314; e-mail: charles.manz@asu.edu.

Henry Mintzberg is professor of organization at the European Institute of Business Administration (INSEAD) in Fontainebleau, France, and at McGill University in Montreal. His areas of expertise include general management, the process of strategy formation, and the design of organization and impact of design on organizations.

Professor Mintzberg won the George R. Terry Award for the best management book of the year in 1995 and is a Fellow of the Royal Society of Canada. His publications include *The Rise and Fall of Strategic Planning: Reconceiving Roles for Planning, Plans, Planners; Mintzberg on Management: Inside Our Strange World of Organizations;* and *The Structuring of Organizations: A Synthesis of the Research.*

Professor Mintzberg can be contacted at INSEAD, Boulevard de Constance, 77305 France; telephone: (33) (0) 1 60 72 40 00; fax: (33) (0) 1 60 74 55 00/01; e-mail: mintzberg@insead.fr.

Allan M. Mohrman, Jr. is associate director and research scientist at the University of Southern California's Center for Effective Organizations. He is a coauthor of *Designing Team-Based Organizations: New Forms for Knowledge Work* and *Large-Scale Organizational Change.* Mr. Mohrman can be contacted at (213)740–9814; fax: (213)740–4354; e-mail: mohrman@alnitak.usc.edu.

Susan Albers Mohrman is a senior research scientist at the University of Southern California's Center for Effective Organization (CEO). She is a coauthor of *Designing Team-Based Organizations: New Forms for Knowledge Work; Employee Involvement and Total Quality Management;* and *Large-*

Scale Organizational Change. Ms. Mohrman can be contacted at CEO: (213)740–9814; fax: (213)740–4354; e-mail: morhman@ceo.usc.edu.

James F. Moore is the founder and chairman of GeoPartners Research, Inc., a business-strategy-consulting and investment-advisory service based in Cambridge, Massachusetts, and author of *The Death of Competition.* Mr. Moore received his doctorate from Harvard University and conducted research at Stanford University and Harvard Business School. His 1993 *Harvard Business Review* article "Predators and Prey: A New Ecology of Competition" won the McKinsey Award for best article of the year.

Linda Moran is senior consultant with Zenger Miller, Inc., a training and consulting firm. She is coauthor of numerous articles, as well as *Keeping Teams on Track* and *Self-Directed Work Teams: The New American Challenge.*

Ed Musselwhite was president and chief executive officer of Zenger Miller, Inc., a training and consulting firm. He is a graduate of Northwestern University's School of Business and began his career as an account executive and marketing manager with IBM. He later cofounded DELTAK, a training company in the data-processing industry that was later acquired by an international publisher. Mr. Musselwhite joined Zenger Miller in 1982. He is coauthor of several publications, including *Keeping Teams on Track; Leading Teams;* and *Self-Directed Work Teams: The American Challenge.*

Barry J. Nalebuff is the Milton Steinbach Professor at the Yale School of Management and an independent consultant. He teaches a wide variety of courses, including competitive (and cooperative) strategy, political-economic marketing and game theory, and decision making. He also teaches a course in negotiation strategy at Yale Law School.

Mr. Nalebuff is the coauthor of *Co-opetition,* with Adam Brandenberger, and *Thinking Strategically,* with Avinash Dixit. His numerous academic papers and articles have appeared in such publications as the *Harvard Business Review,* the *Journal of Law, Economics, and Organization,* the *Journal of Conflict Resolution, World Politics,* the *New York Times,* the *International Herald Tribune,* and the *Washington Post.*

He can be reached by e-mail at barry.nalebuff@yale.edu.

Burt Nanus is professor emeritus of management at the University of Southern California's School of Business Administration and an independent consultant in leadership. He is also a former director of research at UCS's Leadership Institute. Mr. Nanus is author or coauthor of several books, including *Visionary Leadership: Creating a Compelling Sense of Direction for Your Organization; The Leader's Edge: The Seven Keys to Leadership in a Turbulent World;* and *Leaders: The Strategies for Taking Charge,* with Warren Bennis.

David P. Norton is president, CEO, and cofounder of Renaissance Solutions, Inc., a management-consulting and systems-integration firm. Prior to cofounding Renaissance, Norton cofounded and spent 17 years as president of Nolan, Norton & Company, which was acquired by Peat Marwick. He holds a B.S. degree in electrical engineering from Worcester Polytechnic Institute, an M.S. in operations research from Florida Institute of Technology, an M.B.A. from Florida State University, and a doctorate in business administration from Harvard University. He has written numerous articles on performance measurement and strategic management, and he is coauthor of *The Balanced Scorecard.* Mr. Norton can be contacted through the corporate offices of Renaissance Solutions, Inc., at 55 Old Bedford Road, Lincoln North, Lincoln, MA 01773; telephone: (617)259–8833; fax: (617)259–0565.

James O'Toole is retired from the faculty of the University of Southern California's Graduate School of Business and is a former vice president of the Aspen Institute, an international nonprofit educational institute dedicated to enhancing the quality of leadership. During his more than 20 years at USC, he served as director of the Twenty-Year Forecast Project (1973–1983), was editor of *New Management* magazine for six years, and was executive director of USC's Leadership Institute.

In addition to his academic activities, Mr. O'Toole served as a special assistant to Secretary of Health, Education and Welfare Elliot Richardson, and as chairman of the secretary's Task Force on Work in America. Mr. O'Toole has been a consultant with McKinsey & Company, has served as a director of field investigations for the President's Commission on Campus Unrest, and was director of the Aspen Institute's Program on Education, Work and the Quality of Life. He was chosen among the 100 most respected emerging leaders in higher education in an American Council of Education survey and served on the board of editors of the *Encyclopædia Britannica.*

Mr. O'Toole's extensive publication list includes such books as *Leading Change: The Argument for Values-Based Leadership; The Executive's Compass; Vanguard Management;* and *Making America Work.*

Glenn M. Parker is president of Glenn M. Parker Associates, a consulting firm that specializes in creating and sustaining teams and team-based systems. He is the author or coauthor of several handbooks, training resources, and books, including *Cross-Functional Teams: Working with Allies, Enemies and Other Strangers; Fifty Activities for Self-Directed Teams;* and *Team Players and Teamwork: The New Competitive Business Strategy,* which was selected as one of the best business books of 1990. Mr. Parker can be contacted through his offices at 41 Woodlane Road, Lawrenceville, NJ 08648.

William A. Pasmore is a professor of organizational behavior in Case Western Reserve University's Weatherhead School of Management. His research focuses on the sociotechnical systems design of organizations, participation in organizational change, organizational learning during research-and-development activities, and global social change. He has also taught at Stanford University, the European Institute of Business Administration (INSEAD), and the University of Leuven in Belgium.

Professor Pasmore's publications include *Creating Strategic Change: Designing the Flexible High-Performing Organization* and *Designing Effective Organizations: The Sociotechnical Systems Perspective.*

Thomas J. (Tom) Peters is a self-described gadfly, curmudgeon, prince of disorder, and corporate cheerleader. He is also founder and chief of the Tom Peters Group, author and coauthor of numerous books and articles, consultant and speaker, producer of and actor in training films, and host of BBC and PBS specials.

He coauthored his first and best-known book, *In Search of Excellence,* with Robert H. Waterman, Jr. His other books include *Liberation Management; Thriving on Chaos;* and *A Passion for Excellence,* with Nancy Austin.

Paul E. Platten is a vice president and general manager of the Hay Group's Boston office. Mr. Platten, who has done extensive work in the area of executive compensation, received his Ph.D. from New York University. He is coauthor of *People, Performance and Pay.*

Michael E. Porter is the C. Roland Christensen Professor of Business Administration at the Harvard Business School and an independent consultant. His areas of expertise include competitive strategy and international competitiveness.

In addition to his academic and consulting responsibilities, Professor Porter was appointed by President Reagan in 1983 to the President's Commission on Industrial Competitiveness, chaired the commission's strategy committee, and serves as cochairman of the Subcouncil on Capital Allocation of the Competitiveness Policy Council. Among his awards and honors, he won Harvard's David A. Wells Prize in Economics for his research in industrial organization, two McKinsey Awards for best *Harvard Business Review* articles, and the 1980 Graham and Dodd Award of the Financial Analysts Federation. In 1993 he was named the Richard D. Irwin Outstanding Educator in Business Policy and Strategy by the Academy of Management.

Professor Porter has an extensive publication list, which can be accessed through the Internet site http://www.hbs.edu/bios/mporter.html. He is the author of 14 books and more than 50 articles, including the best-selling *The Competitive Advantage of Nations; Competitive Advantage;* and *Competitive Strategy.*

Professor Porter can be contacted at (617)495–6309; fax: (617)547–8543; e-mail: mporter@hbs.edu.

C. K. Prahalad is the Harvey C. Fruehauf Professor of Business Administration, a professor of corporate strategy and international business at the University of Michigan, and an independent consultant.

His first position was as an industrial engineer with Union Carbide India. He has since served as a visiting research fellow at Harvard Business School (1975), a professor and chairman of the Indian Institute of Management's Management Education Program (1975–1977), a visiting professor at the European Institute of Business Administration (INSEAD) in Fontainebleau, France (1981), and most recently a member of the University of Michigan faculty.

Professor Prahalad has published papers and articles in journals such as the *Strategic Management Journal* and the *Harvard Business Review.* He coauthored *Competing for the Future: Breakthrough Strategies for Seizing Control of Your Industry and Creating the Markets of Tomorrow,* with Gary Hamel, and *The Multinational Mission: Balancing Local Demands and Global Vision,* with Yves Doz.

Edgar H. Schein is Sloan Fellows Professor of Management Emeritus and a senior lecturer at MIT's Sloan School of Management. His interests are in the areas of organizational culture, process consultation, organizational learning and change, the research process, and career dynamics.

Professor Schein has been a prolific writer over the years. His articles and papers have appeared in such publications as *Sloan Management Review* and *American Psychologist.* He is the author or coauthor of *Organizational and Managerial Culture As a Facilitator or Inhibitor of Organizational Learning* (MIT Organizational Learning Network Working Paper 10.004, 1994); *The Art of Managing Human Resources;* and *Organizational Culture and Leadership: A Dynamic View.*

Professor Schein can be contacted at his office at (617)253–3636 fax: (617) 253–2660; e-mail: scheine@mit.edu.

Peter R. Scholtes is the founder of Scholtes Seminars & Consulting, a Madison, Wisconsin, consulting company. His postgraduate education and professional experience have been in the area of organizational development. He has shared the platform with Dr. W. Edwards Deming as an instructor and was among the first to combine his expertise in organizational development with Dr. Deming's teachings.

Mr. Scholtes is the author of *The Team Handbook,* which has sold almost 700,000 copies, and is coauthor of the second edition of the book. He has also written several articles, particularly on the controversial subject of the use of performance appraisals. In 1995, *Quality Digest* named him one of the 50 Quality Leaders of the Decade.

Donald A. Schön is Ford Professor Emeritus and a senior lecturer in MIT's Department of Urban Studies and Planning. Dr. Schön, who was initially educated as a philosopher, has been an educator, consultant, and government administrator. During his 20-plus-year tenure at MIT, he served as head of the department from 1990 to 1992. He was also director of the Institute for Applied Technology at the National Bureau of Standards and president of the Organization for Social and Technological Innovation. His recent research focuses on public and organizational learning, professional effectiveness, professional education, and design research.

Dr. Schön's list of publications include *Organizational Learning: A Theory of Action Perspective; Theory in Practice: Increasing Professional Effectiveness;* and *Technology and Change.*

Jay R. Schuster is a partner in Schuster-Zingheim and Associates, Inc., a consulting firm that specializes in pay practices. Mr. Schuster, who holds B.B.A. and M.A. degrees from the University of Minnesota and a Ph.D. from the University of Southern California, is a coauthor of *The New Pay.*

John P. Schuster is a management consultant with and founder of the company that later became Capital Connections, Inc. He is a coauthor of *The Power of Open-Book Management.*

Peter M. Senge is a senior lecturer at MIT, director of the Center for Organizational Learning at MIT's Sloan School of Management, and a cofounder of the management consulting and training firm Innovation Associates, which was acquired by Arthur D. Little in 1995. His area of interest and research is the study of how organizations develop learning capabilities.

Mr. Senge is the author of *The Fifth Discipline: The Art and Practice of the Learning Organization* and coauthor of *The Fifth Discipline Fieldbook: Strategies and Tools for Building a Learning Organization.* He can be contacted at MIT at (617)253–1575; fax: (617)253–1998; e-mail: psenge@mit.edu.

Henry P. Sims, Jr. is a professor of management and organization in the College of Business and Management, University of Maryland. He is the coauthor of *Business without Bosses; The New Leadership Paradigm;* and *Super Leadership: Leading Others to Lead Themselves.*

Douglas K. Smith is a consultant with McKinsey & Company, Inc. He is a coauthor of *The Wisdom of Teams* and *Fumbling the Future: How Xerox Invented and Then Ignored the First Personal Computer.*

John P. (Jack) Stack is the president and CEO of the Springfield Remanufacturing Corporation, a rebuilder of engines and engine components. (See Chapter 6 on motivation for details about Stack's career.). He is the author of *The Great Game of Business.*

Paul Strebel is a professor of business administration at the International Institute for Managing Development (IMD) in Lausanne, Switzerland, and director of IMD's Change Program for international managers. He is the author of *Breakpoint: How Managers Exploit Radical Change* and *In the Shadows of*

Wall Street: A Guide to Active Stock Market Investment. Professor Strebel can be contacted by e-mail at strebel@imd.ch.

Noel M. Tichy is a professor of organizational behavior and human resource management at the University of Michigan Business School, where he has been on the faculty since 1980. Prior to that he was a manager at General Electric's Management Development Institute (1985–1987), an associate professor at Columbia University (1972–1980), and a senior research associate at the Center for Policy Research (1970–1980).

Among Professor Tichy's honors are an Educator of the Year Award from Sales and Marketing International (1994); a Best Practice Award (1993) and the Organization Development Award (1990) from the American Society for Training and Development; and the New Perspectives on Executive Leadership Award from Johnson Smith & Knisely for *The Transformational Leader* (1987). He is a director of the Global Business Partnership and the Global Leadership Program at the University of Michigan Business School. He serves on the board of governors of the American Society for Training and Development and is editor in chief of *Human Resource Management Journal.* He is also on the editorial boards of the *Journal of Business Research* and *Organizational Dynamics.*

Professor Tichy's publications include *Control Your Destiny or Someone Else Will: How Jack Welch is Making General Electric the World's Most Competitive Company,* with Stratford Sherman; *The Transformational Leader;* and *Managing Strategic Change.*

Michael Treacy is a consultant specializing in business strategy and corporate transformation who works with individual corporations and with the consulting firm CSC Index. He is a former professor of management science at MIT's Sloan School of Management and coauthor of *The Discipline of Market Leaders.*

Eric Trist is one of the founders of the Tavistock Institute for Social Research in London. He collaborated with K. W. Bamforth in research at the Haighmoor mines in South Yorkshire and in 1951 coauthored the resulting *Human Relations* article "Some Social and Psychological Consequences of the Longwall Method of Coal-Getting." His later collaboration with Fred Emery resulted in what is known as the sociotechnical systems approach to work design.

Mr. Trist's other publications include *Organizational Choice: The Loss, Rediscovery and Transformation of a Work Tradition;* "The Sociotechnical Perspective" (in Andrew Van de Ven's *Perspectives on Organizational Design and Behavior*); and *Toward a Social Ecology: Contextual Appreciation of the Future in the Present.*

Marvin R. Weisbord has been a manager, consultant, and entrepreneur for more than 30 years. He consulted for government, education, business, and non-profit organizations until his retirement in 1991. He is a founding partner in Block-Petrella-Weisbord, a consulting firm that specializes in restructuring work, and a partner in Blue Sky Productions, a video company that documents innovations in self-management. He coauthored *Future Search* with Sandra Janoff and is the author of *Discovering Common Ground* and *Productive Workplaces.*

Etienne Wenger is a research scientist with the Institute for Research on Learning. He is working on the development of a broad conceptual framework for considering learning as a part of social practices and of the formation of social identities. Mr. Wenger holds a B.S. in computer science from the University of Geneva, Switzerland (1982), and an M.S. and Ph.D. in information and computer science from the University of California, Irvine (1984 and 1990). He can be contacted at the Institute for Research on Learning, 66 Willow Place, Menlo Park, CA 94025; telephone: (415)614–7900; fax: (415)614–7957.

Margaret J. Wheatley is president of the Berkana Institute, a charitable scientific, educational, and research foundation that supports research into new organizational forms. She is also a principal of Kellner-Rogers & Wheatley, Inc., a consulting firm, that focuses on applying natural science principles of self-organization to respond to change and that experiments with organizational redesigns that support speed, flexibility, resiliency, and autonomy. Dr. Wheatley was formerly an associate professor of management at the Marriott School of Management at Brigham Young University.

She is the author of *A Simpler Way* and *Leadership and the New Science: Learning about Organization from an Orderly Universe.* Dr. Wheatley can be reached through the Berkana Institute or at Kellner-Rogers & Wheatley, Inc.: 3857 North 300 West, Provo, UT 84604; telephone: (801)221–0044; fax: (801)221–0055.

Fred Wiersema is senior vice president of CSC Index, a consulting firm that specializes in business strategy, reengineering, and large-scale change. He is a coauthor of *The Discipline of Market Leaders.*

John H. Zenger is chair of Times Mirror Training, the parent company of Zenger Miller and three other training companies. Mr. Zenger, who has a doctorate in business management, taught at the University of Southern California and the Stanford University Graduate School of Business. He is the author of *Not Just for CEOs* and is a coauthor of *Leading Teams* and *Self-Directed Work Teams.*

Patricia K. Zingheim is a partner in Schuster-Zingheim and Associates, Inc., a consulting firm that specializes in pay practices. Ms. Zingheim received an A.B. degree from the University of Michigan and an M.A. and Ph.D. from Ohio State University. She is a coauthor of *The New Pay.*

Index

Albrecht, Karl, 18
archetypes
  drifting goals, 115–16
  escalation, 112
  fixes that fail, 110
  growth and underinvestment, 116–17
  limits to success, 113–14
  shifting the burden, 112–13
  success to the successful, 115
  tragedy of the commons, 110–11
Argyris, Chris, 96, 94, 100–105

balanced scorecard
  four key perspectives, 258–60
  linking measures to business strategy,
    260–61
Bamforth, Ken, 129–32
Bartlett, Christopher, 17, 33–35
Bennis, Warren, 2–3, 27, 29, 39, 42
Blank, Warren, 11–15
Bolman, Lee, 41
Bordas, Juana, 27
Brandenburger, Adam M., and Barry J.
  Nalebuff
  changing the game of business, 218–28
  game theory and business, 217–19

Champy, James, 34–35, 66
change
  employee resistance to, reasons for
    employee rebellion, 56
    failure to align organization with,
      55–56
    fear of more work, 52–53
    habits must be broken, 53–54
    lack of communication, 54
    perceived negative outcome, 52
  failure rates, 48–49
  importance of, 47–48
  large scale, advantages of, 66–67

major organizational change, frequency
  of, 48
successful, ingredients for
  clear vision, 59–60
  communication, 61–64
  convincing employees of needed
    change, 59
  early wins, 60–61
  employee involvement, 69–72
  establish need to change, 57–59
  formula for, 57
  guiding coalition, 64–66
  keep it complex, 66–69
  in search conferences, 72–77
Cohen, Susan, 143
Collins, James, 22, 26
communication, what employees need to
  know, 64
communities of practice, 91–94
compensation
  incentive pay, rules for, 284–86
  pay for competencies, 280–84
  pay-for-skill systems, 278–80
  point-factor systems, problem with,
    274–78
  team system design and, 164–65
  traditional pay, problem with, 274–78
Conger, Jay, 19, 32–33
Conner, Daryl, 56, 57–58, 65
Covey, Stephen, 5–6

Daniels, Aubrey, 263–74. *See also* performance management
Deal, Terrence, 41
DePree, Max, 6–7
DeSimone, Livio D., 35
double-loop learning. *See* learning
Drucker, Peter, 10–11, 39
  knowledge revolutions, 296–99
  post-capitalist society, 294–300

Emery, Fred, 129–32

Farson, Richard, 41, 66
Flannery, Thomas P., 277, 286–87
Forrester, Jay W., 95, 105–9
future search conferences, 72–74
  advantages of, 75–76
  agenda for, 73–74

Galpin, Timothy, 67–69
Gardner, Howard, 30–32
Gardner, John, 8, 10, 41
Gates, Bill, 14
Ghoshal, Sumantra, 17, 33–35
Gilbert, Thomas F.
  behavior engineering model, 239–40
  effective employee information system,
    requirements for, 246
  human competence, formula for calculat-
    ing, 234–36
  information, value of, 245–47
  model for creating incompetence, 241
  performance deficiencies, diagnosis and
    treatment process for, 241–44
  performance improvement potential
    (PIP), formula for calculating,
    236–38
  worthy performance, definition of, 234
Greenleaf, Robert K., 36–39

Hamel, Gary P., and C. K. Prahalad,
  194–203
  core competencies, 196–98
  criticism of, 201–3
  strategic architecture, development of,
    199–201
Hammer, Michael, 49–50
Handy, Charles
  federal organization, 303–7
  job design in federal organization, 308–10
  portfolio living, 311–20
  shamrock organization, 311–17
high-performance organizations
  advantages of, 138–41
  resistance to, 140–41
  versus traditional organizations, 133–38
  See also teams
Hofrichter, David A., 277, 286–87

Iacocca, Lee, 14–15
Isaacs, William N., 90

Jackson, Jesse, 14
Jacobs, F. Robert, 48, 70, 72–74
Jobs, Steve, 15
Jones, Laurie Beth, 13

Kaplan, Robert S., 257–63. See also bal-
  anced scorecard
Katzenbach, Jon R., 22, 27, 60, 138,
  140–41, 151, 167–70
Kets de Vries, Manfred F. R., 10, 40, 42, 52,
  117
Kim, Daniel H., 85–91
Kotter, John, 41–42, 53–54, 58–62, 65

Lawler, Ed, 159–60, 164–66, 168–69, 275,
  280–81, 284, 287
leader roles and responsibilities
  as change agent, 33–36
  managers versus leaders, 16
  role shift
    commander to storyteller, 29–33
    strategist to visionary, 17–29
    systems architect to change agent and
      servant, 33–39
  as servant, versus traditional leader,
    36–39
  as storyteller, 29–33
  as strategist, 17–18
  traditional role, problem with, 33–34
  as visionary, 18–29
leadership
  characteristics of leaders
    Bennis, Warren, 3
    Covey, Stephen, 5–6
    DePree, Max, 7
    Gardner, John, 8
    Namus, Burt, 4
    O'Toole, James, 4
  evaluating potential for, 9
  learning to lead
    education, role of, 41
    experience, role of, 41–42
    failure, role of, 42
    genetics and childhood, role of, 40
    training, 43

natural laws of
  field of interaction, 14
  leadership as event, 14–15
  willing followers, 13
leadership traits
  Drucker, Peter, 10–11
  Gardner, John, 10
  Kets de Vries, Manfred F. R., 10
learning
  archetypes, 108–17 (*see also* archetypes)
  defined, 85
  double-loop learning, 100
  explicit knowledge, 90
  exposing left-hand column and, 96–99
  how learning occurs, consensus
    view, 86
  individual, 85–90
  inquiry skills, 99–105
  key research findings about, 86
  ladder of inference and, 96–97
  microworlds, 118
  Model I, 100–105
  organizational, 91–94
  organizational culture and, 120–25
  psychological safe havens for, need for
    126
  reflection skills, 95–99
  simuworlds, 118
  systems thinking, 105–19
  tacit knowledge, 90
learning organization. *See* learning

managing change. *See* change
Manz, Charles C., 139, 140–41, 147–49,
  160
mental models, 90–91
Micklethwait, John, 201
Mintzberg, Henry, 193
Mohrman, Susan Albers, 141, 143, 154–57,
  165
Moore, James
  businesses as ecosystems, 213–17
  coevolution, stages of, 213–17
  competition, death of, 211–13
Moran, Linda, 163
Morhman, Allan M., 143
motivating people
  antecedents, 264–65

balanced scorecard and, 257–63
behavior engineering model, 239–40
business as behavior, 263–64
compensation and, 274–87
consequences
  defined, 264
  power of, 265
  types of, 265–68
effective employee information system,
  requirements for, 246
extinction, problem with, 269–70
Gilbert, Thomas F., 234–47
human competence, formula for calculating, 234–36
incentives and, 263–87
information, value of, 245–47
model for creating incompetence, 241
open-book management and, 251–56
performance deficiencies, diagnosis and
  treatment process for, 241–44
performance improvement potential
  (PIP), formula for calculating,
  236–38
performance management and, 263–74
positive reinforcement
  power of, 270–72
  tips for using, 272–74
punishment, problem with, 269
worthy performance, definition of, 234
See also compensation
Musselwhite, Ed, 163

Nalebuff, Barry J. *See* Brandenburger, Adam
  M., and Barry J. Nalebuff
Nanus, Burt, 4, 18, 22
Norton, David P., 257–63. *See also* balanced
  scorecard

Open-book management, 251–56
organizational change. *See* change
organizational learning. *See* learning
O'Toole, James, 4, 49–50

Parker, Glenn M., 144, 167–68
Pasmore, William, 47–48, 55–56, 60, 64,
  67, 69–71
performance appraisals, team system design
  and, 167

performance management
  antecedents defined, 264–65
  business as behavior, 263–64
  consequences
    defined, 264
    power of, 265
    types of, 265–68
  extinction, problem with, 269–70
  positive reinforcement
    power of, 270–72
    tips for using, 272–74
  punishment, problem with, 269
Peters, Tom
  businessed jobs, 311
  gotta units, 307
Platten, Paul E., 277, 286–87
Porras, Jerry, 22, 26
Porter, Michael
  competitive forces, basic, 180–85
  competitive strategies, generic, 185–88
  criticism of, 192–94
  growth/share matrix, criticism of, 176–79
  value chain, 189–92
Prahalad, C. K. See Hamel, Gary P., and C.
  K. Prahalad

real-time strategic change events. See future
  search conferences

Schein, Edgar, 120–26
Scholtes, Peter, 160–63
Schön, Donald, 95, 101–2
Schuster, Jay, 280–81
Senge, Peter, 81, 92, 95, 105–19
Sims, Henry P., 139, 140–41, 147–49, 160
Smith, Douglas, 138, 140–41, 151, 167–70
Stack, Jack, 247–56. See also open-book
  management
strategy
  businesses as ecosystems, 213–17
  changing the game of business, 218–28
  coevolution, stages of, 213–17
  competition, death of, 211–13
  competitive forces, basic, 180–85
  competitive strategies, generic, 185–88
  core competencies, 196–98
  game theory and, 217–28
  game theory and business, 217–19

  growth/share matrix, 176–79
  strategic architecture, development of,
    199–201
  strategic planning, problems with, 193–94
  value chain, 189–92
  value disciplines, 204–8
  See also Brandenburger, Adam M., and
    Barry J. Nalebuff; Hamel, Gary P.,
    and C. K. Prahalad; Moore, James;
    Porter, Michael; Treacy, Michael,
    and Fred Wiersema
Strubel, Paul, 52
structure
  federal organization, 300–307
  gotta units, 307
  job design, 308–11
  portfolio living, 317–20
  shamrock organization, 311–17
  See also Drucker, Peter; Handy, Charles;
    Peters, Tom
Stuller, Jay, 202
systems thinking, 105–19

Tavistock Institute for Social Research, 129
teams
  coordination across, 146–47
  cross-functional, advantages of, 144
  development stages, 160–63
  functional versus cross-functional,
    143–44
  getting team unstuck, 170–71
  leaders, expectations of, 151–54
  members
    roles and responsibilities of, 147–49
    skills required of, 156–59
  performance appraisals and, 167
  performance goals, setting, 167–68
  size of, 168
  successful design, tips for, 163–70
  team responsibility chart, 150
  transition to team leadership
    speed of, 154–56
    stages of, 149–54
  types of, 141–43
  See also high-performance organizations
Thatcher, Margaret, 42
Tichy, Noel, 57
Treacy, Michael, and Fred Wiersema

criticism of, 210–11
Hamel and Prahalad, criticism of, 202–3
value disciplines, 204–8
  selection of, 208–10
Trist, Eric, 129–32

vision
  characteristics of good vision, 19
  Churchill, Winston, 21
  definition of, 18–19
  development of, steps in
    five-whys, 26
    handy-dandy vision crafter, 26
    Nanus, Burt, systematic approach,
      23–25
    personal 27–28

Disney, Walt, 20
  examples of, 20–22
Ford, Henry, 20
King, Martin Luther, 21–22

Weisbord, Marvin, 72
Welch, Jack, 14
Wenger, Etienne, 92–93
Wheatley, Margaret, 19
wheel of learning, 87–90
Wiersema, Fred. *See* Treacy, Michael, and
    Fred Wiersema
Woolridge, Adrian, 201

Zenger, John H., 140–41, 163
Zingheim, Patricia, 280–81